Freedom, Inc.

and Black Political Empowerment

Freedom, Inc.
and Black Political Empowerment

Micah W. Kubic

UNIVERSITY OF MISSOURI PRESS
Columbia

ISBN 978-0-8262-2055-4
Library of Congress Control Number: 2015955241

∞™This paper meets the requirements of the American National Standard for
Permanence of Paper for Printed Library Materials, Z39.48, 1984.

Typefaces: Myriad, Minion

Contents

Acknowledgments

I wish to express my sincere thanks to those who made this book possible. I am grateful to the members of the faculty of the Howard University Political Science Department, who provided essential guidance and insight. Daryl Harris gave encouragement, wise counsel, and intellectual stimulation; without his assistance, the theory portions of this book would be greatly impoverished. John Cotman, Michael Frazier, Marilyn Lashley, and Clarence Lusane contributed expertise and critiques that enriched the final work. Abdul Karim Bangura was enormously helpful in constructing the research methodology.

A great friend and proofreader, Pat Gallagher, gave priceless assistance in preparing the manuscript.

Rosemary Lowe, whose friendship and wisdom are treasures to me, and whose activism and courage are treasures to the people of Kansas City, inspired me to pursue this vein of research in the first place. Troy Nash gave me opportunities when others did not, and without his mentorship, friendship, and intellectual engagement, this book would not have been possible. My parents, Joseph Craig Kubic and Donna Kubic, have supported me no matter what, and encouraged me to pursue interests that seemed unorthodox. Finally, my family—Schylon and Garrett—have given me their unwavering support, the strength and confidence required to finish this work. They showed patience and flexibility as I went through the labor pains of writing this work, and for that—and for so much more—they have my love, appreciation, and respect.

Freedom, Inc.

and Black Political
Empowerment

Introduction

Since 1967, when Carl Stokes and Richard Hatcher were elected the first black mayors of large American cities, ever-increasing attention has been paid to the interplay between African Americans and local politics. Considerable effort has been exerted to determine whether the advent of African American mayoralties results in tangible benefits for the black community and to identify the demographic conditions, alliances, and thematic emphases required for black candidates to succeed. Many works explain black success in local electoral politics or at winning satisfaction of local systemic demands as the result of interracial coalitions or the charisma and political skills of individual leaders or both. Failure in these same arenas, it is argued, reflect an inability to form or sustain interracial coalitions (usually blamed on "nationalist" or "overly" race conscious elements within the black community); factionalism and disunity among African Americans; the presence of an urban regime that views black demands as a threat to its economic interests, and so alternately squashes and co-opts the black community; the demobilization of black activists and grassroots populations; or the absence of political entrepreneurs who achieve success through wiliness and force of personality.

What goes largely unaddressed is the role played by local organizations and interest groups in mediating these other tendencies, enabling or precluding black electoral victory or policy success. Machines and the local incarnations of political parties have garnered some attention, but all manner of local political organizations—including interest groups, slating organizations, voters' leagues, and even neighborhood associations—are largely regarded as less effective than the actions of individuals or influentials, so localized as to make research on them nontransferrable and thus unnecessary, or reducible to such labels as "business interests" or "good government reformers," which are supposedly self-explanatory in behavior, motive, and constituency. These groups

[1]

are considered so generic as to demonstrate almost uniform behavior and motives across time and place. Little effort is made at examining how the internal politics of, activities of, or relationships between formal local organizations influence outcomes.

The groups most neglected are local independent political clubs with targeted constituencies, referred to here as local political organizations (LPOs).[1] In nonpartisan races, which include the majority of American big-city municipal elections, LPOs spring up to endorse candidates, mobilize voters, sponsor advertising campaigns, and otherwise do the work that party committees perform in partisan races. In partisan ones, LPOs represent the interests of a specific constituency within the party for the primary, serve as the liaison for the constituency to the party, and influence the turnout of the constituency in the general election. Some also lobby elected officials on issues of concern. Unlike political action committees (PACs), LPOs go beyond endorsing a candidate or donating to a campaign; they do the real work of electioneering, including grassroots organizing and person-to-person contact with voters. LPOs have considerable input and participation from the constituency they serve—not just elites—differentiating them from many traditional election-oriented interest groups. African American LPOs serve to unify black voters into a potent bloc capable of influencing elections and public policy, especially in cities where African Americans are a minority confronted by a hostile or neglectful white majority. In these cases, an African American LPO can serve as the unified political voice of the black community or coordinate political action to achieve the satisfaction of black demands on the system. Yet, these institutions have not received significant scholarly attention or been placed at the center of urban politics analyses of urban politics.

This book takes a different approach. It tells a fascinating story, that of Kansas City, Missouri's Freedom, Incorporated—the nation's oldest surviving black LPO. Through that story, the book makes the argument that local black political efficacy is not achieved primarily through individual campaigns for elective office, the charisma of individual candidates, or even the forging of interracial alliances. Rather, black political efficacy is best achieved through building and maintaining institutionalized black LPOs, which use a formal structure, embrace multiple tactics, including electioneering, and use a "black interests" organizing model. The story of Freedom will demonstrate that even institutionalized black LPOs secure greater efficacy for black communities when they are corporatist, cultivate a highly mobilized base, and engage in strategic bargaining with nonblack political forces.

The Importance of Local Political Organizations in Urban Politics

Although it builds on the scholarly work done in African American politics and urban politics over the preceding six decades, the approach taken by this book in providing an in-depth look at an LPO is a very different from that of most books. Not only have other authors largely overlooked LPOs, but none of the four basic theoretical approaches to the study of urban politics make LPOs the subject of intensive scrutiny. The institutional approach, associated primarily with the work of Edward Banfield and James Q. Wilson,[2] explains political outcomes primarily through the governmental and electoral structures in place. This approach predates the ascendance of black political power in cities, but it treats the failure to win black demands on the system as a product of unreasonable demands or to broader structures, especially machine politics. The institutional approach values LPOs as political actors but oversimplifies them as fixed, uniform, and predictable across time and space, not as living organisms that change in reaction to internal and external factors.

A different problem plagues the way pressure groups models approach LPOs. Since the publication of Floyd Hunter's groundbreaking study on Atlanta in 1953, much emphasis has been placed on identifying "community power structures"[3] or disproving their existence through claims of pluralism.[4] Both ends of the spectrum of the pressure groups approach have generally ignored formal groups and institutions, focusing attention instead on demographic groups or economic categories. Only a few scholars have researched the formal organizations that lobby city officials.[5] This approach is not adequate, because even at the local level, groups are not merely stand-ins for influentials or a particular demographic. Even less is said about how groups and influentials transform their power into votes for favored candidates on election day. Indeed, this perspective mistakenly seems to view elections as ancillary to outcomes.

The political economy approach, closely associated with the terms *urban regime* and *growth machine,* maintains that municipal decisions are driven by the needs of large economic interests. Molotch[6] and Stone[7] both argue that cities are essentially driven by an insatiable desire for economic growth and real estate development and have a dependent relationship on the sources of private capital for those activities. In black-led urban regimes, writes Stone, the black population receives occasional, symbolic benefits in exchange for supplying the votes that keep the growth-centered regime in power. These theorists give short shrift to individual organizations that constitute the regime and are silent on what occurs when elements of the regime come into conflict with one another.

The electoral politics approach explains outcomes as the result of the populace expressing its will at the ballot box. This approach forcefully argues that black interests can be served through participation in electoral politics. The influential work of Rufus Browning, Dale Rogers Marshall, and David H. Tabb is the finest exemplar of this strain of thought. They argue that "minority incorporation," defined as the enactment of policies favorable to minority interests, was achieved only through elections and only by crafting multiracial alliances.[8] These authors are dismissive of protest's efficacy, a stance that is problematic given that others have argued that substantial gains for African Americans were achieved through a dual strategy of elections and protest.[9] Browning, Marshall, and Tabb's findings have inspired a cavalcade of similar research on the importance of interracial alliances to achieving black progress in the urban context.[10] All three authors acknowledge that interracial alliances are usually possible only after black communities achieve high degrees of internal unity, a theme that has been taken up by a number of other authors.[11] Research in this vein can be illuminating, because election results are usually the best available measure of public opinion, but it flattens political maneuvers into a single dimension that does not change until the next election. Lobbying, protest, shifting alliances, and changing public opinion are not reflected in the analysis until the next election comes along and the proverbial deck is reshuffled. Most problematically, the electoral approach views the inherently short-lived campaigns of politicians as the most important unit of analysis. But campaigns do not spring fully formed from the ether; instead, they tap into existing formal and informal infrastructures and sometimes give birth to new ones. These structures outlast the campaign, and influence the direction of multiple campaigns and policy contests simultaneously.

There is merit in each of these frameworks, but more theoretical development is needed to establish the links among interest groups, elections, protest activity, and influentials or regime architects. Greater theoretical attention should be devoted to the role that LPOs can and do play in connecting, coordinating, and shaping all of these forms of political behavior. This book sets out to do just that, because LPOs are an understudied facet of the urban political system. Indeed, this author was unable to find a single book-length study on the activities of these organizations or their role in local political systems.

Nevertheless, references to LPOs are found throughout the literature, with widely varying accounts of their influence. Banfield and Wilson note that these groups formed in many nonpartisan cities to fill roles previously played by political parties.[12] Banfield's collection of studies on urban political systems describes

LPOs in five major cities.[13] Davidson and Fraga show that slating groups in four Texas cities were long-lasting, partly membership-based, and influential in post-election policy.[14] Bridges provides perhaps the most detailed account of the role LPOs played in local politics, showing that in several southwestern cities, reform LPOs ruled supreme, successfully squashed all opposition, and prevented participation by the lower classes that reform movements so often sought to exclude.[15] In stark contrast, Conway found that slating groups were of minor importance and rarely influenced voter behavior.[16]

Black LPOs are even less visible in the scholarly literature. Some have written at length on locally based civil rights organizations active during the freedom movement of the 1960s, but these organizations focused on direct action as opposed to electoral politics.[17] Jennings devoted a book to a "new form" of black activism he saw emerging in America that was most noticeable at the local level, the defining trait of which was its frustration with the managerialism of black elites.[18] Hadley discusses the emergence of a host of black LPOs in Louisiana, especially in New Orleans. Hadley makes special note of the role of ministers in forming and sustaining these organizations; ministers were instrumental in the founding of the earliest groups, but their perceived conservatism led to a decline in influence, which they sought to reverse in the 1980s.[19] Brown and Hartfield discuss two church-based LPOs in Detroit: the Black Slate and the Fannie Lou Hamer PAC.[20] The Black Slate, founded by the Rev. Albert Cleage of the Shrine of the Black Madonna, has been particularly influential thanks to the crucial early support it gave to the mayoral candidacy of Coleman Young.[21] Brown and Hartfield provide one of the clearest descriptions of the work black LPOs engage in, but argue that the influence of the two groups studied is primarily due to their connection with the black church. In most cities, black LPOs are *not* directly connected with a church, although they frequently count ministers among their leaders or membership. The question then becomes, how do these LPOs create the environment of trust and social capital that Brown and Hartfield write is present in the church-based groups? A volume edited by Smith and Harris also argues for the black clergy as constituting an important force in local politics, typically through ministerial alliances that undertake special projects and infrequently endorse candidates.[22]

This constitutes the entirety of existing work devoted to black LPOs. On the basis of this slim bibliography, one might be tempted to argue that black LPOs are not influential. But such a notion is refuted by the frequent references to black LPOs and the organizations' role in works primarily about something else. For example, Burgess gave a great deal of credit to a strong black political organization that existed in "Crescent City," the mid-sized southern city she studied.[23] Atlanta—now regarded the pinnacle of African American political empowerment—owes a great deal to its Negro Voters League, founded in 1948 and influential into the late 1960s. Its sophisticated endorsement strategy, coupled with its ability to guide black voters, allowed African Americans to hold the balance of power in city elections decades before they constituted a majority of the population. Indeed, Atlanta's much-heralded reputation as the "city too busy to hate" during the 1950s and 1960s is partly attributable to the influence of the league.[24]

Black LPOs became even more important as the civil rights movement bore fruit and African Americans gained wider entry into the system. Scholarly pieces on Cleveland's Carl Stokes never fail to mention his founding of the Twenty First District Caucus as a mechanism for winning systemic demands. The caucus was heralded as a national model of black power before a series of unwise strategic moves led to its demise.[25] Chicago has no dominant black LPO, but several smaller ones were important in creating the Task Force for Black Political Empowerment that elected Harold Washington as the city's first African American mayor.[26] Indeed, the absence of a dominant black LPO is partly responsible for the fragmentation of the black community after Washington's death. The Democratic Minority Conference in Los Angeles provided Tom Bradley with networks that would propel the police lieutenant to the city council and the mayoralty.[27] Mel King's Boston mayoral campaigns grew out of years of activism and successive black LPOs, the most important of which was the Black Political Task Force.[28] Amiri Baraka's United Brothers organization, notable for its Pan African orientation, was a driving force behind Kenneth Gibson's election as mayor of Newark.[29] In Houston, the Harris County Council of Organizations influenced the votes of 70 percent of black voters with the issuance of its slate.[30] In Birmingham, Richard Arrington helped form the Jefferson County Citizens Coalition (JCCC) in 1973. Within a year, its endorsed slates garnered over 80 percent of the black vote. For nearly two decades, it was impossible to gain election from a predominantly black district anywhere in that Alabama city without JCCC's endorsement.[31] A successor organization remains in existence today, its endorsement valued even though its influence has declined.

New Orleans represents a special case, because it claims a multitude of black LPOs. The city's organizations include BOLD, COUP, LIFE, and SOUL. These organizations were essential to birthing the city's black political class, and each of the four black mayors either emerged from or founded one of these organizations.

Tensions between the groups and their leaders have been one of the mainstays of the city's black politics.[32]

In short, existing work severely discounts the importance of LPOs in accounts of local and urban politics, providing us with only the barest sketch of what black LPOs do, how they are structured, how they exert influence, how agendas are structured, how they unite and mobilize the black community, how they enter into multiracial alliances, and where they fit in the constellation of pressure groups seeking to impact municipal policy. These questions are particularly relevant in cities that have elected only one black mayor, and where black leadership seemed to subsequently be in disarray. More than anything, research is needed on why, how, and when these organizations grow and prosper or decline and fall.

The Theory of Black Political Efficacy

This book seeks to fill that gap. Using Freedom, Inc. as a case study, this work seeks to explain how and why the organization grew, prospered, and declined. More important, it seeks to illuminate the relationship between the thriving of Freedom, Inc. and the satisfaction of black Kansas Citians' demands on the local political system. As the case study shows, the organization's decline in turn led to diminished black political efficacy.

The positing of just such a relationship between a strong LPO and black political efficacy is the central argument made by this book. To put it another way, in achieving empowerment and efficacy for African Americans at the local level, institutions—not just individuals, campaigns, demographic groups, or governance structures—matter. Furthermore, black political efficacy hinges upon the existence of a particular type of organization. Neither organizational efficacy nor community-wide political efficacy can be attained by just any black LPO; it is not the mere existence of a group or the undertaking of collective action by itself that leads to empowerment. Rather, black LPOs are more likely to be efficacious—and deliver greater efficacy for the black community within which they are nested—when those organizations are institutionalized. Here, the term *institutionalized* means that an LPO is a formal organization independent of any campaign or personality; uses multiple tactics to influence political outcomes including lobbying, protest, litigation, but especially electoral politics; and is oriented around a "black interests" organizing strategy rather than exclusive use of "alliance" or separatist organizing models.

This usage of "institutionalized" differs from that employed by writers like Robert C. Smith and Adolph Reed.[33] Those authors use the term pejoratively to refer to black leaders and organizations in the post–civil rights era, ones that they perceive to have been captured by white corporate interests and more vested in retaining newly gained privilege than in delivering benefits to the black masses. Reed uses the term to refer to black elites that actively politically demobilized the black population in order to minimize threats to their own power. Here, the term is used in a different fashion, to emphasize organizational sophistication, longevity, and independence rather than the incorporation within the white elite as feared by Smith and Reed. Despite the potential for confusion that this terminology creates, it is appropriate to refer to organizations that are formal and independent, that embrace multiple tactics including electioneering, and that use black interests organizing models as "institutionalized" because this is the term used by the eminent scholar Mack Jones to describe a thrust of the early 1970s. Jones used this term to describe the period when African American political leaders and activists devoted substantial energy to creating independent political and research organizations to pursue black interests.[34]

Of course, some institutionalized organizations are better able to respond to changing conditions and deliver benefits for their constituencies than others. Todd Shaw makes this point quite successfully with his Effective Black Activism Model (EBAM); his analysis of Detroit black activism shows that the existence or passion of black activist groups by itself does not result in change.[35] Rather, Shaw's EBAM demonstrates that the demands on the system made by Detroit's black activist groups were most likely to be met when those groups were able to craft alliances, make use of strategic advantages, and employ adaptive techniques. A similar argument is made here; although the existence of an institutionalized black LPO is a necessary condition in attaining local black political empowerment, it is by no means a sufficient one.

The theory of black political efficacy argues that a few factors are necessary if an organization is to be efficacious enough to lead the way towards black political empowerment. First, black political efficacy is highest when there is a *single, corporatist* LPO that serves as the primary locus of black political activity. Multiple organizations, or competing centers of black political power, weaken the credibility, leverage, and organizational efficacy of all of these organizations/centers of power. This is not to say that organizations representative of the particularistic interests of subgroups within the black community cannot or should not exist. It is only to say that "black interests" are more likely to be served when there exists a single, united organizational voice for the black community, which then works to coordinate and mediate the more particular interests of subgroups. The great danger in this is that more marginal subgroups will never see their interests find their way on to the agenda of a single, corporatist entity. Nevertheless, the story of Freedom, Inc., will show that rival centers of black organizational power lead to no one's demands being satisfied by the system.

Second, black LPOs are more efficacious and achieve greater empowerment for the community when they cultivate and sustain a mobilized, grassroots base that can be relied on to vote *en bloc*. As the story of Freedom will show, LPOs can utilize a number of strategies for creating and sustaining these high levels of mobilization and grassroots engagement, including positioning themselves as the primary defender of black interests, denouncing "enemies at the gate," creating a culture of open and transparent decision-making, or maintaining strong alliances with other influential institutions like the black church or black press. Regardless of how high levels of grassroots mobilization are achieved, they are necessary in order for institutionalized black LPOs to gain political power and attain community goals.

Third and finally, black LPOs are more likely to be effective organizations and produce concrete gains for the black community when they are able to engage in meaningful bargaining with nonblack political actors. After achieving success within the black community, black LPOs may gain credibility among whites and civic elites who are willing to bargain for support of their own initiatives. This bargaining produces short-term, strategic, interracial alliances that yield benefits desired by black voters. When these benefits are the result of bargaining by the black LPO, that success imparts even greater power and credibility to the LPO among the black electorate, thus reproducing the cycle. Highly impactful bargaining is most likely to occur when the black population is able to make the difference in electoral outcomes, either because of demographic strength or relative parity among white political forces. It is important to note that the sort of bargaining described here is *not* the result of long-term, ideologically grounded alliances with, for example, white liberals. Bargaining *is* more likely to take place with political forces that are ideologically friendlier to black aspirations—such as white liberals—but the bargaining that actually results in black empowerment is of a decidedly strategic and temporary variety.

To restate, the theory of local black political efficacy that undergirds this book holds that black communities are most effective at securing their demands on local political systems when strong black LPOs are present. Strong black LPOs must be institutionalized ones, that is, formal organizations that are independent, use multiple tactics, including electoral politics, and explicitly organize around black interests. Moreover, black LPOs are strengthened and deliver greater political efficacy for black communities when they are corporatist entities, cultivate and sustain high levels of grassroots mobilization, and engage in successful short-term bargaining.

Although the emphasis on black LPOs and the theory of local black political efficacy are unique to this book, the theory was not plucked from the ether. Existing theories leave little doubt that formal organizations and institutions influence political outcomes. Political science has for decades nurtured a thriving debate on the role played by pressure groups, but all of the theories accept as foundational the concept that formal organizations matter.[36] Organizations are asserted by all of the theorists cited above to be important because they embody, enable, and ease collective action, without which change in the public sphere is impossible. Formal organizations can be vehicles for those with shared interests to conduct research, coordinate strategy, disseminate information, encourage negotiation with leaders, and stimulate mass involvement.[37] All of these tasks are essential if groups are to accelerate the pace of progress or secure political victories. The theoretical claims made by scholars of pressure groups are supported by empirical evidence; if formal organizations were unsuccessful at winning benefits from the system, one would hardly see so many corporate interest groups occupying choice Washington office space.[38]

The contention that the most successful organizations use multiple tactics and include some electoral component is also theoretically and empirically grounded. Pressure groups fall into a number of generic categories: those oriented toward protest; those oriented toward lobbying; those oriented toward political action/campaign work; those oriented toward legal challenge; and those that utilize all of these tactics. The most feared and successful formal organizations are the last group. The National Rifle Association, the AARP, and the American Israel Public Affairs Committee invariably rank among the most powerful interest groups. They accomplish this feat not by virtue of their large membership, but by vigorously lobbying elected officials, bringing lawsuits, mobilizing activists, and maintaining PACs that ensure that those who move against their interests suffer electoral consequences.[39] Moreover, Shaw's EBAM shows us that different tools and tactics are appropriate and effective at different times.[40] Thus, organizations that have a wide range of tools at their disposal and the ability to deploy the tools best suited to the moment are in the best position to create political change.

The contentions that black LPOs and black communities are best served by black interests organizing models, rather than coalition-based ones, and by short-term, strategic bargaining are perhaps controversial. Debate over coalitions vs.

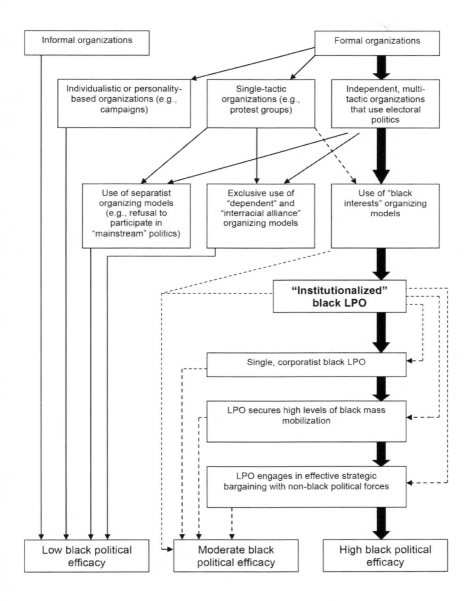

Figure 1. The Theory of Local Black Political Efficacy

independent power politics or "permanent allies" vs. "permanent interests" has been a recurring feature of black politics.[41] The theory of institutionalization outlined here does *not* argue that coalitions are undesirable or unimportant for black interests; indeed, the theory's insistence that strategic interracial bargaining is an important element of success belies such a notion. Indeed, in many cases, coalitions are not just demographically inevitable but patently desirable. However, we should recognize, as Carmichael and Hamilton did in their much-misunderstood theory of Black Power, that alliances inherently include multiple (and competing) interests. Coalitions cannot press for all of the interests of all of their members equally. Some groups within the alliance may routinely be called upon to sacrifice their particular interests "for the good of the coalition," and thus never achieve their goals for entering the coalition in the first place. Groups that are less unified, less powerful, lacking in capacity, or occupy a subordinate position in society are more likely to see their agendas perpetually minimized. If coalition is the exclusive organizing model used by these groups, they are doomed to perpetual dissatisfaction. To win their own demands—and not just be cogs in a machine that produces gains for others—Carmichael and Hamilton recommended that blacks build strong organizations of their own.[42]

It is recognized that a debate exists over what black interests are, or whether black interests and the "black community" exist at all. Only if one accepts a nakedly simplistic individualism wherein African Americans have nothing in common with one another would organizations articulating black interests be unnecessary. Although such people do exist and feel that their interests are best catered to by other color-blind pressure groups, they are a minority of a black community in which a sense of shared fate operationalized in a black utility heuristic is highly salient.[43] Given the pervasiveness of the black utility heuristic—and the fact that many black communities across the country *have* succeeded in defining black agendas, defining black interests is not impossible. Of course, black interests are not always readily apparent nor are they necessarily universal. As Cathy Cohen, among others, has demonstrated, class, gender, and sexuality can all influence what is perceived as a black interest. As a result, what becomes defined as a black interest is highly contingent and conditional. Nevertheless, when race and racism are the predominant context, as has been the case for most, or even all, of American history, then the group interests of African Americans become more readily apparent.

Ronald Walters articulates a similar concept in his study of black presidential politics. Walters argues that black political progress has been impeded in the post–civil rights era because African Americans organize almost exclusively within the Democratic Party. This provides "dependent leverage," which relies on the willingness of the party apparatus to make concessions. Gains are won when blacks find themselves a part of the winning team, but since the primary goal of that team is *not* to produce gains for African Americans, the potential for progress is inherently limited. More productive, he maintains, is "independent leverage," where African Americans possess power outside of any party and where the primary loyalty is not to any party but to black interests.[44] Independent leverage strategies do not preclude long-term alliances or compromise; they maintain that neither alliance nor compromise is a virtue in itself, and that these strategies should be evaluated on the basis of the tangible benefits they will yield. "Black Power" and independent leverage theoretical models assert that the most effective tool for securing black liberation is the creation of independent structures that are accountable to, responsive to, and charged with speaking for the black community. Where such structures are absent, the theory maintains, they are replaced by alliance models that inevitably dilute the presentation of and diminish responsiveness to black interests.

Carmichael, Hamilton, and Walters also lend theoretical support to the contention that that a corporatist entity is most effective. The leverage that these writers envision the black community exerting through its organizing efforts is possible only when a single, corporatist body speaking for that community is present. If there are multiple, rival claimants to be the "voice of the black community," with widely varying views and roughly equal political strength, it is unlikely that any of those groups would see its policy preferences enacted.

The contention that a high level of grassroots mobilization is essential builds most heavily on the theoretical work of Reed.[45] Reed is intensely critical of the path taken by the black freedom movement in the post–civil rights era, which he views as overly fixated on minor concerns of symbolic nationalism and insufficiently class-oriented. Reed would vigorously disagree with the theory of institutionalization's argument for a corporatist LPO (and the term institutionalization itself), but he does identify the demobilization of the black masses as the major impediment to black political success over the past four decades. Reed avers that the demobilization of the masses has given black political leaders the freedom to pursue their own agendas without fear of being held accountable. Absent real mobilization—or an organization to do the hard work of mobilizing—he maintains that African Americans lack a concrete agenda to pursue and have engaged in symbolic politics, like the ultimately fruitless exercise of the

Jesse Jackson presidential campaigns. Although Reed discounts the existence of high levels of mobilization at the local level, his diagnosis of mobilization as an essential ingredient in achieving black political success is one foundation of the theoretical model found here.

Although the work of Carmichael, Hamilton, and Walters provides a theoretical base for the construct of institutionalization offered here, the latter differs from the former in asserting the importance of formal, impersonal, long-lasting organizations and institutions. Earlier authors did not view ad hoc, temporary, informal, or individualistic (e.g., candidate committees) groupings as problematic, provided they achieved gains over their life spans and were vigorous in their advocacy. Walters, for example, heralds Jesse Jackson's 1984 campaign as a model. Important as that effort was, it was inherently time-constrained, ephemeral, and individualistic in a way that the LPOs described earlier are not. Since pressure groups theories inform us that formal organizations designed to be active in the longer-term are essential to the political process, they maximize the efficacy and responsiveness to black interests called for by Black Power and independent leverage theories.

In short, although the theory of black political efficacy is outlined for the first time here, the elements that form it are firmly grounded in the existing literature on black politics. There is good reason to believe that where an institutionalized LPO exists, is a corporatist body, cultivates and sustains a highly mobilized grassroots base, and is capable of engaging in short-term, strategic bargaining, a city's black community will achieve higher levels of political efficacy.

Approach and Organization of the Book

To support the argument that local black political efficacy is most readily achieved through the existence of a strong, institutionalized black LPO, this book tells the story of Freedom, Inc., an African American LPO in Kansas City, Missouri. Since its founding in 1962 by six grassroots leaders, Freedom has become Kansas City, Missouri's dominant black political organization. It is the oldest still-existing black LPO in the nation.[46] Its emergence fundamentally shifted the political calculus in the city by creating an independent vehicle for the development of black political power and pressing black interests. By uniting and mobilizing the black community to forcefully advocate for black interests, Freedom won the adoption of an open housing ordinance, a public accommodations ordinance, a higher level of municipal services in the black community, altered the plan for a superhighway that would have disadvantaged black neighborhoods, and elected scores of African Americans to public office, including two black mayors. Freedom is more than simply a slating group although its influence is felt through the issuance of its black-and-gold Freedom Ballot; it was and is also a pressure group, a protest organization, a civil rights movement, a space for the development of a local black agenda, and the political voice of a largely united black community.

This book presents a comprehensive case study and history of Freedom, Inc. and municipal politics between 1962 and 2007. The book uses a variety of historical sources including primary source documents, contemporary news accounts, and interviews to tell the story of Freedom, Inc. Data were also collected through participant observation. The author worked as a legislative assistant to a Freedom-backed elected official between 1999 and 2007, managed several Kansas City municipal campaigns, and collaborated closely with Freedom on a number of projects. Insights gained and facts learned from these involvements are incorporated into the text and inform the general approach. In addition, the author conducted semi-structured interviews with knowledgeable informants who were assured that no identifying information would be used here and that confidentiality would be maintained. Finally, two indices were constructed to evaluate the efficacy of Freedom as an organization as well as the efficacy of Kansas City's black community. The two indices created here, the Black Political Efficacy Index (BPEI) and the Organizational Efficacy Index (OEI), are described in greater detail in the concluding chapter of this volume, where they are used to test the theory of black political efficacy.

This book proceeds as follows: chapter 1 provides readers with the context in which Freedom arose; it includes information on the historical and political background of Kansas City. Covering the period 1962 to 1968, chapter 2 analyzes the founding of Freedom, the organization's formative years, and its rapid rise to a position of power. Chapter 3 assesses the period from 1969 to 1979, when Freedom emerged as a king maker organization. Chapter 4 explores the period from late 1979 to 1990 and how Freedom coped with a period in the political wilderness. Chapter 5 details the period from 1991 to 2007, discussing the conditions that saw Emanuel Cleaver elected as the city's first black mayor. The chapter also considers the period after Cleaver left office, when Freedom was widely thought to be in decline. Chapter 6 summarizes the key findings and presents a fuller discussion of the two indices that measure political efficacy. Ample evidence is found through these discussions for the theory of black political efficacy, which argues that black political efficacy is enhanced by the presence of strong, institutionalized black LPOs that are corporatist, maintain high levels of grassroots mobilization, and engage in strategic bargaining. Finally, the chapter speculates about the implications of the book and the way forward for black politics in the twenty-first century.

CHAPTER 1

The Context of Black Politics in Kansas City

It would be foolhardy to attempt to explain the role played by Freedom, Inc. in the politics of Kansas City, Missouri, without first providing some context on that city. Aside from the pervasive white supremacy found in every large city in the middle of the twentieth century, were there circumstances in Kansas City's African American community that contributed to the founding of a strong black LPO, in the form of Freedom? How did African Americans, other ethnic groups, and socioeconomic classes relate to one another, especially politically? This chapter attempts to answer these questions in order to better explain why Freedom, Inc. was able to emerge. The political culture of Kansas City was one where long-lasting, formal organizations were dominant actors in local politics and where African Americans were only nominally included in those organizations. African American demands on the system were ignored or rejected, and living conditions for blacks in the city deteriorated through local government action or inaction. As a result, the political context and culture found in Kansas City by 1962, the year of Freedom's founding, was one that made organizing an LPO to pursue the interests of the black community an almost natural step.

From Remote Trading Post to Major American City

Today Kansas City, Missouri is a vibrant city of over 459,000 residents, nearly 138,000 of them African American, that sits at the center of a metropolitan area with over 2 million people, but the city's origins are more humble.[1] Founded in 1850 as the "Town of Kansas," Kansas City began as a small trading post on the bluffs high above the Missouri River. The site's earliest settlers never envisioned a grand future for it. The nearby settlements of Westport, Missouri, St. Joseph, Missouri, and Leavenworth, Kansas were expected to be the major cities, with the Town of Kansas supplying traded goods.[2] With the rapid expansion of the railroads in the 1850s–1860s and the arrival of ambitious young people heading west to make their fortune, the little town's sense of its self and its destiny were radically transformed. In 1853, the Town of Kansas was renamed and incorporated as the grander-sounding City of Kansas. The infant city's geography was such that it was a logical hub for the railroads as they expanded westward. Kansas City's rapid growth in the years after its founding was enabled by the fact that the new city's elite (such as it was; there were no eastern bluebloods among the upper crust of this frontier town) was unified and committed to civic boosterism. It was this united front that allowed Kansas City to rapidly surpass the competing cities of Westport, St. Joseph, and Leavenworth for regional supremacy. The unity found among the leadership class in this period is in marked contrast to the city's politics in later years, when factionalism became rampant.[3]

For the next few decades, Kansas City was a boomtown, becoming a regional finance and mercantile capital. Surrounding rural areas used Kansas City as a launching point for the marketing of their agricultural products, birthing the famous stockyards. The city and the surrounding region experienced relatively consistent prosperity and growth from the 1860s until the Great Depression. The population grew quickly (see Table 1), from just over 4,000 in 1860 to more than 130,000 by 1890. The city's physical boundaries grew with its population, with annexations in 1859, 1873, 1885, 1897, 1909, 1947, 1950, 1957, 1958, and 1959. Even one-time rival Westport was swallowed up by Kansas City. At the same time, Kansas City was developing a national reputation as a gateway to the West and a place of abundant economic opportunity. The Broadway songwriting team of Rodgers and Hammerstein were facetious when they wrote "Everything's Up To Date In Kansas City," but the song's title was not far off the mark. By the dawn of the twentieth century, most of the city's streets were paved (a rarity in American metropolises), electricity was in widespread use, and the city attracted major national events (including the 1900 Democratic convention). As a mark of the city's prosperity, in the 1910s, more automobiles were sold in Kansas City than anywhere else in the United States except New York and Chicago.

At the same time, Kansas City earned an unfortunate reputation for vice. Saloons, gambling parlors, and houses of prostitution grew in popularity and soon became among Kansas City's most common—and lucrative—lines of business. From the 1880s until the early 1940s, even the illegal varieties of these enterprises operated in the open, thanks to a well-developed system of

Table 1. Population of Kansas City, Missouri, 1860–2010

Census Year	Total Population	White Population	White Percent	Black Population	Black Percent
1860	4,418	4,228	95.7	190	4.3
1870	32,260	28,484	88.3	3,770	11.7
1880	55,785	47,613	85.4	8,143	14.6
1890	132,716	118,821	89.5	13,700	10.3
1900	163,752	146,090	89.2	17,567	10.7
1910	248,381	224,677	90.5	23,566	9.5
1920	324,410	293,517	90.5	30,719	9.5
1930	399,746	360,725	89.5	38,574	9.6
1940	399,178	357,346	89.5	41,574	10.4
1950	456,622	400,599	87.7	55,682	12.2
1960	475,539	391,348	82.3	83,146	17.5
1970	507,087	391,496	77.2	112,005	22.1
1980	448,159	312,836	69.8	122,699	27.4
1990	435,146	290,574	66.8	128,768	29.6
2000	441,545	276,006	62.5	142,621	32.3
2010	459,787	272,305	59.2	137,540	29.9

Source: United States Census Bureau. "Table 26. Missouri - Race and Hispanic Origin for Selected Large Cities and Other Places: Earliest Census to 1990." *Historical Census Statistics on Population Totals by Race, 1790 to 1990, and By Hispanic Origin, 1970 to 1990, for Large Cities and Other Urban Places in the United States.* Washington: United States Census Bureau, 1991.

corruption. Although this corrupt collaboration between police and vice was eventually defeated—to the point that contemporary Kansas Citians find it unfathomable that their hometown was ever a vice capital—the specter of this corruption haunted local politics for years to come. As Schirmer has argued, a significant part of the impetus for Kansas City's reform movement in the early twentieth century stemmed from the desire of the city's middle class—the "better class of people," in the insufferably elitist jargon of the day—to rid Kansas City of its justly deserved reputation for all manner of wild living.[4]

The Pendergast Machine

The machine of the Pendergast brothers, "Big Jim" and "Boss Tom," is the most significant factor in shaping the political history and culture of Kansas City. Even today, seventy years after his fall from power, any attempt at modifying Kansas City's system of government is denounced by invoking the legacy of Tom Pendergast. Until the turn of the twentieth century, Kansas City was not a stronghold for either political party. Partly because of the highly pragmatic nature of American politics during the period, partly because of rapid growth, and partly because of near-constant disgust with the performance of elected officials, Democrats and Republicans traded control over local institutions. Both parties had bastions of strength within the city, but neither could rely on a city-wide base and each election was thus hard-fought.[5]

James "Big Jim" Pendergast, the son of Irish immigrants, arrived in Kansas City in pursuit of greater economic opportunities. Struggling at first, his luck took a turn for the better when he placed a winning wager in a horserace. Pendergast used his winnings to open a saloon (which he named "The Climax," after his equine patron) in the hardscrabble "North End." "Big Jim" used his personal popularity to enter politics, as a Democrat, given the partisanship of the local Irish population (and the anti-Irish bigotry of the local Republican Party). After several successful forays into Democratic Party internal politics, Pendergast ran for a seat in the City Council's lower chamber in 1892. He scored a resounding victory in that election and each subsequent one until failing health caused him to retire in 1910.[6]

During his tenure as an alderman, "Big Jim" Pendergast established a rudimentary machine, first in his own ward and then in neighboring ones. By most accounts, even those of arch-antagonist William Rockhill Nelson and his *Kansas City Star*, Pendergast was enormously popular among his constituents. He earned their affection and loyalty by distributing patronage and individualizable benefits like Thanksgiving dinners, but also by being an accountable, responsive, and effective elected official. He used his power to reward friends and punish enemies. Using a sophisticated network of precinct and block captains, he commanded the loyalty of the voters in his ward, producing lop-sided victories for whichever candidate or referendum position he endorsed. This ability to influence voters in contests other than his own gave him outsized influence in Kansas City and Jackson County. The elder Pendergast never controlled more than three of the city's sixteen wards, insufficient to win elections on their own. However, at a time when Republicans and Democrats alternated control over local political institutions, no Democrat could expect to win city or countywide office without racking up large majorities in the Pendergast wards. When opponents of "Big Jim's" faction won Democratic nominations and failed to sufficiently accommodate his interests, the Pendergast machine would withhold its support in the general election and thus send the entire ticket down to defeat.[7]

During the period when the Pendergast organization was led by "Big Jim," it was only one of *many* machines operating in Kansas City. Unlike other big cities of the day, like New York's Tammany Hall, there was no single, hierarchical machine in Kansas City; instead, every primary election was a fierce contest for primacy between competing factions. The existence of multiple factions is a highly significant point, one with great relevance for the eventual emergence of Freedom, Inc. seventy years hence. The political culture that developed early on in Kansas City was one with multiple organizations competing with one another in order to win satisfaction of their respective demands; if existing organizations and factions were not responsive, new ones were formed. With political activity concentrated in factional organizations, it should come as little surprise that the city's black community would later choose to undertake a quest for empowerment and efficacy through a similar vehicle.

It was James Pendergast's younger brother, Tom, who developed the machine into a political legend, with its influence reaching all the way to the White House. "Big Jim" brought his younger brother into politics in the 1890s; as the elder brother's health began to fail, he increasingly relied on Tom to manage the affairs of the family machine. In 1910, voters overwhelmingly chose to send Tom Pendergast to City Hall to replace the ailing Jim. Tom tired of the life of a legislator quickly, but he developed a vision for building a grand political organization in Kansas City. To do so, Pendergast knew that he had to find a way to communicate effectively with voters outside of his rough-hewn, working-class North End base. The wealthier classes living in the city's ever-expanding southern reaches traditionally viewed the factions with disdain.[8]

By playing savvy politics, Pendergast gained a foothold even in the most prosperous of Kansas City's neighborhoods. With the proceeds from his successful concrete and construction business (as well as from illicit payoffs), "Boss Tom" left the North End behind and moved into a mansion on Ward Parkway, the city's most exclusive address. By expanding his political influence beyond the historic home of factionalism, Pendergast became the undisputed boss of the city from roughly 1915 until 1939. It was this extension of his machine into parts of the city where no other faction had ever won support that elevated Pendergast to the top of Kansas City's political pyramid. Although his machine did not win *every* election during that period and much transpired without his consent, "Boss Tom" was the most powerful man in Kansas City and perhaps even in the state.[9]

Throughout his entire time in power, a vigorous opposition existed, although until the late 1930s it met with only limited success. Hard though they tried, the organizations which agitated for reform had precious little to do with the eventual downfall of "Boss Tom." Events like the "Union Station Massacre" (where federal agents were murdered by mobsters in busy Union Station, and the mobsters assisted in their escape by corrupt law enforcement officers) cemented Kansas City's national reputation for criminal activity, causing even some of the machine's loyal defenders to blanche in shame.[10] Missouri's governor—elected as a loyal Pendergast protégé—began railing against the machine and using the full power of his office to attack its foundations.[11] In 1936, the machine became more brazen in its voter fraud activities than ever before. Even Pendergast's opponents conceded that his slate that year was headed to an overwhelming victory by honest means, such that fraud was unnecessary. Regardless, the fraud prompted a federal investigation. That investigation eventually pursued other avenues, one of which resulted in the boss being charged and convicted with tax evasion, from an illegal payoff he received on state insurance contracts. Pendergast was imprisoned, albeit briefly, in 1939 and released only on the provision that he strictly refrain from any political involvement.[12] He died shortly thereafter, and with him so did most of his machine.

What is most perplexing about the Pendergast saga is the fact that he worked diligently to build *organizational* strength, yet the machine did not survive his departure from the political scene. True, prosecutors and machine opponents successfully purged many of Pendergast's immediate subordinates who might have ascended to the role of citywide leader. It is still somewhat surprising that what outwardly appeared to be a well-organized, institutional machine should prove more akin to an ephemeral charismatic movement and dissipate so rapidly after the departure of its leader.

However, the demise of the citywide Democratic machine is less paradoxical when one remembers that Pendergast's accomplishment was the *exception* in local politics, not the *norm*. Recall that the city had long been home to a host of political organizations, each with geographic or demographic niche constituencies. These organizations continued to exist during the years of Pendergast dominance, as well. "Boss Tom's" real accomplishment was the cooptation and inclusion of these factions and organizations within his own infrastructure, not their total displacement. With Pendergast no longer in power, the machine's loyal elements reverted to their hyper-localized, faction-centric pattern. Democratic machine loyalists continued to exist, but conducted their political activities through dozens of political clubs, each with its own boss, constituency, agenda, political tactics, and constantly shifting alliances.

Kansas City did not suddenly become a "machine-less" town. On the contrary, the triumphant reform movement itself became machine-like. Although it arguably never engaged in the corrupt practices that it denounced when undertaken by the dreaded factions (a noun that became a slur), the reform movement and its primary organization, the Citizens Association (CA), became even more central to the city's political life than Tom Pendergast ever was.

The Reform Movement and the Citizens Association

By the middle of the twentieth century, Kansas City's national reputation no longer was one of vice, corruption, and being a "machine" town. To the extent that Kansas City was part of the national conversation during these years, it was because of its apparent success at undertaking political reform.[13] Gone were the days when the city was famous for booze, brothels, and jazz, replaced by a middling reputation for good government and tree-lined boulevards.

Kansas City's ascent from den of vice to darling of reformers was not rapid or easy. Early attempts at reform met with strong disapproval from the voters. As early as 1905, reform-minded citizens attempted to institute a new city charter that would "modernize" local government and minimize the influence of the factions. Like subsequent reform drives, the 1905 effort was primarily comprised of upper-class white men active in the finance, legal, and real estate professions. From the very beginning, the reformers seemed blind to the fact that the demographic profile of their movement, well-to-do, white, professional, disproportionately Republican, and concentrated in the city's far southern reaches, severely hampered their ability to communicate their message in a city where political victory could only be attained with the support of the substantial working class and at least some nominal Democrats. The proposed charter went down to defeat; although it won overwhelmingly in the upper-class wards, it lost just as overwhelmingly in the faction-controlled districts, and voters in the remainder of the city were evenly divided. Several other efforts were made in the 1900s and 1910s, with only one (in 1908) successful, and then only because the proposition gained support from both the factions and the reformers.[14]

After the defeat of yet another reform-oriented charter in 1917, the reformers became passionate about converting to a council-manager form of government. The council-manager system had been created just a few years previously in Dayton, Ohio, to great apparent success. Proponents of the system claimed as its chief virtues that it produced "efficiency," "economy," "science," "professionalism," and "nonpartisanship," all of which comported nicely with what Kansas City's upper-crust had long claimed was necessary in their city. Too often, the Kansas City reformers' idea of "efficiency" was simply that they would have their own way. When working class or poor Kansas Citians, particularly from the factional strongholds, had their own policy preferences enacted, these preferences were by definition "inefficient," "corrupt," or "unprofessional"—regardless of the merits involved. After a lengthy campaign the council-manager system could claim significant support in Kansas City. Machine leaders, self-aware and politically calculating as they were, felt threatened by the prospect of a council-manager system and prevented the move from gaining traction.[15]

But the major breakthrough for "reform" came from the man the movement cast as the chief villain, Tom Pendergast, who came to see the council-manager proposal differently than his factional brethren. When a council-manager charter was put before the voters in 1925, he vigorously supported it. In the Fifth Ward, his base of operations, 1,260 ballots were cast for the charter and only 75 were cast against it. Most other factional leaders followed Pendergast into temporary alliance with the reformers. Although the reform movement was more aggressive than ever, what permitted the 1925 charter (still largely in effect today) to win voter approval was the support of the machine. What caused Pendergast and other machine leaders to support this initiative, when they had opposed past reform efforts? First, Pendergast was preternaturally gifted at reading the public mood. He sensed the charter would be approved sooner or later, with or without him, and knew that his own power base would be strengthened by being on the winning side. Second, Pendergast came to view the council-manager system as an opportunity rather than a threat. Under the pre-1925 system, power was widely distributed in city government and the city council played an important management role. Pendergast cleverly realized something that eluded the reform forces: concentrating power in a single appointed official reduced the burden for a would-be boss. So long as Pendergast could wield leverage over a single individual—the city manager—he would continue to have access to patronage, contracting opportunities, and policy-making, all without the uncertainty of corralling independently elected council members.[16]

As a result, what should have been the crowning triumph of the decades-old reform movement became only an intermediate victory for it. Although popular memory in Kansas City today claims that the council-manager system and a weak mayor are necessary to halt the rise of another Pendergast,[17] the truth is that "Boss Tom's" machine achieved its highest peaks *after* the system was introduced. Kansas City's machine leader proved to be correct in his expectation that he would be able to better control the city manager than the city council.

The reformers quickly realized what they had wrought. The major reformist institutions remained committed to the council-manager system, but took every opportunity to expose corruption within the system and to critique the performance of the machine-oriented officials. At every municipal election, they strove to recapture what they regarded to be the spirit of 1925, with little success. The many visible accomplishments of the Pendergast-oriented municipal government, especially a grand new skyscraping City Hall and balanced books, weakened the reformers even in their upper-class heartland, while they utterly failed to expand their base into the machine-controlled wards. The city administration's accomplishments, especially the balanced books, would prove to be fraudulent, but the fraud was not exposed until after Pendergast had fallen from grace. Between 1925 and 1940, the reformers strove at every election to snatch victory away from the machine and failed miserably on every occasion.

In 1940, with Pendergast languishing in jail, the factions divided, and the machine's city manager in disgrace after his juggling of the municipal books became public, the reformers won the municipal election. This victory was spearheaded by the Citizens Association (CA), created in 1934 from the decaying Citizens League. The CA was the broadest-based of any of the reform organizations; although it was still inattentive to the interests of the poor and ethnic minorities, it cast its net further than the traditional upper-class white Anglo Saxon Protestant world of previous reform groups. Indeed, the CA's principal founder and spokesperson was a rabbi, Samuel Mayerberg. Also involved in the founding of the CA was one of the city's leading African American ministers, the Rev. D.A. Holmes. Inclusion of Holmes did not signal broad black participation in the movement, but it did represent the dawning of awareness on the part of reformers that they needed to expand their electoral base. That new awareness aside, the CA's mission remained identical to that of previous incarnations. In its official history, the contemporary CA describes its purpose in the 1930s and its 1940 romp to victory this way:

> At that time, corruption was rampant at City Hall. Vote stealing, bribery, and "country bookkeeping" were the order of the day. In 1940's [sic] "clean sweep" crusade, the Citizens Association successfully ousted the Pendergast political machine that had a stranglehold on City Hall. This campaign, billed as the "Battle of the Brooms," included a band of 7,500 women who wore badges depicting brooms. The Citizens Association became the dominant force for reform and good government for the next 65 years.[18]

For many years after 1940 the CA *was* the city's dominant political force. From 1940 until 1959, it won every municipal election. Its endorsed candidates won every mayoral election from 1940 until 1971 (and again from 1979 through 1987), and its candidates comprised a majority of the City Council from 1940 until 1959.[19] The CA's only competition for influence came from the *Kansas City Star,* the city's dominant newspaper and unofficial organ of the "reform" movement. The *Star* worked in close, if tacit, cooperation with the CA; CA leaders could rely on having their every utterance glowingly reprinted in the newspaper. The slates of candidates endorsed by the CA and the *Star* were, with rare exceptions, identical from the 1930s until 1979.

During the nineteen-year period when the CA achieved overwhelming electoral victories, Kansas City developed a national reputation for "good government." Reformers were quite pleased with themselves, hailing the fact that the city now lived up to the principles set out in its nonpartisan, reform-minded, efficiency-enabling charter. City manager L.P. Cookingham became a celebrity in municipal government circles as the man perceived as "turning Kansas City around."[20] Although it is certainly true that corruption declined during this period, not all was idyllic. Voter turnout declined precipitously after municipal elections were moved to the dead of winter, there were semi-credible claims that Cookingham used city staff to advance the CA and its candidates, infrastructure decayed, the problems of the poor and working class went largely unaddressed, and the city's primary strategy for stimulating economic growth was to annex land. Still, clear majorities of the Kansas Citians who took the time to vote cast their ballots for the CA slate. That organization was just as highly structured and institutionalized as any club ever bossed by a Pendergast. Like similar reform political organizations in other parts of the country,[21] the CA worked in close collaboration with the dominant local newspaper (the *Star*) and elites in order to retain political control. Although its stated ideals might have been quite different from those embraced by conventional political machines, in its first few decades the CA qualifies as a machine. The CA was aided by the fact that its opponents remained in disarray. There were literally dozens of autonomous political clubs that sometimes worked together, but frequently clashed for no discernible reason.

Like other political machines, even the CA could be defeated. In 1959, it was, to the great shock of local and national observers. With the CA experiencing internal rancor and the six major Democratic factions united for the first time in years, operating under the banner of the "Democratic Coalition," the factions emerged victorious. The Coalition capitalized on the fact that a good number of its CA opponents were "secret" Republicans, in a town that was overwhelmingly Democratic (even in the officially nonpartisan city elections). The Coalition's victory was, predictably, denounced by the *Star* and the CA's allies among the elite.[22] From the moment the Coalition's members took office in 1959 until their defeat in 1963, hardly a week went by without a hostile editorial in the *Star* about the sorry state of local government. Some of the past practices of patronage and police pay-offs returned, the City Council was hamstrung by division and noncooperation between its majority and minority, and the instability resulted in the city going through ten city managers between 1959 and 1963.[23] Some of these difficulties were produced by the resolute refusal of the CA and its allies to enter into *any* compromise with the Coalition; they sought to make the city ungovernable, in the hope that voters would punish the forces nominally in control.

Two major points about the CA should be stressed. First, even with the loss in 1959, the CA was unquestionably the leading political force in Kansas City in the early 1960s. It was the only organization with a citywide base, that had strong allies in the media and business sectors, that was not organized on the basis of personality or charisma, and that was a well-managed, professional, organization. Unlike its would-be competitors, the CA had a large membership, visible leaders, adequate finances, a clear strategy for achieving its goals, and mechanisms for implementing that strategy. In other words, it was a formal organization that used the benefits of structure to produce the outcomes it sought. Second, even with this predominance and the largely symbolic participation of a handful of prominent African Americans, the CA had not managed to significantly expand its influence into new territory or among diverse groups over the preceding twenty years. Working class whites and African Americans were not moved by the ritualistic invocation of reform and good government, while the CA had precious little to say about creating jobs or expanding opportunity for African Americans. As a result, many blacks involved in local politics organized, at the very least, outside of the city's dominant political institution and oftentimes in direct opposition to it.

The African American Experience in Kansas City

If African Americans seem largely absent or invisible in the preceding account, it is for good reason. The city fathers[24] generally behaved as though the city's African American population did not exist; on the rare occasions when the existence of this growing part of the population was acknowledged, it was not by mouths filled with praise. Blacks resided in Kansas City from the very beginning, albeit in small numbers. The first census of the City of Kansas, conducted in 1860, showed 190 people of African descent residing there. Missouri permitted enslavement of Africans, and 166—or almost 88 percent—of Kansas City's black population was comprised of enslaved people.[25] Despite being a slave state, Missouri opted to remain part of the Union during the Civil War—although a rump group, including the sitting governor and a minority of the state legislature, formed a secessionist state government in Neosho. Statewide opinion was divided, but the ostensibly more urbane residents of Kansas City appear to have been on the side of the Union, if primarily for economic reasons. This aside, the city and the state often resembled its southern neighbors in its treatment of African Americans.[26]

With emancipation, thousands of freedmen from rural Missouri made their way to the cities. The African American population of Kansas City jumped from 190 people in 1860 to 3,770 in 1870, an increase of an astounding 1,984 percent. As in other cities, an increase in the black population prompted a backlash from whites unaccustomed to black freedom, scornful of black humanity, and fearful of black economic competition. One of the first manifestations of an increasingly hostile racial climate was the imposition of a rigid pattern of residential segregation. Prior to the 1870s, residential segregation was not rigid in Kansas City—partly because of the city's geography, partly because of the small black population, and partly because, in the artful phrase of C. Vann Woodward, the "strange career of Jim Crow" had not yet been launched. From the 1870s until the 1970s, residential segregation in the city became ever-more rigid, even as the physical space where blacks were allowed to live grew. At first, blacks were generally forced to live in close proximity to the stockyards and rail depot. As the city expanded southward, the most desirable neighborhoods moved southward as well, to J.C. Nichols's master-planned Country Club District and the manses erected along Ward Parkway. African Americans were then permitted, even encouraged, to take up residence in once-genteel, now down-at-the-heels neighborhoods. By the dawn of the twentieth century, the parts of the city where African American settlement were permissible were very firmly defined. African Americans were not welcome west of Troost Avenue, or south of 27th Street. The housing stock was generally of poor quality, often owned by greedy white landlords who charged considerably more than it was worth, and over-crowded.[27]

White Kansas Citians and the local government apparatus used many tools, magnificently described by Gotham[28] to enforce residential segregation. They included complicity by the real estate industry (with practices like steering and redlining), an ill-fated attempt at defining racial residential patterns in city ordinance,[29] price-gouging, and outright violence. Throughout the 1910s and 1920s, attempts by blacks to move into historically white neighborhoods were met by bombings. Dozens of homes newly purchased by blacks were bombed by white racial "purists," anticipating the better-known spate of bombings in 1950s and 1960s Birmingham, Alabama by two generations. Although local newspapers serving the black community, especially the newly founded *Call,* were vociferous in their criticism of this violence, little was done about it. Neither the "reformers" nor the *Star,* otherwise always eager to denounce the machine-controlled police department, mustered up much concern when police turned a blind eye to this pandemic of violence. Even with such dedicated opposition, the geographic space occupied by the black community gradually expanded. Although the black community did not—and still has not—surmounted the western border of Troost Avenue, the southern boundaries slowly moved. Long after violent resistance to residential integration ceased, Kansas City remains highly segregated. Indeed, it ranks as one of only a handful of American cities that is "hyper-segregated."[30]

Although white supremacy was never as crude or overt as might be found in other corners of the country, race relations were not so different from those to be found in cities like Memphis or Little Rock or Chicago. Economic discrimination was rampant. African Americans encountered difficulty in securing employment; when they did, they received the hardest jobs and the lowest wages. Poverty within the black community was both more widespread and more devastating than among whites. City government was just as culpable in this discrimination as were private employers; the few African Americans employed by the City of Kansas City were typically segregated into all-black units and paid lower wages than whites doing comparable jobs.[31] The Kansas City Police Department was frequently assailed by African Americans for racism in hiring as well as policing.

A well-developed system of "petty apartheid" existed from after the Civil War until the mid-1960s. Indeed, in the early 1990s, even the *Kansas City Star* was moved to write of this period:

> People who were not here a generation ago scarcely can imagine how deeply racial segregation was embedded in the fabric of Kansas City. The schools were entirely separate. Blacks were not served in restaurants and were turned away at hotels. In theatres, blacks sat in the balcony. The city closed down the Swope Park swimming pool rather than integrate it [. . .] Blacks simply weren't seen on the Plaza or, indeed, were hardly seen south of 31st street unless they were in a maid's uniform or pushing a broom.[32]

The *Star* itself was no paragon of racial liberalism; news about the city's African Americans was virtually absent until the early 1970s and the rare blacks to grace the paper's pages were usually athletes, entertainers, or accused criminals. The civil rights movement succeeded in winning column space from the paper's editors, but coverage focused on the national—not the local—movement. Downtown department stores would not permit African American customers to try on clothes and would not permit black patrons to sit at their lunch counters. The city's amusement park, Fairyland, was a recurring irritation to local black leaders because, until 1964, it admitted African Americans only on its once-yearly "Negro Day."

Freedom, Inc. would prove instrumental in the eventual dismantling of this petty apartheid, but was a late addition to the constellation of local civil rights organizations. One advantage that Kansas City's blacks did have over their compatriots in cities further south was the vote; although there were occasional attempts to stifle black voter turnout, the disenfranchisement and intimidation campaigns that swept the South from the 1890s through the 1960s did not make their way to Kansas City.[33]

None of this recounting of the reality of racial discrimination should be surprising given the influence wielded by white supremacists. The Ku Klux Klan experienced a nationwide resurgence in the late 1910s and early 1920s; Kansas City was no exception to this trend. Although the KKK's influence was more widespread in eastern and rural Jackson County than in Kansas City proper, for a few years the organization decisively impacted close electoral contests.[34] The KKK faded from the local scene before the onset of the Great Depression, but racist sentiments certainly did not.

As in other cities, pervasive white supremacy and intense racial segregation did produce some limited benefits. Black-owned businesses of all sorts thrived on the east side of Troost, from funeral parlors to restaurants to insurance companies and clothiers. A solid, "respectable" middle-class of entrepreneurs, teachers, ministers, and a handful of professionals was fashioned. As African Americans developed an economic base of their own, limited and fragile though it was, they were increasingly able to speak out against the intolerable conditions in which they found themselves. *The Call,* for example, was founded in 1919 to serve the needs of the city's black population. Although not Kansas City's first black press organ, it would prove to be the most successful and longest-lasting, operating continuously into the present.

Perhaps the most famous consequence of intense residential segregation and white supremacy was the creation of "Kansas City jazz" and the emergence of an entire neighborhood of nightclubs and entertainment venues. The neighborhood around 18th and Vine, in the heart of the black community, became internationally famous as the home of some of the best music, food, and fun to be found. Some of the hotspots that earned 18th and Vine this worldwide reputation were owned and operated by local African Americans. Most of the performers who garnered widespread acclaim, like Count Basie, Dizzy Gillespie, and Myra Taylor, were also African American. Not everyone was charmed by 18th and Vine; the neighborhood's establishments were known for catering to all types of vice (from liquor to illicit drugs to gambling and prostitution), in which they were protected by payoffs to the corrupt police force. The city's reformers were zealous in their denunciation of the neighborhood for its criminality; although their position on making a "clean sweep" of the area did not originate in its racial character, it was enhanced by it. It is not a coincidence that the steady demise of the "Jazz District" began with the reformers' assumption of the reins of power.[35]

The relative isolation of the city's African American population produced a shared experience, a sense of linked fate, a feeling of community, dense intra-community networks, and a series of collective efforts to improve the status of that community. During Reconstruction, African Americans throughout the United States pursued electoral politics as a partial solution to the problems that ailed the community. Blacks in Kansas City were no exception, though the city's small black population prevented the strategy from achieving the same results that it did even on the opposite side of the state, in St. Louis, where the

Liberty League succeeded early on at electing blacks to local and state office.[36] The recognition that the vote might be used to gain power and improved living conditions never faded among black Kansas Citians, even if attempts to capitalize on its power usually ended badly. Leading black citizens organized a number of clubs designed to harness black political power. Political clubs of this kind existed exclusively to engage in electioneering activity, usually on behalf of white candidates, but they were controlled by African Americans. Contemporary commentators doubted the independence of these clubs, claiming that their leaders were "bought and paid for," thus anticipating a claim that would be made about every subsequent generation of Kansas City's black political leadership. The early clubs operated within Republican Party politics. During the years when neither party had a clear advantage in local elections, these African American political clubs were an important part of any Republican's march to victory. As a result, some limited gains—normally in the form of low-ranking patronage jobs—could be attained for the black community in the event of a favorable election outcome.[37] However, the black community's small share of the population, the rise to dominance of the local Democracy, and intense personal rivalries between black leaders prevented any of these black political organizations from attaining primacy or lasting very long.

Indeed, by the 1910s, these clubs were no longer exclusively Republican in their orientation. The local Republican Party was briefly commandeered by a group of xenophobic, intensely racist, anti-Catholic zealots in the 1890s, doing lasting damage to the party's reputation with African Americans. At the same time, the ascendancy of the local Democrats meant that African Americans seeking influence increasingly turned away from the Republicans. By the early 1930s the Republican impulse among Kansas City's African Americans was largely eradicated. In 1926, the GOP won 59 percent of the ballots in precincts with African American majorities. By 1930, the two wards that then had black majorities were giving 52 percent and 60 percent, respectively, of their votes to the Democratic Party. From 1932 on, the Democratic share of the black vote never fell below 60 percent.[38] Also by the early 1930s, the tradition of independent African American political clubs had largely come to an end. Ward and precinct organizations staffed by African Americans persisted, but they were controlled by the Pendergast machine, rather than being independent organizations.

Even after the conversion to the nonpartisan system of local government, black integration into the Democratic machine accelerated in the 1930s and

1940s. The city's reform element had little to say to black Kansas Citians and cared even less. This is not to say that no African Americans were part of the reform movement—the Rev. D.A. Holmes and T.B. Watkins are prominent exceptions—simply that reformism was not the dominant political expression in black Kansas City. African Americans were aware of the disdain in which they were held by the Democratic machine, but opted for minimally attentive disdain over the total disregard of the reform camp. Within the machine, African Americans were forced into a position of subservience. Residents of wards with black majorities were not permitted to select their own precinct captains or committee-people, much less elected officials. All decisions about leadership positions, candidates to support, and policy were dictated outside of the black community. By the 1950s and early 1960s, the city's five wards with black majorities (the 2nd, 3rd, 14th, 16th, and 17th—see Figure 2) were controlled by three white factional leaders: Henry McKissick, Louis Wagner, and Tim Moran. McKissick led the Jeffersonian Democratic Club (JDC), one of the city's six major factional organizations, until 1962. Although led by whites, the club's electoral strength came entirely from black majority wards, especially Ward 2 (which was nearly 100 percent African American in 1961). In 1962, McKissick handed off the reins of power to Louis Wagner, a white assistant prosecutor who lived near Ward Parkway—far away from the wards he "controlled." Wagner's control over voters in "his" precincts was managed through the distribution of petty items like alcohol, food, and shoes.[39] In the almost exclusively black 14th Ward, Tim Moran was the "boss." Moran did not rank as one of the city's top factional leaders; instead, his 14th Ward Democratic Club operated as a subfaction of the JDC, with Moran taking orders from McKissick and Wagner.[40]

Subservient political incorporation within the Democratic machine did yield some infrequent, symbolic benefits for the black community. Kansas City sent an African American state representative—a Republican—to Jefferson City as early as 1928. The individuals sent to Jefferson City from this district, which soon shifted from Republican to Democrat, were reliable cogs of the political machine rather than advocates for independent black interests. In the 1950s, three African Americans served in elective office in Kansas City—two as municipal judges and one as a machine-oriented member of the state House of Representatives.[41] Despite rapid population growth, African Americans in Kansas City lacked representation of even the symbolic variety on the City Council, the school board, the county court, and in the state Senate. Given this state of

Figure 2. Map of Wards and Precincts in Kansas City, Missouri (South of the Missouri River Only) in 1963.

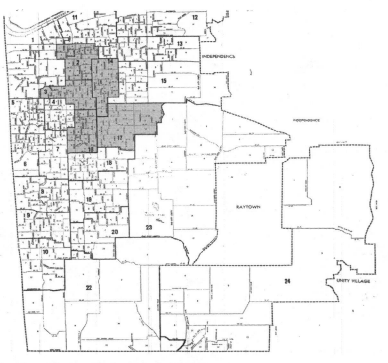

Map Source: Kansas City Star, March 25, 1963.

Note: Wards with African American majorities are shaded in grey, based on the author's calculations. The entire ward is shaded, even if it includes precincts that are overwhelmingly White. The third ward, for example, had only a narrow African American majority but is nevertheless shaded; the bulk of the ward's White population lived in the far western corner of the ward.

affairs, it is understandable that the city's African Americans alternately exhibited *ennui* and disgust with electoral politics.

This disgust was fuel to the fire of the civil rights movement, which intensified in the late 1950s. Scholars have rightly noted that the "civil rights movement" was actually *many* movements, driven by local concerns and local leaders, that were only loosely connected to each other.[42] Most of these local efforts gained minimal media attention, unless they happened to be graced with a visit from one of the "national" leaders that the generally uncomprehending white press wrongly presumed to be in control of a rigidly hierarchical movement. Although the victories in *Brown v. Board of Education* and the Montgomery bus boycott brought new hope, Kansas City was home to civil rights efforts before those momentous events. For example, Lucile Bluford, later editor of *The Call*, attempted unsuccessfully to follow in the footsteps of her friend Lloyd Gaines[43] and integrate the graduate school of journalism at the University of Missouri. During World War II, local African Americans participated in A. Philip Randolph's March on Washington Movement. That movement pressured Franklin D. Roosevelt into issuing Executive Order 8802, which ostensibly prohibited racial discrimination among defense contractors. Just a few months prior to the issuance of the order, *The Call* and *The Kansas City Star* drew attention to the blatantly discriminatory hiring practices of North American Aviation, a defense plant in Kansas City, Kansas that was owned by General Motors. Although North American Aviation did not substantively change its hiring policies as a result of the new Executive Order, local activists still felt as though they had accomplished something worthwhile.[44] The most substantial civil rights activity prior to *Brown* and Montgomery, came from a group calling itself the Committee on the Practice of Democracy (CO-POD). COPOD was founded in 1942 by white liberals with scattered participation by blacks, and was affiliated with the national Congress of Racial Equality (CORE). COPOD first promoted residential integration, then founded a "Fellowship House" where interracial groups could meet (as most public halls in the city prohibited interracial gatherings), and then sought to integrate restaurants and public facilities by dispatching interracial groups to demand service. In 1951, the NAACP succeeded in persuading the City Council to integrate city-owned facilities, including Municipal Auditorium, the airport's restaurant, and the city's outdoor theatre. Civil rights activists also sought the integration of the city-owned swimming pool, but the city refused.

This standoff led to litigation, and during the years that it took for the courts to rule that the city could no longer deny admission to African Americans, the pool was closed to everyone.[45] Local political leaders were adamant that these reforms could not be the precursors to integrated schools or to integrating privately owned facilities, except at the discretion of their owners.

Inspired by *Brown* and by Montgomery, local African Americans began to take ever-more aggressive action against segregation. A new cadre of black leaders (albeit self-proclaimed ones) slowly emerged. These new leaders were young, college-educated, middle-class professionals, or entrepreneurs whose businesses catered to the African American community. At the same time that they worked within the political system, and many had ties to the factions, they began to loudly assert that the "old ways" of relying on the political machines or on the goodwill that whites might accord to individual intermediaries (like black clergymen) were no longer sufficient.

New tactics—sit-ins and protest marches—were adopted by the more activist element of the local African American community beginning in 1957. A municipal Human Rights Commission report found that many hotels and theaters in downtown Kansas City were desegregated, but that the downtown department stores and restaurants were not. A local women's club proposed an active campaign of challenging this segregation; the challenge was taken up by a new organization calling itself the Community Committee for Social Action (CCSA). The CCSA was itself a federation of other organizations, primarily the social and professional clubs of African Americans as well as the local chapter of the NAACP. Although the leadership of the CCSA was solidly middle-class and entirely black, the movement attracted the support of the black working class and some limited endorsement from liberal whites.

The CCSA engaged in a forceful campaign of direct action, concentrating their ire on downtown department stores and lunch counters. None of the city's downtown stores permitted black patrons to try on clothes, none of the lunch counters were integrated, and these same establishments refused to hire African Americans as anything other than after-hours janitorial staff or an occasional warehouse employee. The CCSA demanded immediate integration of the facilities and, more importantly, that the stores commit to hiring large numbers of African American employees. Most of Kansas City's whites were appalled by this new activist strain. Members of the ostensibly progressive "reform" movement could not comprehend what the fuss was about. One of the movement's fawning chroniclers, Kenneth Gray, lamented that the advent of protest was a sign that black leadership lacked the "savoir-faire" of the past.[46]

Still, CCSA's pickets and boycotts of the downtown stores were successful. Black customers stayed away, as did some whites. The sharp decline in business led some stores to accept integration, although they insultingly called for "training" courses for black customers who they presumed to lack the grace and manners required for the fine dining experience of consuming a hot dog at the Woolworth's lunch counter. After the first few stores were integrated without a serious white backlash, the remaining stores followed suit.[47] Even with this progress, segregation remained pervasive. In 1961, the city lost the national convention of the American Federation of State, County, and Municipal Employees because blacks were routinely denied service. The city's convention bureau spokesperson lamented the loss to the *Star,* wondering why the world did not believe that Kansas Citians believed in "liberty and justice for all," since, as he termed it, "only" the city's motels, bowling alleys, hospitals, skating rinks, small restaurants, and recreational facilities were segregated while "most" convention hotels and large restaurants were integrated.

More serious was the fact that one of the major objectives of the CCSA campaign—employment opportunities for African Americans in downtown stores—was unsuccessful. Schirmer maintains that this objective was limited to working class picketers, but interview subjects for this book who participated in the movement disagreed. One long-time activist in the African American community stressed that employment was a major issue of the movement and the marches, but maintained that, "They had been doing marches downtown for years. But the marches didn't seem to help. The way they settled all the marches was, they gave [a prominent African American woman] a job at one of their department stores, to pacify us. Otherwise they never really got much."[48] When African Americans sought help from their ostensible allies at City Hall—especially after 1959, when the Democratic Coalition of which black voters were a part seized power—they received none. Neither the City Council nor Mayor H. Roe Bartle were willing to take further action, believing that the questions of hiring practices and discriminatory accommodations were ones to be resolved by private business owners.

Another node of black political activity was the church, which Carter G. Woodson once called the "all-comprehending institution" and Hanes Walton ranked as one of the most important socializing institutions in black life. Kansas City was no exception. Some churches and ministers embraced the otherworldly, "leave it to Jesus" orientation that is a recurring minor theme in black religious history, but just as many adopted a more prophetic voice. The city's black churches and clergy tended to be critical of the Democratic machine, primarily for its collaboration with vice, but did not embrace the reform movement. Most of the city's ministers were not firmly identified with either the Democratic or reform machines. Instead, they adopted the pragmatic posture of intermediaries. White elites allowed some leeway for these ministers to be respectfully heard when making policy appeals, or to intercede on behalf of individual parishioners in trouble, in exchange for containing black discontent.

A final node of black political activity was to be found in *The Call,* the primary newspaper serving the black community. The newspaper was founded by C.A. Franklin in 1919, and soon succeeded in driving competing organs of the black press out of business. Franklin's paper thrived by adopting a firm editorial line in favor of black interests, if a bourgeois variation of those interests. *The Call* did, in fact, become "Southwest's leading weekly," as its slogan claimed, with a national edition that reached tens of thousands of readers throughout the Midwest and Southwest. *The Call* was also, until the 1960s, a reliably Republican newspaper. In this the paper was increasingly out of touch with its readers even as it became the gold standard for news about Kansas City's black community. The paper grew in circulation and influence under the editorships of Roy Wilkins (later executive secretary of the NAACP) and Lucille Bluford, adopting a more aggressive posture in defense of civil rights. Before the founding of Freedom and the election of independent black officials, *The Call* was one of the few vehicles the city's African American population possessed for expressing discontent or pursuing remediation of its issues. Indeed, the city's first African American mayor, Emanuel Cleaver, once paid tribute to Ms. Bluford by saying, "Miss Bluford will go down in history as one of the most unparalleled African-American personalities in our city. At one time, we had no African-American council members or representatives. All we had was Miss Bluford."[49]

As important as *The Call* was to Kansas City's African American community in the years prior to 1962, it was largely disconnected from other elements of the movement for black progress. The paper reported on the events of black churches, civil rights organizations, and even the black sub-machine controlled by Wagner, but there was no strong alliance between any of these elements. Attainment of substantive victories for African Americans was impeded by this fragmentation and the fact that theoretically allied organizations were in fact working at cross-purposes.

Several points about the black political experience in Kansas City should now be quite clear. First, white supremacy was "deeply embedded" in Kansas City. Outright violence had declined by 1962 and the local civil rights movement had won some victories, but segregation remained more or less in place and black interests went untended. Second, the vote had long been an integral part of black Kansas Citians' efforts to secure change in living conditions and local politics. Organizations were formed and efforts to harness the power of the vote were made; the fact that these had not proven successful inspired disgust and resignation, but did not disengage African Americans from the political process. Third, even with the demise of independent black politics in the 1920s and 1930s, formal organizations remained the primary vehicle for African American political involvement. Finally, prior to 1962, black politics in Kansas City could be described as fragmented, manipulated by white outsiders, and impotent.

This chapter has shown that the political culture of Kansas City was one where formal organizations were the dominant actors in local politics, first in the form of partisan machine politics (Pendergast) and then as reformist machine politics (the CA). African Americans were never incorporated into these organizations. Democratic and reform machines alike systematically ignored or rejected black demands on the system, put African Americans in subservient positions, and were totally unconcerned by the prevalence of virulent white supremacy in Kansas City. Disgust with the system, the slow pace of change, the inadequacy of the local protest movement to fundamentally change the city or win victories on economic issues, and the disregard with which they were held even by "allies" grew among African Americans. As a result, the sense grew that *something* needed to be done differently. The political context and culture of Kansas City in 1962 was such that the organizing of a black LPO was a logical remedy. The founding of just such an organization is the subject of the next chapter.

CHAPTER 2

Tired of Being Political Pawns
The Founding and Early Years of Freedom
(1962–1968)

Before the Dawn of Freedom

The realities of white racism, economic hardship, and political impotence all contributed to the founding of a black political organization, Freedom, Incorporated, in 1962. But these conditions long pre-dated the emergence of that LPO; indeed, they had been present since the founding of the Town of Kansas without ever producing the sort of independent black politics that Freedom would embody. The crucial difference was that the political context of the city—indeed, the entire country—was slowly changing. In Kansas City, as elsewhere, both reform and its agonizingly slow pace led African Americans to explore new strategies for empowerment. Thanks to its own efforts and this changing context, by the end of the decade, Freedom would be relatively institutionalized, corporatist, capable of achieving the mobilization of the African American population, and able to engage in effective short-term bargaining with white political actors. As a result, the city's black community achieved higher levels of political efficacy than ever before.

The local civil rights movement's protest marches at downtown department stores and restaurants were not successful at achieving all of their objectives, but they were a smashing success in prompting local African Americans to consider what a "new Kansas City" would look like and to ponder unorthodox strategies for achieving their goals. The protest marches also showed definitively that the city's African Americans could not rely on white elected officials for assistance. Although some members of the City Council and Mayor H. Roe Bartle insisted that they supported fairness and justice, none became a profile in courage by advocating for immediate and expansive integration. Indeed, Bartle seemed to think that he was doing African Americans a favor simply by deigning to meet with representatives of the NAACP. It became quite clear that the only way that black interests would be regularly heard at City Hall, would be through electing

African American members to the City Council. The sense that an African American councilperson was a necessity was buttressed by the fact that the black population was growing, in both absolute and relative terms; between 1950 and 1960, the city's black population grew by almost 50 percent while the white population declined. Almost a fifth of the city's residents were African American in 1960, yet the community had no real representation in municipal government.

The Redistricting Campaign of 1961

Out of these sentiments sprang a full-fledged effort in 1961–1962 to enact the most significant reform to the City Charter since its adoption in 1925, by altering the composition of the City Council. Although no one could have known it at the time, the redistricting campaign would prove to be the major impetus and an organizational dry run for the establishment of Freedom, Inc.

Since the adoption of the reform City Charter in 1925, Kansas City had been governed by a nine-member City Council. Four members of the Council were elected in districts, four members were elected at-large (with one member required to live in each of the districts), and the mayor was elected at-large to preside over and vote in the assembly. As the city grew, the number of residents per district grew as well. In 1925, there were roughly 75,000 residents in each district; by 1961, each district was home to more than 125,000 people. Even though the African American share of the population was increasing and heavily concentrated in a narrow corridor, there were not enough black votes to sway the results of even one district election (much less the at-large contests) for an African American candidate. Even though the mission was obviously suicidal—at least without the strong backing of either the Democratic factions or the CA, neither of which saw any need for such a mission—by 1961 three black candidates had run for Council under the Charter system, each going down to a lopsided defeat.[1]

A round of major annexations in the late 1950s added huge swathes of sparsely populated territory north of the Missouri River and in the far south of the city. Under the city's existing scheme of districts, these residents had no representation. The CA and the Democratic Coalition alike saw redistricting as an opportunity to curry favor with these new voters in advance of the 1963 municipal elections. All parties agreed that redistricting was a necessity, and moved forward quickly. Mayor Bartle convened a Charter Review Commission, which recommended the 6–6 proposal of a City Council composed of thirteen members: six elected in districts, six elected at-large (one from each district), and the mayor.[2] This was also the favored option of the CA, which argued that the plan balanced parochial interests with the needs of the city as a whole. Others felt differently; individuals associated with the factions organized a Committee for Better Area Representation (CBAR) to press for a system where twelve members would be elected from districts and only the mayor would be elected at-large.[3] Denunciation rained down on the CBAR plan from the CA, the Chamber of Commerce, and the *Star*, all of whom insisted that the twelve district plan was a ploy to ensure permanent factional control of the Council.[4] They asserted that the Democratic factional leaders would gerrymander districts in such a way that the bogey-man of "controlled votes" (a euphemism for faction supporters and African Americans) would dominate elections.[5] CBAR gathered enough signatures to put its plan on the March 1962 ballot, where it competed with the 6–6 plan of the reform set.[6]

For the first few weeks of the debate it went unnoticed in the *Star* or *Times* that African Americans were skeptical of the 6–6 proposal. Yet, the lone black elected official at the city level, municipal judge Lewis Clymer, was one of the earliest CBAR leaders.[7] CBAR experienced substantial internal tension, prompting Clymer and a number of other officials to resign a few weeks later, a fact that did attract the notice of the white press, but he still expressed support for the CBAR proposal.[8] Many African Americans were put off by the political maneuvering taking place in CBAR but still supported the *concept* of more districts with smaller populations. *The Call* first editorialized that both plans had merits and stressed that its top priority was electing an African American to the City Council in 1963. Eventually, however, the paper came out in support of the "6–6" proposal, saying that voting for the at-large seats gave the black community clout it would lack under the "12 district" plan. This was a questionable conclusion even then, but decades of subsequent investigation has shown that African Americans rarely wield as much power in cities with at-large council members as they do in pure district systems. As part of its relentless (and shameless) campaign to defeat the twelve-district plan, the *Star* put the *Call*'s editorial on its own front page. Although they did not say so publicly at the time, some white 6–6 supporters later claimed that the factions intended to draw the boundaries of their proposed twelve districts to ensure that only a single African American would be elected to the Council.[9]

Some African Americans continued to support the twelve-district plan for two reasons. First, the plan's supporters claimed that it would have resulted in at least two, and possibly three, districts sending black council people to City Hall.

Even the handful of African Americans who were members of the CA made it clear that electing a black councilperson was their top priority in 1963.[10] Second, the proposal was strongly supported by the Democratic faction leaders who exercised political control over the wards with black majorities. The five wards with black majorities (see Figure 2 in the preceding chapter) were considered part of the turf of Henry McKissick and Louis Wagner's Jeffersonian Democratic Club (JDC). McKissick and North End faction leader Alex Presta were the two staunchest advocates of doing away with at-large seats on the City Council. McKissick retired before the March 1962 election, turning over the machine's reins to Wagner. Wagner and the other factional bosses knew that their redistricting proposal could emerge victorious only with heavy turnout and high margins from the wards with black majorities. Wagner and his ally Tim Moran gathered the members of the Democratic committee from their precincts (many of whom were white, and some of whom did not even live in the area) and gave them instructions to recruit workers and to distribute cash, food, liquor, and favors, as necessary.

One of the committee people to whom Wagner and Moran turned was Leon Jordan, who had been elected (or, more accurately, selected by Moran) as the Democratic Committeeman for the 14th Ward in 1958. Jordan is a fascinating figure in his own right and not simply because of his later role as one of the founders of Freedom, Inc. Jordan served in the military, was a social worker, was a public school teacher, and, most notably, was a police officer. He joined the Kansas City Police Department in 1936, cultivating a reputation for honesty, integrity, and fairness among blacks and whites alike. In 1947, he left the United States to become the national Chief of Police in Liberia, a post that he held with distinction and to international acclaim for five years. He returned to Kansas City as a police sergeant in 1952, but quickly became disillusioned with the menial work to which he was assigned and by the rampant racism in the city and the police department. After expressing his displeasure with the treatment he was receiving, Jordan became the first African American promoted to the rank of lieutenant. He resigned from the department several days later, upon learning that the "promotion" carried with it no actual duties.[11] Jordan then entered the world of business, working closely with the white owner of the Green Duck Tavern at 25th and Prospect. The tavern's owner, Tim Moran, controlled the 14th Ward—in the very heart of the African American community—and took a liking to Jordan. Jordan bought the tavern from him in 1955, earned his confidence, and won selection as the ward's Democratic committeeman.[12] As a former police officer, Jordan was (mistakenly) assumed by the white factional leaders to be someone who would defer to authority and whom they would be able to control. He apprenticed under white factional leaders for several years, learning from them how the system worked, who was influential and who was not, and the "nuts and bolts" of electioneering. At the same time that he could rely on the confidence of the white factional leaders, Jordan earned the trust and respect of the people who actually lived in the area. Someone who knew Jordan well recalled that, "He was always out there working and struggling for poor people and to help us get our rights."[13]

When Wagner and Moran directed Jordan to produce solid margins for the redistricting effort, the retired police officer adopted a slightly different approach than he had in past campaigns. Rather than simply summoning workers who were blindly loyal to the machine, he instead contacted individuals whom he knew personally and whose loyalty was to the black community. That represented a dramatic departure from the way that black politics had been conducted in the past and was a step toward independence from the factions. Jordan identified roughly twenty people to work the polls in the 14th Ward on the day of the referendum. They were distributed across the precincts and trained in the art of talking to voters and passing out sample ballots.[14] Based on conversations he was having with friends, Jordan already had the idea for an independent black political organization in mind as he planned the 14th-Ward campaign for redistricting in the winter of 1962.

The move to create twelve districts and discard at-large seats on the City Council failed overwhelmingly. Black voters were an important part of the rejection of the twelve-district plan. In all but one of the wards with a black majority, the district proposal lost. In Jordan's 14th Ward, the twelve-district plan did better than almost anywhere else but still lost, 830 to 1,055 votes. The 2nd Ward, the almost exclusively black center of Wagner's JDC, produced one of the few bright spots for the all-district campaigners, providing 1,492 votes for the plan and 514 against it.[15] Black voters' rejection of the twelve-district proposal can be interpreted as a rejection of the factions themselves and of a growing desire for political independence.

Instead, the 6–6 plan emerged victorious. As a result of the redistricting required under that plan, one of the districts—the Third District—had an African American majority. That majority was very slight, just barely over 50 percent, because faction leaders opted to place the bulk of the Wagner-controlled 2nd Ward (and its "controlled" votes) in a different district, with the goal of helping a faction-supported white incumbent. Still, the Third District's slight African American majority meant that at least one and possibly two members of the

Council would be black after the 1963 election, if a black candidate could win support for the at-large seat.

Three things about the redistricting battle would prove to possess lasting importance. First, as noted earlier, the campaign provided Leon Jordan with the embryonic infrastructure of an organization independent of the Democratic factions. Second, it proved once more that the Democratic factions were not reliable allies. Despite the fact that African Americans were a crucial part of the Democratic Coalition's base, its elected officials were unresponsive during the civil rights protests and did little to serve black interests. As if that neglect were not enough, the coalition seemed politically impotent. Continued dependence on the factions, Jordan and his associates reasoned, was thus unproductive both for policy reasons (the community was not benefiting from the alliance) and for pragmatic ones (the coalition would be soon be defeated, and not in a position to provide benefits). Third, the redistricting solution ultimately arrived at provided a new opportunity for black political power. If the tangible gains to be realized from that opportunity were to be maximized, a whole new approach would be required. Black voter rejection of the factions perhaps signaled that the time was ripe for just such a new approach.

"Dignity, Equality, Freedom—Thru Unity"
The Founding of Freedom, Inc.

After the March 1962 redistricting campaign, a new approach—an independent black LPO, Freedom, Incorporated—rapidly materialized. Leon Jordan's disillusionment with the JDC and the Democratic factions in general had been growing for some time. Beginning in 1961, the topic of conversation among Jordan and his friends, most notably funeral home owner Bruce Watkins, was the urgent need for black political independence. They maintained that the pressing needs of the black community were being ignored because African Americans were regarded as a "controlled vote." This circle's analysis of the situation in black Kansas City foreshadows the arguments made several decades later by scholar Ronald Walters in his book *Black Presidential Politics*. African Americans in Kansas City prior to 1962 attempted to use "dependent leverage," hoping that their inclusion in the coalition of the factions would result in tangible benefits for the community. Instead, the factions subordinated black interests to their own and believed the black vote could be cheaply purchased through benefits like liquor, patronage jobs, and the occasional cash payout. Even when African Americans, like state representative J. McKinley Neal, were elected to office, they acted on the orders of factional leaders rather than those of the black community. Jordan's circle held that the only solution was for the city's African Americans to become politically independent. Doing so would result in an increased number of black elected officials and those officials would in turn genuinely advocate for black interests, producing substantive change for the community.

The group centered around Jordan and Watkins was far from alone in holding this sentiment. Local NAACP president Lee Vertis Swinton was scornful of the twelve-district plan, believing that it would bind blacks more closely to the factions at a time when the community sought to chart its own destiny. (Incidentally, Swinton's position endeared him to white elites, enhancing a stature that had been lowered through his involvement in the downtown protests.) African American businessman and CA vice chair Everett O'Neal insisted that black Kansas Citians wanted "graft-free," honest, and independent politics, but (unconsciously) subverted his own argument by then imploring African Americans to join the CA.[16] In the spring of 1962, at the same time that local African Americans had been assured by factional leaders that they would boost the number of local black elected officials, a large number of faction-affiliated black candidates filed to run in the August Democratic primary. Many races had multiple black candidates facing off against a lone, faction-friendly white incumbent; independent-minded African Americans interpreted this as a clear sign that the factions were not serious about increasing black representation and were instead resorting to the time-tested strategy of "divide and conquer" to retain power while still claiming that they welcomed black candidates.

In response, Jordan intensified the conversations about political independence with five of his closest friends: real estate agent Fred Curls, attorney Leonard Hughes, business owner Howard Maupin, chiropractor Dr. Charles Moore, and funeral home owner Bruce Watkins. These men were all prominent in the community, respected for their business acumen, intelligence, personal warmth, and commitment to community progress. The six men met at Jordan's Green Duck Tavern, developing a strategy to, in the words of a longtime Freedom activist, "organize and bring everybody together politically because the [civil rights] marches ain't getting it."[17] The goal was to achieve black political independence, from the factions, the CA, the *Star*, and anyone else outside the community, thereby producing benefits for the African American community that the protest strategy was incapable of securing by itself. The six men had all been involved at least peripherally in politics, though Jordan and Watkins had the most experience. Jordan's background has already been described; Watkins was the stepson of one of the most prominent black Kansas Citians of the 1920s and 1930s, Theron B. Watkins. The elder Watkins had run (unsuccessfully) for elective office, was one of the leading figures in black Republican politics in the Midwest, and played a small part in founding the CA.[18] Bruce Watkins inherited a share in the family's successful funeral parlor, serving as its vice president, but spent much of his time on community projects. In 1956 he ran unsuccessfully for state representative as a Republican.[19] Ironically, Leon Jordan lost the Democratic primary for the same post in the same year, but by the end of the 1950s had joined the 14th Ward Democratic Club run by Tim Moran.[20] Watkins made a name for himself as a caring and community-conscious activist; a close friend of his who followed Watkins into Freedom said of him:

> From the funeral home on, he was always helping people. And whatever he could do to help anybody, he would do it. From the funeral business, if you was short of money, he would try to help you get some way so you could get a decent funeral. When it comes to getting out here with the people, if somebody abused you downtown, he was right down there on it at the courthouse or at City Hall.[21]

All six men were steeped in the Kansas City tradition of factional politics, where a multitude of organizations serving defined demographic or geographic constituencies were major players, alternately competing and collaborating with one another for power. Operating within this political culture, the logical step for the six men to take in the pursuit of political independence was the initiation of their *own* organization.

That is precisely what they did. The six founders called a meeting of all those who had worked with Jordan in the 14th Ward on the redistricting campaign. About thirty people met at the Jordan-owned Carver Theater at the end of April 1962. There they heard a presentation from the six founders about their vision for a new organization, had the massive scope of the work to be done impressed upon them, and were asked to participate. As a result of the meeting, Freedom, Inc. was formally organized to pursue political independence, better representation, enhanced political efficacy, and articulation of black interests in the 14th Ward. In its earliest incarnation, Freedom would concern itself only with politics in the 14th Ward, just one of the five wards in which African Americans were then in the majority. Jordan was named president, Moore became vice president, Curls was appointed secretary, Maupin was elected treasurer, and Watkins began service as chair of the board of directors. On April 27, 1962, the organization received its certificate of incorporation from the state and was officially launched. A short article appeared in the following week's edition of *The Call*,[22] where, if the group's name and logo, one of black hands being loosed from chains, did not make the point clear enough, Jordan explained Freedom's premise:

> One of the main goals of the group will be to follow through politically with the fight so gallantly being conducted by the NAACP, the CCSA [the local civil rights group active in the downtown store campaign] and other groups in the struggle for complete freedom on all fronts. [. . .] We as a group are tired of being political pawns for a few Ward Parkway leaders. As evidenced by the large number of Negroes who have filed to run in the August primary, the same old practice of 'dividing us and ruling us' is apparent.[23]

Although Jordan was the group's leader and chief spokesperson, the other personalities involved made it clear from the outset that Freedom was not organized around him. Curls told *The Call* "we are fortunate to have a leader among us with the vision and courage that Leon Jordan possesses. However, this is no one-man organization. The governing body is composed of men of the 14th Ward who make their living in the 14th Ward and who, therefore, are greatly concerned about area representation of the ward."[24] In this, Freedom differed considerably from its factional predecessors, which were frequently organized around the charisma, economic interests, or political connections of their leaders. Importantly, all six founders were independent, self-employed business people. They relied on themselves and the black community for their incomes, which meant that they could not be penalized by outside interests for their political stances. Just as importantly, since the founders were self-employed, they faced no meaningful restrictions on when and how much political work they could do; if something needed to be done in the middle of a workday, one of the founders could go and do it, something that wage laborers or patronage employees could not do with the same ease. Those intimately involved in Freedom would later cite this independence and freedom of action as being essential to the LPO's initial success, as well as being an important characteristic of successful contemporary leaders.[25] Like the CA, but unlike many of the factions, Freedom was not a personality cult but mission-oriented from the start.

That mission, however, was different from anything else Kansas City had seen before. The slogan adopted by the organization, which has been retained on the

Freedom logo ever since, explains that mission succinctly: "Dignity, Equality, Freedom—Thru Unity." Freedom was organized to advance the causes of dignity, equality, and freedom for African Americans, and saw the path to achieving these goals as being political unity. Jordan, Watkins, and the other founders recognized quite clearly that if African Americans cast their votes in a bloc, they might determine the outcomes of many elections. Especially since the black share of the population was growing, this potential power meant that the African American community could make demands on the system in exchange for their support. This mission, and the total independence from any other group, distinguished Freedom from the handful of other African American LPOs that already existed at this time, like Herman A. Johnson's Mid City Democratic Club[26] or the City-wide Democratic Club (which was not citywide at all). What was needed to realize nascent African American power was an independent organization that would make political decisions based on the best interests of the African American community, to coordinate the effort, to responsibly negotiate with other groups and voting blocs, to educate voters, and to inspire hope in the possibilities afforded by unity. Although the organization refrained from adopting a manifesto or declaring any rigid ideological orientation, seeking from the start to be a "broad church" movement, the desire for autonomy, self-determination, an organization with a black membership and leadership, support for a defined set of black interests, and black unity are all textbook examples of what has been termed *community nationalism*. This is a form of proto-nationalism whose aspirations fall short of Garveyite emigration, territorial independence, or Nation of Islam-style separation. In its structure and intent, though not in an ideological program, Freedom was thus a proto-nationalist organization that differed considerably from some of the other consciously interracial organizations springing up during this period.

Freedom was from the beginning a formal organization intended to be independent and long-lasting, engage in multiple tactics ranging from protest to electioneering, and press for specifically black interests by organizing the black community first. In short, then, Freedom was from the beginning intended to be institutionalized. The important role that this played, coupled with the other elements of the theory of institutionalization, namely the organization's ability to be corporatist, heavily mobilize black voters, and engage in short-term bargaining with other political forces, in promoting black political efficacy can be seen from the story of the first Freedom campaigns for office.

The First Freedom Campaigns (1962–1964)

The first members of Freedom recognized that neither independence from the JDC nor political efficacy for the 14th Ward's residents (much less the broader black community) could be achieved through Freedom's mere existence. Instead, change would come only through a strategy of assiduously courting the black community's support and mobilizing it into action.

The Precinct Captain Infrastructure

Freedom's small founding group therefore immediately went to work at building a grassroots network, using many of the same tactics that Jordan, Watkins, and other politically involved members had learned from factional chiefs. Working quietly—though at least some of the ignorance of Freedom's activities came from opponents who refused to believe that there would ever be a time when black Kansas Citians did not simply do as Louie Wagner and Tim Moran instructed them—Freedom assembled an enviable network of precinct captains within the 14th Ward. As the theory of black political efficacy argued for here avers, this direct link to and mobilization of the community would prove to be a central element in Freedom's success and in achieving satisfaction of African American demands on the system. Long after the factions dissipated, Freedom would continue to maintain a strong infrastructure of precinct captains.

Within a matter of a few weeks, Freedom had precinct captains in place in all eighteen of the ward's precincts. Many of the new precinct captains were involved with Jordan in the redistricting campaign and attended the initial meeting at the Carver Theater, but a handful were attracted to it in the days that followed by the message of black political independence and unity. Importantly, the precinct captains were not just titular activists; they were expected to *work* their precincts and interact with their neighbors. As one person active in Freedom since its earliest days said,

When we started with Freedom, you had a committeeman and a committeewoman to work the ward. They got the poll workers and every poll had a precinct captain. And your captain was the one working the polls, they got maybe two people to work with them. And this is how we worked it. And the committeeman and committeewoman made sure that all that day the polls were manned properly and the people were working. Before the election, the committeeman and committeewoman made sure that the precinct captain worked that ward. And you had to work it.[27]

For that reason, captains were carefully selected. The first eighteen were diverse in gender, age, profession, and political experience. All were appalled by the conditions with which African American Kansas Citians were forced to cope, eager to serve Freedom's cause, hard workers, and, crucially, respected figures in their neighborhoods or professional circles. Tapping into these reservoirs of respect and goodwill allowed Freedom precinct captains to begin approaching their neighbors about political issues immediately and year-round, rather than just around elections. As one Freedom precinct captain explained:

> The point I'm making is Freedom used to have to work the ward. We'd go door to door. And they don't do that anymore. They just go there out on election day. [. . .] And get poll workers from wherever. And the poll workers don't even know how to work a ward. The point I'm saying is the committeeman or committeewoman are not doing what they used to do.[28]

Another Freedom activist, involved since young adulthood, stressed that the fact that Freedom was "around consistently, all year long." This activist emphasized that precinct captains engaged in vigorous door-to-door organizing and phone banking, informing neighbors about the issues and what Freedom was seeking to accomplish.[29] From its founding, Freedom maintained an office; voters were encouraged to drop by and to treat this as a communal gathering space, where political issues could be discussed, gossip exchanged, friendships formed, and strategy shaped.

All of these in-person, precinct-level contacts allowed Freedom to effectively compete with others seeking to influence and communicate with 14th Ward voters. Wagner and Moran's factions were generally absent from the daily lives of their followers, appearing only in the weeks preceding an election and then disappearing into the mist, and in any event increasingly relied on bribes rather than making intellectual, emotive, or interest-based appeals. The CA simply ignored the African American majority wards. The *Star* and *Times* were not widely read in the black community, and *The Call* had a circulation of less than 20,000. Freedom and its aggressive, in-person contact strategy filled a void in political information and activism.

Surviving August 1962
The Partial Victory of the First Freedom Campaign

Creating and mobilizing this network of precinct captains took on urgency in the spring of 1962, because Freedom's first electoral test was just a few months away. Partisan primaries for state and federal offices were to be held in August. A record number of African Americans had filed for office, though many were suspected of being factional plants and serious candidates did not emerge to challenge a number of higher-ranking machine stalwarts, like state representative J. McKinley Neal. At the level of Democratic committee people, though, the competition was fierce. Although not typically high profile, these positions were coveted by activists for their influence over party nominees and policy. Faction leaders had long used their ability to sway outcomes in these low-interest, low-turnout committee person elections to secure influence in the local Democratic Party that was disproportionate to their actual share of the Democratic electorate. Although Freedom did endorse candidates in a number of races, it sought to make its stand in the races for 14th Ward committee people.

Leon Jordan opted to run for reelection as the committeeman from the 14th Ward. Tim Moran, who had effectively run the ward for twenty-five years, sponsored a rival candidate, James Mason. Although Jordan was the incumbent, his chances were thought to be slim since he lacked machine backing. Jordan recruited Rosemary Smith Lowe, a beautician who assisted Jordan in the twelve-district campaign, as Freedom's candidate for committeewoman from the ward. She challenged incumbent Dovie Means, who stayed firmly in the Wagner/Moran camp. The August 1962 campaign in Kansas City's 14th Ward was different than most committee person elections, in that it was assuredly issue-centric. There was only one issue: Should the black community declare independence from white political control, chart its own destiny, and thereby be free to aggressively pursue what the community itself defined as its interests? Freedom's candidates, leadership, and precinct workers framed this choice in the starkest possible terms. A vote for the Freedom ballot was a vote for the black community, while anything else was a vote for the demonized "Boss Wagner" and an exploitative, backward dependence on those with no interest in the community.

Freedom's leaders rightly perceived that the organization's future—and the objective of black political independence—hinged in large part on the August 1962 primary. Moran felt the same way, appreciating that the first sign of weakness in his organization—already built on a shaky foundation of what amounted to absentee landlordism—might cause the entire façade to collapse. All of the usual faction efforts—palm cards, newspaper ads, door-to-door canvassing, and the infamous "walking around money"—were enhanced (with *The Call* later noting that Moran spent more than ever before on behalf of his candidate), even as the faction's leaders refused to seriously entertain the novel notion of black collective agency. Many factional leaders believed that Freedom's calls for independence were simply covert maneuvers by rival whites.

When the ballots were counted, both sides could claim partial victory. Jordan defeated Moran-backed candidate Mason by a decisive margin, 61 percent to 36 percent. Lowe earned 44 percent of the vote and was defeated. African Americans running in other races, including Freedom secretary Fred Curls in a bid to become a county magistrate, were defeated by large margins (although the districts in which they ran either did not encompass Freedom's 14th Ward or took in territory well beyond it). *The Call* took a negative view of this turn of events, headlining its coverage "First Independent Push by Negroes Defeated." The outcome was not so devastating as that headline would suggest, as other coverage in *The Call* did take note that, "Leon Jordan Takes Over 14th Ward From Moran."[30] Contemporary commentators overlooked the most important part of the story, ascribing Jordan's victory to his incumbency and personal popularity. Those factors cannot be denied, but it ignores much of the grassroots mobilization work that Freedom undertook. Focusing on Jordan overlooks the hundreds of votes won by other Freedom candidates; in defeat, they attained more support than any previous group lacking factional sponsorship had. Since Freedom had but four months in which to organize compared to Moran's twenty-five years, the Freedom forces clearly did something right.

Of course, the most lastingly important piece of Freedom's first campaign was not the outcomes in these two down-ballot, obscure races. Instead, what was significant was that Freedom launched a direct attack on the omnipotent factions, did so without white support or assistance, and survived. Even partial victory was sufficient to fuel the Freedom fire, inspiring others to consider the possibility of what could be accomplished through independence. Had Jordan and Lowe both been defeated, there can be little question but that Freedom would have evaporated without fanfare. Jordan's victory—and Lowe's strong showing—indicated that the founders of Freedom were in tune with the popular mood, had at least some of the skills required in order to mobilize that mood, and allowed Freedom to live to fight another day.

Emerging Stronger from Crisis
The 1963 Municipal Election

The 1963 municipal election provided the next opportunity. Although filled with opportunity, the events that transpired during this election also briefly provoked an existential threat to Freedom. Indeed, for a time, it seemed as though the LPO might be torn apart at the seams. Freedom not only survived intact, but emerged much stronger and used the campaign to make the black community's debut as a genuine center of power in Kansas City. That Freedom was not regarded as a force to be reckoned with in the election is demonstrated by the fact that neither the *Times* nor the *Star,* in their otherwise exhaustive coverage of the municipal elections, so much as mentioned the organization's name until after the primary (and then only fleetingly). This would prove to be the last election in which Freedom was considered an afterthought.

A mythology has since sprung up among Freedom activists about the 1963 elections. It holds that the LPO was largely, even exclusively, responsible for the election of both of the first black members of the City Council. The truth is more complex, filled as it is with long-forgotten political intrigues and the uncomfortable fact that an important part of Freedom's strategy was an alliance with its once and future adversary, the CA.

The 1962 redistricting produced one council district with an African American majority. The black majority in the Third District was a narrow one, slightly over 50 percent, but the CA and the Democratic factions all promised that they would put forward slates with African Americans for the district's seats. These promises, coupled with some subtly applied pressure, succeeded in preventing any white candidates from filing for either the district or at-large (where the citywide white majority could easily place a white candidate in office) seats. Still, competition for these seats was fierce; for the March 1963 primary, three candidates filed for the at-large seat and four candidates filed for the district seat. The district seat attracted Freedom founder Bruce Watkins, NAACP President Lee Vertis Swinton, and noted attorney-activist Harold Holliday. The at-large race featured prominent businessman and CA leader Everett O'Neal as well as Dr. Earl Thomas, principal of Lincoln High School, which historically served the city's black students.[31]

Although this cast of candidates guaranteed that the black community would possess symbolic representation on the new City Council, Freedom sought to ensure that the representation provided would be substantive and independent as well. The LPO saw the election as an opportunity to strengthen its position in the 14th Ward, defeat the factions, and assert itself for the first time as a force in the rarified world of municipal politics, largely dominated by the downtown boardroom elites of the CA. Before it could achieve those goals, Freedom was forced to grapple with dissension in its midst.

The race for in-district councilman in the Third District was the crux of the conflict; the primary featured three individuals with long records of activism in the community. Watkins's background has already been described; in the primary, his principal source of formal institutional support came from a handful of labor unions. Swinton was the president of the local NAACP. Although civic elites were not overly fond of his organization, in the course of the civil rights demonstrations, Swinton made many contacts with the elites in the CA. A combination of those contacts and a misreading of the black popular mood that held that Swinton was a sure thing because of his NAACP position caused the CA to endorse the attorney. Later in his career, Swinton would become a supporter of Freedom, but in 1963 he still held back from the LPO. Holliday was regarded as a "radical"; he could usually be relied on to give the fieriest of speeches at any civil rights rally, though he softened his approach somewhat for the campaign. An attorney, Holliday was the first African American to attend the University of Kansas City (now the University of Missouri-Kansas City), and was one of the earliest members of Freedom, Inc.[32]

Choosing a candidate to endorse in this race proved problematic for Freedom, which by spring 1963 was the city's largest all-black political club.[33] It is a testament to the LPO's commitment to collective agency and refusal to become a cult of personality that Freedom did not simply endorse Watkins, who, after all, was the chairman of the board, immediately. Doing so would have provoked an angry reaction from Freedom member Holliday and his supporters, who were adamant that Watkins reneged on an agreement that he would run in the at-large race and leave Holliday to carry the Freedom banner in the district race.[34] Holliday and his supporters intimated that they would withdraw their support from Freedom—permanently—if the club endorsed Watkins or Swinton. Although the Holliday faction comprised a small percentage of the LPO's roughly 300 members,[35] the organization's leadership wisely decided that a vocal split was not in the long-term best interests of Freedom or the broader black community. As a result, Freedom remained neutral in *all* of the municipal primary races.

While the organization itself remained neutral in the primary, the leaders, precinct workers, and members of Freedom did not. Leon Jordan gave Watkins his personal endorsement and was a frequent surrogate speaker for the funeral director on the campaign trail. Of Freedom's eighteen precinct captains, sixteen worked for Watkins. The sole dissidents were assistant prosecutor Gwendolyn Wells (who worked in the same government office as JDC boss Wagner) and Harold Holliday.[36] Watkins's campaign infrastructure was built around the Freedom precinct captains, who applied the same tactics they had used during the summer primary but without the benefit of the Freedom banner. Door-to-door canvassing, telephone trees, and an emphasis on personal contacts were the hallmarks of Watkins's efforts.

Most contemporary political observers considered the energy of the Freedom-centric campaign team and Watkins's own considerable personal charm to be mighty shabby substitutes for the benefits (money, professional political help, and the *Star*'s endorsement) that Swinton's CA backing brought him. Nor was Watkins considered terribly competitive with Holliday, after the latter publicly and gratefully accepted the support of Louis Wagner, Tim Moran, and the rest of the Democratic Coalition;[37] most political commentators were blissfully unaware of the drive for black independence from the factions, and saw the factional support as quite a coup for Holliday. These endorsements would prove to be less than unadorned boons for Watkins's opponents. Using precisely the same message that Freedom employed in the August 1962 committee elections, Watkins labeled both of his opponents pawns of outside interests.[38] In endorsing Swinton in the primary, the *Star* noted Holliday's factional support and racial "radicalism" while ignoring Watkins entirely.

Yet, on primary day, Watkins led the field with 3,523 votes. He was trailed narrowly by Holliday, who won 3,291 votes; Swinton, with all of his supposed institutional advantages, failed to advance to the general election with just 2,562 votes.[39] Watkins's victory in the primary was due largely to his performance in sixteen Freedom precincts, while Holliday's areas of strength were in the precincts still firmly in the Wagner/Moran orbit. Swinton performed well only in precincts with white majorities (where the CA and *Star* endorsements helped), but even there Watkins did better than expected because of his ties to organized labor.

If the primary strained the relationship between Holliday and his erstwhile allies in Freedom, the general election campaign severed it completely. The "radical" lawyer strengthened his relationship with Wagner, going so far as to issue public statements praising the political boss and other factional leaders for the good work he claimed they had done in the black community.[40] Such unambiguous adulation for the political bosses whose activities were the prime reason for Freedom's emergence was more than the LPO's membership could bear. Shortly after the primary, the Freedom board met and formally endorsed Watkins for the Third District seat.[41] On behalf of the club, Leon Jordan issued a statement lamenting what it perceived as Holliday's abandonment of the goal of independent politics.[42] Some Freedom members mourned the break for tactical reasons: they felt as though independent politics would never be attained if the organization initiated a pattern of sectarianism or if rump factions were constantly leaving. They knew intuitively the advantages that a single, corporatist black LPO could have, for both the strength of the LPO and for black political efficacy.

Watkins took to the hustings to denounce the alliance between Holliday and Wagner. In speech after speech, he assailed his erstwhile Freedom colleague. To take just one example, Watkins delivered a speech where he declared:

Within recent months, Mr. Holliday has deserted [Freedom, Inc.] and its aims. He went to Boss Wagner and pleaded to be his candidate. Boss Wagner then announced with pride: 'This is my candidate.' The truth of the matter is that Mr. Holliday is the third-district council candidate of the Independent Voters Association (whose slate he is on) but he belongs to Boss Wagner. I will assure you that I will never sell the citizens of the third district to a boss such as Wagner.[43]

With the Freedom infrastructure formally behind him, Watkins was able to take advantage of the group's headquarters and the precinct captains could officially coordinate their work under the LPO's banner. During this election, and throughout the early period of Freedom's history, the precinct captains and Freedom workers were all volunteers. Freedom's organizational budget was small, with contributions coming mostly from endorsed candidates to pay expenses.

After minimal debate, the CA chose to endorse the funeral director.[44] Although revisionist historians would later claim the CA did so because Watkins was a "sure thing," this claim hardly stands up to scrutiny.[45] The reform LPO had already demonstrated in the primary that it lacked the ability to read the black public mood. Moreover, Watkins placed first in the race by only a few hundred votes while the organizing infrastructure upon which he relied was new and untested. More damning for the case of those who claim Watkins became a shoo-in, the Freedom founder received the endorsement of neither the *Star* nor *The Call*;

the *Star*, normally eager to bless certain victors with its endorsement in order to claim a share of the victory, opted not to endorse any candidate in the general (even though it had previously labeled Holliday a factional tool and a dangerous radical), while *The Call* printed a strong front-page endorsement of Holliday.[46] A much more credible argument for the reformers' endorsement demonstrates Freedom's growing strength. First, given the full-throated support of Wagner/Moran for Holliday, the intensely antifaction CA could hardly choose him as its candidate and maintain any shred of credibility. Second and more importantly, the CA desperately needed entry to the black community for its slate. The mayoral contest between CA candidate Ilus Davis and Dutton Brookfield of the Independent Voters Association (IVA) was expected to be very close.[47] Although a Republican, Brookfield had the vigorous support of Wagner and other Democratic faction leaders active in the black community (Graves 1963a). Despite his alliance with the factional leaders it had so recently denounced, Brookfield also had the endorsement of *The Call*—largely, the paper claimed, because Davis had not been aggressive enough in supporting a public accommodations ordinance during the 1950s.[48] The CA recognized that, in a close election, victory for its candidates could easily hinge on the black electorate. With two traditional pillars of black politics lined up against its candidate, and after a thorough thrashing of its slate in black-majority precincts during the primary, the CA sought out allies in the African American community. Likewise, Freedom had few options in terms of seeking out allies. Aside from its endorsement of Holliday, the IVA was not a legitimate option. Weak though Davis might have been on civil rights issues during his city council tenure, Freedom leaders saw no reason at all to believe that Brookfield would be more enlightened (especially given his dalliances with the John Birch Society). Brookfield's embrace, albeit tentative, of Wagner and other factional leaders made it impossible for Freedom to lend any support to his IVA slate. In short, the interracial alliance—that organizing mode prized above all others by most political scientists—between Freedom and the CA was crafted not on the basis of ideology as Browning, Marshall, and Tabb[49] or Sonenshein[50] would have it, nor on the basis of shared interests, but on the less noble basis of a shared enemy. Once the shared enemy was defeated, the interracial alliance between Freedom and the CA degenerated.

As a result of these overtures from the CA, the first "Freedom Ballot" in a municipal race endorsed the entire CA slate a few weeks before the election.[51] Accepting the CA endorsement and campaigning for the joint CA/Freedom slate muddied Watkins's message from the primary just a bit. Gone were the denunciations of the "downtown" and "boardroom" elites from his primary campaign against Swinton, replaced by harsh characterizations of Holliday, Wagner, and the factions.[52]

The alliance between Freedom and the CA created another issue for the former; namely, it forced Freedom to intervene in the Third District At-Large contest between Everett O'Neal and Dr. Earl Thomas. Thomas was a popular figure in the black community, owing to his tenure as a beloved high school principal. O'Neal was a prosperous entrepreneur and civic activist who won the CA's nod because of his long involvement with that organization. Thomas was driven into the arms of Wagner, the Democratic factions, and the IVA because of the CA's early support for O'Neal. Most figures in the community considered Thomas a much better candidate. Indeed, even the *Star* agreed, making Thomas the one candidate without CA backing to earn its endorsement.[53] Freedom's members were certain that Thomas would win, and that his prestige would help Holliday. Holliday and Thomas shared a campaign office and team (supplied by Wagner and JDC politicos), frequently made joint appearances, and Thomas defended Holliday from Watkins's attacks. This certitude about Thomas's unshakeable popularity among African American voters was what gave Freedom members the most pause before entering an alliance with the CA. Still, members decided that, on balance, the alliance with the CA and O'Neal would do more to help black interests than to hurt them.

When the votes were counted on March 26, Freedom was able to claim a partial victory. In the district race, Watkins won a massive victory over Holliday, 61 percent to 39 percent. In the 14th Ward, where Freedom's efforts were concentrated, Watkins rolled up his most impressive margin. O'Neal did not fare as well, losing to Thomas by a citywide margin of 47 percent to 53 percent. Thomas performed well in areas with both white and black majorities, thanks to the dual endorsements of the *Star* and factions; even as Thomas won the other black majority wards, Freedom delivered a narrow vote victory to O'Neal in the 14th Ward. The remainder of the Freedom/CA ticket swept most of the open city positions. Freedom was unable to deliver victories in the 14th Ward for every single member of its ticket, but did significantly narrow the margin for faction-supported candidates compared to the support those candidates secured in neighboring black majority precincts. Freedom/CA mayoral candidate Ilus Davis, for example, garnered just 22 percent of the vote in the nearly all-black 2nd Ward but 44 percent of the vote in Freedom's 14th Ward heartland (see Table 2).[54] Clearly, then, the variation in black voter behavior in the 1963 municipal elections was attributable to the activities that Freedom undertook in support of

Table 2. 1963 Mayoral Election Results in
Predominantly African American Wards

Ward	Ilus Davis (%)	Dutton Brookfield (%)
2	891 (22%)	3,085 (78%)
3	1,806 (51.1%)	1,733 (48.9%)
14	1,707 (43.6%)	2,208 (56.4%)
16	1,592 (52.8%)	1,423 (47.2%)
17	1,747 (47.5%)	1,933 (52.5%)
Total in Predominantly African American Wards	7,743 (42.7%)	10,382 (57.3%)
Total Citywide	54,717 (51.1%)	52,403 (48.9%)

Source: Kansas City Times – March 27, 1963

its candidates. In most cases, the Freedom endorsement was not crucial to the outcome. One exception was in the mayoral race. Davis's winning margin was just 2,300 votes; Freedom delivered 1,700 votes for Davis in the 14th Ward alone and likely influenced some black voters in other wards.[55]

This generally strong performance by Freedom caused even the scribes from the *Star,* who generally doubted that such a thing as black agency or independence existed, to acknowledge that the "new" organization was well on its way to becoming a power player in municipal politics.[56] Aside from this external perception of change in black community politics, the 1963 election had three other major results. First, the election resulted in the first African American members of the City Council, something that was inconceivable just a few years earlier. Second, it signaled the beginning of the demise of the Democratic factions. Almost completely ejected from City Hall, they would linger for another two decades, but would never again achieve the same level of success in municipal, county, or state politics. The demise of the factions would be hastened by the departure of one of their electoral bases: African Americans. Third, it demonstrated for the first time that black voters were crucial to municipal politics. Not only would two African Americans serve on the Council, where they could demand that attention be paid to black interests, but black voters could provide the margin of victory in many contests where white voters were divided. This was a lesson that many other cities, often with histories of racism equal to or more severe than Kansas City's, had already learned. Black voters would soon use their newfound power to wrest concrete, tangible concessions from City Hall. Freedom, Inc. was at the forefront of those efforts, serving as the convener of discussions for what demands should be made and how they should be pressed.

Beating Segregation at the Ballot Box
The Public Accommodations Ordinance

The leaders and members of Freedom, Inc. realized immediately that they were more successful than a simple review of the 1963 win-loss record might suggest. As a result, they immediately began discussing how to capitalize on the black community's emerging power and strategies for enhancing that power. Jordan and the organization's other leaders began to consider expanding Freedom's operations beyond the 14th Ward. These efforts did not bear fruit until 1966 and beyond. Watkins and other Freedom members made overtures to the other successful African American candidate for City Council, Dr. Earl Thomas. Although Thomas had run on a rival slate, he quickly developed a working relationship with Watkins and Freedom. All of these parties agreed that black interests could only be well served through unity; division among the city's black elected officials, they agreed, would prove disastrous. This operational unity, what *The Call* would term closing ranks,[57] among African American leaders to produce a single, corporatist organization that would be the political voice of the black community would prove crucial to achieving higher levels of black political efficacy.

The black community began an internal debate on the question of what policies its newly elected representatives should pursue first at City Hall. Given that one of those new representatives (Watkins) was a Freedom leader and believed in a consultative, group-based approach to leadership, the organization itself was central to these discussions. Many an evening was spent at the Green Duck Tavern or the Carver Theatre debating whether to pursue efforts against residential segregation, or increased hiring of African American city employees, or increased funding for housing and recreation in central city neighborhoods, or to challenge continuing segregation in public accommodations such as restaurants and taverns. There was never any doubt that all of these issues *must* eventually be raised; the question being debated was simply which to tackle first. An important consideration here was deciding which area was most likely to produce a victory. This emphasis on a "winning issue" arose not because black leaders were frightened of taking on the status quo, sought to appease anxious whites, or because Freedom's members were unwilling to wage a hard fight. Instead, it was because Freedom's leaders, in particular, knew that any concession to black interests by city government would require massive effort on the part of the black community. If those exertions proved unsuccessful, it would be a devastating blow to African American independence and efficacy.

It was soon decided that the first priority should be a strong public accommodations ordinance. Public accommodations had long been important to African American Kansas Citians, who had attempted nearly a decade earlier to secure passage of a strong law. An ordinance was adopted prior to the 1963 elections, but the ordinance was far weaker than versions previously proposed and so therefore did not accomplish much. Public accommodations were also a hot topic in the national debate, with national civil rights organizations pressing for a federal law guaranteeing all people access to any business open to the public.

It is important to note that this process of determining priority issues was driven largely by Freedom, Inc., and would have been impossible without it. In the pre-Freedom days, there was never any discussion of black interests or any internal attempt to discern what the community wanted. The factions simply determined what the agenda would be, and that agenda omitted anything but the most minor and symbolic of concessions to the groups' African American supporters. Freedom changed that by deciding that it would establish its own agenda, through consultation with its hundreds of members and information gleaned from the precinct captain network. The many African American politicians who remained outside of the Freedom fold were compelled to participate in this process—if perhaps half-heartedly—or risk being labeled a Tom-ish tool of the machine.

As a result, Watkins and Thomas consulted with local attorneys to draft a strong public accommodations ordinance. Watkins introduced the resulting ordinance in the City Council in the fall of 1963, just a few months after his election.[58] The ordinance made segregated public facilities and businesses of all sorts illegal, including motels, taverns, restaurants, and recreational facilities. It remains unclear what persuaded the CA-dominated City Council to adopt the public accommodations ordinance, as they did by a vote of 11–2 in the fall of 1963. The members themselves claimed they supported the ordinance out of moral conviction.[59] This seems unlikely, given that the morality of the issue had not changed since the time when some of the very same council members opposed a similar strong ordinance. Most of the city's civic elite, including the CA, the Chamber of Commerce, and the *Star,* supported the ordinance, fearing that a "negative image" would harm efforts to attract conventions and new commerce.[60] Similar concerns about image ultimately moved even the ardently atavistic segregationists of Birmingham to consider some concessions to African Americans, so the possibility that Kansas City's political leaders were influenced by economic concerns should not be dismissed. However, a purely image-conscious and economic argument fails to explain the case. There were no major conventions lost in the months preceding the ordinance's adoption (unlike in 1961 and 1962), and Kansas City was not even an afterthought in the national conversation on segregation while southern movements in Albany, Birmingham, Greensboro, Jackson, and Memphis dominated the news.

Although economics played a role, the best explanation for the adoption of the public accommodations ordinance was that an independent organization emerged to champion black interests. This was the element missing from previous efforts at passing an ordinance. Jordan, Watkins, and other Freedom members did an excellent job of reaching out to other city leaders in advance, reminding them of the crucial role the African American vote played in the 1963 election—and the fact that demographers expected the African American share of the city's population to increase before the 1967 election. The alliance and bargaining that Freedom initiated with the CA during the municipal elections and sustained thereafter proved very effective; it gave Watkins and Freedom entry and clout in CA circles that they would not otherwise have had, resulting in a tangible benefit.

These efforts achieved their desired goal when the ordinance was adopted by the City Council, with only two members (both of them CA adversaries) opposed. The vote represented the first real triumph for black interests in modern Kansas City political history. Freedom's members were euphoric, taking the vote as a sign that their strategy was working. Less than two years after their declaration of independence, the black community was beginning to achieve long-cherished goals. The euphoria was short-lived. Although little formal opposition crystallized during the City Council hearings on the issue, to the point that some white Council members falsely came to believe that the issue was noncontroversial, the ordinance's actual adoption provoked a firestorm among a small, usually depoliticized group: tavern owners. Nearly all of the city's taverns—with a very few tourist- and conventioneer-focused exceptions—were rigidly segregated, and while the "wide-open" days of the Pendergast and frontier era were over, the city still had thousands of these establishments. Tavern owners were irate that the ordinance meant they would be forced to serve African Americans and unexpectedly sprang into action.

Kansas City's reform charter permits both referenda and citizen initiative petitions. As a corollary, any ordinance adopted by the City Council can be temporarily enjoined from implementation and placed on the ballot for voter approval if a sufficient number of signatures are gathered. The tavern owners used their existing trade group to do just that. It was estimated that a majority of the city's tavern owners participated in the effort, gathering signatures directly from patrons in their establishments. Although the petition-gathering effort had little money, almost no political acumen or experience, and formal support only from fringe political elements like the local chapter of the John Birch Society, it nonetheless collected the required signatures in just a few weeks.[61] A special election was scheduled for April 7, 1964.

Most of Kansas City's white civic elite did not take the tavern owners' threat seriously. Accustomed to the CA mode of governance, where civic elites were disproportionately important and the endorsements of the CA, business leaders, and the *Star* were sufficient to generate electoral landslides, these elites regarded the tavern owners' effort as an amateurish exercise predestined for failure. Nor were these elites particularly passionate about the cause of public accommodations. Mayor Ilus Davis, though, was surprisingly passionate about the cause, earning him the lasting praise of Watkins. Indeed, Watkins would later recount how, at a private strategy session, Davis was confronted with the news of the tavern owners' opposition. The mayor "pounded his desk and declared 'I'll be damned if I'll let tavern operators dictate the moral tone of this city.'"[62] Even with the mayor's strong support, the citywide campaign to preserve the public accommodations ordinance got off to a slow start. A campaign committee with the requisite prominent citizens as co-chairs was not formed by Davis until a month before the election, and it counted only one African American amongst its more than a dozen members.[63] Nearly every major political organization in the city came out in support of the ordinance.[64] The city's elected officials made the rounds to speechify in favor of the law.[65] Many prominent clergymen added their names to public pronouncements of the moral necessity of integration and gave sermons on the subject to their congregations.[66] The *Star* repeatedly editorialized for the adopted ordinance (if half-heartedly, constantly emphasizing that Kansas City was already a very tolerant place whose image would be unjustly tarnished if the ordinance was rejected). Still, precious little actual organizing took place for the ordinance among white voters. Few funds were expended until the closing days and the traditional campaign tactics to persuade voters were not used. The Democratic factions joined the CA in offering strong rhetorical support for the ordinance. Since they wished to retain their influence among black voters, they had little choice.[67] Even then, the faction leaders were moved to declare their support only after a scathing public denunciation of them by Watkins generated attention.[68] But the other major constituency of the factions was working class white ethnics, who generally opposed the law. To reconcile the tension, the factions rhetorically embraced the law but did little of their typical electioneering work.[69] This fence-straddling was made publicly defensible by the fact that none of the money raised by the pro-ordinance side was diverted to the factions to pay for "expenses," as was the typical practice.

This rather lackluster approach to the campaign was justified by the pro-ordinance side with claims that the ordinance was overwhelmingly favored by the electorate. There was no need to be more aggressive, they claimed, because Kansas City was a tolerant town and the tavern owners a miniscule minority. Such claims appeared to be warranted when the Civic Research Institute, a local think tank, released the results of a scientific public opinion survey a month before the election. That poll, which noted that its sample seriously underrepresented African Americans, showed almost 53 percent of the electorate voting for the ordinance, just 21 percent opposing it, and 24 percent undecided.[70]

While mainstream white elites considered the outcome a given, African American activists and Freedom members did not. Freedom's membership knew well that many Kansas Citians were likely to be persuaded by the ever-more-explicit racism of the tavern owners and the antiintegration forces. As the campaign progressed, the tavern owners' spokesperson went from simply proclaiming that government should not give mandates to private businesses, to declaring "We are not against Negroes as Negroes, but the association feels that whites, whiskey, and Negroes is a combination that just won't work. Whites and whiskey alone are a combination that is hard enough to control."[71] By the end of the campaign, the president of the tavern owner's association was trotting out the ultimate segregationist canard and fever dream of "miscegenation" as a reason for rejecting the ordinance, writing an open letter to members that termed the ordinance "obnoxious and immoral" because its purpose was "expressly to make it legal for Negro boys to date white girls in public taverns, dance halls, and swimming pools. We, the tavern owners, will express ourselves that we are not ready for this personal intimate mixing of the races in our places of business."[72] Allies of the tavern owners claimed the ordinance was a "plot" by CORE and other outside agitators steeped in "fanaticism."[73] One Presbyterian minister who was a frequent anti–public accommodations panelist resorted to a perverse quasi-class analysis in maintaining that if the ordinance passed, "Negroes will still be second-class citizens, the mayor and his group will be first-class, and the rest of us will be third-class."[74]

Knowing that these sorts of appeals—and even the more niche claims of the John Birchers that the ordinance was "Communist-inspired"—would persuade some white voters, Freedom and other politically active blacks were certain that the ordinance's success would depend on African American voters. Local civil rights organizations convened a meeting to forge a formal coalition to campaign for the ordinance. Dozens of local organizations participated in this effort,[75] ultimately dubbed Operation P.A., but Freedom quickly took the lead, as could be expected given that Freedom chairman Bruce Watkins was the primary sponsor of the ordinance.

Freedom's members determined quickly that the campaign in the black community should not be waged purely under their organization's name. After significant internal debate, it was decided that Freedom would coordinate and cooperate in a broader effort that would unite the LPO with black activists from the faction-controlled wards. Not everyone agreed with this move, feeling that it could compromise the push for independence. At the same time, though, the view that a united front was necessary prevailed. This demonstrates once again the institutionalized nature of the Freedom project; lesser political strategists or individuals less concerned about black interests might have insisted on a go it alone approach, one that would personally glorify Freedom's members. That the organization refrained from such an approach is to its lasting credit. That a debate existed at all, and that the outcome might have been very different, shows that the activities of LPOs are not predestined. Support for black interests need not have compelled Freedom into cooperation with others; internal politics dictated the course of action eventually taken.

The decision to pursue a united front also provided an opportunity to reconcile with Harold Holliday and his followers. Watkins personally recommended that Holliday be named the chair of Operation P.A., which brought Holliday squarely back into the Freedom fold after the contentious municipal elections.[76] Although Operation P.A. was intended to be a united front, Freedom provided most of the organizational and strategic muscle. Holliday supplied some additional organizers from his own campaign and, by all accounts, did a masterful job at coordinating the work. Herman Johnson and Lee Vertis Swinton's Mid City Democratic Club, operating in the JDC stronghold of the 2nd Ward, also were frequently singled out for their relentless organizing. Pleading poverty, the JDC and other factions sent out far fewer workers than they normally would have.[77] Instead, Freedom's now-celebrated precinct captain network sprang into action.

The most important accomplishment of this effort was to register thousands of new African American voters. As was the case elsewhere in the 1960s, voter registration among African Americans in Kansas City lagged behind that of whites. This had obvious consequences for black political power. Freedom had maintained since its founding that black political independence would be more easily attained if the number of black voters increased, because the new voters would be less tied to the factional organizations. However, given the other challenges that the organization faced in maintaining itself, voter registration had not been a high priority. That changed in the 1964 public accommodations vote, when the organization's strategists correctly ascertained that the ordinance would go down to defeat unless the black community was mobilized, with turnout significantly stimulated. In just five weeks in 1964, nearly 5,000 voters were added to the rolls. Eighty percent of the new registrants were African Americans.[78]

Registering voters was not enough. Adding names to the rolls would not be helpful unless those new registrants could be moved to the polls on Election Day. Once again, the Freedom electioneering apparatus proved to be essential. The factions, including the JDC in the typically high-turnout 2nd Ward, did uncharacteristically little to contact their voters even as Wagner and other bosses voiced support for the law. Instead, Operation P.A. and the workers supplied from the ranks of Freedom members took responsibility for door-to-door canvassing, telephone contact, and a multitude of rallies and speeches.

On election day, Freedom and the forces of integration emerged victorious, if just barely. The public accommodations ordinance won voter approval in what was then the second-highest turnout special election in the city's history, 45,476 votes to 43,733 votes, a margin of just 1,743 votes. Integration was favored in just nine of the city's 26 wards, five of which had black majorities. White voters rejected integration, as Freedom predicted they would, and contrary to the expectations of the moderate civic elites who insisted that Kansas City was an unjustly maligned paragon of tolerance, by a substantial margin, with just 38 percent of the voters in white-majority wards supporting the ordinance. There can be no question at all that it was the efforts of Freedom and the black community that produced a victory for public accommodations. In a city where African Americans were just 18 percent of the population, the wards with black majorities produced 27 percent of the total votes and close to half of the yes votes. In wards with black majorities, the margin for the ordinance was 20,827 to 3,130, and most of the dissenting votes came from individual precincts with white majorities.[79] Moreover, it was the voter registration efforts of the winter of 1964 that made the difference, as the number of newly registered voters in the black community who participated in the election far exceeded the proposal's margin of victory.[80]

The Civil Rights Act of 1964 was signed into law by President Lyndon Johnson just a few months after the Kansas City vote, rendering the city's public accommodations ordinance blessedly obsolete. Still, the vote had lasting repercussions that reached far beyond the specific policy implications involved. First, thousands of African American voters were added to the voter registration rolls. Second, the many naysayers in the African American community who insisted that black interests could only be indirectly addressed, through relying on the crumbs tossed off by the factions, were proven wrong. African Americans could organize themselves to produce meaningful change. Third, the vote was the clearest demonstration yet of the key role that could be played by the black community, meaning that elected officials would need to find new ways of interacting with this potential power bloc. Fourth, and most crucially, the campaign demonstrated what was possible when the black community was more or less united under the leadership of a single, corporatist political organization and effectively mobilized. The Freedom-led 14th ward produced the city's most lopsided margin for the ordinance (5,948 to 129) and turned out more voters than every other ward in the city, save one. If segregationists could be beaten at the ballot box through Freedom's efforts, then surely much more was possible. The victory in the public accommodations battle and Freedom's inarguable success at mobilizing black voters for black interests were just the impetus required to enable Freedom's expansion beyond the confines of the 14th Ward, allowing Freedom to become the major vehicle for black politics in the city. This would prove to be a nearly decade-long, and always contested, process, but it would never have begun without this experiment in "united front" politics where Freedom served as first amongst equals.

The Threat of Freedom Made Real (1964–1967)

With several substantial victories under its belt, Freedom was increasingly taken seriously by other political forces. The *Star* began reporting Freedom's endorsements and spoke favorably of the organization, considering it an ally against the factions that were the paper's bête noir. Nonfactional white civic elites saw the organization and its members as a potential source of votes, though they still did not comprehend that Freedom would follow its own course. The factions increasingly saw Freedom as a real threat to their survival. As a result, the four-year period between 1964 and 1968 was characterized by a pitched battle for supremacy within the black community. Freedom and the African American community emerged victorious in these struggles; the community gained both in terms of symbolic and substantive representation. As a result of Freedom's activities during this period, by the end of 1968 it was unquestionably the dominant force in local black politics, had conclusively defeated the factions, and become one of the two major forces in local politics. Within the space of six years, the threat of freedom issued by Leon Jordan and his compatriots in 1962 was made real.

Prelude to Victory
The 1964 and 1966 Democratic Primaries

The activists and leadership of Freedom, Inc. had precious little time to savor the victory of the public accommodations ordinance. Immediately after that April election, the organization began to regroup in order to fight the August Democratic primary election. This election was of crucial importance to the organization. First, Freedom president Leon Jordan opted to challenge long-time state representative J. McKinley Neal, the Kansas City delegation's only African American member. Second and of equal importance, the city's influential congressman, Richard Bolling, faced a stiff challenge from a candidate backed by an unusually cohesive united front of the factions. Third, a confluence of circumstances rendered it possible for one or two additional African Americans to win seats in the Missouri House of Representatives;[81] Freedom intended to wage serious campaigns in these districts.

Jordan's campaign against Neal was undertaken only after considerable debate within Freedom. The campaign was not simply a matter of personal aggrandizement, nor a decision arrived at exclusively by Jordan himself; instead, Jordan consulted with Freedom members and weighed the costs and benefits to the organization and the broader black community before deciding to challenge Neal. With the possible exception of Watkins, Jordan was the most popular figure within the organization. Given his public service and demonstrated political acumen, no one questioned the fact that Jordan would be a formidable candidate and an excellent state representative. Instead, the debate centered on whether it was the right year to challenge Neal. Were Jordan to lose a head-to-head challenge to Neal, the organization's credibility in both the black and white communities would be undermined. After assessing the potential complications, Jordan decided to run. Neal was regarded by Freedom as nothing more than a factional plant who had been woefully ineffective, despite the fact that *The Call* often featured glowing articles about his supposed accomplishments.

Of only slightly less import to the organization, and the black community in general, was the primary challenge faced by Congressman Richard Bolling. As a member of the Rules Committee, Bolling was an influential member of the House. He was the most liberal person the Kansas City area had ever sent to Congress; since his first election in 1948, Bolling had been a reliable vote for the liberal wing of the Democratic Party. He was also one of the most forceful supporters of civil rights in the House, often finding himself on the losing end of a battle with the Rules Committee's recalcitrant Southerners. Bolling was disliked by the old-line factional leaders for these same reasons—in the course of the campaign they would claim that he was beholden to "New York organizations" like the NAACP and Americans for Democratic Action, as well as his refusal to grant them access to his meager patronage.[82] The factions united in 1964 to challenge Bolling, selecting as their candidate Jackson County Judge Hunter Phillips.[83] Phillips was a conservative and unsympathetic toward civil rights, yet Wagner and factional leaders insisted that "their" voters would deprive Bolling of the nomination.[84]

Freedom begged to differ. The membership was united in insisting that maximum effort should be exerted to defend Bolling, who they rightly regarded as a champion of black interests, certainly when compared to the barely closeted segregationist Phillips. To the activists of Freedom, Inc., Wagner and other white bosses were demonstrating the utter contempt and disregard in which they held African Americans. Immediately after it became clear that Bolling would be challenged, Freedom declared its enthusiastic support for the incumbent congressman and began organizing the black community on his behalf.[85] In this, Freedom would be aided by *The Call*. For the first time in its short history, Freedom and the major news organ of the African American community would agree on a candidate.

At precisely the same time, opportunities to elect one or more new African American state representatives emerged. One district had an African American majority, but at factional direction had long been represented by a white man, Harry Goldberg. In 1962, Wagner promised that at the next primary he would support an African American candidate for the post. Goldberg announced that under those circumstances, he would retire. Wagner kept his promise, endorsing factional stalwart Henry Ross to represent the district, which encompassed much of the JDC-dominated 2nd Ward. Freedom endorsed another black candidate in the race, prompting Goldberg to change his mind and stand for reelection in the hope that division in the black vote would provide a path to victory. Another district, in the southern part of the central city, was in transition; the district had only just attained an African American majority, though it remained unclear whether the area possessed a black voting majority. Harold Holliday, now restored to favor within Freedom on the basis of his stellar performance in the public accommodations campaign, was endorsed by the organization to contest the seat against the white incumbent. He was joined by three other African American challengers, causing commentators to believe that the black vote would be fractured.[86]

In the 1964 primary, Freedom pursued victories in all of these contests simultaneously. This required an effort unprecedented in the organization's short history, primarily because it entailed branching out from the 14th Ward into the 2nd Ward (for the contest against Goldberg and Ross), the 17th Ward (for Holliday's race), and other black majority precincts (to aid Bolling). The level of complexity required to organize precinct workers, print literature, and coordinate other forms of in-person contact was of an entirely new order than that employed in the past. Freedom met this challenge by relying on its veteran workers in the 14th Ward, bringing some of the workers from the public accommodations ordinance fight into the organization, and by partnering with the Mid City Democratic Club in the 2nd Ward. Moreover, candidates were asked to supply volunteers to work for the entire Freedom ballot, not just individual candidates. Only through volunteer labor of this sort could Freedom compete with the factions, whose workforces were composed of patronage employees or those for whom the political bosses had done favors. Lacking any patronage of its own, Freedom relied on volunteers to broadcast its message. Although this made the organization's corps of workers somewhat less reliable, it carried the advantage of ensuring that Freedom's workers were true believers.

Waging a serious campaign of this kind also required unprecedented monetary expenditures, far beyond the organization's indigenous capacity for fundraising. Freedom was able to raise the required resources by bargaining with the newly formed Committee for County Progress (CCP), entering into an informal strategic alliance with the group. The CCP was founded by reform-minded Democrats to coordinate organizing and electioneering efforts against the old-line factions. Its express purpose was to deprive the factions of control over Jackson County politics; although reformers had dominated city politics for a quarter of a century, factional control over the county courthouse had never been ceded.[87] In 1964, CCP was intent on electing an antifactional slate of candidates to the few county offices that were up for election that year. Because the organization was an interest group within the Democratic Party and because of the myriad ways in which county patronage was intertwined with state and national politics, the CCP involved itself in that year's state legislative and congressional races. Bolling, with his liberal record, charm, and national influence, was a hero to many CCP members, who vowed to protect him. The CCP's membership understood that if Bolling was vulnerable to and defeated by a factional candidate, than no reform-minded Democrat would be safe ever again.[88]

Given their shared antifactionalism and commitment to the incumbent congressman, CCP and Freedom joined forces to nominate Bolling, an antifactional slate for county offices, and a host of state representatives. Indeed, the CCP-affiliated sheriff even permitted the organization to use his jail for meetings and social events. One Freedom-affiliated activist recalls:

Sherriff Owsley—he was the sheriff at the courthouse—we all had to go to the courthouse to take Bruce [Watkins]'s crew, because he had a big group. So we went to the 11th floor of the courthouse, that was the jail, and that's where [Freedom] went the night of the ballot, to do their entertaining and meet and greet each other. At the 11th floor of the courthouse, at the jail.[89]

CCP was lavishly funded (mostly because of the participation of Jackson County presiding judge Charles Curry, one of the area's wealthiest real estate investors) and, as part of the alliance, supplied Freedom with funds to support its endorsed candidates. As was normal practice, candidates endorsed by Freedom also contributed monies to finance the organization's efforts.

The 1964 primary bore many similarities with the 1963 municipal and 1964 public accommodations elections. In all cases, Freedom bargained its way into a pragmatic, short-term alliance with white "reformers." As in 1963, the basis of that alliance was a shared enmity of the factions. In all cases, Freedom mobilized its precinct worker network, making ample use of person-to-person contact strategies. The message was one of black political independence, stressing that black interests would be served only by dispensing with the factions. As in the past, Freedom was abetted by editorial support from local newspapers. The *Star* endorsed most of Freedom's candidates and its news coverage of the organization's effort was limited, but generally flattering. *The Call* joined in endorsing some of Freedom's candidates, producing an unprecedented level of unity between the two institutions.

This time, however, Freedom's victory was far more decisive. Bolling won the Democratic nomination by a two-to-one margin, achieving a lop-sided result that surprised most local observers. Commentators uniformly attributed the size of Bolling's victory to his huge margins in African American precincts. Even in the 2nd Ward, Wagner's bailiwick, Bolling defeated Phillips. The congressman's largest margins, however, came in the wards where Freedom's influence was strongest, such as the 14th Ward.[90] At the same time, all but one member of the CCP's slate for county office were defeated. In these lower-profile races, the old-line factions still demonstrated strength in the black community.[91] Perhaps most important for Freedom, two of its candidates for state representative were successful. Jordan thrashed incumbent Neal, garnering 3,637 votes (67 percent) to Neal's paltry 1,789 votes (33 percent). Defying all predictions, Holliday consolidated the black vote, winning 2,301 votes to the white incumbent's 1,377 votes. However, Freedom was unable to win a victory for its candidate against Goldberg and Ross; in that race, its candidate placed ahead of Goldberg but trailed Ross by nearly 1,200 ballots. Wagner's endorsement was sufficient to secure the nomination for Ross.[92] After the atrophy of the JDC, Ross would remain in office by building a personal following. Unlike many other African American politicians who clashed with Freedom, he would never reconcile with the organization and would remain inveterately hostile to the LPO until his death.

But the factions were not yet cowed. They sought to regroup and launch an even more vigorous offensive in the 1966 Democratic primary, sparing only Bolling from their wrath. Jordan and Holliday faced faction-backed challengers; apparently unwilling to entertain the idea that Jordan's victory was not just a fluke, the factional forces recruited ex-representative Neal as their candidate once more. Nearly all of the county offices were on the ballot and the CCP recruited a full slate of reform-minded Democrats to challenge factional incumbents. The CCP and Freedom alliance persisted, this time with Freedom bargaining for an African American to be slated for countywide office. As the senior elected official within the Freedom ranks and as the individual with the closest ties to the reform set, Watkins was chosen as this alliance's candidate for clerk of the circuit court.[93]

In nearly every respect, the 1966 election was a repetition of the 1964 primary. Indeed, later observers would come to regard the 1964 primary as a dry run for the historic triumph achieved in 1966.[94] The antifaction message, the crucial role played by CCP in bankrolling Freedom's mobilization efforts, and the factions' unwillingness to change (by refusing to slate an African American candidate) all contributed to an overwhelming CCP/Freedom victory. All but one faction-supported candidate for county office went down to defeat. The reformers were elated, believing this victory to be the culmination of forty years of effort. Watkins thus became the first African American elected official in Jackson County, winning a majority of ballots in all of the wards with African American majorities. That Watkins won a majority in Wagner's 2nd Ward, where the JDC made it clear that his defeat was its highest priority, was considered a major repudiation of "Boss Wagner" even as voters there cast ballots for the rest of the JDC ticket. Jordan's margin in his state representative race increased over two years prior, with the Freedom president now garnering over 80 percent of the vote.[95] Perhaps the most significant part of the 1966 victory was that the factions were deprived of their sole remaining source of power, control over county patronage. Once more, black voters made the difference between victory and defeat for the reform group. Freedom expanded its influence, reaching more deeply into the 2nd, 3rd, 16th, and 17th Wards, even if it could not be said to "control" them in the same way that it did the 14th.

Freedom emerged from the 1964 and 1966 elections immensely strengthened. Although Freedom still could not be said to represent a majority of the city's black voters, in the course of just two elections, it had doubled the number of its members holding elected office, was uniformly saluted as a linchpin in a congressman's victory, further cultivated its ties with the reformist element, and was regarded by nearly every commentator as having been an important component in the defeat of the factions. Perhaps most important, the force of Freedom's argument for black political independence and unity was gaining supporters in areas outside of the 14th Ward. It must be acknowledged that this move to Freedom was not caused solely by the LPO's organizational efficiency or strategic brilliance; instead, the sheer political stupidity of the factions, for example, in insisting on slating the anti–civil rights Phillips at a time when their own survival in black wards was imperiled, was essential. However, as with the public accommodations ordinance, the results of the 1964 and 1966 primaries opened up new possibilities, proved that greater African American representation was possible, showed that organizing even in "controlled" wards could yield positive results, and continued to demonstrate that Freedom was a force with which to be reckoned.

Transforming Electoral Victory into Results
Freedom's Articulation of Black Interests, 1964–1967

As important as defeating the factions or expanding into new territory might have been, they remained a means to an end rather than Freedom's raison d'être. Neither the leadership nor the membership of Freedom lost sight of the fact that the LPO's central objective was to improve the quality of life for black Kansas Citians. Between the time of the approval of the public accommodations ordinance and the 1967 municipal elections, Freedom's members remained vigilant in pressing for black interests. During this period, there were four major issues on which African Americans sought action from municipal government: segregated housing, police conduct, employment opportunity, and improved city services in the urban core. In each case, a member of Freedom was responsible for pressing the issue, in response to the expressed desires and demands of the broader African American population.

Residential segregation had long been a concern for African American Kansas Citians. African Americans sought to expand the boundaries of "acceptable" black settlement, improve the quality of housing stock in which they lived, and create racially integrated neighborhoods. These issues intensified in importance during the 1960s, when the federal government began making large sums of money available for various housing and urban renewal projects.[96] In Kansas City, African Americans were deeply worried that federal monies would be used in ways that would only calcify or intensify existing residential segregation. For example, original plans to build new housing for low-income people called for all of the units to be concentrated in the urban core, even as one of the program's ostensible goals was to expand residential opportunities for this population. On the issue of segregated housing, Bruce Watkins took the lead. He argued forcefully, colorfully, and to significant media attention that public funds should be expended in ways that dismantled residential segregation rather than reinforced it. The Housing Authority of Kansas City (HAKC) eventually agreed to build scattered-site housing for low-income people, with some of the units even located in the newly annexed areas north of the Missouri River. The pressure that

Watkins and other elected officials applied was crucial to securing this concession. Even after the HAKC made its announcement, Watkins continued to raise the issue, to the great discomfort of HAKC staff who said Watkins "can't take yes for an answer."[97]

Watkins and fellow councilman Earl Thomas were instrumental in securing large sums of federal money for urban renewal in the Third District. Of course, urban renewal was not an unvarnished good and in many cities became removal of the dispossessed; in Kansas City, Watkins and Thomas ensured that residents were involved in the process and that funds were spent to rehabilitate existing housing stock rather than for gentrification. Through Watkins's leadership, a consensus was reached among the CA council members on the necessity of spending urban renewal funds in urban core neighborhoods rather than, for example, using the money to underwrite infrastructure in the newly annexed areas.[98]

Another important facet of the residential segregation issue was the increasing turnover in the racial character of neighborhoods. The 1960s were the period of white flight; as African Americans entered neighborhoods, whites fled to the suburbs. As Kevin Fox Gotham has masterfully explained, Kansas City is a prime example of the phenomenon. Neighborhoods transitioned rapidly in the 1960s, with the local real estate industry playing an outsized role in the process. Civic leaders feared what this transitioning would mean for the city's economic and demographic base, but few of Kansas City's elected officials indulged in the sort of craven fear-mongering seen in other cities. Watkins and Mayor Davis both repeatedly made public statements about the need to "live together." Still, residential segregation became more pronounced than ever during the mid-1960s, with the "Troost Wall" definitively becoming the barrier between the city's black and white populations.[99] Watkins's efforts to enact a fair housing ordinance, which would have punished realtors for practices (e.g, steering) that replicated segregation, met with repeated failure. Only after the 1967 municipal elections were behind them did a majority of the council adopt a fair housing law.

The second issue during this period was by far the most controversial. Since at least the 1930s, African Americans had complained of maltreatment and brutality by the Kansas City Police Department (KCPD). Despite the fact that misconduct in the police department was regularly exposed, neither the newspaper nor civic leaders were willing to take allegations of racially disparate treatment seriously. Until Watkins arrived at City Hall in 1963, such claims never made it onto the municipal agenda nor were police officials pressed to respond to the charges. Many black Kansas Citians felt that law enforcement in the city took a turn for the worse with the arrival of police chief Clarence M. Kelley in 1960. Prior to his selection as chief, Kelley was an FBI agent who had led the Kansas City, Memphis, and Birmingham offices. It was during his tenure as station chief in Birmingham that the FBI signed its most notorious informant in the Ku Klux Klan, Thomas Gary Rowe, and Kelley was known to be great friends with Birmingham Public Safety Commissioner Eugene "Bull" Connor. Although the extent of Kelley's complicity with Connor and segregationist vigilantes would not be known until later, Kansas City's African American residents argued that under his leadership fewer crimes in black neighborhoods were being solved, that the department's hiring policies were hopelessly racist (just a few dozen of nearly 1,300 employees were black), that African Americans were frequently harassed by police, and that police brutality against blacks increased.

Kelley conceded that his officers used force more often than in the past, but insisted that it was always provoked. What most irked African American Kansas Citians was that Kelley always, without question, defended the officers regardless of the facts of the case and usually accompanied his defense with snide remarks about those alleging misconduct. Kelley maintained that KCPD hiring policies were not racist; there were simply no "qualified" black applicants.[100] Unfortunately, Freedom's elected officials were unable to achieve any change in the administration of the KCPD. Although funded by the city, the department was administered by the state through a Board of Police Commissioners appointed by the governor. City elected officials thus had limited influence over the department, with even the size of the city's appropriation to the KCPD mandated by state statute. Nevertheless, Watkins and Thomas persisted in drawing attention to what they regarded as racially motivated police misconduct.

The third major policy issue during this period was equality of opportunity for employment in municipal government. Since the Pendergast era African Americans had composed a substantial share of city employees, but tended to be clustered at the lower rungs of the ladder. None of the municipal departments had an African American director and few blacks served even in mid-level management. A similar pattern was to be found in companies performing work on municipal contracts; many had large numbers of African American workers, but they did manual labor and did not reach even into mid-level management, much less ownership. The same was true about volunteer positions on municipal boards and commissions. African American activists in Freedom protested this state of affairs, but those raising the issue were informed that there were simply no qualified applicants. The merit system and city manager form of government meant that council members could not directly intervene in employment decisions, but Watkins and Thomas both took opportunities to speak on the council floor about highly qualified African Americans who were passed over for employment. Freedom members monitored promotions and hiring at City Hall and were quick to bring up the issue whenever they encountered elected officials. Although there was no structural reform to address equal opportunity in hiring, the vigilant attention Freedom members paid to the issue succeeded in producing limited change. By 1967, a handful of African Americans were appointed to more senior-level posts, usually in departments thought to be "black-oriented," though there were still no black department directors and contracting with black-owned or -led businesses remained almost nonexistent. The first black department director was appointed the following year, but even then was named to lead a "black-oriented" department, human relations; that department's charge was to oversee diversity efforts in employment and mediate disputes.

Finally, the city's black elected officials, neighborhood leaders, and activists all agitated for improved city services in urban core neighborhoods. These individuals maintained that the city devoted fewer resources to these neighborhoods than it did to, for example, the upper-income Country Club Plaza. In particular, they argued that roads and sewers in the Third District were deteriorating, that city services were not provided in equal portion there, and that an attitude of neglect pervaded the city's interaction with these areas. In making these arguments, Thomas and Watkins earned the rhetorical support of their colleagues, but little changed in the directives issued to the city manager. Residents reported little change on this issue, except for the influx of antipoverty program dollars that the city was compelled to spend in urban core neighborhoods.

In short, the record of serving black interests in the period 1964–1967 is a mixed one. Limited victories were secured on residential segregation, employment opportunity, and improved city services, while the attempt to challenge police conduct was an abject failure. Black interests were receiving a hearing and being acted upon in an unprecedented, if still unsatisfactory, fashion. In prior years, even limited victories were nonexistent; the very fact that police brutality was being challenged on the floor of the City Council, forcing some attention to be paid to the issue, was a minor-grade triumph. For this change, Freedom should be accorded the credit. While the preceding pages have taken note of individuals (particularly Watkins) who presented the black community's case on these issues, it should be stressed that these were not individual efforts but manifestations of collective agency. Decisions to pursue these particular policy issues were taken only *after* conversation within Freedom, based on feedback received from the LPO's activists on what occupied the minds of their neighbors. Of even greater importance, the systemic demands articulated by Watkins and Thomas were rendered credible to their colleagues only because of the demonstrated influence that Freedom possessed. When they spoke and claimed that an issue was of vital importance to the city's African American population, their claims were reinforced with the implicit (and sometimes explicit) threat that failure to respond would result in retaliation from Freedom.

The Municipal Election of 1967

The perceived potential for retaliation by Freedom was an important component of the 1967 municipal election. Despite the fact that the council had taken several actions that were unpopular with white voters—including public accommodations, fluoridating water, and pushing for daylight savings time (the latter two were overturned by the voters in referenda)—the CA slate attracted only fringe opposition. The council was well regarded for its emphasis on efficiency and economic development, but there still would have been political space for credible challengers to emerge. Instead, the challengers who filed for office tended to be members of the John Birch Society, little-known right-wing activists,[101] and assorted gadflies.[102] The factions chose to abstain from the campaign altogether, in no small measure because they remained paralyzed from the loss of county government the previous summer.

The CA's control of the city was presumed to be firm enough, thanks partly to having bargained for alliance with Freedom for another election cycle, to make any effort at challenging a CA-endorsed candidate quixotic. The CA-Freedom alliance was cemented for another four years through Davis's progressivism on issues of race and by the ease with which G. Lawrence Blankinship was appointed to the vacancy left by Watkins when he took county office. Blankinship was a prominent black businessman, owning the city's largest distributor of African American-targeted beauty products. He was Watkins's personal choice to replace him on the Council, a choice with which Freedom institutionally concurred. After his endorsement by Freedom, the CA voted to endorse Blankinship, and he was unanimously appointed to fill Watkins's unexpired term in December 1966.[103] He was subsequently endorsed by both the CA and Freedom for a full term in 1967, without so much as a hint of discord or disagreement over his service. In addition, Freedom and the CA were united in their desire to end the public service career of Mrs. Harry Hagan, who represented the Fifth District (and who, through her entire public life, went by Mrs. Harry Hagan, rather than using her own first name). Both organizations declined to endorse her and campaigned against her, with Jordan, Watkins, and Mayor Davis all criticizing her vigorously by name. Moreover, in calling for her defeat the CA specifically mentioned her atrocious record on civil rights and issues affecting the black community.[104] Most important, the CA did not react negatively when Freedom endorsed the factional incumbent Sal Capra over a CA-backed opponent in one race. Capra had been one of the most loyal and outspoken supporters of civil rights issues on the council, and Freedom's membership was adamant that he should be rewarded for his courage.[105] Typically, the CA demanded a loyalty oath from its candidates and partners, but it accepted Freedom's decision thanks to the strategic bargain struck by the two LPOs.

The alliance continued to be successful for both parties. Davis won reelection overwhelmingly, with some of his largest margins attained in black-majority precincts. None of the CA-backed incumbents faced serious threats, and all won overwhelmingly (though some commentators were taken aback that the John Birchers won over 30 percent of the vote). Sal Capra won reelection by a healthy margin, a substantial portion of which was supplied by black voters in his district. Freedom was able to take partial credit for that victory, which it badly needed in light of the debacle it faced with Hagan. Hagan won reelection by a nearly two-to-one margin, though her district was 30 percent African American. Although she lost in the black-majority precincts of the 17th Ward, where Freedom's influence was being felt for the first time, she did so only narrowly. Indeed, she captured something close to 40 percent of the black vote in her district, despite the impassioned opposition of Freedom, *The Call,* and the CA.[106] Moreover, it was noticed that the percentage of voters who were black had increased over four years prior, according black voters new clout in citywide, if not district, races. In short, the power of Freedom and the black community was reaffirmed though not enhanced by the 1967 elections. As the new council term began and as 1967 turned to 1968, nearly everyone believed that the next four years would be much like the last four. How terribly, terribly wrong that prediction would prove to be.

1968: The Year of Turmoil, Tragedy, and Triumph

The year 1968 is now regarded as one of the most tumultuous in modern history. It was a year marked by two major political assassinations—those of Martin Luther King Jr. and Robert Kennedy—war in Vietnam, and hundreds of disruptive protests around the world. Kansas City, long removed from its days as a wide-open capital of vice and now regarded as a sleepy outpost of Middle

America, would not be exempt from the dramatic events of the year. For the first and only time in its history, Kansas City would be rocked by an urban rebellion.

The Urban Rebellion

As in other cities with large black communities, the rebellion began in the aftermath of the assassination of Martin Luther King Jr. Unlike in other cities, there was no immediate violent reaction in Kansas City. Instead, there were several days of nonviolent protest marches and church services. The city's leading elected officials expressed sincere sadness about the murder, with Leon Jordan saying that, "I am too bitter to comment. I am waiting for the enforcement of the laws we have on the books [. . .] They're going to shoot the country to hell if they don't get a hold of those bigoted people on both sides—and we have them on both sides."[107] On April 9, the day of Dr. King's funeral in Atlanta, many school districts—including the one across the state line in Kansas City, Kansas, which had a large African American population—opted to cancel classes, either out of respect for the slain leader or to avoid predicted trouble. The Kansas City, Missouri School District (KCMSD) did not cancel classes, offering instead an hour-long memorial service; this decision proved to be a mistake. Many African American students simply stayed away from school that day, others left class once the funeral began, and others still engaged in angry though nonviolent protest on the grounds of their high schools. With the district's superintendent out of town, principals of three high schools with black majorities—Central, Lincoln, and Manual—opted for an early release, hoping that it would satisfy protesting students. Instead, thousands of African American students began to congregate at Central High School, where a hastily organized march to City Hall began.

Throughout the march, the demonstrators were nonviolent, with only isolated incidents of minor trouble like broken windows (and these not necessarily attributable to the demonstrators). Elected officials and older politicians, including Bruce Watkins and Alvin Brooks (who became the first black department head when he was named to lead the new human relations department earlier in the year), as well as several players for the Kansas City Chiefs professional football team joined the marchers along the way. At one point, Mayor Ilus Davis joined the marchers. He gave a poorly received speech, with some students believing that he was attempting to contain them in black-majority neighborhoods and stymie their desire to march to City Hall, before he attempted to lead the marchers the rest of the way to City Hall. His presence unsettled the more militant black activists, most notably Lee Bohannon, an up-and-coming leader of a small youth activist group. Bohannon challenged the mayor's presence, saying "I don't want a white man in front of me. I want a black man." The mayor was also embarrassed when police officers blockading downtown refused to let the march he led pass. The assembled marchers came to the conclusion that even the city's mayor lacked the ability to control the KCPD; only a direct call from Mayor Davis to Chief Kelley enabled the marchers to pass.

At City Hall, the marchers heard speeches from civil rights activists and elected officials. Several speakers were shouted down, driven from the speaker's platform by boos and heckling. Still, the event remained nonviolent, if restless. A police cordon ringed the protesters, with black activists later maintaining that the officers seemed eager to attack. Sensing that the event could rapidly go awry, Watkins, clergymen, and youth leaders persuaded most of the gathered masses to disperse, either to return home or to attend hastily scheduled activities, including a dance in the basement of Holy Name Church at 23rd and Benton. That evening's edition of the *Star* practically crowed in announcing that Kansas City had escaped the violence and "rioting" other communities encountered on the same day.[108]

Not long after the *Star* landed on doorsteps, violence broke out. Precisely how the violence began remains a point of contention. The official report of the Mayor's Commission on Civil Disturbance would judge that the crowd was dispersing, though a handful of "agitators" called the police names and threw a few rocks, until a black man climbed on the hood of a police car with the intent to attack. From there, chaos ensued. Police officers—almost exclusively white, since the KCPD's 1,300 member officer corps was just 5 percent black at the time—were quickly launching vigorous "enforcement" measures against any African American they encountered. Measures taken by the police inflamed the situation, with police assaults on bystanders provoking previously nonviolent individuals. This included the brutal beating of two black priests who were attempting to disperse the youth. Actions taken by the police seemed to fuel the fire (figuratively as well as literally, with fires being set across the city in short order), with the community particularly aghast at the widespread use of tear gas. The first tear gas canister was thrown at City Hall as the situation there degenerated; police would later claim—though the mayor's commission found no evidence to support the claim—that a tear gas canister had been stolen earlier in the day, and that this first use of the hated weapon was by militants seeking to cause trouble.

In what was perhaps the most egregious example of the police contributing to rather than mediating tension, eight tear gas canisters were tossed through an open window into the basement of Holy Name Church. The church's basement was housing a dance, organized by clergy, youth activists, and DJs from KPRS, the city's black-owned radio station, with the intent of providing a venue to keep restless youth off the streets. The police later claimed that they were attempting to disperse a crowd of "rioters" across the street, who sought refuge in the church basement. The police log showed that the department was well aware of the dance taking place in the church, but police opted to throw the canisters into the facility anyway. The Mayor's Commission on Civil Disturbance later held that there was "no justification whatever" for the incident.[109]

As one might expect, word quickly spread about the use of tear gas on innocent, nonviolent black youth attending a church dance. Violence spread as a direct result, and soon the neighborhoods of the urban core were awash in fires, overturned cars, and looting. Commercial stretches in the black community were looted, vandalized, and sometimes set aflame, though anecdotal evidence suggests that establishments posting signs reading "Soul Brother" or "Black Owned" were passed over by the urban rebels. Mayor Davis declared a state of emergency, imposing a curfew and granting the police "emergency powers." Missouri Governor Warren Hearnes, who had put the National Guard on alert the day of King's assassination, sent in thousands of troops to restore order. After a full day of disruption, it seemed as though the police and National Guard had succeeded in restoring "order," though only by employing brutal tactics in an indiscriminate fashion against any African American they encountered. But the next morning trouble resumed, first at Lincoln High School. There, students were normally prohibited from entering the building prior to the ringing of the first bell. The principal refused to make an exception on this day; patrolling police and National Guardsmen were generally ignorant of this practice and became aggressive when they saw students "loitering" on the school's lawn. The students reacted to the police presence with epithets and a few scattered rocks; the police responded with more tear gas, throwing several canisters into the school itself. Even more serious was a rash of sniper shootings targeted at police patrolling the black community; the sniper shootings caused police and troops to "crack down"— again using tear gas canisters—and produced further outrage from young black Kansas Citians.[110] It was later proven that at least some of the snipers were white supremacists from outside the community. They sought precisely the outcome that was achieved, a crackdown in neighborhoods with black majorities and additional violence.[111]

Order was fully restored after two days, but the National Guard stayed in place to ensure that it was not a false "peace." The rebellion was swift but immensely consequential: six people (all African American men) were killed, eighteen people were injured by police, eighteen people were injured by persons unknown (or unattributed), 26 law enforcement officers were injured, sixteen people were treated for conditions stemming from the tear gas, 312 buildings were damaged, $915,000 worth of property damage was done, 98 cases of arson were identified, and 1,042 people were arrested.[112] Perhaps the most significant casualty was the self-righteous and complacent attitude of Kansas City's white civic leaders, who had long prided themselves on the city's supposed tolerance and healthy race relations, insisting "it can't happen here." In the aftermath of the rebellion, many civic leaders claimed that greater attention must be paid to black communities to avert "the urban crisis." The Mayor's Commission on Civil Disturbance echoed the popular sociological line of the times, attributing the "riot" to a "long history of social and economic tensions and frustrations, which have established an *emotional state among Negro ghetto residents that can be triggered into mass disorder and violence by the occurrence of an otherwise comparatively unimportant incident."*[113]

Welcome as the rhetoric of equality for African American citizens was, it was always encountered by ringing endorsements of the work done by Police Chief Clarence Kelley. But to most black Kansas Citians, Kelley and Gov. Warren Hearnes were the clear villains of the episode. African American leaders maintained that a brutal and unnecessary police overreaction was the cause of the entire incident, which was made worse as the municipal response grew militaristic. While Mayor Davis won plaudits from nearly everyone, including Freedom, for several reassuring television appearances and apologies for the wanton use of tear gas, Kelley and Hearnes refused to admit any mistakes. Indeed, in a joint television appearance with Davis at the height of the crisis, Kelley went out of his way to contradict the mayor, defend the use of the tear gas canisters, and to antagonize the black community. Kelley and Hearnes were applauded by whites for their "strength" and "rapid response." Indeed, even as the Mayor's Commission regularly and accurately conceded that police overreaction and misconduct were prime causes of the events of April 1968, the report saluted Chief Kelley as "a capable and competent Chief of Police. He is honest and fair, has real integrity, and is highly respected generally by the policemen under his command, including the Negro policemen."[114] The report went on to say that the KCPD's real problem with the black community was not one of misconduct or racial inequality, but public relations. Suffice to say, the activists of Freedom, Inc., not to mention the city's more militant activists, had a very different opinion.

The Fair Housing Ordinance

At first, it seemed like the rebellion might have another, unexpected casualty: Kansas City's recently adopted fair housing ordinance. The egregiously high levels of residential segregation and the rapid white flight of the mid-1960s had long been a concern for Freedom and its representatives at City Hall. When Watkins departed the City Council in January 1967, his Freedom-selected successor, G. Lawrence Blankinship, became the most visible advocate for taking municipal action against residential segregation. Indeed, the beauty product distributor's passion for this issue was an important factor in Freedom's decision to endorse his application for the vacant council seat and his election to a full term in April 1967.

After the municipal general election in April 1967, Blankinship continued the crusade for a new "fair housing" ordinance. It penalized various techniques employed by residential realtors to influence the "racial character" of neighborhoods, including the infamous practice of "steering" and the even more notorious method of "block-busting." Given the dominant role that the real estate industry played in producing and reproducing residential segregation in Kansas City,[115] this focus was well placed and farsighted. It also, unsurprisingly, provoked vigorous opposition from the realtors' organization. Even with the dedicated opposition of the realtors, right-wing organizations, and many neighborhood organizations, the council unanimously adopted the ordinance in the summer of 1967. Once more, Freedom's alliance with the CA proved its worth; the most vigorous supporters of the ordinance were Blankinship and Mayor Davis, who persuaded the remaining CA council members to cast votes in favor. These members were reminded of the support that their reelection bids had received from black voters in general and Freedom in particular, while Davis insisted that the question was one of basic morality.[116]

Although even the ordinance's supporters conceded that it was weak and did little to proactively promote integration, it had a large number of passionate detractors. As with public accommodations earlier in the decade, a rump group of self-interested business figures (in this case, the real estate industry) quickly organized a petition drive to put the ordinance to a public vote. The required number of signatures was collected by Christmas and the ordinance, whose implementation was delayed while the referendum process took place, was put on the April 30, 1968 ballot.[117] The real estate industry was better funded and better organized than the tavern owners had been; an industry political organization paid for numerous advertisements in the local newspapers, using scare tactics to convince voters that the ordinance would fine or jail them for renting or selling a home to any white family.[118] Such allegations bore not even the faintest resemblance to the truth, of course.

Even the most confident supporters of fair housing were shaken by the urban rebellion, which took place just a few weeks before the scheduled fair housing vote. White public opinion was overwhelmingly hostile to the rebellion and, by extension, became even more antagonistic than usual to anything regarded as something that African Americans desired. The ordinance's supporters became convinced that the law would be overturned by the voters, carried away on a massive wave of white backlash. Contemporary polling data showed that white Kansas Citians' reaction to the rebellion was overwhelmingly negative: 67 percent of white Kansas Citians felt that the rebellion would hurt blacks in the long run, 58 percent said that blacks in Kansas City were already treated fairly, and 52 percent said that the city's blacks should devote less time to protesting and more time to "earn[ing] the rights of American citizens."[119]

The attention of Freedom, Blankinship, Davis, Watkins, and others shifted to finding some way to avoid the April 30 vote without substantively retreating on the cause of fair housing. For once, activity in the nation's capital proved constructive and presented a solution. In the aftermath of Dr. King's assassination, a long-stalled civil rights bill with strong fair housing language (much stronger than anything in the Kansas City law) passed both houses of Congress and was signed into law by President Lyndon Johnson. The passage of that civil rights bill would render Kansas City's own fair housing ordinance moot, though the federal law would not take effect for several years. Even the symbolic defeat of the local ordinance and a four-year lag time on implementation of the national act would have been disastrous not just for the cause of fair housing, but for further progress on other local black interests. After several brainstorming sessions among Freedom's membership, Watkins publicly suggested—and the council quickly concurred—that the local fair housing ordinance be repealed and immediately replaced by adopting the provisions of the federal law. With this action, the April 30 referendum was cancelled, as the ordinance to be voted upon was stricken from the books.[120] This stroke of genius accomplished all of the objectives of the black community, Freedom, and white allies like Mayor Davis: it avoided the embarrassment of defeat at the polls, denied a victory to some of the most dedicated opponents of the ruling coalition, accelerated the timetable for implementation so that local action was not purely a response to a federal mandate,[121] continued the momentum for civil rights, and made the local law on fair housing even tougher than it would have been had the Blankinship-authored ordinance survived the referendum.

The Aftermath of the Rebellion
Triumph over the Factions and Freedom's Increasing Militancy

Beyond the issue of fair housing, the urban rebellion of 1968 had serious implications within the black community and for Freedom, Inc. Faced with the death of six African Americans and millions of dollars in damage, the city's black community was radicalized. Although the members and leaders of Freedom, Inc., could not have predicted the events of April 1968, the LPO's mission, structure, and reputation permitted it to respond in a politically effective way. "Militant" groups like a Black Panthers chapter led by Pete O'Neal attracted significant attention, support, and influence, though not actual members. Whether to stave off the threat posed by these more militant groups or because its members were genuinely caught up in the same radicalizing wave, Freedom itself became more aggressive in its rhetoric and action. Since the LPO was already among the most "radical" of the political organizations in the black community, this shift did not appear to be, and was not, empty posturing.

The precinct captain network once more proved its worth, as distributor and source of information as well as a mobilizer of the masses. Freedom members and leaders were visible in the community during the rebellion and in its aftermath; they appeared to be deeply rooted in the community, to understand and share the frustrations of the broader black community. Watkins seemed to especially sense this anger, but tried to channel the collective frustration into involvement in the political process, repeatedly invoking what came to be his trademark phrase: "Don't get mad, get smart." In addition, Freedom's leaders—especially Jordan—were able to keep the lines of communication open with the more militant youth leaders, even if a generational chasm did inhibit them from fully cooperating with one another. Freedom's leaders were instrumental, for example, in securing city employment (in Model Cities) for the brother of Panther leader Pete O'Neal. The city's radicals were never co-opted by Freedom, and some refused to communicate with the LPO. Emanuel Cleaver, for example, was brash, newly arrived from Texas, and led the local chapter of the Southern Christian Leadership Conference (SCLC), believing existing civil rights groups were too conservative and accommodationist. Although Cleaver was personally fond of Jordan, he "was determined not to join" Freedom, because he regarded it as nothing but a black political machine, not nearly "radical" enough for his worldview.[122] In this, Cleaver was atypical, and the ability of Freedom to keep open the channels of communication with more militant elements would be crucial in permitting the organization to not just survive but be strengthened by the changing ideological currents of the period.

Strengthened Freedom was, because the August 1968 primary provided the final, decisive victory over the factions. Having finally come to the realization that their ability to ever again wield influence in Jackson County or Kansas City was dependent on regaining their lost African American support, the factions campaigned vigorously to crush Freedom. One component of this strategy was to oust Jordan from office; still believing that Freedom was primarily the personal organization of its president, the faction leaders concluded that if Freedom's leader could be defeated or humiliated, the organization would follow. In 1968, Wagner and other factional leaders arrived at the belated realization that Jordan was personally popular and his past victories were not flukes. The factions failed to realize that it was not just his personal charm or famous firsts that made Jordan popular (indeed, the community was rife with gossip about Jordan's personal failings); it was the battles he chose on behalf of African Americans. Failing to appreciate this crucial distinction, the factions recruited a candidate even more popular and famous than Jordan: Satchel Paige, the Hall of Fame pitcher of the Negro Leagues and major league baseball. Paige, who was born in the district and lived there all his life, had earlier cast his lot with the factions by accepting a no-show job as deputy sheriff.[123]

Paige made no speeches during the campaign, but the factions undertook a lavish advertising campaign on behalf of him and the rest of their "True Negro Democratic Ballot." Turning the traditional Freedom attack on the factions on its head, newspaper advertisements asked black Kansas Citians, "Would you vote for these White Bosses—Uncle Toms—who are interested in serving the interests of the White community alone?" Taking advantage of the Freedom alliance with CCP, Jordan, Watkins, and Holliday were portrayed (verbally and graphically) as "Charley Curry's Puppets (CCP)." In a vicious bit of *ad hominem* attack, newspaper ads labeled Jordan as "The Leer," Watkins as "The Smear," and Holliday as "The Sneer."[124] Black voters were not persuaded by these tactics. The effort to rebrand the factions as the true voices of racial progress and Freedom as the captive of white bosses may have been daring, but it was blatantly false. While

Paige's athletic accomplishments may have won him popularity and accolades, they did not win him votes. Jordan garnered an impressive 1,894 votes to Paige's paltry 308 votes.[125]

Jordan had won before, however, and so it was not his victory—even over a celebrity challenger—that was the most important outcome of the 1968 primary. Instead, the results of other races showed Freedom's ascendance. Herman Johnson, then president of the local NAACP branch and previously the president of a rival black political club in the 2nd Ward, joined Freedom and was its candidate for a state representative's seat; he won overwhelmingly against a factional candidate. Johnson's victory on the Freedom ballot was important because it signaled the end of separate ward-based black political organizations as well as recognition that Freedom was the dominant, corporatist black LPO. From this point on, black organizational challengers to Freedom would attempt to fashion community-wide bases or personal followings, rather than employing the old pattern of operating within specific ward or precinct territories. Harold Holliday sought to become the Kansas City area's first black state senator; the district in which he ran had a white majority, but Holliday came agonizingly close to victory through Freedom's efforts on his behalf. Most significant of all were the elections with arguably the lowest stakes, those for the Democratic central committee. These elections served as indicators of organizational strength and reproduced that strength by making party resources available to the victorious groupings. In these crucial races, all but one of Freedom's candidates for the committee won. By far the most important of these races was in the 2nd Ward, long considered the personal fiefdom of Louis Wagner and his JDC. Watkins ran for Democratic committeeman from the 2nd Ward against a Wagner-backed incumbent. The county official's popularity and Freedom's enhanced presence in the ward carried Watkins to victory, 1,099 to 773, and so effectively ended the JDC's control over the ward.[126]

For the factions, the 1968 primary was an utter disaster. For Freedom, the primary was the long-awaited complete triumph. There was no partial victory this time. With only one minor exception, wherever African Americans were in the majority in Kansas City and Freedom contested the race, its candidate was successful. After the August primary, the competition among organizations for preeminence among black voters was conclusively settled: Freedom had won. The factions were never again able to command any loyalty; increasingly lacking the patronage with which they once wooed voters and workers, their former supporters began migrating either to Freedom or to their own personal organizations, and the white-controlled factions rapidly shriveled away in the black community. Black political unity was not yet achieved, as a substantial minority of African Americans still cast ballots for Freedom's adversaries, but the LPO could for the first time be said to represent a majority of the city's African Americans in all of the black-majority wards. Freedom was now a black community wide organization and would, from this point on, always be described by commentators and journalists as the "dominant" black political organization in Kansas City. It had effectively managed to become the single, corporatist political voice of the city's black community.

Indicative of Freedom's new preeminence, community-wide influence, and militancy were the LPO's actions in the November 1968 elections. Warren Hearnes, the Democratic governor who many Freedom activists considered personally responsible for the rebellion's six deaths, stood for reelection. While all of the old-line Democratic factions enthusiastically endorsed Hearnes for reelection, Freedom did what would have been unthinkable just a few months earlier and for the first time endorsed a Republican in a partisan race. When the endorsement was announced, most commentators ridiculed the action. These commentators insisted that African Americans were delusional to believe that Hearnes, as opposed to black people themselves, was responsible for the events of April. They maintained that Freedom lacked the clout to persuade blacks to vote for a Republican candidate for governor at the same time that Richard Nixon and Spiro Agnew headed the GOP's ticket. Come election day, it was those doing the ridiculing who were embarrassed. In the three black-majority wards where Freedom was most active and influential, Hubert Humphrey won 14,349 votes (90 percent) to Richard Nixon's 1,315 votes (8 percent) and George Wallace's 199 votes (2 percent). At the same time, the incumbent governor won just 5,881 votes (39 percent) to the Republican nominee's 9,151 votes (61 percent) in those same precincts, even as Hearnes racked up a statewide victory margin over 60 percent.[127] There ceased to be much doubt that Freedom was the single-most important influence on, and representative of, thousands of Kansas City's African American voters.

A Power for the First Time

The six-year period between 1962 and 1968 was clearly an important one for Freedom, Inc. and for Kansas City. This was the foundational period for Freedom, where it moved toward becoming an institutionalized organization: it was formally organized, independent, engaged in multiple tactics, and used a black interests organizing model. The organization was not yet fully institutionalized, because it remained overly dependent on the personalities of Leon Jordan and Bruce Watkins. But this was only because the organization was young; it consciously set for itself the goal of achieving full independence from any person or campaign. The LPO managed to survive and thrive by mobilizing the community through a precinct captain network as well as savvy use of bargaining to create strategic short-term interracial alliances. Consistent with the theory of black political efficacy argued for here, in the process, the LPO secured the satisfaction of some black demands on the system. Where Freedom did fail, and where attempts to enhance black political efficacy failed, it was in large part because there were rival claimants to the title of "voice of the black community," in the form of the factions and other ward-based black LPOs. Still, even this began to change. It can be fairly said that in 1968, Freedom became that single, corporatist LPO unifying the black community for the first time. Likewise, by 1968 the black community in Kansas City had become a power for the first time.

CHAPTER 3

"Don't Get Mad, Get Smart"
Freedom, Inc. and Balance of Power Politics
(1969–1979)

Many contemporary observers now regard the 1970s as the period when Freedom and the city's African American community reached their highest levels of efficacy. These claims are not just nostalgia for a Black Power paradise that never was; Freedom's organizational efficacy and the black community's political efficacy *were* greatly heightened during this period. During the 1970s, Freedom increased the number of black city council members, proved crucial to two mayoral victories, and was instrumental in a number of important policy victories for the African American community. These successes stem from the fact that Freedom became fully institutionalized during this period, retained a strong claim on being the corporatist political voice of the African American community, effectively mobilized black Kansas Citians, and engaged in strategic short-term bargaining with nonblack political actors.

At the same time, however, there were also devastating losses, including the election of a black Republican hostile to Freedom to represent the LPO's Third District heartland, the agonizing defeat of Bruce Watkins in his trail-blazing run for mayor, the departure of a dissident group within Freedom that briefly threatened the LPO's position, and continuing decline in the quality of life in urban core neighborhoods. Moreover, some of the first signs of organizational calcification and decay that would later hamper Freedom's efficacy and reputation become visible during these years.

Both the triumphs and the defeats were outgrowths of the LPO's core strategy during this era: to use strategic bargaining and effective mobilization to make black voters the balance of power in local politics. As will be seen below, this balance of power, or kingmaker, strategy possessed strengths and limitations for both Freedom's organizational efficacy and the political efficacy of Kansas City's black community.

Balance of Power Politics

As the name suggests, a balance of power strategy is one where a group seeks to take advantage of division in the rest of the electorate to maximize the gains the group receives from the political system. If, for example, the white electorate is evenly divided in its support for candidates or parties, a relatively unified black voting bloc can play the decisive role. In such instances, it may be logical for the competing candidates or parties to effectively bid for black support, with each trying to outdo the other in terms of the promises they make to attract that support. The black community thereby benefits both in seeing the election of its favored candidate and in having extracted the maximal concessions from that candidate as a condition for black support. Given that all individuals and groups expect some sort of demand satisfaction in exchange for their support, what differentiates a conscious balance of power strategy from normal politics is the former's aversion to long-term alliances and its complete conditionality. That is, for those practicing balance of power politics, a prior record of sympathetic action or shared ideology or even personal friendships is woefully insufficient to guarantee support in the present. In this sense, balance of power politics represents the ultimate expression of what Ronald Walters has referred to as independent leverage.[1]

The advantages of a balance of power strategy, or kingmaker politics, seem so abundantly clear that the reader would not be remiss in asking why this strategy is not always adopted by African Americans. There are several reasons and several ways in which the approach can go terribly wrong. First, a kingmaker approach depends on the nonblack electorate being divided in such a way that the black vote is decisive. Where the nonblack electorate is largely unified or the black vote insubstantial, there is no balance of power for African Americans to wield. Second, this approach assumes that affiliation with "black interests" will not produce a backlash among the white supporters of the candidate favored by blacks. This is demonstrably untrue; whether in municipal politics[2] or national politics[3] elected officials frequently see precipitous declines in their white support when they are viewed as supporting black interests. Indeed, rather than out-bidding one another for black support, candidates may do the opposite and compete to see who can rain more calumny down on African Americans, in order to win larger shares of the white vote. Third, as a practical matter, maintaining absolute independence and refraining from entering into alliances are not as simple as they sound. Politics is indeed a transactional business, but it is also a human one. Relationships and trust count for something, even among the most hard-nosed and cynical of professional politicians. Even with these limitations, though, conditions are sometimes apropos for kingmaker strategies to produce significant benefits for the groups that employ them.

Freedom's Adoption of a Balance of Power Strategy

Freedom, Inc. did not issue any formal statement of policy declaring that it would henceforth employ a balance of power strategy to achieve its goals. Nevertheless, a careful review of public statements by the LPO's leaders and of the decisions made by the LPO on candidates and issues supports the label. Use of a kingmaker approach was not foreign to the LPO; after all, Freedom attempted in past elections to be a decisive factor in the victories of its favored candidates. However, in those instances, the LPO's behavior was dictated not by balance of power politics, but by its enmity with the factions. Ridding the black community of the factions was Freedom's central goal between 1962 and 1968. Although Freedom engaged in strategic bargaining with the CA to maximize its concessions from the reform bloc, balance of power politics was not in effect because there was nothing that most factional candidates could have offered that would have won them Freedom's support.

With the humiliation of the factions in 1968 and their evaporation from the black community thereafter, defeating the factions ceased to be either a logical or politically resonant core strategy for Freedom. A new overarching strategy was called for, and the activists in Freedom perceived balance of power politics as well suited to the circumstances they faced. Watkins regularly exhorted his audiences, especially young people, with the phrase, "Don't get mad, get smart." That is, rather than acting out of emotion, engaging in empty symbolism, or participating in destructive behavior, African Americans should be politically calculating and use the ample power that they already possessed. Rather than being taken for granted by any group, including the CA or the CCP, black Kansas Citians should demand something in exchange for their support.

At the dawn of the 1970s, the city's politics were more muddled than ever before; as one interviewee described it, "the whole world was changing."[4] Although the factions in the black community were comatose, they remained influential in the declining-but-still-vote-rich North End.[5] Elsewhere in the city, the factions were withering away but their supporters were not yet reconciled to the CA. The CA itself was, despite its nonpartisan character, facing unprecedented tension between its partisan Democratic and Republican members. Thanks to annexations in the north and far south, thousands of voters without firm grounding in municipal politics were being incorporated into the body politic. These annexations made the city both more Republican (thanks to voters in the far south) and more conservative (as the voters in the Northland tended to be old-fashioned, rural, conservative Democrats or working-class). The annexations added a geographic dimension to policy, as the newly annexed territories would hereafter always be in a battle with the more-established parts of the city for municipal funds and services. The net effect of all of these circumstances was that the city's white voters were relatively evenly divided on political questions, with tensions existing between Democrats and Republicans, reform and faction, and Northland and south of the river. Freedom, Inc. realized that it could effectively use its influence with, connection to, and representation of the city's African American voters to wield the balance of power in exchange for concrete benefits for the black community.

For example, the city's leadership almost unanimously endorsed a ballot initiative to increase the local earnings tax[6] from one-half to one full percent. The additional funds would be used to hire more police, renovate fire stations, and initiate a free garbage collection program. Freedom, Inc. chose to remain neutral on the proposition after "Watkins suggested the black community should support the boost if a part of the income could be pledged for spending there. But there was no public reaction by city leaders." Watkins lambasted the plan to hire police by saying "We want more policemen free from bigotry and racism" and the garbage collection program by stating, "How amusing it is to many minority people with the new thing of ecology and pollution—a fact of life they have lived with since birth."[7] The clear point of Watkins's public statements on behalf of Freedom on the issue was to compel other city leaders to pledge a certain share of the tax's revenues to African American neighborhoods. When no such pledge was forthcoming, Freedom sat on its hands.[8] Later in the decade, when the council moved slowly in filling a vacant seat representing the black-majority Third District, a Freedom councilmember held out the prospect that black voters would retaliate by withholding their badly needed support for an elite-favored package of bonds.[9] Or, if we expand our purview beyond municipal politics for just a moment, there is the case of the 1972 Democratic presidential nomination. In that case, *The Call* and Bruce Watkins both used the phrase "balance of power" to describe Freedom's role and strategy in determining the outcome. At local nominating conventions, regular Democrats supporting Muskie and liberals supporting McGovern were deadlocked. Freedom members ultimately aligned behind the regulars, granting them victory. The regulars promised to send two Freedom delegates to the national convention, while the liberals would send only one. Since no black Kansas Citian had ever possessed a full vote at the Democratic National Convention, this was regarded as a significant concession, secured only by the use of a kingmaker strategy.[10]

Roiled by Tragedy: The Murder of Leon Jordan

Unfortunately, Leon Jordan, the man most responsible for Freedom's founding and success, did not live to see the fruits of the new strategy. Just three weeks before the August 1970 Democratic primary, in which he was expected to trounce his "militant" opponent Lee Bohannon, Jordan was murdered. The 65-year-old state representative was shot three times while leaving his Green Duck Tavern at 1:10 am on July 15. The shots were fired at close range and witnesses told police that the assailants were three black men who sped away in a brown Pontiac.[11] The murder made front-page news and stunned the entire city; testimonials on Jordan's wisdom, courage, commitment to black interests, and unique ability to relate to both established power brokers and young militants filled the news pages and poured in from nearly every officeholder in the state. Freedom members were simultaneously pained at the loss of their friend and leader, appalled by the brazenness of the murder, worried about the future, and infuriated at the apparent political motivation of the deed.

Although the police launched an investigation, Jordan's murder went unsolved for four decades. Several people were arrested or indicted in connection with the murder, but all were released or acquitted. During the four-decade interval, speculation on the cause of and criminals behind Jordan's murder was rampant. Accounts of what "really" happened range from political intimidation, to retribution for Jordan's clash with mob-aligned members of the Missouri House (including one incident where he punched another member in the mouth), to his zero-tolerance policy for the drug trade in his neighborhood, to supposed complicity in that trade, to robbing the politician of some valuable jewelry he supposedly had in his possession that evening, to his being murdered by the Black Panthers.[12] In 2010 the Kansas City Police Department was pressured by local civil rights activists into reopening the case (although some activists were reluctant to do so, feeling that unsavory details of Jordan's personal life, like his penchant for purchasing stolen jewelry or adulterous affairs, might emerge). The reopened investigation found that some of the crucial evidence in the case, notably the murder weapon, had disappeared. The gun was later found being used by KCPD officers who were unaware that it had been improperly removed from an evidence locker decades before. This sort of shoddiness in the initial investigation notwithstanding, the police and *Star* reporters closed the case in 2011. That investigation made a case that the murder weapon was provided by the mob,[13] with the murder itself committed by James "Doc" Dearborn, leader of an African American underworld group known as the "Black Mafia." Dearborn, who was murdered in a motel in 1985, was among the men indicted in the 1970s for Jordan's murder, but released.[14]

Although prosecutors claimed that the evidence for the involvement of Dearborn and the mob is clear, they acknowledged that the motive for Jordan's murder and the individual who ordered it remain shrouded in mystery. Police and prosecutors believe that the murder may have been ordered by mob leaders because of Jordan's clash with a mob-affiliated state representative and his interference with underworld business activity in the inner city. Few Mafia figures from that era are still alive, and the one individual who seems to have concrete knowledge about the motive is serving time in federal prison and refuses to comment.

Regardless of what the actual motive for Jordan's murder was, most black Kansas Citians saw it as a political assassination. Harold Holliday, Jordan's colleague in the Missouri House and then Freedom's vice president, told the *Star,* "If this act was intended to throw fear into the members and leaders of Freedom, Inc., they missed the point. Every time they strike down one of us, ten of us will rise to carry on the job."[15] Mamie Hughes, married to one of Freedom's founding members and later a county legislator, told an interviewer six years after the killing that it was "planned because somebody felt, I believe, that they would destroy an organization and a people."[16] Even Jordan's primary opponent, Lee Bohannon, saw a plot to deprive black Kansas Citians of a great leader; he cautioned that, "We cannot let a crisis such as this divide our community. White people have long appointed and picked our officials and representatives. I refuse to be appointed to a position or office at the expense of a black man so known and respected throughout this community."[17]

The impact of Jordan's death on Freedom was immense and immediate. Many Freedom leaders and lower-profile members wondered if there was a plot afoot to target black political activists, or if the streets would erupt in rage as they did two years earlier. One longtime member and close friend of Jordan recalled of the days following the murder, "It was scary. 'Cause they didn't know what was going to happen. And they didn't know what the gangs were gonna do. And it was just scary."[18] Freedom collectively and consciously chose to persevere without altering its orientation or behavior in any way. If Jordan's murder was politically motivated, the LPO refused to be cowed.

A second issue was how to cope with the upcoming Democratic primary. Although few of the primary races were seriously contested, Jordan's death left a gaping hole on both the black-and-gold Freedom Ballot and in the LPO's election strategy. Jordan's death might be presumed to result in the automatic nomination of his opponent, the militant Bohannon. But Freedom leaders were understandably reluctant to allow the young activist to win without a fight, and Bohannon himself had too great a respect for Jordan to desire victory in that way. Jordan's widow, Orchid, was persuaded to run in her late husband's stead. Freedom quickly retooled its overall campaign, producing compelling newspaper advertisements and printed literature that stressed the need for unity in this time of crisis and the personal sacrifice that Leon Jordan made for the cause of equality. The swiftness with which this dramatic turn-about in strategy and messaging was accomplished is itself a testimony to the increasingly professional and sophisticated nature of Freedom's electioneering efforts. Freedom's candidates, including Orchid Jordan, all won overwhelming victories in that August primary; Orchid Jordan would go on to serve in the Missouri House of Representatives for sixteen years.

The third and final issue needing immediate attention was the future of Freedom itself. Jordan was the driving force behind the LPO's founding, its most popular personality in the black community, and someone who commanded respect from a broad cross-section of the community. His death might be presumed to result in the LPO's collapse. The *Star* and *Times* often referred to Freedom as "Leon Jordan's organization," as though it were nothing more than a personal following. Given that so many of the city's political clubs were nothing but personality cults, this is not surprising, but far from the truth. From the beginning, Jordan and the other founders sought to make Freedom more than a personal fiefdom. Although formal power was concentrated in the organization's officers, especially its president, informal power was widely distributed. Jordan and his fellow officers well understood that Freedom's power came only by virtue of its ability to simultaneously represent and influence the masses. Decisions were only taken after a broadly consultative process.

Of course, what drew members to Freedom was not primarily the personage of Leon Jordan, but a commitment to using politics for the advancement of black interests. Jordan himself keenly recognized that the organization must be about more than him, or Watkins, or any of the other marquee-name leaders. That much is evident from the aggressive way in which he sought to recruit capable and committed young people. It was Jordan who reached out to Emanuel

Cleaver, as well as future councilmen Charles Hazley and Richard Tolbert. Without these recruiting efforts by Jordan, Freedom might have lacked the ability to persist.

All of these factors together meant that Jordan's tragic death did not create an insoluble vacuum in the organization. Bruce Watkins was able to easily step into the role of president, Harold Holliday took over from Watkins as chairman of the board, and Freedom's activist workers continued to perform their duties as they always had. Although Watkins became the public face of the organization, internal responsibility and power became more widely dispersed. The organization's board took on a greater role in setting policy and other individuals rose to fill the strategy-plotting gap left by Jordan's death. Rather than causing Freedom to disband, the founder's death produced an even stronger organization. Indeed, in the aftermath of the 1970 tragedy, Freedom could be said for the first time to have become a fully institutionalized LPO.

Charting an Independent Path: The 1971 Municipal Elections

Even though the transition to new leadership was relatively smooth, considerable uncertainty still existed over whether Freedom would continue to wield influence in the future. The first real test came during the 1971 municipal elections, where Freedom decisively proved that it was a force with which to reckon. That spring, Freedom succeeded in ousting two incumbent black council members, provided the winning margin for the successful mayoral candidate, and nearly elected an African American candidate in a district with a white majority. Most impressively of all, it did so over the combined opposition of the CA, the *Star,* *The Call,* and influential members of the black business and religious elite. In the 1971 elections, Freedom truly charted a wholly independent, and, to its erstwhile allies in the CA, unexpected, course. Such impressive success was achieved through an open and transparent endorsement process, a clear and convincing message, savvy alliance building, and, most importantly, the existence and effective use of strong mobilization of the black electorate. For all this success, though, the 1971 election saw the beginning of several patterns that would plague Freedom ever after: allegations of corruption, claims of electoral misconduct, and charges that the organization was motivated by self- rather than community interest. Evidence for these assertions was paltry at best and fabricated at worst in 1971, as the claims were made by those Freedom spurned with ample justification. Irrespective of this lack of evidence, Freedom's opponents quickly latched on to these claims and have since repeated them so often over the decades that they have become part of the conventional wisdom of Kansas City's elites.

Freedom's top priorities were the races for the council seats from the Third District. The Third District remained the only one of the city's six districts with an African American majority; the size of that majority had increased due to redistricting and white flight, such that African Americans made up over 70 percent of the district's population.[19] Both incumbents, G. Lawrence Blankinship in the district seat and Dr. Earl Thomas in the at-large seat, were supported by Freedom at the 1967 election and both sought reelection in 1971. As early as fall 1969, however, it became clear that neither incumbent would receive Freedom's support in 1971. The decision not to endorse either Blankinship or Thomas shows quite clearly that Freedom did not take an essentialist or narrowly parochial view of what constituted black interests; if the organization had been interested only in shallow symbolism, it could quite easily have endorsed the two men and avoided a bruising struggle. But between 1967 and 1971, the incumbents had come to be viewed by a substantial portion of the black population as ineffectual racial moderates, even conservatives.[20] Blankinship, a successful distributor of beauty products for African American consumers, was considered by his critics to be more interested in using public office to expand his business than in advancing black interests. Thomas was by then a septuagenarian and overwhelmed by exhaustion; Freedom members considered it folly to rely on him to lead any fight.[21]

Both men ultimately ran for reelection by pointing to the fact that they were not rabble-rousers and that their style was to work behind the scenes, rather than by making a scene. But Freedom's membership demanded a more vocal and activist defense of black interests; the old, pre-Freedom ways of quietly negotiating for crumbs had little appeal in the era of "Say It Loud, I'm Black, I'm Proud." In this sense, a clash in the style of leadership demanded was as important as substance in Freedom's decision to withdraw support from the two black incumbent council people. Blankinship later claimed that the break occurred because he refused Freedom's directive to support a white candidate for municipal judge over a black candidate. Freedom insiders vigorously denied the charge.[22] Even if the charge were true, however, it would demonstrate that Blankinship's style was not consistent with the culture of Freedom, where elected officials were expected to support the decisions that were collectively made by the group. If individual elected officials began to openly defy the group, then the unity which was the foundation of the LPO's power and credibility (in both black and white circles) would be lost. Outsiders would take advantage of disarray and multiple power centers in the black community, rather than a single corporatist one, to avoid satisfying the demands of any of them.

What is certain is that Blankinship and Thomas were regarded by Freedom's members as ineffectual. Blankinship was praised for his work on passing the fair housing ordinance in 1967, but was thought to have done little in the four years thereafter. Although the incumbent maintained that he had secured substantial federal funds for the district, his opponents charged that those were funds that *had* to be spent in high-poverty urban core neighborhoods and that Blankinship played a negligible role in the process.[23] In both of his terms, Thomas was regarded as milquetoast, willing to follow the leadership of his in-district colleague; without Watkins there to aggressively raise black issues, Thomas was thought to have retreated into the background.

One of the oldest saws of electoral politics, though, is, "You cannot beat something with nothing." In order to provide something to counter what it perceived as ineffectual, accommodationist incumbents, Freedom actively recruited candidates in both races. The candidates the organization recruited in the fall of 1970 demonstrate quite clearly the open, mass-based, and transparent nature of the LPO during this period. Rather than selecting individuals who already served in elective office, or who were longtime insiders, or who came from established political families, both of Freedom's Third District candidates were under the age of thirty and had come to the LPO's attention through grassroots or precinct-level electoral activism. Charles Hazley, a 29 year-old employee of Hallmark Cards, was endorsed to run against Blankinship. Richard Tolbert, a 26 year-old consultant with a master's degree from Yale, was selected as the organization's candidate against Thomas. Tolbert, in particular, was regarded as a rising star; he was eloquent, well educated, urbane, and Leon Jordan's protégé. After just a few campaign appearances, political observers were touting him as the person most likely to become the city's first black mayor.

In 1971, Freedom was not content to contain its activities to the Third District. Racial turnover in the adjacent Fifth District had become more pronounced, such that roughly 40 percent of the district's population was African American. Freedom strategists felt that a black candidate could not win in the district race, especially after redistricting in early 1970, when district lines were drawn so as to reduce the African American share of the district's population.[24] However, they did hold out the hope for victory in the at-large race, where black votes from elsewhere in the city might be enough to nudge a capable black candidate to victory. The decision to enter a Freedom-backed candidate against a white candidate in the at-large race was a daring one, given that just three years before the city's electorate seemed poised to reject fair housing, but demonstrates the balance of power orientation of Freedom strategic thinking during this period. For its candidate, Freedom selected Harold "Doc" Holliday, Jr., the 27 year-old attorney son of the state representative and Freedom supporter-turned-opponent-turned-chairman.[25] The attorney's youth and passion were viewed as being points in his favor, emblematic of the organization's desire to share power with a new generation.

Freedom promptly proceeded to mobilize support for Hazley, Holliday, and Tolbert. Within the precincts with African American majorities, the LPO followed its now-standard procedure of mobilizing the electorate through the precinct captain network, recruiting volunteers for aggressive door-to-door contact campaigns, printing literature, use of telephone trees, holding rallies and meet and greet coffees in the homes of prominent citizens for the endorsed candidates, and seeking the support of black elites, especially the clergy.[26] Although the Freedom candidates engaged in the sort of retail politics that is essential to success at the local level, both Third District candidates would be charged by their opponents, not entirely unfairly, of dodging joint appearances. Hazley devoted more energy to knocking on doors than to appearing at candidate forums with Blankinship. When these events were held in the Third District, Bruce Watkins, who was demonstrating his commitment to the "Dump Blankinship" movement by personally serving as Hazley's campaign manager, was often sent as a surrogate; Hazley's absence and the effective transfer of Watkins's substantial popularity to the young candidate infuriated Blankinship, who constantly complained about it to the press.[27] Freedom's efforts on behalf of its candidates were hampered by the opposition of segments of the African American elite. Blankinship, and to a lesser extent Thomas, was a bona fide member of the black bourgeoisie. Some compatriots in that class sympathized with the preference for a less activist approach to black interests, saw no reason to "undermine" a "successful black man," or were simply too entwined with the Blankinship business interests to oppose him. The incumbents received support from prominent clergy, black business people, and even a handful of youth activists (notably the charismatic Bernard Powell of SAC-20, whose career would be cut short by assassination nearly a decade later). These supporters charged, without a shred of evidence, that the "Dump Blankinship" movement was launched by white outsiders using black surrogates because Blankinship was "too effective" or "too independent."[28] *The Call* editorialized that Blankinship and Thomas were both good men doing good jobs and so should not be replaced; in addition to this editorial endorsement, the newspaper carried numerous front-page hard news stories that cast Blankinship in an immensely favorable light while ignoring Hazley's existence. Since Holliday was opposing two white candidates, he received the paper's support.[29]

Still, the apparent division within the black community over the Third District races, with Freedom on one side and members of the small black elite on the other, complicated the LPO's attempts to win support for its candidates outside of the black community. Support from outside the community was important in both the district and at-large races, for different reasons. In the district race, almost all of the ballots cast would come from within the black community but most of the funds raised to wage a professional campaign came from outside of it. Attracting white support for Hazley would therefore be important to minimize Blankinship's financial advantage. In the at-large race, white votes would be necessary to secure Holliday's election. As in the past, the endorsement perceived to be crucial among white voters was that of the CA. Freedom leaders active in the CA, especially Watkins, lobbied aggressively for the black LPO's candidates to be endorsed by the reformers. In an attempt to strike a hard bargain, Freedom said it would refrain from endorsing any member of the CA council slate unless its priority candidates received reciprocal endorsement. Some members of the CA, primarily those already loath to cooperate with the "firebrands" in Freedom and who far preferred "their" black leaders to be accommodationist, claimed to be appalled by such low politics, conveniently forgetting that Kansas City elections had long been characterized by strategic gambits of this sort. Unease over the LPO's new assertiveness, the existence of relationships between some of the incumbents and CA board members, and Freedom's stance in the mayor's race combined to make this gambit unsuccessful. After a heated floor debate, the CA opted to overturn its screening committee's recommendation of Thomas in favor of Tolbert, but ratified decisions unfavorable to Hazley and Holliday.[30] The CA's refusal to break with Blankinship—with an overwhelming vote in his favor— and subsequent remarks by CA members that questioned whether Freedom was representative of the black community[31] ensured that there would be no formal alliance between the two LPOs in 1971.

Any potential for alliance with the CA was imperiled long before the council slate decisions were made, however, when the "reform" organization opted to endorse Dutton Brookfield for mayor.[32] When Republican businessman Brookfield ran against CA favorite Ilus Davis in 1963, the CA declared with certitude that a vote for Brookfield was a vote for corruption, factionalism, and municipal disaster. Eight years later, with only a controversial tenure as chairman of the Jackson County Sports Authority (which was overseeing the construction of two stadia for major league sports franchises) added to his resume, Brookfield was heralded by the CA as the change agent the city desperately needed. Brookfield's success in capturing the CA endorsement demonstrates the internal turmoil that organization was encountering during this period. The organization had always been strongest in the well to do areas around the Country Club Plaza, which were then the most heavily Republican precincts in the city. As the association's membership base atrophied in response to the diminishing threat posed by the once-feared factions, the relative importance of these Republican members increased. In an unprecedented fashion, the association's Republican members came together to deliver the endorsement to their partisan ally, Brookfield.[33]

During the CA screening process, Freedom loudly averred that it would not ever endorse Brookfield for anything. Watkins regularly and passionately declared his view that Brookfield was a racist unworthy of black support.[34] Freedom instead supported Dr. Charles Wheeler, a lawyer and doctor who had been elected county coroner and then a county judge on the CCP ticket.[35] Wheeler narrowly lost a campaign for presiding judge in Jackson County in the summer of 1970. Reformers had soured on Wheeler, claiming that he was needlessly confrontational.[36] Before entering the mayor's race, Wheeler publicly stated that he cared little about winning the CA endorsement (a blasé attitude that, coupled with his statement that he would prefer a strong mayor form of government to the reform system, did not aid him in winning that group's support). Freedom's commitment to Wheeler put it in confrontation with the CA, whose members claimed to be shocked that the black LPO was not following the CA's lead. Such a dismaying denial of black agency demonstrated that, unlike Ilus Davis, the new leadership of the CA understood nothing about Freedom's purpose or aspirations.

Since the CA refused to grant Freedom's demands on behalf of the black electorate, Freedom engaged in bargaining with a new set of white partners; the result was a hastily cobbled together group of Democratic partisans including the desiccated old-line factions. Although present, the factions played a role in the Wheeler campaign in name only. Still, the partisan nature of this alliance and the participation of the factions earned a reproof from the *Star,* ever eager to transform a municipal campaign into a battle between the righteous white hats of the CA and the evil factions.[37]

As usual, the *Star* largely echoed the CA endorsements. The city's paper of record endorsed Brookfield, who it had stridently denounced eight years earlier, while denigrating Wheeler, a longtime foe of the *Star*.[38] Surprisingly, the newspaper endorsed Hazley, Holliday, and Tolbert. Although the editorialists saluted the service of the two incumbents, they argued that the challengers possessed great promise.[39] In spite of this alignment on the council slate, the paper's news coverage of Freedom during the campaign was wholly negative. Where reporters in the past had regularly referred to Freedom as an "organization," shortly after it became clear that the LPO would endorse Wheeler rather than Brookfield, news stories began routinely referring to Freedom as a "faction."[40] Given that the newspaper had spent several decades turning that noun into the most vile of slurs, this new characterization was damning. From *The Call*, most of the individuals on the Freedom ballot received no help whatever. The primary newspaper serving the black community enthusiastically endorsed Brookfield over Wheeler (as it had done eight years earlier), making it a point to reject Watkins's characterization of the candidate as a racist.[41] Freedom's inability to forge a constructive working relationship with the black press would be a source of irritation during this period, even if it only rarely materially influenced outcomes. The *Call*'s latent hostility toward Freedom was something of a puzzlement to Freedom activists, who expected the paper to view it more favorably given its long crusade for African American political independence. The best explanation for the two institutions' inability to cooperate during this period is perhaps that the newspaper remained nominally Republican,[42] while Freedom was becoming more strident in its Democratic partisanship.

The campaign was a hard-fought and vitriolic one. As in past elections, Freedom's efforts to mobilize black voters depended on a strong message, this time capitalizing on voter frustration with the status quo. The candidates featured on the Freedom ballot were said to be those assertive enough to deliver results for black voters. Freedom advertisements and literature counseled voters that if they were upset by neighborhood decline, poor public services, and a lack of diversity in city administration, Blankinship and Thomas should be retired. Brookfield was labeled a racist and a Nixon clone; nearly every Freedom statement about Brookfield stressed his Republican affiliation and drove home the point that black Kansas Citians would be badly hurt by the expansion of "Republican racism" into municipal government.[43] By contrast, Wheeler was praised for his campaign promise to ensure that "I see as many city trucks in the inner city as I do on the Plaza" and for stressing the importance of the black vote to his campaign.[44] Essential to the Freedom campaign's message was the claim that the organization was indigenous to and representative of the black community, a claim that no other LPO could make. The Citizens Association, for example, was rebranded in much Freedom literature as the "White Citizens Council Association," a clever, if ferocious, attack on the racism that Freedom members saw in the CA's endorsement decisions.[45]

Those who bore the brunt of these attacks never succeeded in formulating an effective response. Blankinship insisted that he was effective, running on the slogan "Others promise, Blankinship produces."[46] The incumbent was clearly on the defensive; on those occasions when he moved to the attack, the charges he leveled did not resonate or were obviously absurd. For example, he claimed that Freedom was the captive of a white-led "Dump Blankinship" movement. Of Wheeler, the councilman said, "The days of the plantation bosses is long past and your vote for me Tuesday will say to the white outside agitator, Dr. Charles B. Wheeler, that your 'divide and conquer' program will not work any longer in the black community; we are making our own decisions."[47] Thomas seemed to be missing in action throughout most of the campaign. Brookfield angrily denounced the charges of racism, citing the fact that 40 percent of his company's workforce was African American, that he won 60 percent of the black vote in his 1963 mayoral bid (although he neglected to mention that these votes were "delivered" by white factional bosses), and wrapping himself in the endorsements of D.A. Holmes and *The Call*.[48]

Most interesting from a historical perspective, though, was the clear attempt by the anti-Freedom forces to paint the LPO with the brush of illegitimacy and illegality. Until the 1971 election, Freedom was almost unanimously regarded by the reformers as being a force for good, even if the two groupings did not always agree. However, Freedom's decision to go its own way in the 1971 elections marked the end of that cozy relationship. The LPO had always been criticized from within the black community, but in the past such criticism came from African Americans whose subservience to the white-led factions rendered their opinions suspect. In 1971, criticism came from African Americans who were independent of the factions, but resented the influence that Freedom wielded. Black and white critics both alleged for the first time that Freedom was nothing but a faction, was motivated by self- rather than community interest, sought to reestablish the worst practices of bossism, or was controlled by outside interests.[49] Moreover, the LPO was accused of using illegal tactics to retain its position of power. On the day of the municipal primary, for example, G. Lawrence

Blankinship accused his erstwhile-mentor Bruce Watkins of attempting to bribe one of the former's poll workers. Watkins was accused of offering a teenage girl passing out Blankinship ballots $3 to give him her ballots and go home. Watkins admitted to jokingly telling the girl that she was distributing the wrong ballots, but strongly denied offering any bribe.[50] In testimony before the Board of Elections, Watkins made a claim that African American voters consistently rejected efforts by poll workers to give them any sample ballot other than the Freedom one. In defending himself, Watkins said of the "Community Ballot" being distributed by the Blankinship forces, "You couldn't give the ballots away. Why would I try to buy them?"[51] Nothing came of the Blankinship complaint, but the stigma of engaging in questionable practices would hereafter adhere to Freedom. The LPO did not meekly submit to these allegations, but rebutted them at every opportunity, adeptly turning the arguments made against it. Perhaps the most skillful rebuttal of all came when Bruce Watkins revealed in a public speech that Freedom had been offered tens of thousands of dollars to double-cross Wheeler in the closing days of the campaign. Watkins angrily maintained that no amount of money would cause the LPO to work for the election of the "Republican racist" Brookfield and that the black vote could no longer be "purchased."[52] Although the Brookfield campaign denied that any such offer had been made, Freedom's rejection of the overture suggested that the LPO was not for sale.[53] The substance of the myriad charges and counter-charges can be dismissed as the natural product of the heat of a campaign. What is more important is that accusations of various forms of chicanery would become a defining feature of the Freedom experience; these accusations were never accompanied by real evidence, but seeped into the public consciousness.

Despite the opposition of the CA, *The Call,* many prominent African American clergymen, and most of the black business class, Freedom succeeded in deposing the two Third District incumbents. Richard Tolbert won more votes than any other candidate in the municipal elections, defeating Dr. Earl Thomas by the crushing margin of 69,534 (75 percent) to 23,539 (25 percent). Third District voters did not accept G. Lawrence Blankinship's arguments for his own effectiveness, opting for the more vocal approach promised by Charles Hazley by a healthy margin of 6,783 (56 percent) to 5,269 (44 percent). In the Fifth District At-Large race, "Doc" Holliday came agonizingly close to victory. He lost to his white opponent by just 2,086 votes out of almost 95,000 cast; given the circumstances, with Holliday running from a white-majority district against a well-regarded white candidate, that he came so close was a small victory in itself.

Holliday nearly succeeded in large measure due to his strong showing in the Freedom wards.

In the crucial mayor's race, where Freedom and Bruce Watkins staked their institutional and personal credibility, respectively, on black voters rejecting the "Republican racist" Brookfield, Charles Wheeler won by a resounding margin, 57,870 (55 percent) to 46,469 (45 percent). Wheeler won all seven wards in which Freedom then operated (see Table 3), accumulating 12,042 votes (63 percent) in those wards to just 6,781 (36 percent) for Brookfield.[54]

Considering that Brookfield won 60 percent of the African American vote in his earlier campaign (albeit with the help of the factions), Freedom deserved credit for the turnabout. Indeed, the number of votes that Wheeler received in the Freedom wards was larger than his margin of victory. Freedom could legitimately claim that it was the kingmaker in the mayor's race. Freedom also supported five other successful candidates for the City Council. The *Star* chose, somewhat disingenuously given the fact that its mayoral candidate had been defeated for the first time in history, to paint the results as a victory for the CA. The paper's postelection headline read, "Wheeler, 8 Citizens Victors."[55] *The Call* headlined its

Table 3. 1971 Mayoral Election Results in
Predominantly African American Wards

Ward	Charles Wheeler (%)	Dutton Brookfield (%)
2	1,563 (71.1%)	636 (28.9%)
3	1,489 (68.6%)	682 (31.4%)
14	2,053 (68.2%)	957 (31.8%)
16	1,630 (62%)	1,000 (38%)
17	2,045 (67.8%)	973 (32.2%)
18	1,722 (60%)	1,156 (40%)
19	1,531 (52.6%)	1,377 (47.4%)
Total in Predominantly African American Wards	12,033 (64%)	6,781 (36%)
Total Citywide	57,870 (55.5%)	46,469 (44.5%)

Source: Kansas City Times – March 31, 1971

coverage, just as fairly, "Wheeler And Freedom Win City Election," as eight of the thirteen successful candidates carried the black LPO's endorsement.[56]

The election results showed that if Freedom could not accurately claim to represent the *unanimously* shared perspective of black Kansas Citians, and the significant, if insufficient, vote of confidence in Blankinship demonstrated that unanimity was not present, the LPO did possess a better grasp of and deeper connection with African American Kansas Citians than did any other local institution or LPO. There were no real or credible rivals to it in terms of voicing black political interests. Although many of its candidates emerged victorious, the CA was humiliated by its loss in the mayoral race. In purely local politics, Freedom was clearly on the ascent while other LPOs were on the decline. Freedom's kingmaker strategy succeeded on election day, but it remained to be seen whether G. Lawrence Blankinship was correct when he claimed that the Freedom candidates would only make promises rather than producing results.

Freedom Scorned: Filling A Council Vacancy in 1974

More will be said later about how Freedom's influence was utilized, mobilized, and tested on black policy interests during the first half of the 1970s. Here it suffices to say that some significant policy victories were won through Freedom's activity and influence. But in other respects, the influence of Freedom and the broader black community were neither as expansive nor as decisive as the election results might suggest. Despite the fact that Freedom provided the crucial margin of victory in several 1971 municipal races and despite the fact that a majority of the council members were elected with Freedom's support, the LPO increasingly saw itself cast as the villain in municipal politics. This view, and the limits it imposed on Freedom's influence, was best demonstrated in 1974, when the City Council moved to fill a vacancy.[57]

A vacancy was created in January 1974, slightly more than fourteen months before the expiration of the council term, when Richard Tolbert resigned his seat as the council member for the Third District At-Large. Tolbert, whose political career seemed so promising in 1971 that he was being heralded as a future mayor or even president, quickly proved to be a major disappointment to his backers, which included all of the city's major political organizations. Although Freedom's members did not regret their aggressive action in replacing the well-intentioned but lethargic Thomas, they must have regretted recruiting Tolbert as that replacement. Within a year of his election, the young councilman's behavior became embarrassingly eccentric and erratic, with Tolbert absenting himself from the council's weekly business sessions, where pressing issues were discussed in an informal setting. Claiming that the sessions were a waste of time because he was not allowed to pursue his own agenda, Tolbert held his own, sparsely attended, alternative "Citizens Business Session" in the council chambers at the same time. This bit of absurdity was followed in rapid succession by his founding of a new political organization to compete with the CA and Freedom (which he launched while standing in front of a photograph of Leon Jordan), condemnation of a bloc of "Pharisees" among his council colleagues whom he threatened to sue, talk of appointing his own mock city council to rival the real one that he regarded as ineffective, using a city-owned car for nearly six weeks without informing anyone that he had taken the car (discovered only when the vehicle was towed), an announcement of a later-abandoned mayoral bid, lawsuits from creditors over thousands of dollars in unpaid bills, claiming he was going to build a downtown sports arena, introducing an ordinance to impeach himself (ostensibly to force his detractors to go on the record against him), and voluntarily ceding his vote on the council after a poll showed that citizens felt officials under criminal investigation (as he was for the unpaid bills) should not retain their seats. Although Tolbert maintained that he wished to remain a member of Freedom, the LPO's board formally censured the rogue councilman. Tolbert responded by adding Watkins and Holliday to the ranks of the "Pharisees" and saying, "Father, forgive them, for they know not what they do." After all of this, it came almost as a relief when Tolbert simply disappeared for three months, with colleagues, friends, family, and the press all at a loss as to his whereabouts and unable to make contact with him. When he finally did return, at the end of January 1974, it was simply to provide a letter of resignation from the council.[58]

The City Council moved quickly to fill the vacancy, with the application process opening and closing in a matter of weeks. Freedom moved even more rapidly; Tolbert resigned on a Friday and by the following Monday, Freedom's board authorized an endorsement of another youthful candidate, Michael Myers. Myers, just 32 years old, worked as an extension agent for the University of Missouri, was a mayoral appointment to an important urban renewal agency, and considered a rising star within the organization. Watkins and Freedom-affiliated incumbent Hazley called a press conference at City Hall to announce Myers as the LPO's choice, where the candidate was simultaneously endorsed by Mayor Wheeler.[59] In the past, as Freedom and its allies would repeatedly point out, vacancies were filled with individuals selected by the political organization that sponsored the candidacy of the person being replaced.[60] Freedom leaders interpreted this norm to mean that the black LPO should play the leading role in selecting Tolbert's replacement and acted accordingly, especially since the vacancy existed in Freedom's Third District heartland. An early and strong endorsement for Myers was intended to dissuade other candidates from entering the race. Instead, the action angered several members of the City Council, who claimed that Freedom and Mayor Wheeler should have refrained from endorsing until the application process was closed.

Endorsing Myers so early in the process demonstrated once more the generally independent, anticliquish approach that characterized Freedom's internal culture. Not only did the organization again endorse a youthful candidate who lacked deep roots in the black bourgeoisie or the white political establishment, Freedom passed over other potential candidates with deep roots and personal popularity inside of the organization to do so. Most notably, Freedom rejected the city council ambitions of Herman Johnson, a successful realtor, former NAACP branch president, and former Missouri House member.[61] Johnson ran with Freedom's blessing in both of his House campaigns and in an unsuccessful 1972 bid to become Kansas City's first black state senator.[62] Johnson remained in the council vacancy race until the bitter end.[63] Other candidates included a businesswoman who based her candidacy around the need for a black elected official who was not "beholden" to Freedom and a former city employee. The remaining major candidate was Joanne Collins, a moderate Republican member of the state human rights commission who lost a 1972 race for county legislature and whose husband held a regional civil rights post for the Nixon administration.[64] Despite being active in dozens of local civil rights and social organizations, Collins's views on municipal issues were unknown until the interview stage of the selection process. The moral indignation of some council members notwithstanding, other local organizations also rapidly expressed a preference for individual candidates. The New Breed Council, an organization for black Republicans that failed miserably in its efforts to be a counterweight to Freedom, promoted Collins.[65] The Baptist Ministers Union and several other activist African American groups supported Myers.[66] *The Call* editorialized in favor of Collins and Johnson, maintaining that Tolbert had demonstrated that youth had no place in the City Council.[67] The CA reviewed the qualifications of all the candidates and, without explicitly endorsing anyone, proclaimed Johnson "highly qualified" while finding that Collins and Myers were "qualified."[68]

Just a few weeks after Tolbert's seat was vacated, the council tried to meet to interview and then appoint a successor. However, the council's attempt to hold this meeting in secret, over the opposition of Mayor Wheeler, quickly derailed the process. Council members claimed that they merely wished candidates to have the luxury of complete honesty and some protection in the event that there were embarrassing episodes in their past.[69] In the interval between the aborted meeting and a court ruling (prompted by a *Star* lawsuit) that the council must meet in public to fill the vacancy, it was revealed that Myers was on probation for a drunk driving conviction (the product, by all accounts, of an isolated incident of poor judgment). This was the embarrassing revelation that apparently prompted some members' desire for a secret process.[70] Despite the public attention given to Myers's situation, when the council reconvened, Freedom's candidate received five votes on the first ballot. Collins also received five votes (three of them originating from a united front of the council's Republican members). After multiple ballots and a bit of caucusing, Myers and Freedom were scorned when Collins's supporters succeeded in cobbling together the seven votes required for her appointment.[71] Collins's appointment was historic; she became the first black woman, and only the third woman of any race, to serve on the City Council at a time when women members were often excluded from social events to which the male members were invited.[72]

Collins professed to be shocked by her selection, the coalition of Collins supporters felt gratified by their ability to check Freedom's power, and Freedom's members felt outraged and betrayed. Watkins characterized the vote as a "slap in the face of the black community" and said "[The council members] turned around and more or less told us where to go."[73] A sense of betrayal was not entirely unjustified, given that several council members elected with Freedom support now rejected its nominee. Freedom members were understandably further outraged when a handful of council people, notably Leon Brownfield, the crucial swing vote that brought Collins her victory, and the district councilman for the increasingly black Fifth District, made it explicit that their action had everything to do with sending a message to the black LPO.[74] Brownfield said on the record, and other members stressed off the record, that their votes were intended to be a rebuke to Freedom and Wheeler's alliance with it. Among the organization's supposed sins were its "arrogance" and "aggressiveness" in promoting its candidate, the LPO's refusal to tergiversate on its position toward the city's state legislative agenda (elements of which it had instructed its state representatives to oppose), and for its overall approach to politics, which was regarded as too independent for comfort. The general impression conveyed was one of displeasure that black Kansas Citians were now successfully advancing black interests through use of the same political tools that were long regarded as the exclusive purview of whites. To his lasting credit, in-district councilman Charles Hazley welcomed and cooperated with his new colleague despite the hostile climate. The two Third District council people would maintain an amicable, warm, professional relationship, even as Freedom immediately declared that its top priority for the 1975 election would be defeating Collins in her bid for a full term.[75]

Hindsight shows us that there is likely nothing that Freedom could have done to secure a more favorable outcome. Still, the whole affair was instructive in three important ways. First, it demonstrated clearly that the kingmaker strategy could provoke a harsh, counterproductive reaction. It was the use of this strategy, the accompanying demands that it placed on officials in exchange for support, and the resulting success that contributed to the overwrought gnashing of teeth about Freedom's hardball tactics even among supposed allies. In this sense, the strategy might prove to be unacceptably limited. Second, it confirmed once more the conviction of Freedom activists that the city possessed a toxic and paternalistic racial environment. Elected officials from outside the area effectively condemned normal lobbying and campaign behavior because those engaging in the behavior were African American. Third, the incident demonstrated that the balance of power strategy could still be effective. Myers had, after all, attracted support from four white council members who owed their offices to black voters. Discouraged as the Freedom activists were, they resolved to mobilize even larger numbers of black voters in 1975, in order to gain even more influence.

Politics Can Be Bittersweet: The 1975 Municipal Elections

Freedom thus threw itself headlong into the 1975 municipal elections several months earlier than it would normally have done so. An early start was necessary, because the jockeying for position, alliance-building, and deal-making between groups that were the life's blood of local politics were already well underway. Mayor Charles Wheeler was running for reelection and his two major challengers believed that the incumbent's relative popularity could be overcome only by initiating their campaigns early; others felt compelled to follow their lead in the down-ballot races. Moreover, Freedom was now operating in five wards (Wards 2, 3, 14, 16, 17, and 18) which meant that more time and energy was required to cover this expansive territory. Freedom set four goals for the 1975 elections: 1) Defeating Joanne Collins for a full term; 2) Electing a third black member to the City Council, in the personage of Bruce Watkins; 3) Electing Charles Wheeler to a second term as mayor; and 4) Securing a strong majority of Freedom allies on the Council, through a careful and calculating endorsement strategy.

The Black Community Speaks?: The Effort to Defeat Joanne Collins

Freedom's leadership and activist membership were incensed by the appointment of Joanne Collins to represent the Third District. Her appointment was regarded as a slap in the face, not just because she came from outside the ranks of Freedom in a district where Freedom was the dominant political actor, but because her worldview was thought to run counter to that of her Third District constituents. Collins was a moderate, even liberal, Republican, and was well liked by many within Freedom, who appreciated her charm, outgoing personality, and unquestioned commitment to public service. But at a time when Richard Nixon and the Republican Party more generally were fast adopting the infamous Southern Strategy, even nominal affiliation with the GOP was anathema to those within Freedom. Much of Freedom's electoral strategy in the municipal elections was driven by the effort to defeat Collins. All of the LPO's bargaining was based on this race; although Freedom sought support for all members of its slate, the key demand it made of those pursuing Freedom's endorsement was enlistment in the battle against the Republican councilwoman.

Myers, Freedom's candidate during the selection process, was passed over in 1975. The LPO's members felt that only a better-known, experienced candidate could succeed and, in any event, the revelation of Myers's conviction for drunk driving was embarrassing to everyone concerned. Bruce Watkins personally recruited Mamie Hughes as Freedom's candidate, making her the first woman ever slated by Freedom in a city race, while Myers became the manager of the coordinated Freedom campaign in the Third District.[76] The growing women's movement was felt within Freedom, where many of the most dedicated activists—but few of the endorsed candidates—were women. Tensions between the largely male leadership and an increasingly female base of workers would become much more serious during the 1980s. Hughes was a dynamic and well-respected Jackson County legislator in her second term representing a district that was basically coterminous with the city's Third District.[77] She was a former schoolteacher who was then married to Leonard Hughes, a founding member of Freedom.[78] Hughes had many advantages as a candidate: she was popular among Freedom's African American base, although not well known outside of the black community she had the respect of many influential whites, she could be relied on to consistently and passionately defend black interests, and her gender neutralized whatever slight tactical advantage might accrue to Collins from voters who valued a woman's presence on the Council.[79] This time, unlike in 1971, there was no pressing need to accommodate restless, militant youth, for by 1975 the radical black youth movement in Kansas City had been extinguished.[80] Hughes's major liability was that she was not overly interested in serving on the Council. She ran because Freedom members asked her to, but her "heart was not really in it."[81]

Since the seat in question was an at-large one, Freedom's support would not be sufficient to send Collins packing. The LPO set out to drum up support for its candidate, with the CA, even in its weakened form after the outcome of its 1971 mayoral endorsement, still the most important target. The CA of 1975 was but a shell of its former self. While most of the city's influential people, including the most visible of Freedom's leaders, like Holliday and Watkins, retained a loose affiliation with the organization, the CA's aura of invincibility had been punctured, the ever-growing irrelevance of the factions deprived it of its raison d'être, and the mutual hostility that existed between the mayor and the CA diminished the political benefits to be extracted from involvement with the reform group. As a result, the organization began to lose much of it what made it so powerful: its institutional character. Its meetings became less frequent, the regularity with which it analyzed and declared positions on municipal issues declined, the membership rolls fell, the ease with which personal and partisan followings could dictate the body's actions increased, and the LPO gradually ceased to be a permanent organization as opposed to one that emerged in quadrennial campaign seasons. Even with these limitations, the organization's historical credibility and potential emotional appeal were such that perfunctory affiliation remained a must for many of the city's politicos.

In 1975, the CA was taken over by supporters of liberal councilman Joseph Shaughnessy. Shaughnessy, a young architect who was close to many of the city's neighborhood organizations, was elected to his first term as an at-large councilman four years earlier with Freedom's support.[82] The councilman was notable primarily for the intensity of his ambition (and the yawning gulf between that ambition and his observable political talent), having declared his candidacy for mayor after just three years in the public eye. Capitalizing on the disarray in which the organization found itself in the wake of the Brookfield debacle, Shaughnessy installed one of his loyalists as CA chairman.[83] The organization's powerful executive board was also stacked, so that a plurality of its members consisted of Shaughnessy supporters.

Freedom sought to use this context to its advantage in securing support for Hughes. But it was confronted by the facts that a majority of the council members who selected Collins were strongly allied with the CA, remained supporters of Collins, and both Freedom and CA bête noire Wheeler had harshly criticized the CA for masterminding the scorning of Freedom in the vacancy drama. Collins's forceful critique of Freedom, which would become one of the centerpieces of her campaign, appealed to the many CA members who were antipathetic to the black LPO because of that incident, because of broader discomfort with the sort of black empowerment it was making possible, or because of jealousy/fear that Freedom was supplanting the CA as the city's most influential LPO. These factors, coupled with the fact that Republicans held seats on the candidate screening committee and executive board disproportionate to their number in the general membership, conspired to give Collins a strong vote of confidence from those two bodies. Under the CA bylaws, endorsement recommendations by those entities required the ratification of the Board of Governors, a body with over a hundred members. The Board of Governors could overturn an endorsement recommendation made by the smaller groups, but only with a supermajority of 60 percent or more.

When the Collins recommendation came to the floor at the Governors meeting, it was the subject of intense debate. "Doc" Holliday, now a county legislator in addition to serving as Freedom's chairman, gave an impassioned and eloquent speech nominating Hughes, calling her highly qualified and the true choice of the black community. Collins gave an equally impassioned speech saying that Freedom was not representative of all of the city's African Americans and that minority voices within that community deserved representation on the council. (Curiously, this sentiment of political catholicism and the drive for proportional representation was never mentioned by the CA where white candidates were concerned.) Collins supporters also averred that the incumbent had "earned" a full term and that Hughes was irresponsible in running for the council just a few weeks after winning reelection to the county legislature. Heated though the debate was, the speechifying was mostly for show.

Although nearly everyone expected Freedom to endorse Mayor Wheeler for reelection (except for Shaughnessy, who somehow came to believe that he would be the black LPO's candidate), the organization refrained from making a public endorsement in that race prior to the CA meetings in order to give it maximal bargaining leverage.[84] Given the intense mutual hostility that existed between the CA and Wheeler, the incumbent mayor stood no chance of winning the reform group's endorsement. Shaughnessy, on the other hand, stood a very good chance indeed, but still faced a challenge from a conservative council woman from the Northland, Sarah Snow. Snow made it a point of regularly expressing her disapproval of Freedom, her personal distaste for Watkins, and her high regard for Collins. In this context, Freedom sought to make a kingmaker bargain within the CA. It would instruct its members of the Board of Governors to vote for endorsing Shaughnessy, in exchange for Shaughnessy backers favoring Hughes. When it came time to vote, this strategic gambit very nearly succeeded. Indeed, it was the procedural quirk demanding a 60 percent super-majority that saved the CA endorsement for Collins. Hughes fell a single vote short of the 60 percent requirement.[85] Since defeating Collins was Freedom's top priority, the rejection of Hughes—particularly after many of her detractors coupled it with harsh language about Freedom—poisoned the relationship between the CA and Freedom for the rest of the campaign cycle. The relationship of 1963 or 1967 was long gone, never to return.

The Hughes campaign pressed on, gaining support from most of the other groups that were isolated or alienated by the anti-Wheeler sentiment of the CA. These groups included the now-skeletal remains of the factions, several of the larger labor alliances, the ad hoc "Democrats for Progress" group formed to assist Wheeler, and—important to the effort in the Freedom wards—the largest of the black ministerial alliances.[86] Not among the number of the Hughes supporters, though, were *The Call* or the *Star;* the former opted to endorse both women running for the seat while the *Star* chose Collins by saying that both women deserved to be in elective office, and the only way to achieve that goal was by keeping Collins at the city and Hughes at the county.[87]

Important as the Collins-Hughes race would prove to be, the campaigns of the two women were not notable for presenting competing visions or policy platforms. The campaign was conducted instead on matters of style; but even this distinction was not great, as both women were warm, professional, and put audiences of all races at ease. During her brief time in office, Collins had done little to provoke controversy. She did an almost unparalleled job of making the rounds with her constituents—she was a member of more than fifty organizations, something of which she was still proud decades later, and, on matters concerning the Third District itself, almost always voted the same way as Freedom member Charles Hazley.[88] However, by her own admission, she preferred to work in the background, to mediate, and to negotiate quietly. That was certainly not the style of Hazley, who was vocal in his defense of black interests, persistent in pursuing them, and quite willing to go out of his way to frustrate his white colleagues if doing so might yield benefits for his constituents. Collins built her campaign message around her amiability and mediatory role, arguing that this made her more effective than the militant Freedom could be. Hughes stressed her record of accomplishment at the county legislature and her commitment to public service. When addressing African American audiences, she would add that she was a Democrat and could be counted on to vigorously advocate for black interests.[89]

More important to the campaign was the role of Freedom itself. Collins sought an audience with Freedom to make her case, something that was only grudgingly given. When it became clear that even her friends within the organization would be loyal to Freedom rather than to her, Collins embraced Freedom's opposition and effectively transformed the organization itself into an issue. Picking up where Lawrence Blankinship left off four years earlier, Collins assailed Freedom as mendacious, self- rather than community-centered, corrupt, and representative of only a narrow sliver of the black community. She went much further than Blankinship ever had, by charging that what influence the organization did possess was owed to intimidation. The masses did not support Freedom's positions, leaders, or candidates purely of their own free will, she claimed. Instead, they did so because they were threatened with the loss of jobs, seeing their businesses suffer, being excluded from various social organizations or leadership positions, or even being subjected to violent reprisal if they did not. As portrayed by Collins backers in the daily press, Freedom was little more than a cliquish band of petty thugs devoted to protecting its own limited privileges.[90] Comments of this sort did little to endear Collins to Freedom, Inc.

In the specific case of Hughes, this line of attack was not wholly successful. Elegant and energetic, with a demonstrable record of accomplishment in improving public services, what open-minded voters saw in Mamie Hughes simply could not be reconciled with the image of inner city tin pot tyranny. Hughes and the Freedom campaign team always expected to lose among the white voters most susceptible to anti-Freedom rhetoric. Hughes countered the attacks by repeating over and over that Collins was the choice of white outsiders, not African Americans or residents of the Third District, and that she was out of touch with the concerns and aspirations of black Kansas Citians. This message sought to win votes for Hughes from some white liberals while primarily appealing to black voters who would then presumably give Hughes a large enough margin in the Freedom wards to carry her to victory.

When this theory was tested during the city's nonpartisan primary, the results did not bode well for Hughes or Freedom.[91] Rather than the tight race expected by all, Collins romped to victory, racking up six thousand votes more than her challenger. She was especially strong in the Northland, where her personal friendships with Northland council members Harold Hamil and Sarah Snow translated into voter support.[92] With only a month between the primary and general elections, the Freedom team was forced to react quickly. Hughes, Holliday, Watkins, and Myers diagnosed the problem as low black voter turnout. Black voter turnout was always higher in the general election than in the primary, so this was expected to close some of the gap between Collins and Hughes. More serious, though, was that fact that Hughes's margins even in the Freedom strongholds were underwhelming. Hughes typically won these precincts by ratios of 2:1, instead of the 3:1 or 4:1 her campaign anticipated and required.[93] Once more demonstrating the shameless mendacity of the Star, hard news articles appeared after the primary claiming that by receiving 35–40 per cent of the black vote, Collins showed that she was indeed the choice of the black community and that Freedom's assertions to the contrary were absurd. One account overlooked its own reporting that Collins expected to win 50 percent of the black vote by going on to say how pleased the candidate was with her showing of 40 percent.[94] The Star's inability to make the mathematical distinction between majority and minority aside, Freedom members felt that the lower-than-anticipated margins were attributable to a lackluster campaign by Hughes. At the time and decades later, many involved in the campaign believed that Hughes, accustomed to running in a county legislature district where Freedom endorsement was tantamount to election, took victory for granted and did not work as hard as she could or should have.[95]

It was in this context that some of the most infamous actions in Kansas City political history were taken. Freedom distributed thousands of copies of a piece of literature that boldly proclaimed Joanne Collins to be Kansas City's "Great White Hope."[96] The piece described the circumstances of her appointment to the council and attributed to her a host of unpopular, conservative, Republican, and "anti-black" positions. Collins was outraged by the piece, which she felt was unfair and misrepresented her views.

Hughes and her backers were not the only ones casting epithets about, however. Collins herself did not engage in, encourage, or even have knowledge of this behavior as it was happening, but a quiet smear campaign against Hughes was initiated by persons unknown. A rumor rapidly spread that Hughes, whose skin complexion was light and whose hair was "straight," was not black, but Native American or even white.[97] These persons unknown depicted Collins as the only black candidate in the race. It is no coincidence that this rumor circulated *only* in the black community, as its intent was to dampen enthusiasm for Hughes among black voters. Smear campaigns of this sort are common, but this particular rumor was uncommonly pervasive and effective. Indeed, in what ranks among the saddest moments in the city's political history, Hughes, whose entire public career was dedicated to improving the lives of African Americans and who was quite proud of her racial identity, was reduced to writing an open letter to *Call* readers where she denied the rumors and declared herself "a PROUD BLACK WOMAN" (capitalization in original).[98]

The outcome of the Collins-Hughes race was uncertain to the very end. A devastating blow was dealt to Freedom when Collins eked out a 1,877-vote victory in the general election, largely on the strength of her showing in the Northland. With Collins still winning about 40 percent of the black vote (see Table 4), Hughes's margins in the Freedom wards were not enough to overcome the incumbent's strength elsewhere.[99] Collins would never again be seriously

Table 4. 1975 Third District At-Large City Council Results in Predominantly African American Wards

Ward	Joanne Collins (%)	Mamie Hughes (%)
2	742 (41.5%)	1,044 (58.5%)
3	711 (39%)	1,103 (61%)
14	841 (38.7%)	1,330 (61.3%)
16	841 (38%)	1,373 (62%)
17	832 (37.1%)	1,413 (62.9%)
18	1,026 (44.8%)	1,266 (55.2%)
19	1,240 (52.3%)	1,133 (47.7%)
Total African American Wards	5,392 (38.4%)	8,662 (61.6%)
Total Citywide	34,629 (51.4%)	32,755 (48.6%)

Source: Kansas City Times – March 26, 1975

challenged in sixteen additional years of service.[100] While Freedom had insisted that Collins's election would be disastrous for African Americans, she proved to be generally supportive of Freedom positions on Third District issues. Indeed, a dedicated Freedom activist who worked relentlessly for Hughes conceded years later, "We didn't lose *anything* by having Joanne there."[101] Another person active in politics at the time recalls that by 1983, Collins had reconciled enough with Freedom that the LPO endorsed her for reelection and she nearly became an official member of the organization, going so far as to write out a check for her membership dues.[102] At the time, though, Freedom activists were devastated and at a loss to interpret the results. Fortunately for the morale of the organization's members, other contests had outcomes more to their liking.

The Return of Bruce Watkins to Municipal Politics

Without a doubt the most important of these other contests to Freedom activists occurred in the city's Fifth District, where Bruce Watkins sought to return to the City Council. Watkins resigned from the body in 1966 upon his election as Jackson County's circuit clerk; his election to that post made him the first black elected official in Jackson County history. Watkins was reelected to the county office in 1970 and served a successful term as the first African American chairman of the Jackson County Democratic Committee. The adoption of charter government in Jackson County did away with the circuit clerk as an elective office after 1974.[103] The president of Freedom, Inc. was far too popular among the black electorate and was too useful as an intermediary for bargaining with white elites for him to simply fade away. Watkins briefly entered races for state senate and county executive, but neither of these campaigns went beyond the natal stages.[104] In retrospect, both of those brief bids seem to have been designed to give Watkins and Freedom additional leverage with the other candidates running for those offices. By the fall of 1974, it became clear that Watkins would mount a serious campaign to return to the City Council. He would do so not only for reasons of personal ambition and to retain his influence within Freedom (which practically demanded an elected official as its president), but to increase the black presence on the City Council. The African American share of the city's population was increasing rapidly but there had been no similar increase in the black presence in municipal elective office. Freedom was determined to see that change and, as the city's most popular African American politician, Watkins was a consensus choice for the candidate most likely to possess appeal outside of Freedom bailiwicks.[105]

The city's decennial redistricting process placed Watkins's residence in the Fifth District, but no African American had ever won a council seat in any district other than the Third. Freedom had been critical of the redistricting process because boundaries were gerrymandered in order to dilute the black vote within the Fifth District. The best-laid plans of the gerrymanderers went awry. The racial turnover in that district's neighborhoods accelerated, rather than being staved off by the semi-permanent white control envisioned at the time of redistricting. While the district was 40 percent black in 1971, by 1975 African Americans were thought to constitute about 55 percent of the population. For Watkins, the difficulty was that the *voting* population of the district was thought to remain closer to 40 percent African American.[106] Recalling that "Doc" Holliday very nearly won the at-large seat four years earlier on the strength of black votes in other districts, Watkins originally intended to pursue that office. That the incumbent, C. Harold Mann, was a resolute foe of Freedom and that a citywide campaign would enhance Watkins's profile in advance of the mayoral campaign that he was already contemplating made the at-large post all the more attractive. Watkins's plan was complicated when the incumbent surprised the political community by announcing he would not stand for reelection. Deciding to play a game of musical chairs, the in-district incumbent, Leon Brownfield, announced he would run for the at-large seat instead of the one he already held. Brownfield's decision to switch seats was partly motivated by a desire for a higher citywide profile, partly by fear that the district's increasingly black electorate would look askance at his conservative Democratic politics, and partly out of pure spite toward Watkins and Freedom. In the fall of 1974, a host of emissaries reached out to Brownfield on Watkins's behalf, in the hopes of convincing the incumbent to pursue reelection to the in-district seat. Before the Collins endorsement caused Freedom to break with the CA, many of that organization's luminaries sought to negotiate with Brownfield on Watkins's behalf. These efforts were to no avail. Friendly white elites then made clear that if Brownfield would not budge, they would reluctantly support the incumbent councilman. Brownfield chaired the Council's legislative committee, where he was regarded as indispensable. Watkins bowed to the inevitable and opted to run for the in-district seat.[107]

Even more drama and uncertainty accompanied this move. The Fifth District was thought to have a white voting majority. One white candidate, an activist named Lawrence Ferns, was running for the in-district seat.[108] Speculation ran rampant that the voting would be racialized and Watkins would consequently lose a general election face-off. However, there was doubt as to whether Watkins would advance to the general election. The primary featured a third candidate, a prominent black clergyman and civil rights activist named Emanuel Cleaver.[109]

Cleaver was the founder and executive director of the local chapter of the Southern Christian Leadership Conference (SCLC), pastor of a small congregation in the predominantly white United Methodist Church, perhaps the most prominent face of radical politics in the city, and a master at obtaining publicity. The young minister had marched with Dr. King in Selma and previously worked for the local Young Men's Christian Association, but had resigned with a furious denunciation of the organization's institutional racism. At the SCLC, he organized a local version of "Resurrection City" in Mill Creek Park to bring attention to the plight of the poor and dispossessed.[110] He resigned from the SCLC in order to run for City Council, but did so under duress, claiming that unnamed opponents brought pressure to bear on the organization's board.[111] Cleaver described himself as a Christian "revolutionary" and was radical in comparison to the city's elected officials.[112] With his Afro hairstyle, modish wardrobe, and rhetorical flourishes, Cleaver in 1975 appeared to be the very image of black militancy, but his radicalism was always of the consciously multi-racial variety rather than being oriented toward black nationalism. A 1970 bid for the state legislature ended in defeat, but Cleaver had since become much more prominent. Hardly a week went by without generous news coverage of his personal activism or actions being taken by the SCLC under his leadership. Cleaver possessed an undeniable charisma, a unique ability to communicate with audiences, and a rare talent for grand gestures that guaranteed media coverage. In light of all that, speculation was rampant that the African American vote would be divided and Watkins might not advance to the general election. Opponents of Watkins even suggested that Cleaver might have the upper hand because, they maintained, African Americans in the Fifth District were disenchanted with Freedom.

Watkins had not become the city's most successful African American politician through pure luck. He and his campaign team worked hard, said and did the right things, and capitalized on more than a decade's worth of favors owed him to win the support of nearly every major political organization in the city. Freedom made its support known early.[113] The organization's president could depend on its support under any circumstances, but the alternatives of a white candidate without noticeable sensitivity toward black aspirations and a prominent black Freedom antagonist were dismal from Freedom's perspective. As part of the effort to salvage the CA-Freedom alliance and because Watkins was the most qualified candidate in the race, the CA overwhelmingly endorsed him on the same evening that it formally backed Collins.[114] The Democratic factions lined up behind Watkins, though more because of his support for Wheeler than out of any enthusiasm for the candidate himself.[115] The *Star* endorsed him as the most qualified and capable candidate. The *Call,* too, was supportive of seeing Watkins return to City Hall. Even the major black ministerial alliances endorsed Watkins, although a few clergymen opted to personally stand with Cleaver, their fellow man of the cloth.

The campaigns relied primarily on door-to-door contact with voters, none of them spending exorbitant amounts. The tenor of the campaign was positive. Watkins emphasized his experience and understanding of the political system, Cleaver stressed his idealism and interracial activist base, and Ferns campaigned on the idea of strengthening neighborhood associations' roles at City Hall. Racialized voting was universally anticipated but, to their credit, none of the candidates indulged in racist appeals.[116] The only note of negativity expressed came, and then only rarely, from Cleaver, who made clear that he had little use for Watkins. The substance of Cleaver's criticism was vague, but seemed to be based on a general suspicion of Freedom's pragmatic bargaining and a specific grudge that Watkins was a late but transformational addition to the in-district fray.[117]

Even with all of this drama percolating in the underbrush of the campaign cycle, the primary results were a surprise. Watkins placed first with 2,905 votes, Ferns trailed narrowly with 2,509 votes, and Cleaver was eliminated from the contest by placing a distant but respectable third with 1,598 votes. Balloting was heavily racialized, with Watkins and Cleaver drawing almost all of their votes from African Americans and Ferns almost all of his votes from whites.[118] This in itself was not a shock, but the fact that the black candidates collectively commanded a majority of the votes was; a black candidate was supposed to have a difficult time winning in the district because of a small black voting population. Cleaver professed to be flabbergasted by the racial nature of the balloting, saying that he had anticipated a more multiracial character in his own support than actually materialized. Cleaver's hope for an interracial movement in the Fifth District, whose white residents tended to be lower middle class and conservative, was naïve in any event; the candidate's reputation as, in the words of one voter, a "loud-mouthed militant" and the fact that some whites confused him with the infamous Eldridge Cleaver certainly did not help.[119]

Little changed in the month between the primary and general elections. Freedom workers redoubled their efforts, Watkins and Ferns devoted more energy to retail politics, and the tone of the entire affair remained resolutely positive.

After publicly agonizing, Cleaver announced that he would cast his ballot for Watkins but could not bring himself to ask his supporters to do the same.[120] Bad blood between the two men clearly existed, but Cleaver was savvy enough to recognize that declining to support Watkins would strike a blow to his future political ambitions. Firmly committed to the narrative that whites made up the district's voting majority and that Cleaver was a candidate with interracial and Freedom-loathing support, despite the dubious evidence for both propositions, the media continued to speculate that Watkins would meet electoral defeat. Cleaver was adamant that "most" of his supporters could not support Watkins, though the strength of their antagonism was surely over-emphasized for bargaining purposes, and the press believed him. When the votes were counted, the initial assumptions about the Fifth District's electorate were disproven. Fear of racialized voting patterns proved to be well founded; Watkins drew most of his support from precincts with black majorities, Ferns drew most of his support from precincts with white majorities. Crucially, African Americans represented a majority of the district's voters. Watkins was initially reluctant to run in-district out of fear that blacks would be outnumbered on election day, but it was the district's changing demographics which provided his salvation. The Freedom president garnered 5,251 votes to 4,605 votes for Ferns.[121] Watkins individually and Freedom collectively were gratified by the victory, because it accomplished three major goals. Watkins's victory returned a strong voice for black interests to City Hall, provided Watkins a platform for political involvement and interacting with white elites, and handily defeated a serious challenge within the black community to reassert Freedom's place as the corporatist political voice of that community.

A Sure Thing: Freedom's Support for Charles Wheeler

Freedom's other significant victory came in the mayor's race, where Charles Wheeler stood for reelection. Wheeler's first term had some successes for which the mayor could claim credit, including the new Kemper Arena, downtown construction, and completion of a new airport. These accomplishments and his own personality combined to make Wheeler generally popular. Among the mayor's strongest supporters were African Americans. Wheeler won the support of black Kansas Citians through a number of high-profile appointments, including making Charles Hazley the first African American to chair a City Council committee[122] and naming Dr. Jeremiah Cameron, a vice president of the NAACP and Lincoln High teacher, to the prestigious Parks Board, by advocating for increased expenditures and services in urban core neighborhoods, and by taking occasional walking tours of the inner city.[123] Wheeler typically found himself on the same side of issues as Freedom, most notably on the council vacancy question, and only rarely publicly dissented from the LPO's views. Indeed, the only issue on which Wheeler and Freedom publicly disagreed was over city manager John Taylor. Wheeler entered office wanting to fire Taylor (claiming, tautologically, that the city manager should be fired because he supported the city manager system of governance), but Freedom members joined a majority of the Council in refusing to terminate the manager.

Wheeler irrevocably alienated a moderately sized but massively determined group of detractors. This group included most members of the CA (who were unable to forgive their defeat in 1971 and who did not appreciate the mayor's unwillingness to approach them on bended knee for reconciliation), a sizable contingent of the city's Republican minority, and many Northland residents, who, two decades after annexation, felt that they were shortchanged in the provision of city services. Four years earlier, the central criticism of Wheeler's foes was that he was difficult to get along with: too prickly, too prone to argument, lacking in charm, and too likely to go his own way rather than to forge a working majority. What a difference four years, and political expediency, makes. In 1975, Wheeler was accused by the very same critics as being too easy to get along with, too ready with a smile and a quip, all charm and no substance, a showman rather than a policy-maker, and possessing a severe deficit of that vague but universally revered quality known as leadership.[124] Critics were further irked by the fact that Wheeler used his open door policy to successfully portray himself as the mayor for the "little man," in contrast to the generally upper-class background and concerns of his detractors. Wheeler's populist appeal was regarded by his critics as one more iteration of what they perceived as his buffoonish, clownish, and frivolous nature. The entirety of the evidence for this assertion was that, as part of a promotional stunt for an event to be held in the city, Wheeler "wrestled" (actually, it was more of a brief hug) with a live bear in the mayor's office at City Hall and that he displayed a collection of hats given to him while in office.[125] Most voters seemed to think that these stunts demonstrated a sense of humor—something which prior mayors, for all their many virtues, did not have in abundance.

Wheeler was challenged by two sitting members of the City Council. One challenger was the aforementioned young liberal architect, Joseph Shaughnessy, who was in his first term on the City Council. The other contender was Sarah Snow, a homemaker and conservative Democrat, who was twice elected to an in-district seat representing the Northland. Snow was only the second woman to win a seat on the City Council, the first woman (and the first Northlander) to make a bid for the mayor's office. Neither challenger possessed the citywide profile, legislative accomplishments, signature issue, or the political talent required to run a successful mayoral campaign. Both appear to have made the oldest and most devastating mistake possible for a political candidate: they confused the discontent with Wheeler that was pervasive in their own narrow circles for the mood of the general public.

Freedom intentionally withheld its mayoral endorsement until after the CA endorsement process was complete. It did so in order to maximize its leverage in the council races, with the hope of trading support of Shaughnessy for the CA's mayoral nod for votes in the council endorsements. Shaughnessy demonstrated himself to be an utter naïf when he confused this sort of bargaining for actual support. There was never any real doubt that Wheeler would be Freedom's mayoral candidate, although Wheeler himself claimed differently.[126] Wheeler had a strong record on issues of importance to black Kansas Citians, had been a reliable ally for Freedom, and had publicly said for months that he would not even consider running for reelection unless he could be assured of Freedom's support.[127] This last should be taken both as a mark of respect for the black LPO's influence and a sign of great confidence that he would be the organization's candidate. Even if Wheeler's record had not been as strong as it was, Freedom had no incentive whatsoever to dump Wheeler as they had Blankinship and Thomas four years earlier. Except in the fevered imaginations of the mayor's irreconcilable critics, Wheeler was a sure thing for reelection. Freedom was savvy enough to realize that fact and make itself as integral to the effort as possible, in order to claim a larger share of the patronage and policy benefits to be distributed.

Lacking the same sort of citywide infrastructure that the CA provided for its nominee, Shaughnessy, Mayor Wheeler set out to create one. After significant negotiation among themselves, the mayor's backers produced an organization that they christened Democrats for Progress (DFP). DFP emphasized the mayor's strong partisan affiliation at a time when the national Republican Party was at a low point. DFP consisted of an alliance between Freedom, the remaining factions, organized labor, and several Democratic clubs which typically avoided municipal politics. The latter, which normally managed their own voter outreach plans and independently mobilized precinct workers, agreed to pool their workers on behalf of the DFP slate. DFP made independent expenditures on behalf of the mayor and his slate and served as a financial middle-man, passing funds to its organizational allies (like Freedom). Freedom bargained with the other DFP organizations to ensure that its Freedom ballot was identical to the DFP slate; this ensured that Hazley, Hughes, and Watkins were all prominently featured on the DFP sample ballot.[128]

Neither of Wheeler's challengers could compete with the combined strength of the forces that united in DFP. Shaughnessy had the considerably weakened CA, some neighborhood associations, and a devoted crew of youthful volunteers. Snow had no organized support outside of the Northland.[129] The *Star* chose to remain neutral in the primary (breaking with its tradition of endorsing the CA candidate), while Wheeler captured *The Call*'s endorsement before the primary.[130] Typically, challengers would compensate for such a dearth of organized support by creating a clear contrast with the incumbent, highlighting issues on which they disagreed. Demonstrating an absence of basic political skill, neither Shaughnessy nor Snow did that. Instead, Shaughnessy continually criticized the mayor for a supposed lack of leadership. The challenger claimed that Wheeler should have been more active in settling a teachers' strike the previous year, despite the fact that Kansas City schools were wholly autonomous of city government. Snow also assailed the mayor for lack of leadership, but at least chose to focus her ire on items which were nominally within the mayor's purview. Snow called for the city to "get back to basics" and focus on improving the quality of its much-maligned basic services (e.g., road maintenance, water, plowing snow), though without explaining how this could be achieved. This "back to basics" mantra would quickly become one of the fixtures of local politics; from 1975 onward, nearly every municipal campaign season or ballot initiative would feature some invocation of the need to improve basic services. Neither challenger succeeded in inspiring a widespread revolt against Wheeler's leadership. The attacks of the challengers were so tepid and ineffectual that Wheeler campaigned, without any noticeable backlash, on the absurd premise that a mayor was entitled to a second term unless he grossly underperformed. Moreover, he asserted that his job in the campaign was not to raise issues or talk about his vision for the future, but only to respond to specific criticisms raised by opponents about his record.[131] This combination of ineffectual attack by the challengers and willful disengagement by the incumbent did not serve to excite the voting public. In retrospect, however, it did serve as the first example of how vapid the municipal political debate was when deprived of the ripe chestnut of faction-versus-reform. Whether this emptiness was a product of the local political culture—as shaped by the *Star*'s obsession with the factions, or the result of the city charter itself, which considered city government a business where the "real" decisions were to be left to efficiency-minded, apolitical staff, is not clear.

What did become clear in the February 1975 primary was that the CA was no longer the dominant force in local politics. Wheeler was favored to win, but he exceeded expectations in the primary by receiving more votes than all of his challengers combined and ran 25 percentage points ahead of his closest competitor. Wheeler trounced his challengers in the Freedom wards. Even more embarrassing for the CA, Shaughnessy finished a few hundred votes *behind* Snow and was eliminated from the contest, despite having dramatically outspent her. This marked a new low for the once-dominant reform LPO, as it was the first time in the organization's history that its mayoral candidate failed to advance to the general election.[132]

The CA attempted to regroup, but without success. Still blinded by its collective hatred of Wheeler, made only more intense by the electoral humiliation inflicted on Shaughnessy, whose friends retained their leadership positions within the CA, the LPO chose to endorse Snow in the general election (over the opposition of every single black CA Board member). Virtually no one else followed the organization's lead, though a few CA stalwarts (like Dutton Brookfield or the real estate heir Miller Nichols) did their organizational duty and contributed to Snow's meager treasury.[133] Even these individuals were not inspired by the Snow candidacy. The *Star* swallowed its distaste and endorsed the incumbent; though it had kind words for Snow's council record, it bemoaned her lack of vision, sometimes prickly persona, and narrow regional focus.[134] Although Snow sought to broaden her base, the fact remained that she was a regional candidate. Her issues and priorities reflected that of the middle-class, conservative Democratic, quasi-suburban, hostile-to-City-Hall, nearly lily white Northland that she represented on the council.

While Snow did not inspire any but her most devoted Northland backers, her candidacy did move the membership of Freedom. The black LPO had already declared itself for Wheeler, of course, and had ample reason to support the mayor. Even if it did not, though, Snow's candidacy would have been sufficient to move the organization into action. The council woman was Freedom's most implacable foe in the city's legislative body. She regularly praised Joanne Collins, denounced Bruce Watkins (whose "style" of politics she did not care for), and unambiguously stated that she had no use for Freedom or its endorsement.[135] Reflecting her conservative orientation (and the fact that her district's black population approached zero), Snow was a foe of urban renewal, Model Cities, social services supplied by the municipality, and almost any increase in expenditures for the urban core. Except for Joanne Collins, she consistently opposed naming

African Americans to appointed office like municipal judgeships, though never for expressly racial reasons. In short, Snow was not the least bit sympathetic to black aspirations and her election would have marked a decidedly regressive step for black interests. Snow was portrayed by Freedom as the clear enemy of the black community, though the potency of the attack was weakened by her limited potential for victory.[136] Devoid as the general election contest was of issues—indeed, in a sign of how empty of substance the campaign was, the biggest issue was Wheeler's refusal to participate in television debates with Snow[137]—the heated rhetoric employed by Freedom against Snow and the CA slate provided the only bit of interest in the election in the black community.

Black voters did turn out in reasonably large numbers to help give Wheeler a crushing victory over Snow, 45,110 votes (59 percent) to 31,860 (41 percent). The CA was further humiliated by the fact that its candidate lost even the typical strongholds in the upper income areas by large margins. Snow won in her Northland stronghold, but the region comprised less than 1/6 of the total vote and her margins there were not commanding in any event. The true key to Wheeler's victory was his overwhelming support in the five Freedom wards, where the mayor accumulated 10,744 votes to Snow's 2,953 votes.[138] Although Snow's obvious hostility to black interests might have produced such large margins for Wheeler anyway, Freedom was granted the credit for mobilizing the community in the Freedom wards to vote for Wheeler. A swing to Snow by Freedom voters would have deprived the mayor of his entire margin of victory.

For Freedom, Inc., the 1975 municipal elections were bittersweet. The LPO achieved some remarkable victories, including the reelection of a sympathetic mayor, staving off an intra-community challenge to return Bruce Watkins to the council, and having provided support to a majority of the newly elected council members. But there were also devastating losses, especially Mamie Hughes's narrow defeat and the loss of Sal Capra in the second district.[139] Capra's district had few African Amiercan voters (indeed, it was home to some of the highest-performing precincts for George Wallace), so the loss did not reflect directly on Freedom, but the councilman had routinely supported black interests in the past. Freedom endorsed Capra over his youthful challenger, Robert Hernandez, who became the first Latino elected official in the city's history.[140]

Press coverage of Freedom focused on its role in Hughes's loss instead of its part in the Wheeler and Watkins wins, questioning whether Freedom sat on its laurels or even whether the LPO would survive. Of course, Freedom leaders noted that any time the organization lost a single election, its critics scurried to suggest that its demise was imminent.[141] More careful observers would have noted that, despite the immense political capital fruitlessly invested in the Hughes candidacy, Freedom emerged from the elections as the predominant LPO in the city. Where in the past Freedom shared that title with the CA, the reform organization was critically weakened after the Shaughnessy-Snow debacles. No other LPO could begin to compete for the title. Other organizations were too small, too localized, or lacking in any sort of formal orientation (e.g., DFP, which everyone expected to disappear immediately after the elections). Only Freedom possessed an institutional character, a convincing message, a clear constituency, and had delivered victory to the mayor. The question to be faced as the 1975 elections receded into the past was whether others would recognize Freedom's enhanced power and how they would react. Would Freedom's proven influence over voters result in benefits for the African American community? Or would the LPO's political opponents rage against it, feeling threatened by it, committing themselves to containing its influence, and devoting their energies to stymieing its initiatives?

Defending Black Interests in the 1970s

Freedom's influence was unquestionably enhanced by its key role in the 1971 and 1975 elections. The institutionalized nature of Freedom, its status as a corporatist "voice of the community," ability to mobilize large numbers of black voters, and its willingness to engage in short-term bargaining all contributed to enhanced black political efficacy during this period; both Freedom and the broader black community benefited from tangible policy outcomes. Four major, recurring issues were of crucial importance to black Kansas Citians during this period: crime and the conduct of the Kansas City Police Department (KCPD); the Model Cities program; municipal services in predominantly African American neighborhoods; and diversity in municipal employment, contracting, and appointive offices. This list necessarily omits what was perhaps the most burning issue in black Kansas City during the 1970s, the trials and travails of the Kansas City, Missouri School District (KCMSD). Throughout the decade, virtually every edition of *The Call* carried yet another installment in the district's ongoing drama with controversy alternately focusing on desegregation, decentralization, disinvestment due to white flight, and diversity among the district's administrative and teaching staffs. Litigation against the district by civil rights and black empowerment groups was nearly constant during this period.[142] However, the KCMSD is independent of municipal government (and, indeed, contains only a fraction of the city's geography and total student population, with fourteen other districts in the city limits) and so falls outside of this book's focus on city government.

Before moving on to a discussion of the policy issues, a brief discussion about Freedom's approach to influencing policy during this period is in order. At the dawn of the 1970s, the executive board of Freedom routinely met to issue formal position statements on municipal issues. Formally declaring a position ensured that the LPO's affiliated and allied City Council members were not perceived as lone rangers, but rather lent the force of Freedom's collective strength to the debate. This formal process, which required a majority vote of the executive board and was always a collective action, did not occur at predictable intervals. Although the LPO consistently declared a position on various referenda and ballot initiatives, it also, sometimes without warning, would declare an official position on an upcoming ordinance or even a city issue that did not have an ordinance attached to it. Sometimes Freedom's board would declare a position on an issue in an attempt to set the agenda, rather than merely responding to it. As part of this position-taking, Freedom commissioned (or used) professional reports on and analyses of local conditions, like when a Freedom-commissioned research report asserted that inner city residential properties were over-assessed, inflating the tax paid by African Americans.[143] These analyses provided intellectual support for the policy proposals made by the LPO. Issuing research reports and declaring formal positions on issues were consistent with Freedom's desire to be a space for black political debate, to be a sophisticated advocate for black interests, and to be thought a leader in local politics. These activities reflected the fact that, under Jordan and Watkins, Freedom acted on the conviction that symbolic representation was necessary but not sufficient. As the 1970s progressed, formal position-taking on municipal issues became less common and the commission of independent research ceased entirely. Several longtime Freedom activists bemoaned the fact that active lobbying by the organization itself ceased to be a priority in the late 1970s. Individual Freedom members remained active on policy, taking stands in their own names in support of black interests, but the organization itself retreated from a formal role in the policy process. At the LPO's regular meetings, members were still regularly treated to presentations on important policy issues (and presenters treated to grueling cross-examination), but these discussions no longer resulted in a formal recommendation on the policy in question. Instead, in the latter half of the decade, Freedom concentrated its energies ever-more-exclusively on electoral politics, both on behalf of individual candidates and for ballot initiatives. Elected officials affiliated with Freedom were still expected to "do the right thing," or suffer the consequences at the next election, but no longer could routinely rely on the added strength (or stigma) imparted by a clear directive from the LPO on what constituted the "black community's position."

Policing Crime, Policing the Police: The KCPD and the Black Community

As was recounted in chapter 2, the black community had long maintained a tempestuous relationship with the KCPD. During the 1970s, this relationship became even rockier. Deterioration in the relationship began shortly after the 1968 rebellion, when there seemed to be little potential for even greater hostility between black Kansas Citians and the KCPD. Chief Clarence Kelley, demonstrating yet again that he was utterly insensitive to or apathetic about the concerns of African Americans, took several steps regarded as antagonistic. The most important stemmed from the chief's conviction, discredited by every sentient being that devoted any time to studying the event, that the 1968 rebellion was the handiwork of a group of dangerous black radicals, including the Black Panthers, the SCLC, and other civil rights groups. Fearing that, left unchecked, the radical elements would agitate Kansas City into a dystopia, Kelley created a special police squad whose sole duty was to monitor radical activity. The squad—comprised largely of white officers, if only because nonwhite officers were few in number, attended public events hosted by "radical" voices, noting who was present, taking down license plate numbers, and otherwise attempting to simultaneously record the incident and intimidate attendees. Freedom leaders were irate when they learned of this practice, and became even more so when some of the LPO's elected officials addressed meetings that were monitored. Kelley dismissed the criticism and continued to bask in the adulation of white citizens.[144]

If anything, Kelley enhanced his surveillance of local radicals, greatly contributing to the demise of militancy in the city. Perhaps the most successful of his intimidation efforts involved the local chapter of the Black Panthers, founded and led by Pete O'Neal. As a result of relentless hounding by Kelley, the local chapter never grew beyond twenty or so members, despite operating the wildly popular Free Breakfast Program. Local clerics who provided some operational support to the Panthers, most notably United Methodist minister the Rev. Philip Lawson, found themselves splayed across the pages of the newspaper thanks to information fed to the press by police. In 1970, Kelley's relentless paranoia about the Panthers was rewarded with several days of congressional hearings devoted to exploring the overwhelming threat to internal security posed by the two dozen Kansas City cadres. Several KCPD officials testified to the destructive nature of the Panthers, as did black civic leader and former council candidate Everett O'Neal (no relation to the Panther leader). Their testimony was countered by state representative Herman Johnson, then still firmly allied with Freedom, who made plain that he regarded the hearings as a farcical waste of time.[145] Congressional hearings aside, Kelley's vigilant pursuit of the local Panthers—which, after a bout of the sectarianism that ultimately plagued so many nationalist groups of the era, changed its name to the Sons of Malcolm—succeeded by 1972 in sending O'Neal into exile, reducing the organization to perhaps five members, and shattering the social programs through which it had attained prominence. Freedom and the Panthers were not allies during this period; Freedom activists regarded the Panthers as naïve and occasionally gangsterish, while the Panthers considered Freedom's electoral work to be the rankest form of selling out. One of the few things they agreed on was that the KCPD's harassment was shameful and racially motivated.

Percolating black discontent with the KCPD came fully into the open when, in 1973, Richard Nixon nominated Chief Kelley to be director of the Federal Bureau of Investigation. Many local residents and elites were delighted by the choice, with even *The Call,* which had long been critical of the chief, saying that it was an honor for a local person to have been selected.[146] Bruce Watkins and Freedom were not among them; they were livid. Immediately upon the announcement of the nomination, Freedom released a statement denouncing Kelley for an "unyielding position on law and order [that] contributed fuel to the fiery 1968 riots instead of quenching them."[147] Watkins was granted permission to testify at the nomination hearings; officially representing Freedom, he tore into Kelley as having produced an environment of unrest, refusing to take steps to integrate the KCPD, refusing to believe that "his" officers ever committed acts of brutality, and for being racially insensitive. Watkins was joined by a handful of other black activists, but otherwise stood bravely alone.[148] White Kansas Citians, including supposed allies of black interests like the local American Civil Liberties Union, praised the chief and asserted that African Americans were overreacting to minor slights.[149] Kelley was confirmed by the Senate without a single nay vote and with the support of Missouri's two Democratic senators, over whom Freedom could presumably wield some influence.[150]

Kelley's departure from the local scene[151] proved that tension between the black community and the KCPD existed because of institutional features, not just a personality clash with the chief. Subsequent police chiefs embraced lower profiles than Kelley had and were more amiable with African Americans, but pursued polices that were just as hated. Three major critiques of the KCPD existed in the post-Kelley era, and all were restatements of arguments long made by black Kansas Citians. The first critique centered on the ongoing pattern of abusive treatment experienced by African Americans at the hands of the police. During the 1970s, hardly a month went by without *The Call* featuring a front-page story about relatively blameless African American citizens being harassed, brutally assaulted, or otherwise mistreated by police officers. Although *The Call* typically gave more coverage to these incidents when the victims were respectable members of the black bourgeoisie, as when Bruce Watkins's diabetic brother, Warren, was viciously beaten by police during a routine traffic stop and then found guilty of causing the beating by a hostile judge who disregarded the testimony of multiple eyewitnesses—police brutality cut across class lines. As during the Kelley years, the police administration always stood behind the officers, labeling victims and their advocates as troublemakers.[152]

The second major critique centered on the lack of diversity to be found in police ranks. Kelley responded half-heartedly to agitation during the 1960s and early 1970s for a more diverse force by creating minority recruitment programs, but many African Americans maintained that the commitment to these programs was less than sincere under Kelley and his successors. Skepticism about the genuineness of the police administration in pursuing a force that better represented the population it served was warranted, given that by the end of the 1970s, African Americans still comprised just 6 percent of uniformed officers.[153]

The third major critique of the police was that they were lackluster in providing actual policing in urban core neighborhoods with large populations of non-white people. Crime, especially violent crimes like homicide, rose dramatically during the 1970s, but many black Kansas Citians felt that the KCPD was unconcerned when the victims were African American. African Americans certainly did not embrace the law and order mantra espoused by Nixon and Agnew, which was frequently only a thin excuse for racism, but did want the KCPD to devote more energy to cultivating healthy relationships with neighborhood residents, more effort to addressing systemic issues that could stop crime before it started, and more resources to solving crimes in the urban core.[154]

Freedom, as an organization and through its individual members, was at the forefront of all three of these critiques. Watkins remained, as he had in past years, the outstanding voice against police brutality, but he was now frequently joined by Charles Hazley. Both used their public platforms to agitate for reform in police conduct. Freedom itself did not issue a formal position on the issue (the LPO's opposition to police brutality was self-evident) but it was a frequent topic of discussion at membership meetings. More important, candidates' responses to the issue were determinative when it came to receiving Freedom's endorsement.

As in the 1960s, even the most persistent agitation by Freedom resulted in minimal concrete change. No objective study of police brutality in Kansas City during this period exists. The number of high profile brutality incidents actually increased during the 1970s, though this does not necessarily imply that police brutality itself increased. It may be, for example, that journalists covering the crime beat during this period were more interested in police brutality stories than their predecessors. Or it may be that changing norms made brutality less acceptable than in the past, such that individual incidents produced greater concern. What is clear, though, is that African Americans active in politics during this period were convinced that the situation was not improving. In regards to the criticism that the police force was insufficiently diverse, the KCPD did enhance its recruitment efforts. However, black and Latino observers continued to assert that these efforts were devoid of commitment and, in any event, the statistics did not appreciably improve during this period. In regards to the criticism that black communities were inadequately policed, the only real action taken was by the community itself. African American activists, most notably Alvin Brooks (the first black city department director), founded the Ad Hoc Group Against Crime in order to get citizens involved in the fight against crime.

If Freedom and the black community were indeed ascendant on the local political scene, as preceding sections have argued, what accounts for the imperviousness of the KCPD to this change? It is true that police departments have almost always proven to be the institutions most recalcitrant to reform; nearly every black mayor in the country has encountered controversy when attempting to reform police departments.[155] It is also certainly true that the KCPD had its share of ardent defenders, including most of the city's white elected officials and civic elites. These explanations are insufficient. What fleshes out the explanation is to recall that the KCPD is not under municipal control, but state control. Although the entirety of the department's budget was contributed by the city (with a minimum contribution guaranteed under state law) and the mayor serves as an ex officio member of the Board of Police Commissioners, the Board's four other members are appointed by Missouri's governor. As a result, perhaps the most controversial unit of Kansas City's government, whose policies could and should be discussed by the city's elected officials, was essentially removed from the local discourse, impoverishing the debate and constraining the remedies available. Political realities in the state have meant that Kansas City has rarely elected one of its own to live in the governor's mansion and most governors have been conservative. During the period considered in this chapter, three men served as governor: Warren Hearnes, Christopher Bond, and Joe Teasdale (who became the only Kansas Citian in recent memory to hold the office). None of these men were considered friends of Freedom, which opposed each of them in either the primary or general elections,[156]or of the broader black community. As a result, few of the police commissioners they appointed were willing to challenge the police administration. Even those commissioners who were sympathetic to black aspirations, like Ilus Davis (appointed after his mayoral tenure) or black law professor Gwendolyn Wells, lacked the power to force change; the police board was a prestige appointment, but was treated as a rubber stamp for KCPD leadership. The Board had no incentive to modify its own behavior, since it could not be held accountable by the citizenry. Given all this, it is not surprising that the serious criticisms of the KCPD made by African American Kansas Citians in the 1970s went essentially ignored.[157]

Model Cities

The second major issue area in the 1970s concerned the Model Cities program. Begun as an initiative of the Lyndon Johnson administration, the program sought to invest considerable resources in cities, to fund a variety of social and economic projects that would tackle poverty and address the burgeoning "urban crisis."[158] As a result of political machinations that deprived Model Cities of its original conception of being a pilot program operating in a handful of cities, Kansas City received tens of millions of dollars in the early 1970s. The city created a new Model Cities department to administer the funds, as well as a host of neighborhood-level elected bodies to stimulate participation from the populations served by the programs (in keeping with federal mandates about participation). Model Cities dollars were to be spent in high-poverty areas. In Kansas City, the areas that qualified were almost entirely to be found in the urban core, in neighborhoods with African American majorities. Black Kansas Citians were excited about the potential for Model Cities to significantly improve the quality of life in the neighborhoods in which they resided.

Kansas City did spend the bulk of its Model Cities monies in neighborhoods with black majorities. The funds were spent to support a wide variety of programs, including job training, youth activities, anticrime efforts, indigent health care, low-income housing, and other direct social services. But it took a great deal of effort on the part of local African American activists to ensure that funds were spent in this manner; the Model Cities budget was a persistent source of low-level tension on the city council and in the municipal bureaucracy. Elected officials who did not represent areas where large amount of Model Cities dollars were spent attempted to divert resources into the neighborhoods they did represent, making arguments varying widely in their sensibleness to justify these actions. Bureaucrats faced with tight budgets of their own regularly sought to divert Model Cities resources into their own departments, arguing that some facet of the work performed by their division was consistent with the antipoverty mission. These efforts rarely succeeded, because they were vigorously opposed by a coalition of antipoverty and Freedom activists, though these two categories were neither mutually exclusive nor mutually inclusive. Activists upset about Model Cities funding priorities frequently received coverage in the local press, occasionally causing sufficient embarrassment to the administration as to modify its behavior. More importantly, though, Freedom's influence in the city council ensured that Model Cities was always a high priority issue. The LPO's delegation consistently asked questions about progress, steered more resources into urban neighborhoods with large African American populations, and ensured that the Model Cities department's directors were African Americans sympathetic to the program and its purposes. Allies on the council were informed in no uncertain terms that there would be repercussions for elected officials who reallocated Model Cities funds outside of the high-poverty areas for which it was intended.[159]

This success was made clear when the Nixon Administration terminated the Model Cities program entirely, ordering municipalities across the country to close out the program at the end of 1973. At the prompting of Charles Hazley and Freedom, the city retained most functions of the old Model Cities Department in a new Department of Urban Affairs.[160] Although the old citizen participation scheme disappeared in this conversion, the program staff and many social services remained, with the city funding them through discretionary grants. The tension once found in Model Cities over federal grant money continued under the new system. Freedom attained great success in advocating that Model Cities produce maximal benefits for urban black residents.

Municipal Services in Urban Core Neighborhoods

Similar, if less pronounced, success was achieved on the issue of municipal services. African Americans living in the city's urban core had long maintained that they received an inadequate share of municipal services. Potholes went unfilled, traffic lights went unmended, and water pipes went unrepaired. In the winter, the area's streets were the last to be plowed. In the summer, weeds and grass on vacant lots were allowed to grow wild. These conditions were not experienced citywide, nor were they the result of inadequate resources. To residents of the city's southwest corridor, around the Country Club Plaza district, these conditions would have been entirely foreign. This disparity prompted Charles Wheeler to make his statement that, as mayor, he would ensure that there were as many city trucks in the urban core as on the Plaza.[161]

Wheeler did not deliver on that promise, but progress was made. Longtime residents of the area and contemporaneous accounts concur that there was some improvement in service delivery in urban neighborhoods during the 1970s. The mayor and city council, led by Freedom members, insisted that greater attention be paid to nagging basic service issues in these areas. They expended additional funds on long-needed infrastructure improvements and located new city facilities in underserved urban neighborhoods. Elected officials and Freedom were joined in this by other pressure groups, especially neighborhood clubs distressed by the trajectory of their immediate areas and activist organizations like SAC-20. Successive city managers, fearful that their jobs were in jeopardy, attempted to win support from these blocs by stressing their attempts to create parity in service delivery. African Americans were not alone in calling for improved services, so the modest improvement seen in this area should not be chalked up solely to Freedom. The city's political environment was one calling for improvement on this issue, with the back to basics message earning support from a wide cross-section.

Freedom also had remarkable success in utilizing the city's ballot initiative elections to improve services in the urban core. By city charter, the City Council was not permitted to impose any tax increases on the citizenry or issue bonds by itself. Instead, the Council could only submit proposals for tax increases or bond sales to a public vote. As the city's needs expanded in the 1970s while its revenue model failed to meet those needs, ballot initiatives became quite frequent. As a condition of supporting the proposed taxes or bond issuances, Freedom would engage in bargaining with the proposers so that the initiatives contain specific benefits for the black community. For example, when bonds were being issued to build new city facilities, Freedom made certain that the list of projects to be funded by the bonds included improvements in urban core neighborhoods. Several proposals would have initiated new services for residents, but would have done so on a trial basis beginning in a handful of neighborhoods. Freedom intervened on several of these occasions, threatening to withdraw its support unless the new services were offered on an equitable basis. The threat of withdrawing support was taken seriously, based on Freedom's past record of influencing voters. The threat was particularly potent in bond elections, where state law required that two thirds of the voters support these measures in order to secure passage. When just one third of the electorate could defeat any proposal, the quarter of the voters who could be influenced by Freedom could take on great importance.[162] Sometimes the Freedom strategy was not successful. As a condition of its support for issuing bonds to benefit the city's new airport and other projects important to the white civic elite, Freedom demanded that the council also submit ballot measure that established funding mechanisms for neighborhood revitalization. This concession was granted, but the ballot measures were separated from those benefitting the airport and downtown projects. Voters could pick and choose which projects they supported, rather than having to vote for or against the entire package. The electorate supported the bonds for the airport, and rejected everything else, including favored projects of the corporate elite and the Freedom proposals. Black voters were strong supporters of all the measures, which Freedom recommended they approve, but not enough to overcome the two-thirds threshold required.[163]

The major defeat experienced by Freedom on basic services came at the hands of the state rather than the city. Since the advent of the national highway system and the development of a commuter culture, local officials had sought to build an expressway from the city's far southern reaches directly into downtown. Transportation planners employed by the state and the metropolitan planning organization charted a route for this highway, US-71, which cut through the heart of the black community. The massive project would displace thousands of low-income African American residents, and almost no one else. When this plan was first proposed in the 1960s, African Americans were irate but impotent to stop it. Only a lawsuit by those who would lose their homes restrained the project's progress. Freedom was strongly opposed to the US-71 route, especially since, as initially proposed, the expressway contained not a single entrance or exit in the black community. White city leaders generally supported the plan, though the implacable opposition of Freedom did lead to some dampening of enthusiasm. The city itself had no real voice in the decision-making process and white city officials used this fact to disclaim responsibility. Instead, the decision was made by the state and the metropolitan planning organization. These entities responded in limited fashion to the concerns of the black community, consenting to slight modifications of the route, to the addition of entrances and exits in the black community (so that the highway would not totally isolate these neighborhoods), and to a slight increase in compensation for displaced residents. Even these concessions would not have been made in the absence of organized pressure from Freedom and its cooperation with other organizations, at both the municipal and state levels of government. As with the KCPD, Freedom's influence over a seemingly local matter was stymied by the fact that the decision was made by the state. The LPO's influence in Jefferson City was growing, but still outmatched by the representatives from rural areas or St. Louis. Litigation and the massive scope of the project would delay the completion of US-71 for two decades, but the expressway would be eventually completed, after even more modifications. In an irony lost on many, a major segment of the highway was named the "Bruce R. Watkins Parkway."[164]

Diversity at City Hall

The final issue area that dominated municipal politics during the 1970s, that of diversity at City Hall, was the easiest one on which to take action. Not coincidentally, it was also the area in which the greatest success was achieved. Since its founding, Freedom had argued that increasing the number of black elected officials, appointed officials, and government employees would have symbolic and substantive benefits. Operating under the theory that symbolic success would naturally lead to substantive victory, Freedom devoted considerable energy in the 1970s to increasing the number of black appointed officials and high-ranking city employees. The LPO's municipal elected officials pursued the promotion of black city employees and the recruitment of highly qualified African Americans from outside of the civil service. At Freedom meetings, elected and appointed officials were constantly queried about statistics on African Americans as a share of the city workforce and as a share of upper management. Endorsement decisions incorporated progress on this question; indeed, one major reason that Freedom passed over Blankinship and Thomas for reelection in 1971 was the abysmal progress the two had made on diversifying the city's upper level management and appointive offices. Of course, in placing such stress on this issue,

Freedom was not acting out of altruism. It sought to position itself as a dispenser of municipal patronage (limited as that category might be, given the city's reform charter) and create or solidify its ties with the African American elites most likely to be appointed to civic boards. These ties would enhance the LPO's capacity, accumulate political favors owed to it, and more firmly ground it in the elite class most likely to engage in political activism and maneuvering. Being a provider of patronage, whether of the employment or appointive/prestige variety, also was thought to be something that would persuade the average black voter to cast his or her ballot for Freedom candidates. This was thought to be the case both because individuals would want access to the patronage and because they would be impressed by the scope of the LPO's influence and record in promoting black interests. The holding of this belief was best exemplified in a multi-page newspaper advertisement that Freedom took out to celebrate its tenth anniversary; that spread, which was featured in *The Call,* pictured every single elected official, government employee, and appointed official that owed his or her position to Freedom.[165]

Although the bid to increase African American representation in municipal employment and appointive office fell short of demographic proportionality, it did achieve success. Entering the 1970s, only one African American served as director of a city agency (Alvin Brooks at the Human Relations Commission) and almost none were in senior management.[166] By the end of the 1970s, the ranks of black senior managers numbered in the dozens and were to be found in nearly every city department. Several African Americans had served as department directors, though they still usually led departments focused exclusively on "black issues" (e.g., Human Relations or Model Cities/Urban Affairs) rather than agencies with citywide responsibilities.[167] An African American was appointed as assistant city manager (the number two position in municipal administration) in 1971, initiating a pattern that continues into the present where at least one African American is always to be found among the ranks of the assistant city managers.[168] An NAACP study found that the city discriminated against women and other minorities, but acknowledged that progress was being made.[169] After consistent pressure from Charles Hazley, the city adopted a more stringent policy on diversity in its contracting operations. Similar progress was made on the city's numerous boards and commissions, which previously included only a marginal African American presence. Ilus Davis was the first mayor to appoint more than a token black member to city boards, but the greatest stride forward was made by Wheeler. Immediately upon taking office, he appointed Dr. Jeremiah Cameron, a teacher at Lincoln High and vice president of the local NAACP branch, to the Board of Parks and Recreation Commissioners.[170] The Parks Board, which also administered the city's famed network of tree-lined boulevards, was considered the most prestigious of all appointments and had long been the bastion of the civic elite. Cameron promptly began a massive transformation of the department, forcing it to grudgingly become more responsive to the needs of African Americans, Latinos, and low-income people. Wheeler appointed African American representatives to nearly every major board, including those related to economic development, housing, planning/zoning, and social services. During his eight-year tenure, African American presence on these appointed bodies went from negligible to significant. Wheeler also made history by naming the first African American to chair a committee of the city council, making Charles Hazley the chairman of the powerful Planning and Zoning Committee from 1971 to 1979.[171] Committed as he may have been to the cause of equity, Wheeler did not make these appointments solely because of a passion for justice. His relationship with Freedom, and specifically his reliance on the black vote that it represented, depended on him appointing highly qualified African Americans to city posts. That political expediency was involved is indicated by the fact that the pace of high-profile African American appointments made by Wheeler decelerated during his second term, as it became clear that Freedom would not support Wheeler for a third term. For example, Wheeler became part of a coalition that replaced a retiring black municipal judge with a white one, leaving the court without a single African American member.[172]

In short, then, the 1970s saw considerable gains made by black Kansas Citians in the policy arena. Freedom, Inc. was *the* major actor in achieving these gains, either working directly in its own name or through individuals whose election it championed. Considerable success was achieved in preserving Model Cities and community development grant funds for underserved black neighborhoods, directing federal funds toward pressing needs, improving municipal services and infrastructure in urban core neighborhoods, and altering the complexion of the city's workforce and appointive officeholders. Efforts to make the police department more responsive and to significantly alter the destructive plan for US-71 met with failure, but these failures could largely be chalked up to an absence of adequate influence at the state rather than the local level. These gains for black interests did not convert Kansas City into a paradise for African Americans. At the very same time that these victories were being won, much was going wrong for the urban core and neighborhoods with black majorities. These neighborhoods were experiencing increased crime, increased unemployment, white flight, disinvestment, failing schools, and other devastating social conditions. Although some of the responsibility for these negative trends must be laid at the feet of local leadership (including the members of Freedom, Inc.), these conditions were largely the product of national or global forces over which local leaders had no control and few alternatives with which to adequately counter them. Even as we praise Freedom's important role in advocating for black interests, we should thus be mindful not to romanticize this period or the success which the LPO attained in it.

Building a Mass-Oriented Institution: The Internal Politics of Freedom, Inc. in the 1970s

Neither election victories nor policy successes would have been possible had Freedom not built itself into a highly effective LPO. During the 1970s, the organization did much to mobilize its grassroots base, forge alliances with other black leaders, and to establish itself as a credible corporatist voice for the majority of the African American community. Indeed, the 1970s mark the period when Freedom was most integral to the life of the black community. It also marks a period when the organization rapidly became more sophisticated, professional, and institutionalized. Partly because of the intensity with which its critics attacked it as the tool of a small, self-interested, cliquish elite, Freedom was compelled to take aggressive action to define itself as open, transparent, and community-conscious. More than at any other time in its history, the organization was during this period mass-oriented, though not necessarily mass-based. Freedom engaged in many activities during this period that encouraged widespread community involvement, that were designed to make the organization a force on which the populace could rely even in the years between elections, and that aggressively and effectively mobilized the black community. These facts warrant its designation as mass-oriented, but the persistently low number of actual members and the concentration of power in the board mean that the designation of mass-based was out of reach.

The most important of the tactics Freedom used to mobilize and cultivate a connection with the black electorate was the precinct captain network. These individuals continued to be carefully selected, were expected to deliver the vote in their precincts based on hard work and continual communication with the residents of their territory, and were highly valued by the Freedom leadership.[173] They were expected to relay information about the mood of their constituents on a regular basis, so that Freedom might collectively respond in the most effective manner. Precinct captains were expected to cooperate closely with Freedom's other campaign workers to distribute literature, knock on doors, telephone neighbors, and cover polling locations with the Freedom ballot on election day. But other tactics adopted by Freedom were equally important to securing the support the LPO required in order to be effective. The organization held regular meetings at Freedom headquarters; these meetings were open to the general membership as well as the public and were used to discuss organizational business, upcoming campaigns, and pressing issues in the black community.

Consistent with its heritage as a competitor to the old-line Democratic machines, one important way that Freedom developed a strong relationship with its support base was through the distribution of informal social welfare. Particularly at major holidays like Thanksgiving and Christmas, baskets of food and other necessities would be distributed to residents of the wards in which Freedom operated.[174] The LPO's elected officials and executive board joined together to collect and/or donate these baskets, which were distributed out of the Freedom office. As when the Pendergast machine used a similar tactic, no commitment of support was extracted from recipients of the baskets but their distribution produced goodwill in the community. The holiday basket distribution conveyed the impression that Freedom cared deeply about the plight of the less fortunate and would match its political rhetoric with action.

Freedom made itself open and accessible by regularly hosting events for the public. Throughout the 1970s, the LPO typically hosted a free picnic every summer. With an ambience that more often resembled a family reunion than a political function, attendees were treated to food, games, live entertainment, and the occasional political speech. The picnics were widely publicized, covered by the press, and usually attended by in excess of a thousand people. The picnics allowed loyal supporters to be recognized for their work, gave elected officials and Freedom leaders an opportunity to interact with residents in an informal setting, and conveyed the impression that the organization genuinely cared about its constituency.[175]

In a more overtly political vein, Freedom hosted rallies and meet and greet events during the campaign season. These events were not as heavily attended as the food and fun-oriented picnics, but gave voters the opportunity to hear from the entire Freedom slate at once. Freedom used these events to motivate its support base, to solicit volunteer workers for candidates on the Freedom ballot, and to broadcast the LPO's message for the campaign cycle.[176] One such preelection rally featured a performance by the world-famous Count Basie and his orchestra, luring a large crowd.[177]

Perhaps Freedom's marquee noncampaign activity in the 1970s was the Leon Jordan Memorial Dinner, held annually beginning in 1971. The Jordan Dinner annually attracted in excess of a thousand paying attendees, including the members of both the black and white elites and many of the state's elected officials. Held in a downtown hotel ballroom, the event was celebrated for its use of famous musical acts and for bringing nationally known speakers to give the keynote address (including Tom Bradley, Bill Clay, Bill Cosby, and Coleman Young, among others). In conjunction with the dinner, Freedom members organized day-long seminars (similar to the Congressional Black Caucus's legislative weekend) to discuss the most pressing issues facing black Kansas City. The seminars featured some of black Kansas City and black America's leading politicians (including, one year, the entire membership of the Congressional Black Caucus), intellectuals, and journalists, who were lured to Kansas City because of their esteem for Freedom and its accomplishments. Although sponsored by Freedom, the Jordan Dinner and Seminar were organized by a volunteer committee composed not only of Freedom diehards but by a who's who of the local black elite. The Jordan memorial events garnered support from such a wide cross-section of the community because Jordan had taken on iconic status (with his portrait gracing Freedom literature and a park named in his honor) and because the substantial proceeds were devoted to college scholarships for African American students who showed promise.[178] The ability to attract high-profile figures from the national political scene imparted credibility and importance to the LPO, while the seminar discussions imparted to it an aura of being a thought leader, and the scholarship fund that the events supported indicated that Freedom was genuinely concerned about the community rather than petty self-promotion. However, there was a clear deterioration in the caliber, prestige, attendance, and fundraising success of the Jordan memorial events in the latter half of the 1970s.

The Jordan events raised tens of thousands of dollars for charitable purposes. At the same time, Freedom's own financial position was not particularly stable. During the campaign season, the LPO relied on endorsement fees from candidates on its slate, or contributions from supporters of those candidates, to finance its operations. This business model was shared by all of the city's other LPOs. The organization had no full-time staff, relied on volunteer labor (mostly supplied by candidates as a condition of their endorsement), and expenditures were concentrated in printing and advertising. Still, this funding model opened Freedom to an attack which would be made with increasing frequency as time passed, namely that the imperatives of organizational survival meant that endorsements were sold to the highest bidder.[179] There is no concrete evidence to support this assertion, which first bubbled up into public view in the 1970s, but there is no doubt that Freedom's extreme dependence on endorsed candidates for funds weakened its independence and its credibility.[180] Still, the organization made some significant efforts during the seventies to create an independent financial base for itself. Membership fees were always assessed, but the modest amount of the fee and the relatively small number of dues-paying members (usually a few hundred) meant that this was not a substantial source of revenue. Fundraisers were held regularly throughout the decade, including the aforementioned rally that featured Count Basie as a headliner. Despite the success of these occasional efforts, Freedom never developed an independent financial base. The organization remained reliant on contributions from candidates, was never able to finance lavish campaign efforts, and rarely maintained more than a modest balance in its treasury. Still, the 1970s represented the last time that the organization made efforts to forge an independent financial base; by the dawn of the 1980s, Freedom no longer hosted any fundraising events for itself.

At the same time, Freedom was becoming more sophisticated in other ways. The quality of the materials it distributed to the public, whether policy research, newspaper advertisements, or campaign literature, all improved appreciably during the decade. The ad hoc way in which the group conducted business became more formal and more democratic. Crucially, though, this transition did not take place because organizational sophistication was abstractly regarded as a virtue, but in direct response to internal political turmoil within Freedom. Moreover, the very existence of this tension amply demonstrates that Freedom was not a dictatorship or a personality cult, but a broad-based and dynamic organization with an internal politics all its own.

Cleavages within the organization first became apparent when Bruce Watkins, Freedom's president since the 1970 assassination of Leon Jordan, left the post in the fall of 1975. Watkins's personal popularity within the organization and the broader community was such that he could have remained president if he so chose, but some discontent with his leadership was discreetly percolating. This discontent primarily derived from the loss in the 1975 campaign against Joanne Collins, but also from clashes in personality and ambition. Rather than subject the organization to the instability that even a discreet fight over leadership might produce, Watkins opted to retire. His decision was also consistent with the push to make Freedom sustainable over the long term, neither reliant on nor dedicated to the advancement of any one individual but committed instead to the pursuit of black interests. Watkins was replaced as president by Harold "Doc" Holliday Jr., then a Jackson County legislator and Freedom's chairman. With Holliday changing seats, city councilman Charles Hazley became the organization's new chairman. Rosemary Lowe, the Democratic committeewoman for the 14th ward who had been an activist within the organization since its inception, became vice president. Lowe's ascension to the vice presidency marked the first time that a woman held high-ranking office within the organization. In explaining his departure from the presidency, Watkins cited the need for new leadership, his own dedication to his new council position, and the desire to build a statewide version of Freedom.[181] The election of black members to the Missouri General Assembly from the Kansas City area was distinctly helpful, but these individuals were not always able to curry the necessary influence with statewide elected officials. African American voters in Kansas City and St. Louis (where the African American community was and is terribly divided) often found themselves on opposite sides in Democratic primaries, limiting the influence of both communities. Freedom leaders saw great value in attempting to apply the Freedom model to a statewide vehicle for African American politics. Watkins intended to personally oversee the creation and development of this vehicle. It ranks as one of the great tragedies of Freedom that nothing ever came of this idea.

Although the transition to new leadership demonstrated organizational growth and the cultivation of institutionalization on Freedom's part, it also proved disastrous. After a short honeymoon period, discontent with Holliday's leadership became pervasive. The president's constantly growing chorus of critics alleged that Holliday's leadership style was authoritarian, high-handed, and concentrated power in the hands of a small band of allies. Critics frequently tagged Freedom under Holliday as "a one-man show." Many of the activities mentioned above, including community outreach events, fundraisers, and the Jordan memorial functions, declined in frequency during Holliday's brief tenure. Moreover, under Holliday's presidency, some of Freedom's women activists, who said they did the bulk of the real work in the organization, felt alienated and ignored. Decades later, some who were active in the LPO during this period also alleged that Holliday indulged in some chicanery with the Freedom treasury.[182]

Even with unhappiness over Holliday's leadership rippling through the membership, nothing happened to rein Holliday in until after the 1978 Democratic primary. Before the primary, Freedom successfully prevailed on Governor Joseph Teasdale to appoint the elder Holliday to a vacant Jackson County judge's seat. Harold Holliday Sr. then ran for a full term in the 1978 primary. The same job was being sought by the youthful Leonard Jonas Hughes III (son of municipal court judge Leonard Hughes Jr. and county legislator Mamie Hughes). Hughes claimed that he had been promised Freedom's support for the vacancy and subsequent campaign, but that Harold Holliday Jr. had double-crossed him in order to benefit the latter's father. The campaign that followed was a negative one. Hughes used photographs of Leon Jordan and claimed that, if the Freedom patriarch were still living, he would be supporting the youthful candidate. Orchid Jordan and Bruce Watkins denounced this literature as deceptive and disagreed with their premise, particularly when Hughes joined together with Herman Johnson in his primary campaign against Orchid Jordan.[183] An increasingly nasty and personal dispute played out in the pages of *The Call*, with Hughes—the grandson of a Freedom founding member, no less—calling Freedom a "clique" that took its base for granted, attacking Watkins and Orchid Jordan (while still beatifying Leon Jordan), and saying that Freedom had been "perverted from a noble dream and turned into a nightmare."[184] Leaving aside for a moment the irony of Hughes attacking a Freedom "clique" while belonging to a family that would universally be considered as being among the group's elite, the many charges leveled by the young candidate against both Hollidays and the LPO as a whole resonated with some. The typically invisible race for a magistrate's seat became the most high-profile campaign of 1978 and a referendum on whether Harold Holliday Jr.'s Freedom was a one-man show. A majority of voters apparently felt that it was, because Hughes eked out the barest of victories.[185]

Hughes's victory was a shock to the sachems of Freedom. For the first time since Freedom's ascent, one of the LPO's candidates lost a race in a black-majority district. Not only that, but the defeated candidate was the father of Freedom's president, one of the organization's grand old men, and was beaten by a candidate who ran on an explicitly anti-Freedom platform. Hughes had already been expelled from the LPO by Harold Holliday Jr., and, interpreting his victory to mean that he was the new power broker in black politics, quickly set to organizing his own rival organization. With great fanfare, Hughes named his new organization the Leon Jordan Memorial Political Club, but ultimately bowed to pressure and rechristened it People In Politics.[186] This marked the first serious split in or organizational challenge to Freedom from within the black community, one that the more organizationally committed members of Freedom were not willing to endure lightly. By this time it was common knowledge that Watkins intended to wage a mayoral campaign the following year, an effort in which a vibrant and united Freedom would be essential.

An open revolt broke out against Holliday's leadership, even though all acknowledged that the president was, in the words of one longtime Freedom insider, "one of the most politically astute people in Kansas City politics."[187] The opening salvo was fired by the women of Freedom. Immediately after the election, all of the LPO's Democratic committeewomen met at the home of Rosemary Lowe. They unanimously agreed to a statement, released to the press, expressing no confidence in Holliday's leadership. The Women of Freedom, as the ad hoc group was known, called for Lee Vertis Swinton to replace Holliday as president and for Lowe herself to replace Hazley as chairman.[188] Holliday attempted to stave off the rebellion, but had alienated so many, that action had to be taken.[189] The largely male executive board refused to accede to the specific demands of the women's group. Nevertheless, within a week a compromise was reached wherein Watkins returned to the presidency, Harold Holliday Jr. saved face by returning to a symbolic chairmanship, and Lowe remained vice president.[190] The episode conclusively demonstrated that democracy was alive within the organization and that, at least for the moment, cliquishness would not be rewarded. More important, though, the rampant dissatisfaction with the old leadership resulted in a significant improvement and democratization of the LPO's structures. The executive board, which held most of the decision-making power, was to be expanded from two dozen members to over sixty members. Women had long been underrepresented on the executive board, but were to see their numbers increase dramatically (though not yet proportionally) in the larger body. This promised expansion never transpired, as demonstrated by the fact that in 1980 the board still comprised 27 members.[191] Most significantly of all, a screening/nominating committee was formed with members drawn from within and outside of the board. In the past, endorsement decisions had been made by the executive board and the elected leadership in a relatively informal process. Although these decisions were reviewed and discussed by the general membership to varying degrees, the executive board's exclusive purview over this area concentrated great power in its hands. Creating a screening committee resulted in Freedom's most important activity, political endorsements, becoming more formalized, with presentations, questionnaires, and interrogation by the committee all gradually becoming norms. These qualities created a more sophisticated, responsive, in-depth, and greatly improved process and LPO.[192] The creation of a nominating committee contributed both to the democratization of the organization, but could also give the president considerable power. One former Freedom leader had this to say about the nominating committee:

> One of the president's most significant powers is to appoint the nominating committee. Generally speaking, I would draw upon persons who had experience at that level of government to serve on the committee. If the race to be endorsed was the county legislative race, than I was able to draw on former members of the Jackson County legislature. Likewise the City Council races, you draw upon people who have served on the City Council. The size and composition of the committee are within the prerogative of the president. They make a recommendation [to the full Board]. Appointing the committee, the president has the potential for a lot of influence in what that recommendation looks like.[193]

Changes to the leadership and substantive reforms to the LPO's structures appeased many of the internal critics. Watkins, in particular, used his considerable charisma to convince disgruntled activists that Freedom's mission remained as important as ever and that he would personally ensure a new dispensation. Reform did not heal the breach with Hughes and his People In Politics coterie; the new judge was convinced that he possessed a constituency, was certain that Freedom was dying on the vine, and was thoroughly enjoying his time in the limelight. Hughes himself refrained from overt involvement with the organization after he took office, pleading the necessity of judicial neutrality, but remained supportive of his creation and stocked it with loyalists. As the 1979 municipal elections approached, one of the most urgent questions in political circles was whether the Hughes forces would fight those elections with Freedom, or against them. Irrespective of what other LPOs would do in 1979, Freedom emerged from 1978's internal power struggle as a more democratic and accountable organization. Since Freedom's power relied upon its ability to convince black voters that its candidates were the ones that would best advance their interests, a more democratic, accountable, and mass-oriented organization also meant a stronger and more effective one.

Testing the Limits of Balance of Power Politics: The 1979 Municipal Elections

Freedom would require all the strength and effectiveness it could muster, for the 1979 municipal elections proved to be the most hard-fought in local history. Observers unanimously agreed that the results would shape Kansas City's fate for the coming decade. Black Kansas Citians saw them as particularly important, since Bruce Watkins made it clear that he would wage the first campaign by an African American for the mayor's office. Other races were also important to Freedom, including the first serious challenge to Charles Hazley, Emanuel Cleaver's second bid for the council, and bargaining with white allies over other positions on the council. Freedom emerged from 1979 paradoxically weakened and strengthened. It succeeded once again in electing a council majority and decisively defeated the upstart People In Politics group on its home turf, but the overwhelming defeat of Watkins demonstrated the limitations of balance of power politics and the persistence of white supremacy.

The Bruce Watkins Campaign

Bruce Watkins's campaign for mayor was unquestionably the most important one Freedom had ever sponsored. The campaign was perceived to be a proxy for Freedom's potency in the black community, a Watkins win promised to take "black power" to an entirely new level, there was high enthusiasm and optimism among African Americans over the potential for progress, and a belief existed that a black mayor would succeed in addressing pressing issues facing African Americans and low-income residents. Most important, the campaign would be used to test the limits of balance of power politics. In the past, black voting power had been used to add to the inadequate strength of white allies in exchange for something. Now, Freedom sought to attempt to use its voting power to take the leading, not supporting, role, compelling its would-be allies to support a black candidate for mayor in exchange for Freedom's support in down-ballot races.

Watkins began talking about running for mayor shortly after his return to the city council in 1975, but did not announce his candidacy until the summer of 1978, the very same week in which he returned to the presidency of Freedom.[194] Watkins had long coveted the mayor's office, but many black Kansas Citians firmly believed that the time had come for the city to elect an African American mayor. Other cities in its size class, including Atlanta, Cleveland, and New Orleans, had all achieved this milestone. Moreover, African Americans in political milieus were increasingly frustrated by continuing inaction by white allies on some of the community's top priorities, like the conduct of the KCPD. While cognizant of the fact that a fully race-conscious mayoralty could not be achieved, activists did feel that an African American mayor could yield tangible benefits for the black community. If the time was indeed ripe for a black mayor, Watkins was the natural candidate. He was well liked and respected by all sectors of the African American community as well as by white liberals, was a successful businessman, and had experience in government. No other African American in the city possessed the same high profile, stellar reputation, experience, and charisma. No other African American leader in the city possessed Watkins's national reputation. He was frequently called upon to appear across the country on panels about the "new black politics."[195] Watkins's national reputation was affirmed once more when his campaign launch featured Detroit Mayor Coleman Young as a special guest.[196]

Watkins was taken seriously because it was presumed that he would command the overwhelming majority of the black vote, but Freedom's internal turmoil suggested to some that his margins among African Americans would not be substantial enough to carry him past the primary. A tough race was expected, because the mayoral field was crowded with high-profile candidates. Charles Wheeler opted to try and make history by seeking an unprecedented third term in office. Wheeler's second term lacked the achievements of his first and seemed to validate criticisms of the mayor as erratic. The most notable aspects of his second four years in office were a lethal illegal fireman's strike which was prolonged by Wheeler's intransigence, a half-hearted bid for the Senate, and a quixotic campaign for the 1976 Democratic vice presidential nomination that made the mayor a national laughingstock. Capitalizing on Wheeler's unpopularity to mount their own campaigns were the two city councilmen from the prosperous Fourth District: Richard Berkley and Joel Pelofsky. Berkley was the district councilman for the southwest corridor, a wealthy executive in his family's Tension Envelope Corporation (one of the world's largest manufacturers of envelopes), and a former chairman of the Missouri Republican Party. Berkley was known for his affability, his sunny optimism, and for holding hundreds of town hall meetings with his constituents every year. Pelofksy, by contrast, was best known for his acerbic demeanor. The at-large member for the Fourth District, Pelofksy was one of the council's most liberal members and the favorite of some unions.[197] Pelofsky and Wheeler had both been championed by Freedom in the past, resulting in some idle media speculation that they might attract an appreciable level of African American support.

If Watkins had not entered the race, Freedom would have faced a difficult decision in its endorsement. Such speculation aside, there was never the least bit of doubt that Watkins would be Freedom's candidate for mayor. Freedom made its own public announcement of support for Watkins shortly after the New Year, although it still went through the formalities of bringing the other candidates before the screening committee. This was the right thing to do from a process perspective, but also afforded the LPO an opportunity to evaluate the other candidates in the event that Watkins failed to advance to the general election. Berkley was anathema because of his Republicanism. Pelofsky was too cerebral and confrontational, such that he was not regarded as particularly effective, though his positions were in alignment with Freedom. Wheeler's luster had worn off because of his increasingly erratic behavior and because he no longer was a reliable supporter of black interests. In his second term, Wheeler became more unreliable by the day in battles over the police department, spending federal money earmarked for high-poverty areas, and appointive office, including defending an all-white panel of nominees for municipal judge that resulted in the court having no black members for the first time in a quarter of a century.[198] It was no coincidence that Wheeler distanced himself from his erstwhile allies in the black community at precisely the same time that Watkins's candidacy became more certain; the mayor became ever more blatant in criticizing the organization by name.[199] There can be no doubt that Wheeler sought to compensate for a predicted loss of African American support to Watkins by cozying up to white voters.

Of course, Watkins's support among African Americans extended beyond the activist confines of Freedom, Inc. Even with his decades of relationships and life in the public eye, the funeral home owner and councilman spent the two years preceding the municipal elections cementing his relationships with different elements within the African American community. He well knew that unity would be essential if he were to have the slightest hope of victory. African American business elites were cultivated, with Ollie Gates (owner of the largest black-owned business in Kansas City, Gates and Sons Barbecue) serving as the campaign treasurer and charged with reaching out to his fellow entrepreneurs. Clergy support was solicited early and religious leaders were given an important role in mobilizing voters; nearly every African American minister of any prominence publicly endorsed the Watkins campaign.[200] One unit of the campaign committee did nothing but mobilize younger African Americans, stressing the historic nature and race-conscious qualities of the Watkins campaign, in the hopes that convincing these typical nonvoters to turn out on primary day would boost the candidate's chances. A number of profession-specific support groups organizing lawyers, teachers, and beauticians, among others, were also created. Any tension that might have once existed with *The Call* evaporated, with the paper giving enormous amounts of column space to a multi-part biographical series on Watkins and a regular "Keeping Up With Watkins" feature.[201] All seemed to be swept up in the possibility that Watkins might actually win. Indeed, the only publicly expressed dissent of any consequence among African Americans came from black Republicans and those associated with People In Politics. The latter never publicly opposed Watkins, but were decidedly ambivalent about his ambitions and, it was claimed, entered into a tacit alliance with the Berkley forces.[202] Both sets of dissidents possessed the good sense to realize that Watkins's candidacy was wildly popular among African Americans and was energizing the community; they thus refrained from publicly mobilizing against Watkins himself.

Freedom was not the only LPO whose endorsement was determined, informally at least, well in advance of the official process. Three of the four major candidates (Berkley, Pelofsky, and Watkins) had ties to the CA, whose endorsement was still sought even after its humiliation four years earlier, but none were as strong as those held by Berkley. The CA remained strongest in the Fourth District, Berkley's home territory, and his personal profile as a community-minded business executive corresponded perfectly with the organization's traditional preferences. Although some concern was expressed about nominating a Republican for mayor in a Democratic city—after all, the last Republican business executive nominated by the CA was Dutton Brookfield, whose campaign was not a smashing success—Berkley's personal charm, deep ties to the city's elites, and support from some leading Democrats (including the mortgage banker/political moneyman James B. Nutter and the political consultants Jerry Jette and Pat Gray) assuaged these doubts.[203] As though Berkley's long-standing status as a favorite of the CA was not enough, the CA's membership had serious qualms about the other individuals in the race. Pelofsky was too liberal, too confrontational, and regarded as unwilling to engage in the behind-the-scenes compromise that characterized local politics. Wheeler was a nonstarter because of his long-troubled relationship with the CA. Freedom, and Watkins by extension, never reconciled with the CA after their 1975 dispute; indeed, if anything, the antagonism between the two groups hardened. Several of the CA's African American members were also associated with People In Politics, and this set conspired to deny Watkins whatever slim hope he might have held of receiving the reform group's blessing.[204] To the surprise of no one except an unduly optimistic subset of Watkins boosters, Berkley was named to lead the CA ticket in 1979.[205] Other endorsements were distributed amongst the candidates, with Berkley receiving the support of most business groups and executives, Wheeler allies reactivating the dormant Democrats for Progress, and Pelofksy garnering union backing. The net effect of these fragmented endorsements was to create uncertainty about what the general election field would look like, with all four candidates able to present credible arguments for their advancement. In the face of this uncertainty, the *Star* refrained from making an endorsement in the primary, though it did print a glowing statement of appreciation for Wheeler.[206] This is not to say that the paper remained neutral; while Berkley, Pelofsky, and Wheeler received frequent coverage, Watkins rarely received so much as a mention except when he appeared at all-candidate events.

As had become typical of municipal elections, there was little distinction in the policy positions of the candidates. Wheeler insisted that it was the job of the challengers to raise issues and his task to defend his record. By now disillusioned with the mayor and finding the alternatives credible, the press did not acquiesce to this absurd position as it had four years earlier. More important, the three challengers brought forth the mayor's weaknesses, with a vengeance. But beyond this, the campaign was fought on matters of style and image. Wheeler was cast as the buffoonish showman, Berkley as the consensus-seeking technocrat, and Pelofsky as the increasingly out-of-fashion liberal crusader. Watkins was simply the "black candidate," although some of his opponents initiated a whisper campaign to label him a subservient tool of the Democratic Party factions. Watkins had served as a party functionary, including a tenure as Jackson County Democratic chairman, but the charge of subservience to the factions rang false.[207]

During the primary campaign, Watkins saw little reason to attempt to slough off the "black candidate" label. Instead, his strategy was to maximize his showing among African American voters in order to win the primary, something that required a race-conscious campaign and mass mobilization. While never trading in racially chauvinist or nationalist rhetoric, Watkins did wage a race-conscious effort. His primary campaign was essentially handed over in its entirety to Freedom to operate, putting heavy emphasis on using the sophisticated campaign machinery the LPO had constructed to make multiple direct contacts with voters in black-majority precincts. The Watkins campaign also placed great stock in the efforts of clergy, young people, and its cheerleaders in the black press. None of these efforts could be successful, certainly not in the crucial area of boosting black voter turnout to parity with white turnout, unless Watkins had something of substance to say to African American voters. He did. Stressing his lengthy public record, Watkins built his bid around pledges to meaningfully address crime while devoting more city attention to the aged and the poor. These pledges were not racially specific, but they spoke powerfully to the issues of most concern to black voters. Moreover, Watkins and Freedom printed numerous newspaper advertisements imploring African Americans to fight for "Bruce," just as he had fought for them. Even with this effort, there were some who alleged that Watkins was spending more time courting white voters than black ones. *The Call* chastised this sentiment, blasting it as false and politically naïve.[208]

African American unity, the diligence of Freedom activists, and Watkins's cunning strategy combined to produce a primary victory for "the black candidate." That Watkins earned nearly 24,000 votes (27 percent), placed first in the primary, and ran ahead of his nearest competitor by more than a thousand votes came as a great shock to the white political cognoscenti, who expected Watkins to, at best, place second.[209] Watkins and his supporters were heartened by the fact that he would face Richard Berkley, the second-place finisher, in the general election. Berkley's history of deep involvement in Republican politics was presumed to be a major impediment to his chances in the overwhelmingly Democratic city, one that Wheeler and Pelofsky (who placed third and fourth, respectively) would not have faced.

Just one month separated the primary and general elections, and Watkins was forced to scramble during this period in order to compensate for the strategy he adopted during the primary. By focusing almost exclusively on mobilizing the black vote in that race, Watkins lagged far behind Berkley in building an infrastructure in other parts of the city, particularly the vote-rich Fourth District. Despite the short timeframe, Watkins set about building a campaign infrastructure in other parts of the city. For the first time in history, neither mayoral candidate would possess a truly citywide infrastructure; Berkley understandably exerted little effort in the Freedom wards while Watkins ignored the more conservative Northland. To construct his political infrastructure and reach voters outside of the Freedom heartland, Watkins relied on allies within the Democratic Party. After the defeat of their initially favored candidates, DFP, most labor unions, and even the factions shifted their support to Watkins.[210] Defeated primary candidates Wheeler and Pelofsky, too, rallied to Watkins's side.

In the absence of much actual disagreement on municipal issues, this caused the general election to take on a partisan tone, at least where Watkins was concerned. He hammered Berkley again and again for his Republican ties, arguing that to elect a Republican as mayor would place Democrats at a disadvantage going into the 1980 presidential elections, and for what he called Berkley's "anti-labor" positions.[211] Many argue that Watkins took the partisan argument too far, such that it began to backfire. In the waning days of the campaign, he succeeded in bringing then-Vice President Walter Mondale to Kansas City to stump on his behalf. The visit was initially heralded as a major coup for Watkins, but the Berkley campaign capitalized on the visit as an attempt by outsiders to dictate the outcome of the election, as a waste of money (security costs for the visit were borne by the city), and on the growing unpopularity of the Carter administration.[212] Three decades after the election, insiders in both campaigns pointed to the Mondale visit as the biggest mistake made by either candidate in the race.[213]

Berkley and his team emphasized the candidate's relative moderation and the nonpartisan character of the race. They countered Watkins's attacks by accusing him, not entirely unfairly, though with a false naïveté, of violating the spirit of the charter by converting the race into a partisan one; they knew full well that Berkley would lose if the contest became one about partisan affiliation. As much as possible, they sought to maintain the focus on Berkley as an affable, consensus-building, and can-do candidate. But the Berkley campaign had no compunction about attacking Watkins, particularly his service as Jackson County circuit clerk, where it was alleged that he was spendthrift. Surprisingly, the *Star* did not serve as a cheering section for Berkley in these attacks. Normally among the first to bemoan the introduction of partisanship into the city election as the first step of creeping Pendergastism and a reliable ally of the CA, the daily newspaper endorsed Watkins, albeit tepidly.[214]

The Watkins camp was content with even a milquetoast endorsement by the *Star,* feeling that it would be sufficient to secure the 35 percent of the white vote he would need to win. Only a relatively low share of the white vote was required, because Freedom's efforts within the black community were redoubled. African Americans were genuinely excited about Watkins and mobilized by his campaign, as demonstrated by the high rate of participation in the voter registration efforts Freedom initiated. The Freedom campaign team was *not* taking black voters the least bit for granted but instead taking elaborate steps to make multiple contacts with every potential black voter. A veritable army of volunteers was recruited to canvass African American neighborhoods for "Bruce," a coordinated effort was made for clergy to exhort their congregations to vote for Watkins, and tens of thousands of pieces of literature were distributed highlighting the historic nature of the candidacy as well as the Watkins message. To his credit, Watkins made the same promises to black audiences as he did to white ones: that he would crack down on crime (targeting the "punks" who caused trouble) without cracking heads the way the KCPD did, to spend more funds on neighborhoods, to do more to care for the aged, and expand opportunity for the poor.

One other theme was frequently, if implicitly, present in the Watkins/Freedom interactions with black potential voters: the necessity for high black voter turnout to compensate for anticipated white racism. To his lasting credit, Dick Berkley did not go the route that so many other white candidates facing their city's first major African American candidate for mayor did. Unlike Sam Yorty or Seth Taft or Sam Massell, Berkley did not employ racist or even racial language. There were a few oblique references to opposing school busing and the criticisms of Watkins's tenure at the county, both of which some African Americans felt had racial overtones, but these blanched in comparison to the rhetoric employed in other cities. Of course, given the gargantuan fundraising advantage that Berkley held over Watkins—made possible by Berkley's many close friends in the corporate elite and a generous infusion of his own personal fortune—the former had many reasons to feel confident about his prospects.[215]

Just because the opposition did not engage in race-baiting did not mean that racism was absent from the campaign. When asked directly by the press, Watkins always denied that he believed that white racism would hinder him from winning the mayor's office. Even privately, Watkins apparently felt that there were enough whites, barely, who would be more motivated by partisanship than bigotry to send him to the 29th floor of City Hall. Strategists for the campaign believed that the interracial alliances provided by the endorsements of the *Star,* the factions, and the unions would be sufficient to carry Watkins to victory. This optimism was badly misplaced, as even Watkins conceded on election night.[216] One longtime political insider who worked the 1979 Watkins campaign remembered:

> I knew that we were losing when I went with Ronnie DePasco [a longtime white politician from the North End—ed.] to some little hole-in-the-wall bars and heard guys say stuff like, "Ronnie, I'm not putting in my crops." He called them crops, talking about his garden, because it was spring by then and people were planting gardens. And Ronnie asked him why, and he'd say, "Because if that n——wins, I'm moving."[217]

One longtime resident of the urban core recalled that the racial environment became quite tense, even "nasty," during this period, despite the absence of any overtly racist language emanating from the candidates.[218] Many speculated that the leadership of labor unions and the factions were unenthusiastic about the candidate and so failed to campaign for him, especially in ways that would have mitigated any racism that might have existed among their memberships.

Freedom's volunteer-staffed, hard-working, and enthusiastic mobilization effort among black voters proved incredibly successful. The LPO managed to turn out African American voters and to convince them to pull the lever for Bruce Watkins as their champion. In the six Freedom wards, the LPO's mayoral candidate accumulated 27,949 votes (89 percent). The Freedom wards also had uniformly high turnout, with every ward registering higher voter turnout than every single non-Freedom ward in the city. Indeed, the 14th ward—Freedom's traditional heartland—saw voter turnout reach the stunningly high figure of 71 percent (see Table 5). Unfortunately for Watkins, white voter turnout was also unusually high, if not to the level seen in the Freedom wards, and whites were hostile to his candidacy. Overall, more votes were cast in 1979 than in any city election since the "clean up campaign" of 1942. Watkins received just 52,796 total votes while Berkley received 73,358 votes, allowing Berkley to become the city's first Jewish mayor. Despite the endorsement of nearly every Democratic

Table 5. 1979 Mayoral Election Results in
Predominantly African American Wards

Ward	Richard Berkley (%)	Bruce Watkins, Sr. (%)	Turnout %
2	405 (10%)	3,697 (90%)	63.6%
3	415 (8.4%)	4,513 (91.6%)	63.4%
14	123 (2.4%)	5,078 (97.6%)	71.8%
16	221 (3.8%)	5,549 (96.2%)	69.0%
17	898 (15.5%)	4,911 (84.5%)	66.8%
18	1,388 (24.8%)	4,201 (75.2%)	61.0%
Total in Predominantly African American Wards	3,450 (11%)	27,949 (89%)	65.8%
Total Citywide	73,356 (58.1%)	52,796 (41.9%)	57.2%

Source: Kansas City Times – March 28, 1979

organization in Kansas City, white Democrats abandoned Watkins en masse. The first major African American candidate for mayor of Kansas City received perhaps a quarter of the white vote, far short of the 35 percent required.[219] Watkins and his campaign team were devastated, many of them coming to the belated realization that race had proven fatal to the respected and popular councilman's bid.[220] Freedom activists analyzed the outcome and determined that "what went wrong for Bruce was that he was African American."[221] As one activist who was close with the Watkins family said, "Most [African American] people felt that he had earned the right, if you can say right, to be mayor. And that it wasn't his lack of qualifications to be mayor but the fact that he was black, that he did not get to be mayor. And there was a lot of resentment over that."[222]

Reasserting Freedom's Position in Black Majority Districts

For all its failures, the Watkins campaign was not fruitless. Instead, it was essential in turning back the threat posed to Freedom in the two black-majority districts by People In Politics. Neither of the two at-large council members for these districts, Joanne Collins and Leon Brownfield, both of whom we encountered earlier as Freedom antagonists, faced serious challengers, because Freedom determined that neither could be beaten.[223] The in-district races were altogether different, with Charles Hazley in the Third District facing the most pressure.

Hazley sought a third term on the council, running on his record as a savvy negotiator and backroom operator.[224] Never noted for his oratory, in his second term, Hazley became a force to be reckoned with at City Hall. When others balked at taking steps favored by the black community and/or Freedom, Hazley had a knack for finding the perfect pressure point; he would cannily withdraw his support from even the most major of projects until some concession was made to what he perceived to be African American interests. Quite predictably, this approach irked some of Hazley's colleagues as well as those whose pet projects were put on hold until the bargain was struck.

Hazley was also unpopular with a segment of the African American population, mainly those who departed Freedom to form People In Politics, owing to his tenure as Freedom chairman. People In Politics recruited its young president, assistant city prosecutor Clinton Adams, to run against Hazley. In a clear example of the deep ties Freedom had to even those segments of the community that opposed it, Adams held his job with the city only because Hazley and Watkins had intervened on his behalf when his supervisors attempted to discharge him. The outspoken attorney nonetheless campaigned hard against Hazley. He attempted to wage a campaign from a left and nationalist flank, accusing Hazley of selling out black interests. Unlike the mayoral race, the Hazley-Adams contest was conducted in the realm of issues. Perhaps the most important and recurring issue was Hazley's support of municipal approval and subsidies for Kensington Place, a housing development that catered to a middle-class and affluent clientele, to be constructed in a deeply impoverished neighborhood of the Third District. Hazley argued that revitalization of the urban core would be possible only if the flight of the African American middle class was staved, which in turn was possible only if suitable housing was available. Adams charged that the expenditure of city funds in support of the project was a give-away to the privileged class and that Hazley had forgotten poor and working-class African Americans.[225] Although there was some merit in the arguments of both candidates, it was unfair of Adams to paint Kensington Place as the centerpiece of Hazley's legislative record. The incumbent councilman had supported and pressed for numerous other initiatives that primarily benefitted less prosperous Third District residents.[226]

Despite the fact that he campaigned against Hazley from the left and in nationalist fashion, Adams garnered support from the CA and most white political elites. Since these groups were in conflict with Freedom, backing Adams had more to do with their enmity toward the LPO than any great love for the young lawyer.[227] Of course, the endorsement of the CA and other white elites were of little help in the black majority Third District. Adams's most significant supporters came from within the People In Politics group, including Judge Hughes. In the opening salvo of the campaign, Adams also succeeded in luring Lee Vertis Swinton—former president of the local NAACP, unsuccessful candidate for council in 1963, county legislator, and then a Freedom stalwart (such that the "women of Freedom" even recommended him for president of the LPO)—as his campaign treasurer. Adams worked in the same law firm as Swinton and had a personal friendship with the man, but the latter's departure from the Freedom fold still came as something of a shock.[228]

With the CA, white corporate leaders (and campaign financiers), and People In Politics lined up against him, Hazley could rely only on his own legislative record, some limited labor support, and Freedom's political infrastructure. As part of the coordinated Freedom campaign, the volunteers who blanketed the Third District for Watkins rendered the same service for Hazley. The Hazley-Adams race was the first real opportunity to test the influence of People In Politics and to discern whether their claims that Freedom was decaying were true. If People In Politics was to be believed, Freedom had lost the credibility that was the basis of its support from African American voters. Unfortunately for Adams and People In Politics, their claims proved to be vastly overinflated. On election day, many Third District voters refused to so much as accept a copy of the People In Politics sample ballot, opting instead for the traditional black and gold Freedom ballot instead. Hazley crushed Adams, winning 10,491 votes (70 percent) to the upstart's 4,498 votes (30 percent).[229] Although Adams and People In Politics hurt themselves with black voters because of their ambivalence over the Watkins mayoral candidacy, the real basis of Hazley's overwhelming victory was his strong identification with Freedom and his record of service. Defeat did not chasten Clinton Adams, nor did it put an end to his activism. He turned his sights to the school district instead, where he would prove to be a controversial but effective voice for African American students. In the process, he became unpopular with the same white elites who supported his candidacy in 1979.

A dissimilar battle played out in the Fifth District. Since Bruce Watkins won the in-district council seat in 1975, population shifts had turned the district into one with an unambiguous African American majority. The Rev. Emanuel Cleaver, who sought the office in 1975 as a "loud-mouthed radical" who found the political pragmatism of Freedom distasteful, again contested the seat. This time, though, he dispensed with the flamboyant wardrobe, was no longer closely associated with SCLC, expressed confidence in the political system rather than a Christian revolutionary movement, and, most importantly, made his peace with Freedom. Reconciliation flowed in both directions and was predicated on pragmatic grounds. Cleaver had learned that his desire for political office and the power to make social change that the office conferred was unlikely to be sated unless he came to a suitable understanding with the political system broadly and Freedom in particular. Freedom saw in Cleaver a charismatic and intelligent potential leader, one who shared a commitment to the same interests as the LPO. Cleaver had already proven his persistence and that he had a constituency; unless he was brought into the Freedom fold, he had the potential to be a consistent irritant. Since the long-standing distance placed between Freedom and Cleaver originated in style and personality rather than substance, it made more sense to join forces. They did precisely that, with Cleaver selected over several other African American candidates by the Freedom screening committee early in the 1979 campaign cycle. Cleaver was an enthusiastic supporter of the entire 1979 Freedom ticket, including Watkins.[230]

In the primary, Cleaver sailed ahead of several black and white challengers. In the general election, his challenger was a white candidate, Bill Richardson. Richardson was a labor leader who hoped that African American turnout would be depressed enough to make a Cleaver victory impossible and who Cleaver charged with repeatedly using racist tactics.[231] In order to retain its credibility as a political force in the Fifth District, Freedom needed to convince African American voters that Cleaver would defend their interests and then ensure those voters turned out on election day. If Cleaver were to lose in the Fifth District, it would be interpreted by insiders as a sign that Watkins won four years earlier only because of his personal popularity and as a mark of Freedom's impotence in the district.

Cleaver and Freedom succeeded in this mission by focusing on neighborhood issues of concern to the African American majority, channeling the minister's considerable charisma, and coordinating a massive grass-roots voter contact effort. Like Hazley, Cleaver was aided by the palpable enthusiasm felt in black communities for Watkins, which stimulated turnout. Cleaver finally won elective office, defeating Richardson by the comfortable margin of 11,758 votes (58 percent) to 8,380 votes (42 percent).[232] In later years it would be argued by some that Cleaver attained political success purely through his charm and way with words. Such a claim is belied by the facts. Without the infrastructure and credibility conferred by Freedom, Cleaver's political campaigns, which relied only on his oratory and personal magnetism, were failures. Once the Cleaver persona was wedded with Freedom's organization, success was obtained.

Pragmatism in Other City Council Campaigns

Even a highly effective and motivated black LPO could accomplish precious little in a city where African Americans comprise just 30 percent of the population if it lacked nonblack allies. Nearly every major candidate for city council actively sought Freedom's endorsement. Freedom had earned credibility and respect, albeit of the grudging variety, from white politicos, otherwise this sort of courting would not have taken place. But Freedom remained committed to its balance of power approach, and so would only endorse candidates in races where there were an appreciable number of black votes to be influenced. In the primary, outside of the black-majority districts, Freedom opted to endorse candidates in only two districts.

But during the general election, the LPO took an entirely different tack. In order to cement the support (worthless though it ultimately proved to be) of unions and Democratic leaders for Watkins, Freedom bargained with those groups to drop from its ballot all of the candidates it had endorsed in districts without black majorities. The candidates it had previously endorsed were all opposed by the unions and Democratic leaders, white, and considered by Freedom to represent diversions of scarce resources. The official Freedom ballot would feature only Watkins, Hazley, Icelean Clark (in the Third District At-Large race), and Cleaver. In hindsight, one can question the wisdom of this bargain but at the time it seemed to be a sensible thing to do. However, this bargain led to one of the election's most controversial incidents. On election day, an anonymous ballot that bore some resemblance to the official Freedom ballot (and used the word Freedom) but featured the dropped candidates was distributed at some urban core polling places. Freedom leaders insisted that they were the victims of mischief. Some observers, including the daily press, suggested none too subtly that the phony ballot was distributed because the opponents of the dropped candidates had not paid Freedom an endorsement fee, ignoring the logical gap in this sequence: that Freedom had not endorsed the "betrayed" candidates *or* their opponents who were dropped from the general election ballot.[233] No evidence ever emerged that Freedom was involved in the distribution of the phony ballot, much less that it was distributed because a payoff was not made. Nevertheless, the incident marred Freedom's relationship with the three "betrayed" candidates, all of whom won election despite the supposed treachery, and served as another example of the increasingly harsh and cynical view which political insiders and the press adopted about Freedom.

Effects of the 1979 Municipal Election

The 1979 elections were thus a mixed bag for Freedom, Inc. Although there were some successes for the organization, there can be little doubt that the LPO's members were generally depressed about the results and felt that the election had been their least successful involvement in municipal politics to date. Pessimism on this scale was not in order. Together, the Hazley and Cleaver victories demonstrated that Freedom remained the trusted political voice of a majority of the African American residents of the Third and Fifth Districts. Their elections proved the rebuke of Holliday in 1978 to be anomalous, rather than the first salvo in Freedom's disintegration. Instead, the 1979 elections led to the disintegration of People In Politics. From an auspicious beginning in 1978, the upstart LPO had departed from the scene by the time of the 1983 municipal elections. African American voters expressed their confidence in Freedom's credibility, candidates, leadership, and policy solutions, utterly disproving the claims made by the dissidents. While the organization remained far from perfect, the resounding victories given to Watkins, Hazley, and Cleaver by African American voters demonstrated that Freedom remained the primary political voice of the black community and the crucial actor in pressing for black interests in local government. Moreover, despite the victory of its own mayoral candidate, the CA did not reclaim its once-preeminent place in local politics. The organization was not considered a factor in Berkley's victory; the new mayor's success was attributed to his charm, financial advantage, and the existence of racism. The CA's endorsement was an afterthought in this equation. Even in defeat, Freedom remained the city's most important LPO.

Some degree of pessimism was in order, given the thumping that Watkins received. At first, Watkins's loss was tragic to Freedom's members because it meant someone that they loved and cared about suffered an ignominious defeat. But much more was at stake—and lost—than the political career of Bruce Watkins. For the first time since its founding, Freedom would be excluded from the new mayor's coalition. Watkins's loss demonstrated two limitations of the balance of power strategy. First, it relied on division among white voters. Where no such division was present, and white voters cast their ballots almost uniformly, Freedom could not be instrumental in victory. Second, white racism was still ingrained in the community's psyche. When African Americans took the leading role in a political battle, the battle became racialized, and no amount of interracial bargaining would to attract white voter support. Freedom's ambitious plan to use balance of power politics to lift itself to power was thus unsuccessful in 1979. The loss was particularly devastating in that Bruce Watkins would pass away from cancer a little more than a year later; his frequent exhaustion on the campaign trail, which had been chalked up to a grueling pace, had been something much more serious.[234]

Even with this sad ending to the decade, the 1970s saw Freedom make an enormous leap forward in its efficacy as an organization. This enhancement in its organizational power is attributable to the LPO becoming fully institutionalized, effectively mobilizing the black community, and engaging in strategic short-term bargaining with nonblack political forces. For most of the decade, the LPO also successfully positioned itself as the corporatist, organizational voice of the black community, even as there were multiple individual detractors from this position, inside and outside of the community. This enhancement in Freedom's stature resulted in significant gains on policy issues important to the black community. Although success was not guaranteed and there were failures, particularly where the KCPD was concerned, black demands on the system were more likely to be satisfied than ever before.

CHAPTER 4

In and Out of the Wilderness
Freedom, Inc. in the Berkley Years
(1979–1991)

Freedom exited the 1970s paradoxically stronger and weaker. The LPO's ability to mobilize African American voters had never been so great, but due to the failure of the Watkins candidacy the LPO found itself more excluded from the corridors of power than at any time since its founding. Freedom survived this wilderness period by focusing its energies outside of the municipal arena, acting pragmatically to restore broken alliances, capitalizing on the personal popularity of its elected officials, and tapping into the reservoirs of trust and credibility it had spent two decades accumulating among its black mass base.

By the end of the decade, though, it was clear that Freedom was not the same organization it had once been. This was especially true in the policy arena, where the LPO withdrew from the policy-making process in favor of maximizing the operational independence of individual elected officials. Decline was also visible in Freedom's vaunted electoral politics apparatus, with the organization suffering a handful of high-profile defeats within the black community, experiencing atrophy in its volunteer base, and no longer able to mobilize black voters in the way it once did. These changes are attributable to the organization's loss of credibility with some African Americans and to the LPO's remaking of itself, shunting its erstwhile emphasis on mass mobilization and a mass base aside in favor of a more professionalized and narrow approach.

In the Wilderness: Freedom's Exclusion from
Municipal Power, 1980–1986

In the immediate aftermath of the failed effort for Bruce Watkins, there were precious few who thought that Freedom's time had passed. The organization's strength in neighborhoods with African American majorities was undeniable, even if some observers did begin to question whether Freedom's organizing model and political strategies were capable of producing the same benefits they had in the past. There was recognition within Freedom that change was in order, as the scope of the LPO's exclusion from municipal power became clear. One of Berkley's very first actions was to name Lee Vertis Swinton to the prestigious Parks Board; since Swinton had publicly broken with Freedom earlier in the year, the move was widely interpreted as a swipe at the black LPO.[1] Berkley later proved himself to be a magnanimous victor by appointing Watkins to the Parks Board after Swinton had to resign the post to run for elective office.[2] Before that gesture, though, Berkley made it clear that he would reward his friends and punish his enemies. Despite entreaties from *The Call* and a group of black ministers to retain Charles Hazley in his powerful post as chairman of Planning and Zoning, Berkley removed Hazley as the committee's chair and installed him instead as chair of the newly created and meaningless Education Committee.[3] While these moves were entirely consistent with the normal practice of electoral victors, they nonetheless antagonized Freedom and infuriated Hazley, who would become one of the mayor's most relentless critics.[4] Berkley's leadership style was to seek consensus among his council colleagues. This approach made it impossible for Berkley to fully exclude Freedom—nor did he want to do so—but there was never any doubt that Freedom could not expect any favors from the mayor's office. Moreover, unjustly tarnished with the reputation of political impotence, Freedom's blessing was no longer as actively sought-after as it had been just a few months earlier. Berkley and civic elites allied with him refused to involve Cleaver, Hazley, or Freedom in the planning of or campaign for a major 1981 sales tax program to fund infrastructure; when the plan was presented for a public vote it failed for lack of African American support.[5]

The onus of restoring Freedom to its glory days fell to the LPO's newly elected leadership. In 1979, Watkins and Holliday ceded their positions to a younger generation of leaders. In 1980, Watkins was replaced as president by 38-year-old Phil Curls, a well-liked and savvy political operator first elected to the state House of Representatives on the Freedom ballot in 1972. Holliday's replacement as chairman of the board was Cleaver, then just 36 years old.[6] This continued the tradition of Freedom's leadership being supplied by current elected officials, with the president's and chair's offices divided between two different levels of government. The Curls-Cleaver team's immediate charges were to prepare for upcoming biennial partisan elections and to develop a strategy for coping with the new reality at City Hall. They succeeded famously at the former but had less luck with the latter.

Focusing on Non-Municipal Politics

In politics, the surest way to avoid the dreaded tag of "loser" is to stop losing. Tagged as a "loser" because of Watkins's poor 1979 showing, Freedom felt compelled to move quickly to reassert its political strength. With the next municipal elections still fours year off—and the other levels of government equally as important to its operations and mission (though not the focus of this book)—Freedom opted to concentrate its limited resources on winning battles at the county, state, and federal levels rather than flailing against the Berkley administration.

Unbridled by the structural realities of local politics, like at-large elections that were unfavorable to black candidates, Freedom achieved considerable success with this strategy. In 1980, Freedom succeeded in boosting its influence in the county and state legislatures. One of its most high-profile victories came in a state senate race. Lee Vertis Swinton, last encountered as a Freedom antagonist through his support for Clinton Adams, reconciled with Freedom yet again. Facing incumbent white senator Mary Gant in the Democratic primary, Freedom's support for Swinton in the multicandidate race was the crucial element in the former NAACP president and county legislator's victory. Swinton became the first African American state senator from the Kansas City area.[7] Freedom also turned back a challenge to one of its incumbents and increased the size of the black delegation to the state House by three; the three new state House seats were won when Freedom candidates defeated white and Latino incumbents.[8]

More important, political observers of all stripes were impressed by the organization—and had its importance impressed upon them—during the 1982 congressional race. In that year, Freedom secured its greatest triumph to date by sending an African American, Alan Wheat, to represent Missouri's Fifth District in Congress. African Americans comprised just a fifth of the district's population, making Wheat only the second modern black congressman (after Ronald Dellums of Oakland) to represent a white majority district. Rep. Richard Bolling retired after 34 years of service, setting off a mad scramble for his seat. Eight candidates entered the Democratic primary. Several African Americans expressed interest in running for the seat, but Freedom's early intervention on his behalf ensured that Wheat was the lone black candidate. Wheat was just 31 years old, an effective three-term state representative, chairman of the Missouri House's urban affairs committee, and had been deeply involved in Freedom and local politics for a decade.[9] Wheat came to Kansas City as a taxi cab driver, but "walked into [Harold] Holliday [Jr.]'s office and asked him to represent him on [a legal case].

Holliday took a liking to him. He was president of the [Freedom] board at the time, said you ought to run for state representative."[10] Wheat's campaign relied on his strong appeal in the Freedom wards. The near-unanimous support given Wheat in the Freedom wards coupled with a smattering of support from white liberals were enough to propel him to the narrowest of victories during the primary. Wheat had already called his opponent to concede the race when the last batch of precincts delivered him a victory.[11] Those who participated in the campaign recall that attendees at Wheat's election night watch party believed he had lost as the late television news aired. Only a few stragglers still remained at the party as it became clear that Wheat had actually won, but as they celebrated they were rejoined by those who had departed in despair. In the strongly Democratic district, Wheat would go on to win a solid victory over Republican state representative John Sharp. The contest was free of racial rhetoric or excessive rancor, though it was difficult to persuade some Democratic officials to back Wheat.[12] Wheat underperformed compared to other Democrats in the district, suggesting that race was still relevant, but the outcome also implied that in strictly partisan races (unlike the officially nonpartisan municipal races) an African American candidate would not be deserted in droves as Watkins had been. Freedom was credited with having elected a congressman and, in a change of fortunes that demonstrates the swiftness and inherent disloyalty of politics, more than recovered its erstwhile reputation as a force with which to be reckoned.[13]

Victories at the county, state, and federal levels were impressive, but they were made possible as a direct result of a temporary withdrawal from the thrust and parry of municipal politics. Such a strategy was self-evidently one that could not work during the municipal campaign itself, meaning that Freedom was in a quandary in 1983.

The 1983 Campaign

In 1983, Mayor Richard Berkley stood for reelection. Berkley's conciliatory style, sunny disposition, seeming ability to be present at every community function with more than two attendees, and oversight of a number of major development projects all contributed to the incumbent's popularity with Kansas Citians.[14] The mayor's handling of one of the city's most devastating tragedies—the July 1981 collapse of a skywalk at the Hyatt Regency Hotel, which resulted in 114 deaths—added to his appeal.[15] Despite this widespread popularity, Berkley was not universally beloved. Echoing the sentiments expressed about Wheeler eight years earlier, Berkley's critics maintained that he led "from behind" and that his mantra of "seeking consensus" was but justification for milquetoast indecision.[16] Some partisan Democrats remained infuriated that a Republican had captured the city's top office and were convinced that if the mayor faced a semicompetent white Democrat in the general election, Kansas City's normal partisan inclinations would return.[17] Freedom had an abundance of reasons to shower Berkley with disfavor: his defeat of Watkins, his exclusion of Hazley and Cleaver from positions of power, the distance he placed between himself and the organization, and his continuing affiliation with the Republican Party (albeit its moderate wing) during a time when Ronald Reagan's White House was declaring war on a generation of gains won by the civil rights movement.

Politics can be unpredictable, such that Berkley's popularity might have been seriously challenged with the right candidate. The field that emerged did not contain such a candidate. Only two serious challengers filed against Berkley: Joe Serviss, a two-term at-large councilman elected with Freedom support, and former mayor Charles Wheeler. Kansas Citians were less than enthused by these options; Emanuel Cleaver captured the public mood when he told the *Times,* "We have kind of a boring field of candidates."[18] Berkley captured the CA endorsement early while Freedom opted to endorse Serviss in the race. It did so with a visible lack of passion, with the bulk of its endorsement statement devoted to attacking Reaganism and, by extension, Berkley.[19] Serviss was the most tenable of the candidates for Freedom. Berkley was not an option and Wheeler was by then a laughingstock, with the city's politicos referring to him (in homage to the then-newly released film) as "E.T." for his eccentric behavior.[20]

In hindsight, it might have been best had Freedom declined to make an endorsement at all, because Serviss did not wear well on the campaign trail. He aggressively and incessantly attacked Berkley, especially for a scandal related to the issuance of building permits (over which Berkley had no control). This negative campaign was not well received even by the mayor's critics, much less by the Berkley-backing *Star.* Serviss himself would concede after the campaign that his strategy misfired badly, and he often faced accusations, including those in *Star* editorials and cartoons, of behaving childishly.[21]

More seriously for Freedom, the LPO's endorsement was not universally lauded within the black community. Although Freedom itself had been excluded from the governing councils of the Berkley administration, the mayor made some effort to reach out to an alternative set of African American leaders, primarily the clergy. This outreach was not particularly substantive, but it accomplished its purpose of making selected ministers feel respected and included. As a result, one of the largest associations of African American clergy, the Baptist Minister's Union (BMU), endorsed Berkley several days before Freedom made its own choice known. The BMU traditionally, but not always, supported the Freedom ballot. Tellingly, one of the BMU's leaders said the endorsement should be taken as a comment on Freedom, saying, "It means Baptist ministers are independent. That's what it means. We're not obligated to support anyone."[22] The BMU was quickly joined in its endorsement by the African Methodist Episcopal Church Alliance.[23] These moves came as a surprise to Freedom leaders, with the drama playing out in the press. Freedom retaliated by claiming the BMU endorsement was improperly made, reflected the views only of a minority of the membership,[24] or had been purchased.[25]

The entire incident fed into the narrative that division existed within the African American community. Speculation abounded as to the cause of the disagreement. Some averred that the BMU action was a declaration of independence because Freedom had taken the clergy for granted for too long. Others theorized that the Berkley forces paid off the ministers, something that the Berkley campaign and the ministers firmly denied.[26] This interpretation is questionable, since no evidence ever emerged of such a deal. It is also frankly racist, as it was nothing more than a continuation of the long-standing assertion that every political action taken by African American Kansas Citians was driven by corrupt payoffs rather than by black agency. There is no question that the Berkley campaign did provide funds to an ad hoc organization created by the ministers to support the mayor, to pay costs to distribute literature and carry voters to the polls, but that was standard practice for all groups and candidates. Still others insisted that the BMU endorsement was a reaction to the deal Serviss had made with Freedom, where he agreed to provide funds to the LPO for its efforts on his behalf in the black community. These observers failed to understand that this was the typical arrangement by which all of the city's LPOs financed their activities and that the fiscal note was attached only after an endorsement decision was made; these critics wrongly insisted that Freedom's deal with Serviss was corrupt, and that the BMU was only reacting to it. The most likely explanation, though, is simply that the ministers were cultivated by Berkley and were being pragmatic, knowing full well that he would likely win. They were not bound within the same antagonistic framework as Berkley and Freedom.

Freedom could do little to downplay the division, because the organization's membership was not enamored of Serviss (or anyone else). Freedom members were not fond of Berkley, but had little desire to demonize him, hence, the attempts to make the mayoral battle a proxy fight over Ronald Reagan's agenda. The LPO also lacked resources with which to approach the community on behalf of Serviss. Volunteers could not be found in abundance as in prior years, leading to a partial conversion to a model using paid campaign workers.[27] An adequate number of workers could not be paid, literature could not be distributed, and the advertising budget could not be met, because Serviss welched on his deal with Freedom. Although he originally agreed to provide Freedom with $40,000, Serviss wrote only two checks, one for $10,000 and one for $5,000, both of them intended for the primary. The $5,000 check bounced.[28] Aside from the obvious operational problems this created, the bounced check did little to endear Serviss to Freedom.[29]

The net result was that Berkley sailed through the primary, winning more votes than all of his challengers combined. It also helped that he alone of the three candidates had a clear message: That he was "a good man doing a good job."[30] Wheeler's perceived buffoonery was preferred by more voters than Serviss's attacks, eliminating the Freedom candidate from the race. Even more embarrassing for Freedom was the fact that Berkley won even in its traditional bailiwicks, although more narrowly than elsewhere, with Serviss placing second in the Freedom wards.[31] This gave rise to a sentiment that would be oft-repeated in the years to come, namely that the endorsement of the clergy was more important than that of Freedom. This proposition is questionable at best, since the clergy were divided in 1983, and simply wrong at worst, given Freedom's triumph over clergy-backed candidates in the past and in the future. A more accurate statement is that Freedom's influence with black voters was strongest when it operated in a united front with the most high-profile African American clergy or ministerial alliances, and impaired when a united front was not present.

With its original candidate eliminated from the general election, Freedom reluctantly endorsed Wheeler and did little on his behalf. Freedom did organize a news conference on Wheeler's behalf where prominent African American clergy endorsed the Freedom slate and denounced the dissident ministers. The Rev. Charles Briscoe, a former president of the school board, declared, "While this is not an endeavor to rubber stamp Freedom's activity, we in the black community know and will not forget that Freedom Inc. gave to this community a political power and savvy that we did not have before. We will not stand idly by and see this organization discredited."[32] To the surprise of no one, Dick Berkley went on to resoundingly defeat his predecessor in the general election. The incumbent spent lavishly, four years later, he still had over $170,000 in debt from the 1983 campaign,[33] to attain a 59 percent majority.[34] In the general election, the myth that the African American ministers were the real political power in the community was belied. On the strength of the endorsement of Freedom and *The Call*, Wheeler won the eight wards with black majorities. They were the only wards Wheeler won.[35]

One reason that Freedom was ambivalent about the mayor's race was that the bulk of its energies were being exerted in the Fifth District's at-large council race. That race saw a young African American attorney, Mark Bryant, challenge long-time incumbent councilman Leon Brownfield. The Fifth District's population was increasingly African American (by 1983, more than 60 percent of the residents were African American); Brownfield won election in the past through the support of white voters and by using his position as the city's top lobbyist to pressure viable would-be challengers (like Watkins in 1975) out of the race. With Cleaver, Collins (who Freedom endorsed for the first time), and Hazley all facing token opposition, Freedom was excited about the potential for expanding the number of black council members to four, making their number more proportional to the city's black population.[36] Electing a fourth black member would have the added benefit of displacing Brownfield, a thorn in Freedom's side since at least the 1974 appointment of Joanne Collins to the City Council. Freedom actively recruited Bryant into the race. Moreover, Freedom strategists largely coordinated all elements of the Bryant campaign and made his election the LPO's top priority. Capitalizing on discontent and bad press resulting from Brownfield's dictatorial management of the city's lobbying efforts (including sole discretion over a $100,000 slush fund used to entertain state lawmakers), Bryant's supporters even succeeded in denying Brownfield the CA endorsement.[37]

The Freedom leaders met with the leaders of the CA and labor groups to strike deals on many candidates, trading its support in other races for a reciprocal endorsement of Bryant. The CA's endorsement of Bryant was secured because "Freedom endorsed Jim Heeter [a candidate in another council race—ed.]. Now [Freedom] endorsed Jim Heeter because Citizens Association had endorsed Mark Bryant, and it was a trade between the organizations."[38] The 1983 Freedom ballot contained a nearly full slate of municipal candidates, unlike the sparsely populated 1979 iteration, expressly so that the black LPO would be able to make more deals of this kind.[39]

Just as important, Freedom succeeded in unifying the black community behind Bryant, despite the presence of another African American candidate in the primary race.[40] The clergy that had rejected Freedom's leadership in the mayoral race gladly accepted it here, despite the fact that the other black candidate in the primary was the mother of a popular minister. Brownfield's supporters attempted to create dissension within the community, even convincing the *Star* to print a false report that the black clergy were abandoning Bryant, but since the race was characterized by none of the ambivalence found in the mayoral contest and the imperative of a fourth black council member was clear to all, this tactic was a dismal failure.[41] While the LPO sat on its hands in the mayoral race, it actively mobilized the community for Bryant. One person active in the 1983 campaign recalled that there was "a realization in the African American community that it was more important for us to coalesce behind the candidacy of an at-large African American than the mayoral election. So despite the differences over the mayoral candidates, everyone coalesced behind [Bryant's] candidacy in the African American community."[42] Aided by endorsements from the *Times* and *Star,* which objected to Brownfield's handling of the city lobbying operation,[43] Bryant defeated Brownfield in a major upset.[44] It would be hyperbole to assert that Freedom was exclusively responsible for his victory, especially in light of the LPO's middling record in 1983, but it did play an outsized role.

At the end of Dick Berkley's first term in office, Freedom was little better off than when it began. Although there was something to celebrate in electing a fourth African American and a third Freedom member to the council,[45] Freedom remained excluded from the Berkley coalition. The persistence of this situation was untenable, not only because it impaired the advancement of black interests but because being deprived of access to power hampered the organization's ability to sustain itself.

Coming Out of the Wilderness
Transforming Freedom: The 1987 Campaign

This became clear during the 1987 municipal elections, when Freedom's involvement was driven almost entirely by pragmatism. The abandonment of even a pretense of standing on principle would prove controversial and, in some ways, marked the transition away from the organization's attempt to truly mobilize the black community into becoming a professionalized standing campaign apparatus. In 1987, Richard Berkley attempted something at which no previous Kansas City mayor had succeeded: to be elected to a third four-year term.[46] Previous mayors, including H. Roe Bartle and Charles Wheeler, had suffered ignominious failure when they campaigned for a third term. The discouraging historical odds aside, Berkley was as popular in 1987 as he had been in 1983, a feat he accomplished by deftly managing to avoid controversy and "making blandness a political plus."[47] Most serious potential candidates for the office mulled it over and determined that challenging Berkley would be a suicide mission. Among the candidates who passed on a challenge to Berkley was Emanuel Cleaver, who opted instead to run for a third term on the City Council.[48] The only candidate to throw his hat into the ring was Jim Heeter, a corporate lawyer and first-term councilman holding the at-large seat from the prosperous southwest corridor. Four years earlier, Heeter had defeated incumbent councilwoman (and future mayor) Kay Waldo[49] with Freedom's support.[50]

If anything, Freedom had more reason to oppose Berkley in 1987 than it did in 1983. During the 1983–1987 council term, the mayor sponsored an ordinance transferring authority for a federally funded jobs program from City Hall to the private sector; this move was perceived by African Americans as an attack on the program's black director and a way of depriving poor residents of the urban core of badly needed services. The five minority councilpersons launched a four-hour filibuster that eventually resulted in a compromise plan conceding most of the demands made by African Americans.[51] The mayor also angered African Americans when he pledged to ensure that the city never again did business with an organization of minority contractors, which had supplied business incubation services to the city until questions arose about its operations. Black elected officials did not oppose terminating the organization's contract, but they objected to the "polarizing" tone the mayor adopted during the whole ordeal.[52] Berkley's record on symbolic issues was no different from these more substantive ones. When first elected in 1979, the mayor angered Freedom by stripping Charles Hazley of his chairmanship of the powerful Planning and Zoning committee. After his reelection in 1983, Berkley went even further and removed Hazley (as well as Freedom's strongest nonblack ally on the council, Bobby Hernandez) from the committee entirely, slights that the appointment of Cleaver as the committee's chair could not mend. Berkley's relationship with Hazley, poor to begin with, deteriorated further. Berkley also removed fellow Republican Joanne Collins, whose relationship with Freedom had by then become quite amicable, from her committee chair, in part for suggesting that the mayor should have cooperated more closely with Hazley and Freedom.[53] Hazley and Hernandez formed a bloc on the City Council, successfully maneuvering to direct more projects, services, and city funds into their districts and, more broadly, to lower-income residents.[54] Between 1983 and 1987, Hazley and Hernandez effectively constituted a second power center at City Hall, winning more battles than they lost. Hazley frequently faced down Berkley, who he said was "doing nothing for the minority communi-ty."[55] When coupled with the mayor's Republicanism, there seemed to be reason for Freedom to oppose Berkley on principle.

Principle was offset by other factors. First, the mayor did a much better job of talking to and consulting with Freedom after 1983, even if he did not take the organization's advice or follow its preferred course of action. One person in Freedom's inner circle during this time recalled, "Dick Berkley did come around and try to work with us. He got better over time."[56] Second, in observance of that core law of politics that one cannot beat something with nothing, Heeter was a less-than-thrilling candidate. Although young, energetic, and a relatively liberal Democrat, Heeter was untested in political combat, regarded as an ineffectual legislator, had a slight citywide profile, and was not well liked by his colleagues.[57] Cleaver, in particular, nurtured a strong dislike for the mayoral candidate. This clash owed much to a shared ambition for the office on the 29th floor of City Hall, but the two men's characterizations of one another were still quite nasty. Cleaver's friends attested that he "hate[d]" Heeter, while Heeter went on the re-cord to say, "I don't hold Emanuel in very high regard as an elected official. He seems to me to be one of the most self-serving individuals I've met at any lev-el of government."[58] Heeter lacked a viable network in the city's political elites. Most damning of all, Heeter did not have a base of voter support to which Free-dom could add, with the possible exception of the politically fragmented group known as young urban professionals or yuppies, of which Heeter and his attor-ney wife were considered prime examples.[59] Third, it seemed likely that the very same ministers' groups that ignored Freedom to go their own way four years earlier would again endorse Berkley, regardless of what Freedom recommend-ed. That was something that Freedom leaders were eager to avoid. Finally, there was the fact that Berkley's genial style of leadership made him popular with the electorate at large, and not unpopular with most African Americans, such that he seemed poised for an overwhelming victory.

Into this context strode Emanuel Cleaver, who unexpectedly gave Berkley his personal endorsement in early January 1987. The move came as a surprise even to other Freedom leaders like Charles Hazley, who, when told of the en-dorsement only shook his head in distress and said, "Man, oh, man."[60] Specu-lation abounded as to Cleaver's motives, with some claiming that Berkley had promised to name Cleaver mayor pro tem in exchange for his support.[61] The bad feeling that existed between Cleaver and Heeter, Cleaver's desire to ensure that there would be no incumbent running for reelection in 1991 to clear the field for himself, and a genuine conviction that Heeter was ill suited for the office also contributed to the move.[62] Although he had by then vacated the position of Freedom chairman, Cleaver continued to exercise great influence within the organization, particularly over new president Archie Welch, who was one of Cleaver's parishioners at St. James United Methodist Church.[63] Cleaver was personally popular with Freedom members but, more important, he was regarded as the black elected official most likely to ascend the political ladder; as such, many felt the organization should take steps that would accelerate that climb. (There were also some who adopted the "crabs in a barrel" approach toward Cleaver and sought to halt his rise.) To the chagrin of Berkley's enemies, Freedom endorsed the incumbent early in the process, just one week after the CA conferred its own endorsement upon the mayor.[64] The real rationale behind the decision to ignore Berkley's partisan affiliation and tension-fraught relationship with black legislators was bluntly put on the record for journalists. It is worth quoting at length from an extensive profile that the *Kansas City Star Magazine* wrote about Cleaver, which showed him to be the mastermind behind the endorsement:

[Cleaver's personal endorsement of Dick Berkley] caught many people by surprise, and it was meant to [. . .] [Cleaver] admits he was playing for a much bigger pot. The endorsement plan emerged from a series of meetings with Archie Welch, Dianne Cleaver and several others. The key issue, said Cleaver recently, was "how to make Freedom the main character in the municipal elections and make sure we ride away at the end with the winner." The obvious answer was to pick the likely winner and then do everything possible to make sure he won [. . .] The elegance of the move is what struck politicians such as Jerry Riffel, who, though remaining neutral in the mayoral race, assessed it as "brilliant." He understood that Cleaver was looking beyond 1987. If it worked, Cleaver would strengthen Freedom Inc., consolidate his own base, emerge as a king maker, severely damage his most visible future opponent, and walk away with a pocketful of political IOUs.[65]

Essentially, the organization's leadership agreed with Cleaver that Berkley was a shoo-in for victory. Freedom would be better off being part of that victory instead of another losing effort, in order to restore its much-darkened aura of invincibility, to gain access to the individualizable perquisites distributed by the mayor, and, theoretically, to wield greater influence over the policy direction in which Berkley would steer the city.

The arguments for endorsing Berkley may have been sound, but there can be little doubt that the decision to back the incumbent marked a moment of transition for Freedom. As an organization of politicians, not philosophers, dreamy-eyed idealists, or even traditional civil rights activists, the organization had no inhibitions about engaging in bargaining in order to make its endorsements. But in the past, those trade-offs were made in service of some immediate-term priority, like the election of office-holders attuned to the needs of the community or a particular policy stance. In 1987, no such trade-off was in sight; none of the council members representing black majority districts were seriously challenged and no policy concession was to be wrested away in exchange for support for Berkley. Berkley was endorsed purely because it was assumed that he would win, with a hope and a prayer that being part of his coalition would bring substantive benefits to the black community. Unlike in the kingmaker days of the 1970s, no policy promises were publicly extracted and there was no sense that the black community would provide the balance of power in the election. This extreme form of pragmatism marked a departure from the black interests-based mass mobilization of earlier years. Rather than organizing the African American community on behalf of shared interests, Freedom provided an army of paid campaign workers to approach African Americans on Berkley's behalf. The organization's role in the election resembled nothing so much as a political consulting firm, offering advice on how Berkley could best tailor his message to appeal to black voters and then executing that strategy, choosing its candidate based purely on electability rather than principle. As one Freedom leader described the organization's orientation from this point forward, "There was already an infrastructure there that [candidates] could use to man and staff a campaign in the African American community."[66] This is not to argue that Freedom somehow sold out or that this strategy was ill advised; the former is absolutely false and the latter is a judgment about which reasonable people can disagree. It is only to argue that the Berkley endorsement represented the culmination of a significant transformation in the way the LPO conducted its business.

One of the reasons for endorsing Berkley over Heeter was to avoid the painful split of four years earlier, when some ministers went their own way. Although the endorsement brought Freedom onto the same page as *The Call*,[67] the ploy did not succeed overall, because some prominent names in the Freedom orbit publicly dissented. Former state representative Orchid Jordan, Leon Jordan's widow, and Bruce Watkins Jr., son of the late mayoral candidate, refused to back Berkley; they created a new organization called Freedom Founders, Inc. whose first and only act was to endorse Heeter.[68] Prominent African American Democratic elected officials and party leaders also announced their support for Heeter, on the basis of shared partisanship.[69] The Freedom members who clashed most with Berkley demonstrated a distinct lack of enthusiasm for the LPO's candidate. These desertions demonstrated an unprecedented breakdown in the organization's discipline and ability to exercise internal control; such widespread desertion was simply unheard of in the 1960s and 1970s. Freedom did not sit idly by in the face of such rebelliousness. One state representative who sat on Freedom's board of directors, Vernon Thompson, was expelled from the organization for his endorsement of Heeter, which violated the LPO's policy that all directors support the entire Freedom slate.[70] The black elected officials who endorsed Heeter were bluntly accused of "selling out" the black community in exchange for cash, ironically the very same charge that the dissidents made to explain Freedom's endorsement of Berkley. Freedom did a more effective job of making this charge stick, not least because it made the "sold out" attack the centerpiece of its municipal campaign and put the message in the bluntest (and most ad hominem) terms possible.[71]

Nor did the endorsement of Berkley help restore Freedom's relationship with the CA. Although Freedom's endorsement came after the CA had already given its backing to the incumbent, it was well known in political circles that Freedom would soon follow the urgings of Cleaver and Welch.[72] In the past, this sort of leverage might have been used to produce a favorable outcome in council races. Not so in 1987, when the CA refused to endorse either Charles Hazley or Freedom ally Bobby Hernandez for reelection. Hazley faced only nominal opposition while Hernandez was in a tough fight.[73] In explaining the CA's decision, chairman Robert Lutz said of Hazley and Hernandez, who had served on the council for 16 years and 12 years respectively, that they did not "[come] up to our minimum standards of what we want for a council person." The two men were unpopular with the white political elite because they possessed an uncommon mastery of the legislative process and bureaucracy, which they used to deliver benefits for the residents of their districts rather than to advance the agenda of the elites. These elites explored the idea of instituting term limits on council members, expressly for the purpose of denying Hazley, who was unbeatable in his district, continued influence. Lutz, a well-to-do white resident of the southwest corridor, even arrogantly asserted that Hazley represented only "certain interests" in his district and implied that the councilman was corrupt.[74]

By 1987 the CA was nothing but a shell of its former self, but its condescending treatment of Hazley and Hernandez caused that organization's relationship with Freedom to sink to a new low at precisely the time when alignment in the mayoral race should have brought the LPOs closer together.

In every other respect, the Freedom strategy was successful. Despite hiring a celebrated political consultant from Washington, DC,[75] using an aggressive public relations strategy,[76] and claiming that he would invest his life savings in the campaign,[77] Heeter's bid for the mayoralty was a fiasco. The campaign was plagued by constant missteps, held back by Heeter's inability to connect with voters, and suffered from a lack of a real message or issue with which to attack Berkley. Berkley ran on the visible progress the city was making, with the city then in the midst of a downtown construction boom, adding several skyscrapers to the skyline. After losing the dry run primary[78] by 30 percentage points,[79] Heeter adopted an increasingly combative, negative, and partisan approach. Berkley was forced to attack in kind, something which the normally pleasant and conflict-averse mayor was loathe to do. The discourse descended to a childish hurling of insults, with Heeter blamed by the Berkley-backing *Star/Times* and neutral observers for "polluting an election" and running the nastiest race in memory.[80] Attempting to bludgeon Berkley into defeat, Heeter himself became the subject of a potent attack when it became clear that his campaign and its reviled negative ads were single-handedly financed by a $270,000 "loan" from a controversial local millionaire.[81] Those funds were spent on highly negative television advertisements, as well as passed on to intermediaries within the black community for purposes unknown.[82] The Heeter campaign pursued a strategy in the black community that can only be called tacky and deceptive. His campaign placed a series of expensive advertisements that featured the names and artists' renderings of prominent African American leaders (including Leon Jordan, Bruce Watkins, Alan Wheat, and other living black elected officials in the city who actually supported Berkley), implying that they endorsed Heeter, "the Democrat for mayor." This childish approach was a major factor in *The Call's* decision to pass over Heeter.[83] To counter the cavalcade of television attacks, Berkley loaned his campaign several hundred thousand dollars, in what became one of the most expensive races in Kansas City history. Neither the money nor the Freedom endorsement seemed particularly necessary, for Dick Berkley won the general election in a rout, with 62 percent of the vote.[84] The mayor also won the Freedom wards by 20 percentage points (see Table 6), though his victory was so large that losing them would not have altered the outcome.[85]

Table 6. 1987 Mayoral Election Results in
Predominantly African American Wards

Ward	Richard Berkley (%)	Jim Heeter (%)
2	917 (69.3%)	406 (30.7%)
3	1,228 (59.8%)	827 (40.2%)
14	1,267 (59.8%)	853 (40.2%)
16	1,018 (58.2%)	732 (41.8%)
17	1,358 (60.7%)	878 (39.3%)
18	1,174 (61.1%)	748 (38.9%)
27	1,353 (61.2%)	858 (38.8%)
28	842 (51.3%)	798 (48.7%)
29	1,174 (64.6%)	643 (35.4%)
30	1,225 (62.2%)	746 (37.8%)
Total in Predominantly African American Wards	11,556 (60.7%)	7,489 (39.3%)
Total Citywide	50,992 (62.3%)	30,841 (37.7%)

Source: The Call – April 3, 1987

Freedom achieved its goal of being part of the winning coalition, sending a candidate about whom it was tepid back for a third term at City Hall. The hope and prayer that Berkley would be more responsive proved to be more than an idle fantasy. Berkley repaid his debts by recommending Cleaver as the mayor pro tem (a recommendation unanimously accepted by the council), restoring Hazley to the chairmanship of the Planning and Zoning Committee, and adopted a leadership style that made it easier than ever for Cleaver, Hazley, and Hernandez to drive the agenda at City Hall.[86] Freedom ameliorated its recent reputation as a loser in municipal politics, catapulting itself to the foreground in a way that would prove useful as the city confronted a multitude of issues of concern to African Americans.

The Transition Away from a Mass-Oriented Organization: Freedom's Internal Activities and Politics in the 1980s

During Freedom's time in the wilderness and its reemergence as part of the governing coalition at City Hall, the LPO was transformed. Reed has written about how the black community was demobilized in the 1970s and 1980s,[87] as black elected officials began to concentrate power in their own hands and became more vested in the maintenance of the political system than in transforming it. A similar, if less extreme and self-interested, version of this phenomenon transpired within Freedom over the course of the 1980s. The mass orientation and commitment to high levels of community mobilization found in previous decades were abandoned, though not consciously. The loss of the mass orientation and an ethos of mobilization had consequences for how the organization operated, leading it to become a smaller cadre of activists whose pursuit of black interests was heavily tempered by pragmatism and, on occasion, by self-preservation. Instead of remaining in constant communication with a grass-roots base, the organization began to be active almost exclusively during election season and limited its activities to providing candidates with an insta-infrastructure in the Freedom wards. This transformation also radically altered how Freedom was perceived, by both the African American community and whites.

Changing Leadership

Freedom's leadership changed several times over the course of the 1980s. The first change came in 1979 and was necessitated by Bruce Watkins's departure from active political life. Watkins had little time left in his exceptional life, but saw clearly the need for Freedom to move on and contemplate an existence without his pervasive involvement. He accepted a position with the federal government that demanded his withdrawal from leadership in political groups.[88] This was a healthy move that promised to open the organization up to a new generation of leaders and members. Two members of Freedom's younger generation, both under forty, were elected to the principal leadership posts: state representative Phil Curls became the president and councilman Emanuel Cleaver became chairman of the board. Both were popular, savvy, and effective legislators in their respective domains; their election seemed to suggest that Freedom would "modernize" and respond to the emerging needs of the 1980s. Indeed, the Curls-Cleaver era was replete with successes, including the election of the area's first black state senator and first black congressman.

By the end of 1984, neither Curls nor Cleaver wished to continue in their official roles at Freedom. Curls understandably became preoccupied with his new role as a state senator, while there was speculation that Cleaver sought to distance himself from the organization in preparation for a future mayoral campaign. The organization elected as its new president Archie Welch, a businessman considered close to Cleaver, and as the new chair, clergyman and Jackson County legislator James Tindall. Welch's ascension to the presidency marked the first—and at the time of writing, only—time that the post was held by someone outside of electoral politics. Welch would later become a controversial figure, owing to his company's pursuit of government contracts,[89] but at the time his election was interpreted as a sign of growth on Freedom's part. Some believed that the change in leadership meant that Freedom would develop a stronger alliance with black business, become less tied to the personal political aspirations of whichever elected official happened to be serving as president, and would be driven by a business-minded insistence on vaguely defined "results." Instead, the signal achievement of Welch's presidency was the 1987 endorsement of Dick Berkley.

Welch and Tindall served lengthy terms, from December 1984 until August 1990. The leadership team could claim some significant victories, but was effectively driven from power after the August 1990 Democratic primary. Freedom's slate of candidates and favored ballot initiatives won large votes of approval within the black community at that time, but suffered resounding defeats overall. Freedom's candidate for Jackson County executive lost by a two to one margin, an African American county legislator named Carol Coe lost her reelection campaign to future U.S. senator Claire McCaskill by a whopping 31,000 votes, and Kansas City voters approved a tax for the local zoo over Freedom's opposition. Although Freedom remained dominant within the black community, its leverage in local politics appeared so radically diminished that *The Call* openly talked of Freedom's "future [being] questioned."[90] Talk of the organization's demise was a spectacular over-reaction, but Welch and Tindall nevertheless were blamed for the disastrous outcome. Welch, in particular, was criticized for the increasingly demagogic nature of Freedom campaigns, for an insular and cliquish approach to leadership, and for a growing perception that Freedom's endorsement was for sale. These critical sentiments were not universally shared. Nevertheless, Welch did not help himself when he argued that Freedom did not "lose" the 1990 primary (a demonstrable falsehood) and "that his reign would continue until he and Board Chairman James Tindall decide to step down. . . [Welch said,] 'When we decide on a leadership change, we will announce it.

Tindall told me he will not change until after the city elections in February, 1991. I do not plan to step down until after the November elections.'"[91] Such declarations seemed to suggest that Welch and Tindall served at their own pleasure, rather than that of the membership, and were not warmly received. An internal coup bubbled up and less than two weeks after making that bold declaration, Welch suddenly found that his business affairs required his full attention. He resigned as Freedom president in August and was replaced on an interim basis by former president Phil Curls.[92] Tindall's resignation followed shortly thereafter, but no interim chairman of the board was named. Curls would lead Freedom into the 1991 municipal elections.

In some respects, the new leadership teams in place during the 1980s represented Freedom's open and democratic qualities. None of these leaders were part of Freedom's first generation, though Phil Curls was the son of Freedom founding member Fred Curls. This period also saw the long-promised expansion of the board of directors from 25 to 66 members; this expansion was achieved in part by granting all African American elected officials automatic seats on the board. However, the leadership remained male-dominated; despite the fact that several African American women held elected office in Kansas City, none ascended in Freedom beyond the rank of vice president. As the decade wore on, the novelty of new leadership evaporated. Young people and women active in Freedom increasingly complained that they were not valued by the organization and that an old guard of Freedom leaders and elected officials was making it impossible for new faces to emerge.[93] Criticism of Freedom's leadership would become increasingly common in the late 1980s and early 1990s. Indeed, knowledgeable informants almost uniformly pointed to this period as the beginning of Freedom's decline and laid the blame squarely at the feet of a succession of board members called unimaginative, self-interested, insular, cliquish, or even corrupt. In the 1980s, this sense was still nascent, but perceptions of the organization's commitment to its base were definitely changing and not for the better.

Demobilization and the Weakening of the Grassroots Base

One reason that perceptions about Freedom's belief in mobilizing and connecting to its grassroots base were changing is that the organization did less in the 1980s to cultivate that base than it had in past years. The organization claimed 400 dues-paying members in 1990[94] and still actively recruited members, but the lines of open, free-flowing, and constant communication with "average voters," the hallmark of the LPO's early years, faded. At the same time, the organization withdrew from many of the community activities that endeared it to less politically inclined individuals and served as mobilizing tools.

One obvious manifestation of this tendency was the change in Freedom's newspaper advertisements. From 1962 until 1979, Freedom's print ads were usually full-page affairs that featured the Freedom ballot as well as several paragraphs communicating the organization's message for the campaign. Often visually attractive, the ads discussed issues and gave readers a reason to support the candidates featured on the Freedom ballot. From 1980 onward, the ads only sporadically made any effort to communicate a message or rationale for voting the Freedom ballot. Instead, the print ads now typically featured nothing but the ballot, apparently on the arrogant theory that the LPO did not need to explain its choices or give voters a reason a support to the selected candidates. Although one should not make too much of this, it did signal a change in the LPO's traditional approach of respectfully requesting support from the community.

The precinct captain network that was Freedom's pride and joy during the 1960s and 1970s gradually shriveled into obsolescence. Although precinct captains were sometimes still appointed and Freedom still took great pride in its roster of ward committeemen and committeewomen, the genuine work that these individuals were expected to perform lapsed into insignificance. Although always elective, these posts became titular and honorific rather than tied to vote-delivering performance. Without the extensive information network that it once possessed, Freedom's members and leadership were forced to become ever more dependent on their own sense of the community's mood. This was not necessarily counterproductive, as most of the group's members did have a proverbial finger on the community's pulse, but it did make it more difficult to engage in the forms of reciprocal communication that build trust and lead to electoral support. No longer expected to work their wards, committee people also no longer were expected to supply volunteers to engage in electioneering. The financial demands made on endorsed candidates simultaneously increased, such that candidates ceased to feel much responsibility to supply Freedom with volunteer workers for the organization's activities. After all, went the common refrain, "What am I paying them for?" As a result, the LPO began to move away from a tradition of relying on volunteer labor for its canvassers and poll workers and instead began paying people to perform these tasks. While volunteer labor continued to be used whenever possible,[95] over the course of the 1980s, being compensated for this work became the norm and a whole class of seasonal campaign workers was birthed. While the shift from volunteer to paid labor may have simplified some of the more difficult aspects of campaign management, many knowledgeable informants maintained that it simultaneously weakened commitment to the organization, caused average voters to view Freedom workers with more suspicion than in the past, and weakened the LPO's reputation for being community-oriented. Said one knowledgeable informant, "In the early days [. . .] it was volunteer-driven. People were passionate, they wanted to be involved in the organization, they wanted to make a difference. [Later] you [had] to pay people to go out and make change. That is one of the most disappointing, god-awful things I've ever seen."[96]

This change also made it nearly impossible for the organization to take any sort of mobilizing action outside of the campaign season, because the funds required to pay workers were only available at those times. Rather than a grassroots organization ready to spring into action upon a moment's notice, the perception grew that Freedom was but a small core group of political elites that would spare candidates considerable trouble and assemble for them an infrastructure to use in communicating with Black voters. Over the course of the 1980s, Freedom thus became less mass-oriented and more of a professionalized political organization.[97]

Contributing further to this transformation was the gradual disappearance of many of the activities designed to connect Freedom with the community and encourage widespread public involvement. Over the course of the decade, the LPO dispensed with its distribution of holiday charity baskets as a regular practice. Also appearing less frequently on the roster of activities were Freedom-specific fundraisers, as the organization became even less reliant on funds raised within the black community and more dependent on endorsement fees from candidates. Voter registration drives became sporadic,[98] and the "food and fun" festivals that enhanced Freedom's reputation were no longer frequent events.

Freedom continued to hold its regular monthly membership meetings at its headquarters, which were open to the public, although attendance declined from its high in the 1970s. The annual picnic was continued, though it was no longer a must attend event on black Kansas City's social calendar. The organization also continued to hold election-eve rallies, often featuring musical performances and held at churches, though they were not the extravaganzas they once had been and held less interest for those not deeply immersed in politics.[99] Not much was done to engage the younger generation of African American Kansas Citians, for whom the names Leon Jordan and Bruce Watkins meant little and the ritualistic invocation of past Freedom successes like the fair housing ordinance lacked resonance. The organization's youth auxiliary (originally called Young Freedom) was allowed to lapse before being refashioned in 1982 as Youth for Freedom, but proved to be just a paper organization.[100] The Leon Jordan Memorial Dinner, once the highlight of black Kansas City's political and social season, became a shadow of its former self and then ended entirely.

The public events that Freedom did sponsor no longer seemed to energize the public in the way they once did. They were increasingly gala affairs, catered more narrowly to the paid membership and the political elite rather than the broader public. Freedom held a successful gala dinner, attended by more than 500 people, to commemorate its 25th anniversary. The dinner was accompanied by a seminar on challenges facing black families, but both events were smaller and more exclusive than similar ones held in the previous decade.[101] A gala awards dinner two years later attracted just 300 people.[102]

The decisions to dramatically contract the activities and programming sponsored by Freedom were consciously entered into; cancellation of various events and practices was not due to a lack of funds or interest. Instead, the LPO collectively decided that these programs did not contribute to Freedom's central mission of electing favored candidates to office. The absence of these features was self-evidently harmful to Freedom's long-term prospects and hastened its transition into a professionalized LPO.

Corruption and Ethics Issues

Perhaps the development that did the most damage to Freedom's reputation and ability to mobilize the masses was the proliferation of unethical behavior within its ranks. When asked, nearly every person interviewed for this book acknowledged that Freedom's reputation for integrity was less-than-pristine. Most who held that opinion maintained that this reputation began in the 1980s, with a few saying it began in the 1990s. However, it should be stressed that, when pressed, interview subjects were unable to provide a single specific instance during this period where Freedom itself acted in unethical ways.

The movement away from volunteer to paid workers and the explosion in the scale of resources demanded by that move has provided some fodder for those crying foul, with these critics asserting (by their own admission, without evidence) that monies were diverted or went "missing." Likewise, the increasing reliance on endorsement fees (the almost exclusive source of Freedom operational funding until Missouri campaign finance law was changed in 2010) caused some to assert that Freedom's endorsement went up for sale to the highest bidder. Interviewees who were active in this period recalled that discussions with Freedom about its endorsement invariably included discussions about the money that candidates could contribute to the Freedom effort. Said one candidate, "I also remember we discussed a price, you know, what Freedom wanted. And it was $5,000."[103] One longtime critic of the organization maintained that a trend began during "Doc" Holliday's presidency in the late 1970s but accelerated in the 1980s where

taking money and being all about money is the big thing, the bag-men. They started the practice of giving support to people who really didn't deserve black support, because they were hostile to what were perceived as black issues. But really, the taking of the money. The white business community bitched about it, but they found it much easier to just funnel the funds through Freedom than to try and set up something else.[104]

Some claimed that the difference between Freedom and similar organizations on financial matters was that "they wanted the money first and that was more important than maybe where the candidate stood."[105]

Those active inside Freedom, and a large number of interviewees outside the organization, many of whom were not sympathetic to the organization, feel differently, and vigorously reject this perception as just that, a false perception. They maintain that only those candidates whose compatibility with the group's agenda was already assured ever made it to the phase where money was discussed. These interviewees noted that claims of being for sale are an inherent risk in a fundraising system that relies on payments from candidates, but that it ought to apply to all parties who operate in this way. One interview subject makes a point repeated by many others, noting that the Citizens Association "had to fund their campaigns the same way we had to fund our campaigns, with candidate contributions. When Freedom did it, it was a political payoff. They never say that about Citizens."[106] This suggests that at least some of the allegations about Freedom's supposed unethical behavior are part of a long-standing racist narrative about African Americans as uniquely criminal or venal, with their votes for sale.

However, corruption and unethical behavior were present among some of the individuals active in Freedom during the 1980s. Several of these incidents received considerable press attention—one might say disproportionate attention, compared to the sins of some white politicians active at the same time—and invariably mentioned the perpetrators' affiliation with Freedom. Since Freedom had vouched for the integrity and credibility of the perpetrators, it was not entirely unfair for the LPO to shoulder some of the blame when things went awry.

The first incident of misbehavior worth recounting concerns Lee Vertis Swinton. Swinton was the dynamic former president of the NAACP, who broke and reconciled with Freedom several times before becoming the first black state senator from Kansas City under its banner. In 1983, Swinton was indicted by a secret grand jury. The state senator was accused of stealing thousands of dollars from an estate of which he was the executor.[107] Swinton ultimately pleaded guilty and was forced to vacate his seat in disgrace.[108] A 1983 special election saw Freedom president Phil Curls elevated from the state house to the senate in Swinton's stead.[109]

A second incident involved Harold Holliday Jr. The former Freedom president and chairman was then serving as a Jackson County legislator. In addition to his duties in elective office, Holliday was the president of the Leon Jordan Scholarship and Memorial Fund. The fund was an independent nonprofit organization, the successor to the old Jordan memorial dinners. At the instigation of Freedom's members of the Jackson County legislature, the fund received grants from the county totaling several hundred thousand dollars, which were to be distributed as college scholarships to deserving young students. Beginning in 1983, the fund was consumed by controversy. First, it was revealed that most of the scholarship recipients were the children of African American elites. Although there was no means test associated with the scholarship, the perception was that the fund was being operated for the benefit of the already prosperous rather than those in need. Questions about Holliday's administration of the fund multiplied, with some alleging that he awarded scholarships to students in order to win favors from their parents.[110] The situation became much worse when Holliday was convicted of stealing $1,625 from the fund. The following year, the Internal Revenue Service revoked the fund's tax-exempt status after finding that it had been used to benefit Holliday and his associates. A report issued by the IRS claimed that Holliday had embezzled $21,000 from the fund, in addition to the monies he had already been convicted of stealing.[111] The incident ended Holliday's promising career. Freedom collectively and through its leaders initially gave Holliday unqualified support; as details about mismanagement leaked out, his colleagues stood by him and resisted the efforts of the Jackson County Legislature to expel him.[112]

Management of the Jordan Scholarship and Memorial Fund was the source of even more trouble a few years later. In 1987, Bruce Watkins Jr., son of the Freedom founder, pleaded guilty to stealing from the fund.[113] By that point, a grand jury was investigating why more than $60,000 was missing from the fund's coffers.[114] The incident was embarrassing because of Watkins's family ties, of course, but the younger Watkins was not crucial to the organization. Freedom had declined to endorse him in a bid for state representative the previous year (he lost to the Freedom candidate) and, only a few weeks before his indictment, he participated in the formation of the new "Freedom Founders" organization.

Charles Hazley pleaded guilty in 1988 to failing to file federal tax returns for three years. Hazley had paid the taxes in question on time (and was even owed a refund), but failed to file the official federal tax forms. The councilman resigned his chairmanship of the Planning and Zoning Committee.[115] Hazley served twenty-five days in a federal penal institution for his mistake, but since the offense was a misdemeanor rather than a felony he was not forced to vacate his seat.[116] Nor was there an outcry in the black community to force Hazley to resign; on the contrary, most leaders and average voters petitioned Hazley to remain in office.[117] One white political insider recalled a party celebrating Hazley was held at Freedom headquarters shortly after the councilman's return from prison; this insider explained that this was the point at which the subject lost confidence in Freedom.[118] Hazley remained in office until the end of his term.

Yet another incident concerned Carol Coe, who, with Freedom's support, replaced Holliday in the Jackson County Legislature.[119] Coe never shied away from a fight. She became controversial with the first question she received upon entering the legislature: the *Star* asked her about the Holliday scandal. She replied, "If he stole it, he deserved to have it. . . And I believe my neighbors feel the same way. . . . For as much of a contribution as his family's made to this community, $1,500 is no money. They should have given him that."[120] Coe maintained—with some justification—that she was assailed by whites (and the *Star*, which nurtured an irrational obsession with her every move) for standing up for black interests. But Coe also created problems for herself when she cast the deciding vote that denied the chairmanship of the Jackson County Legislature to Freedom board chair James Tindall,[121] leading to her taking a "leave of absence" from the LPO's board.[122] Later in her term, Coe was accused of taking a bribe in exchange for influencing a county contract.[123] A law enforcement investigation found that the charges were baseless,[124] but the allegation nonetheless was damaging to Coe and

Freedom. The legislator would break with the LPO many times before reuniting with it for an unsuccessful reelection bid in 1990.

While several instances of unethical and illegal behavior (or allegations thereof) were percolating within Freedom's ranks during the 1980s, the closest the organization itself ever came to an allegation of wrong-doing came in 1983, when it was featured on a list compiled by the prosecutor's office of 34 Kansas City political clubs that had not filed newly required campaign finance reports. The *Star* singled out Freedom and two other clubs in its story on organizations that were in "frequent violation of the law," omitting the fact that 31 other clubs had not filed the reports. The *Star*'s coverage of the story likewise neglected to mention that Freedom did file the report, albeit tardily, and was not on the more serious list of political clubs that could be charged with ethics violations.[125]

The constant assertion that Freedom's endorsement was for sale took a toll. Since this assertion was typically made only by those who lost the endorsement, by way of explaining why their otherwise self-evidently superior qualifications had not carried the day, many voters put little stock in the allegations. The fact that Freedom did accept contributions from candidates it endorsed gave some reason for pause. This was not the case among a majority of black Kansas Citians in the 1980s, but the fact that an increasing number of politically astute African Americans were publicly making this argument suggests that there was some segment of the population to which it was credible, compelling, and reason enough to look skeptically upon Freedom. This perception also gained traction among white elites, who found it a convenient way of explaining why their own preferences were not mirrored in those expressed by Freedom.

Black Kansas Citians refused to abandon the organization on the basis of these incidents, not least because there was reason to believe that the publicity that attended them owed something to racism. Indeed, a broad front of black community organizations (Freedom was not among them, though some individual members of the LPO participated) launched a well-publicized and reasonably successful boycott of the *Star/Times* because they regarded the daily papers' coverage of African Americans as insensitive at best and racist at worst. The boycott forced the papers' leadership to the negotiating table.[126] Although the papers did not make public concessions regarding their news coverage, some who worked for the papers insisted that thereafter they trod more lightly where the black community was concerned.[127] Still, there can be no doubt this pattern of behavior undermined trust in Freedom and weakened the connection of the LPO to its voter base.

The 1980s, then, were a period of dramatic internal transformation for Freedom, Inc. An entirely new generation of leaders controlled the organization, with different priorities and different tactics. Much of the programming and many activities employed in the past to cultivate mass support were abandoned. Instead of a vast network of volunteers committed to the organization's mission, Freedom used paid workers in service of pragmatic politics. This professionalized orientation certainly had its advantages (particularly in mastering the mechanics of electioneering), but it also meant that Freedom had strayed from its organizational roots and effectively demobilized the black community. This sort of change is what made state representative Jackie McGee and county legislator Carol Coe—two political figures who admittedly had an axe to grind, since Freedom declined to endorse their 1988 campaigns—feel empowered to declare that "Freedom, Inc. has a proud history in the black community but that during past elections, there has been an erosion of community confidence in the organization."[128]

For all of these changes, a majority of black Kansas Citians continued to put their faith in Freedom. It remained difficult for any African American to be elected to office without Freedom's support. Even African Americans who held office and had personal followings found it difficult to return to elective office without the LPO's blessing. The reasons for the black electorate's ongoing confidence in Freedom are not hard to discern. The LPO had done much good work in the community, was still the primary intermediary with white elites, and had secured for the black community unprecedented political power. With the exception of Joanne Collins and state representative Jackie McGee, every black elected official in Kansas City was affiliated with Freedom and affirmed its necessity, its virtue, and its influence. Popular officials like Cleaver and Hazley always paid deference to the organization and stressed to their constituents that they owed their personal successes to the LPO. Most of all, Freedom had built up vast stores of trust over the years. Even if the events of the mid-1980s called some of the LPO's actions into question and depleted these reservoirs, an abundance of credibility as the single, corporatist, political voice of the black community remained.

Policy Making and Black Interests in the 1980s

Although it did not represent a straying from the organization's roots, Freedom's approach to policy issues did change during the 1980s. The organization continued to provide a forum for the discussion of pressing issues facing the black community, but otherwise withdrew from the formal policy-making process.

One African American policy-maker lamented that more could have been accomplished if Freedom had provided support at City Hall, saying, "I felt like I had worked so hard during the course of the campaign to cultivate a relationship [with Freedom]. And [. . .] I felt like I had made a new friend. And when I got elected, my friend left me! In other words, there was no real engagement."[129] With one major exception, unless the policy in question was subject to a public vote (as with the issuance of bonds or modifications to the tax structure), the LPO did not issue position statements on specific issues. Policy remained important to the organization, as candidates continued to be evaluated based on their positions on issues impacting the black community, but Freedom ceased to act as an interest group competing for attention in the policy-making environment. Instead, Freedom interpreted its role in the policy process as consisting of electing supportive individuals to office, holding them accountable for their actions (or inaction) in office, and endorsing or opposing ballot measures. It also played an important role in convening elected officials and giving them a forum to work out a strategy. Said one longtime activist and Freedom insider:

> The Freedom elected officials would meet for breakfast about every other weekend, talk about everything that was coming up. There was a lot more hanging out, on the weekends, in the clubs. Yeah, it was socializing and drinking [. . .] but they also were cutting deals. They socialized, that brought them closer together, helped them work together. They'd get together before any big deal at City Hall and work out a plan, what they were gonna do, how they were gonna do it [. . .] Freedom did that, brought those folks together.[130]

This transition to a less visible approach is attributable to three factors. First, the organization's ranks within the City Council were larger than they were in the 1960s and 1970s. The institutional imprimatur of Freedom was necessary to convey seriousness when Bruce Watkins or Charles Hazley sat as the LPO's sole member on the City Council, but less so when more Freedom members held seats. Second, the leadership decided that direct involvement in the policy process was a diversion of scarce resources from the group's primary work in electioneering. Freedom still took credit for the work done by its elected officials, but regarded its own part in the struggle for black interests to consist only of evaluating which candidates would best advance those interests.

Third, and most important, the Freedom team at City Hall was so strong and well regarded by colleagues within the organization that more explicit involvement by the LPO seemed excessive. Even when deprived of formal power by the Berkley administration, Charles Hazley, Emanuel Cleaver, and Mark Bryant were influential. Cleaver commanded respect and influenced outcomes through the force of his personality and his ability to attract media attention, using both of these attributes to leverage gains for the black community. He also had the remarkable ability, in the words of one interviewee, "and this is definitely a compliment, to walk in the rain without getting wet."[131] Hazley became immensely powerful by developing a mastery of the legislative process, establishing close relationships with the municipal bureaucracy, and possessing an uncanny knack for identifying pressure points that could be used to force concessions to black interests.[132] Hazley's lengthy service on the council added to his power, as did the growth of his personal and professional friendship with colleagues Bobby Hernandez and Joanne Collins. In the late 1980s, Hazley and Hernandez were virtually unstoppable at City Hall. The two shared a commitment to the same principles and populations, primarily low-income Kansas Citians and "minorities," as well as a gift for political maneuvering; these shared qualities infuriated their political opponents, who would consistently enter policy battles in the belief that they were in an unassailable position only to find Hazley and Hernandez besting them. As one interview subject said of the mid- and late 1980s, "Charles Hazley and Bobby Hernandez more or less ran things at City Hall."[133]

The two men's ability to control outcomes at City Hall was enhanced by the election of the sympathetic Mark Bryant and the elevation of Emanuel Cleaver to the post of mayor pro tem. Joanne Collins was also a vital part of this team. She thrived on the sort of public meetings and neighborhood visits that Hazley eschewed. Her amiable persona, negotiating style, and relationships with some who would not give Hazley (or Freedom) a hearing proved important to achieving gains for the African American community. The collective ability of the Freedom delegation plus reliable allies Collins and Hernandez to shape policy was confirmed in 1990 by James Kemper, scion of the region's biggest banking family, who said that "there is no question that the minority council people and a contingent of labor supporters [were] running the City Hall."[134] The Freedom-Hernandez relationship was not a group alliance between the African American and Latino communities, but a personal alliance between Hernandez, Hazley, and Freedom leaders. No great effort was put into cultivating a deeper interracial alliance. Once Hernandez left politics, the relationship between Freedom and the Latino community ended.

The ability of Freedom members (and Hernandez) to steer municipal policy outcomes was abetted by the hands-off leadership style adopted by Berkley in his third term. From 1987 to 1991, Berkley was frequently out of town, delegated important policy decisions to designated council members, and consciously sought out consensus rather than taking strong positions. This hands-off approach created a vacuum in the policy process, which Cleaver, Hazley, and Hernandez eagerly filled[135] to the significant benefit of the black community.

Freedom as an institution did not involve itself in the policy process during the 1980s, but it still is worth discussing the impressive policy accomplishments of the organization's representatives at City Hall. There were five issue areas of significant and continuing interest to African American Kansas Citians during this period: the relationship with the KCPD, diversity in city employment and contracting, neighborhood development, term limits for elected officials and the election system, and the tension between combating white supremacy and permitting free speech. With few exceptions, these issues did not make their way into the discourse of the decade's municipal campaigns. Nonetheless, the need to address these issues shaped the local government agenda, if only because the Freedom members of the City Council insisted upon it.

Crime and Policing

Crime and policing remained major concerns in the 1980s. Consistent with national trends, neighborhoods with large black populations experienced surges in their crime rates and the levels of black-on-black crime similarly increased. Community leaders, including the Freedom members of the City Council and the organization's allies in civil society, articulated the need for a more strategic response on the part of the KCPD. It was frequently asserted that the department was not doing all that it could to effectively police urban core neighborhoods, preferring to concentrate its scarce resources in upscale and tourist-friendly areas like downtown and the Country Club Plaza.[136] Police officials denied those charges. The KCPD remained under state control, inoculating it from reforms that municipal officials might have desired. Nevertheless, the fact that the Freedom legislators frequently commented on and inserted themselves into the debate over police policy produced limited change at the department. Most important was the fact that the police developed a working relationship with the Ad Hoc Group Against Crime, the citizens' organization founded by Alvin Brooks and other African American leaders.[137] Despite the fact that Brooks was himself a former police officer, there was initially reluctance on the part of police to work collaboratively with Ad Hoc. The organization's persistence, the trust that many African American residents placed in the group's leaders, the glowing media profiles that were written about Ad Hoc, and the support of black elected officials succeeded in changing this. Developing a working partnership with Ad Hoc was only one sign of the fact that the KCPD was becoming less insular and devoting slightly more attention to its relationship with the African American community.

This does not mean that criticism of the KCPD dissolved. Incidents of police brutality and the shortage of African American police officers, especially high-ranking ones, both remained subjects of continuing concern. High-profile incidents of brutality declined over the course of the decade, only to return to the headlines in devastating fashion in 1990. The cause of the decline in brutality is something about which we can only speculate. In addition, there was little appreciable increase in the diversity of uniformed officers.[138]

Whether the KCPD's more inclusive approach to policing accomplished anything to improve safety or reduce crime is open to debate. What is not subject to argument is the fact that this improvement was the result of constant agitation by black activists and elected officials. Just one example of this clout is the fact that, in 1981, newly elected Governor Kit Bond considered appointing Clarence Kelley to the Board of Police Commissioners. A universally negative reaction from African Americans resulted in the idea being shelved. Instead, black board member (and former Freedom member) Gwen Wells was reappointed. Although these sorts of changes might seem to be—and were—quite modest gains, they were still more than Kansas City's black community had ever before wrested away from the KCPD.

Diversity in City Employment and Contracting

The second major municipal policy issue for African Americans was another long-standing one, ensuring diversity in the city's hiring and contracting practices. Progress on this front was slow but steady, the result of constant pressure and questioning from Freedom's elected officials. Charles Hazley and Mark Bryant were particularly passionate about ensuring that African Americans were proportionately represented in the city's workforce, among senior management, and in the pool of city contractors. For the first time the City Council adopted, at the instigation of the Freedom members, an affirmative action plan for municipal employment, with special focus on diversifying the ranks of senior management.[139] During the 1980s, the number of black senior managers rose appreciably. African Americans became directors of departments outside of the stereotypical handful; most notably of all, an African American became chief of the Fire Department in 1981.[140] In addition, one of the most powerful people at City Hall was Assistant City Manager James Threatt, an African American. Although he was second in the hierarchy of the municipal bureaucracy, Threatt's long tenure with the City, relationships with elected officials, and control over federal grant funds sometimes permitted him to exercise power equal to that of the city manager.[141] Controversially, Threatt often used that power to expend funds in urban core neighborhoods. The *Star* published a shoddy exposé which claimed that city loans for urban development were made to friends of Threatt and never repaid. Black leaders considered the charges trumped up and an example of racist bias at the paper. The expose was nonetheless used to justify Threatt's removal from operational control over federal grants and housing policy.[142] Although discrimination in municipal employment still existed in the 1980s, the level of discrimination was less than that found in the private sector and municipal government provided a path for upward mobility for working and middle-class black Kansas Citians.

Greater progress was made in city contracting. Although a policy to ensure that minority-owned businesses received a share of city work had been implemented during the 1970s, monitoring was paltry and the consequences for noncompliance were minimal. The policy was an administrative one, rather than one adopted by the City Council, depriving it of the force of law. As a result, minority-owned businesses received a miniscule share of work performed on public projects. In 1984, pressure from Freedom's elected officials resulted in the passage of a city ordinance with minority contracting requirements.[143] Hazley and Hernandez succeeded in enhancing monitoring and imposing more severe consequences for noncompliance. These council members had no compunction about bringing the legislative process to a screeching halt or killing major developments if firm guarantees about minority utilization were not met. In one notable case, Hazley and fellow members of the board of the Downtown Minority Development Corporation (DMDC) stared down the mayor, a major hotel corporation, New York financial wizards, and a coterie of Kansas City's corporate elite who were attempting to purchase a struggling hotel built with funds originally loaned by the DMDC. The hotel purchasing group and its supporters refused to make an offer that would adequately pay back the DMDC loan, which if not adequately repaid would compromise the organization's ability to continue offering loan programs for minorities. The hotel deal fell through because neither side was willing to compromise, indicating that Freedom's elected officials at City Hall were deadly serious about expanding access to economic opportunity for minority-owned businesses, even at the expense of marquee projects desired by the city's growth machine.[144] In another instance, Freedom and its elected officials refused to support a 1983 sales tax for capital improvements unless it was joined by a requirement that the resulting jobs be filled by Kansas City residents. In the past, these construction jobs were often filled by residents of the suburbs, a disproportionately white population. Mandating that Kansas Citians do the work on these projects would thus benefit city residents in general and African Americans in particular. The gambit by Freedom's elected officials succeeded, in that the local-hiring requirement was adopted by the council and was part of the campaign for the tax. After the tax passed, Freedom was "double-crossed" by Mayor Berkley, who imposed a moratorium on the local hiring requirements by claiming they were too onerous.[145]

Unlike Atlanta, Kansas City never experimented with joint venture arrangements or some of the more aggressive means of promoting black-owned business.[146] Still, the steps that the city did take—under pressure, not voluntarily or out of a sense of altruism—significantly increased the amount of work done by African American-owned businesses on public projects. The strong focus that Hazley, Bryant, and to a lesser extent Cleaver placed on this issue could be interpreted as stemming from a middle-class bias. There is a hint of truth in such an accusation, because the beneficiaries of expanded contracting opportunities were middle-class. But Freedom's elected officials pursued many other goals besides diversity in contracting, goals whose benefits accrued substantially to low- and moderate-income Kansas Citians.

Neighborhood Development

Another recurring issue for black Kansas Citians was the attempt to cope with declining conditions in urban neighborhoods. The deterioration in urban neighborhoods, including declining populations, job flight, falling property values, minimal investment, scarce entertainment and retail options, rising crime, and an explosion in visual blight, was nothing new. Nor was it exclusive to Kansas City, as urban neighborhoods throughout the United States experienced similar decline due to trends outside the control of any municipal policy-maker.[147] Nevertheless, Freedom's City Council delegation used the limited tools available to it to mediate this decline.

They did so primarily by directing additional City funds to projects in urban core neighborhoods and luring private investment into the area. Freedom's elected officials instigated the creation of an enterprise zone in the heart of the city's black community.[148] Freedom's elected officials intervened to spend local and federal grant funds on housing developments serving low- and moderate-income people, believing that a shortage of high-quality housing stock contributed to flight from the urban core.[149] Only a substantial contribution from the city permitted a community development corporation (CDC) to develop a much-needed shopping center in the heart of the urban core. When constructed, the Linwood Shopping Center was considered a revolutionary achievement that would herald the revitalization of the surrounding neighborhood. It did indeed briefly bring new vitality and hope to the area.[150] (Twenty-five years later, the center is only partially leased and its ambitions of catalyzing neighborhood-wide rejuvenation forgotten.) Consistent with national trends, local elected officials passed many of their funds for neighborhood development through CDCs. This strategy resulted in the construction of many new residential units and some strip shopping centers in the heart of the urban core, but many of the grantees proved to have serious problems with financial accountability. Allegations of corruption were frequent.[151] These problems were not as widespread as alleged (or, at least, firm evidence was not forthcoming), but their existence reduced the impact of the substantial expenditures approved by local elected officials.

Another means of addressing declining neighborhood conditions was ensuring that these areas received a fair share of capital improvement dollars. Past infrastructure programs devoted more resources to new neighborhood infrastructure needs or to commercial centers, rather than repairing crumbling infrastructure in urban core neighborhoods. As a condition of support for infrastructure programs, especially those requiring a public vote because they were financed through new taxes or floating bonds, Freedom and its elected officials demanded that the black community receive a fair share of the dollars spent. Demands of this sort had been made in the past, with middling but increasing success. In the 1980s, Freedom and its allies wielded enough power at City Hall to ensure that promises made were promises kept. Although still woefully inadequate to meet the need, neighborhoods with black majorities did receive an increased share of infrastructure spending during the 1980s.[152]

The insistence that the black community receive a fair share of neighborhood development dollars frequently brought Freedom into conflict with other segments of the population. For example, in 1990 civic leaders were convinced that the city's future as a regional economic hub and convention destination depended on renovating the Kansas City Zoo. Zoo backers succeeded in placing a dedicated tax to support the remodeling on the ballot. Although the zoo is physically located within the black community, Freedom opposed the measure on the grounds that it did little to alleviate conditions in neighborhoods and diminished the likelihood of voter approval for a ballot issue that would deal with those pressing needs. Emanuel Cleaver publicly broke with Freedom to support the tax. The zoo tax lost overwhelmingly in the Freedom wards, but won everywhere else, so the tax was approved.[153] A ballot proposal to finance housing rehabilitation and other needs of the urban core was permanently stymied, just as urban core leaders had predicted.

Perhaps the most important attempt by black elected officials to reinvest in urban core neighborhoods came in 1989, when Emanuel Cleaver proposed a sizable capital improvements plan. Known as the "Cleaver Plan," the proposal would raise and spend $114 million on projects identified from the outset: $50 million for flood control for Brush Creek, which benefited the silk stocking district and stretched into black communities east of Troost Avenue; $20 million for construction of a new arena for the American Royal rodeo and livestock show; $24 million for road improvements in the Northland and far south; and $20 million to build an International Jazz Hall of Fame, Negro Leagues Baseball Museum, and new housing at 18th and Vine, in the heart of the African American community. The jazz hall of fame and baseball museum were envisioned as the centerpieces of a revitalization of the 18th and Vine neighborhood, once the world-famous home of Kansas City jazz but in 1989 just another struggling urban neighborhood. Redevelopment of 18th and Vine had long been a priority for residents of the surrounding area and African American elected officials, but no progress had been made toward this aspiration because funding could not be identified. Voters were presumed to be unwilling to approve financing for a supposedly niche cultural attraction like a jazz museum.[154]

The Cleaver Plan became the single most controversial and important legislative proposal of the 1980s, subject to months of heated debate. The plan proved controversial for two reasons. First, Cleaver used an innovative approach that allowed the city to borrow against future sales tax revenues to finance the package. This permitted the council to approve the improvements itself, rather than submitting them to the public for a vote. Second, the plan was vigorously opposed by white civic elites, because it conflicted with their own $1.3 billion dollar proposal for capital improvements. That plan was developed in secret by corporate executives without a scintilla of public input, would levy a new tax, would make nearly all of its expenditures downtown and in the Northland, and its existence was revealed to the public only when it became clear that Cleaver's proposal was on the verge of passage.[155]

In the one major exception to its withdrawal from the policy-making process during this period, Freedom became actively involved in the battle to pass the Cleaver Plan. Working closely with Cleaver, Freedom secured support for the plan from eighteen other African American community organizations. The organizations announced their public endorsement of the Cleaver Plan in one fell swoop, and then vigorously lobbied public officials and civic elites on its behalf.[156] Freedom president Archie Welch declared that Freedom and the black community would withhold its support from a ballot initiative to fund improvements to the convention center—a cherished goal of civic leaders—unless the council approved the Cleaver plan.[157] This sort of hardball chagrined the *Star,* which condescendingly lectured Freedom for making a "foolish threat," but proved effective. Based on Welch's threat and amendments to the original plan that added improvements for the Northland, the council adopted the Cleaver Plan on a vote of 9–4.[158] The African American members of the body were Cleaver's strongest supporters in moving his proposal forward.[159] Through discussions held under the auspices of Freedom, these elected officials were involved in the planning stages of the initiative from the very beginning, to the extent that the Cleaver Plan was regarded as "an outgrowth" of Freedom, Inc.[160] Approval of the Cleaver Plan halted the rival, secret $1.3 billion proposal in its tracks, earning Cleaver the temporary enmity of a large portion of the corporate elite.[161] Regardless of the tantrum thrown by the elite, the Cleaver Plan was an appropriate bookend for the decade. Like many other actions taken by Freedom's council delegation, it brought investment into the urban core which was nevertheless insufficient to stave off some visible signs of neighborhood decline.

Term Limits and the District System

One issue in which Freedom, its elected officials, and its constituency were not successful was preventing term limits for municipal elected officials. Until the 1980s, council term limits were never discussed. Faith in the democratic process ended, however, when Charles Hazley and Bobby Hernandez were repeatedly returned to office, by healthy margins, over the near-universal objection of white elites. Frustrated by their inability to defeat the two men, irate that they exercised so much power at City Hall, and fearful that other council members might become similarly inoculated to the opprobrium of local elites, a group of corporate executives and white political activists banded together to place a term limits proposition on the ballot. These activists made no secret of the fact that the primary goal of the initiative was to end Hazley and Hernandez's service, because they regarded the two as corrupt and disapproved of their policy agenda. Despite widespread public dissatisfaction with the City Council (especially Hazley and Hernandez, who opinion polls showed were as wildly unpopular with white voters as they were beloved in their respective districts), it took three attempts before the term limits advocates were successful. The first attempt did not make it onto the ballot. A second try in 1989, bankrolled by a local construction magnate and supported by the CA, would have limited officials to three terms and expanded the mayor's powers. The primary spokesperson for the anti–term limits campaign, wealthy white attorney (and future mayoral candidate) Dick King, openly decried the call for term limits as the product of racism. Freedom mobilized black voters by emphasizing that the proposition was an attempt to deprive minority communities of power that took a generation to accumulate. The proposition lost by a little more than 11,000 votes, thanks to the Freedom wards, where the measure lost by 10,562 votes.[162] The third effort, which limited elected officials to two consecutive terms (but allowed additional terms to be served, if there was a one-term interregnum), received overwhelming support citywide, owing to the *Star*'s endorsement and its appearance on the regular general election ballot (as opposed to the low-turnout special election held in 1989), but lost in the Freedom wards.[163]

Freedom and its elected officials were irreconcilably opposed to term limits. The reasons for their opposition were obvious. First, the proponents of the initiative explicitly argued that term limits would "get rid of" Hazley and Hernandez.[164] The feeling that white outsiders were attempting to dictate who represented African American and Latino Kansas Citians was omnipresent and justified. Second, lengthy service of elected officials was the primary means by which Freedom and the black community achieved progress during the 1980s. It was experience and familiarity with the system that permitted Bryant, Cleaver, and Hazley to maneuver in the ways they did, particularly when Freedom was in the wilderness, that maneuvering was essential to black progress. African Americans feared that term limits would deprive them of one of the few advantages they possessed in pressing their demands on the system. Third, those directly impacted by the initiative were influential within Freedom and the community and, understandably, used that influence to protect their own interests.

Despite this opposition, the term limits proposal passed in 1990 by an overwhelming margin. Freedom then initiated legal action to stop the implementation of the new law, with Charles Hazley, Bobby Hernandez, former Freedom vice president Rosemary Lowe, and several Latino activists from Hernandez's district as plaintiffs.[165] The suit argued that the term limits law would unconstitutionally disadvantage African Americans and other minorities, by harming their ability to elect a candidate of their choice. Courts ruled against the plaintiffs and in favor of the term limits law, meaning that all five minority members serving on the council in 1990 (Mark Bryant, Emanuel Cleaver, Joanne Collins, Charles Hazley, and Bobby Hernandez) would be forced into retirement after the 1991 elections.

In response, Freedom sought a change in the city's electoral system. Since 1961, the city had been divided into six districts, with six members elected from within districts and six members, one per district, elected at-large. As has already been seen with the case of Joanne Collins, this system meant that at-large members might be elected to represent particular districts despite the opposition of residents of that district. A 1991 proposal advocated by Mark Bryant and Freedom would have instituted a pure district-based system, eliminating the at-large seats and instead electing twelve members from twelve districts. Supporters argued that this reform would make council members more in touch with neighborhood concerns and increase black representation on the City Council. Bryant's move to present voters with the option of amending the charter at the 1991 municipal elections was rejected by his colleagues on a 6–4 vote (three members, including Bryant himself, were absent when the vote was taken). Opponents maintained that at-large seats were necessary to guard against parochialism and that the current system had served the city well.[166]

White Supremacy and Free Speech

A final policy issue is worthy of brief note, though the outcome was more ambivalent than anything mentioned thus far. During the 1980s, the local cable system, American Cablevision, had a franchise granted by the municipal government. In exchange for operating a public access channel, American Cablevision was granted a monopoly in the city. The station offered its airwaves to groups that wished to produce and broadcast their own original programming. One group that sought to broadcast a show on the station was a local branch of the Ku Klux Klan (KKK). Station administrators first denied the request on the grounds that the KKK broadcast did not meet a requirement that content be locally produced, since the racist propaganda the KKK proposed airing was produced by the national body. When the branch offered to locally produce new, but equally vile, content, American Cablevision asked the City council to release it from its contract. Instead of a public access channel the system would offer a community access station, with the distinction being that the station could exercise discretion over which content could be aired on the latter but not on the former. The City Council agreed. This solution proved far from tenable, as the American Civil Liberties Union and the KKK filed a lawsuit. It became clear, as any civil libertarian could have explained to the council from the outset, that the city would lose the free speech claim in court. The City Council was forced to vote on whether the public access station should be restored, which might mean allowing the KKK to broadcast its program. African American council members, especially Cleaver, railed against restoring the channel, but the City Council nonetheless did so on a vote of 7–3. The city settled out of court with the ACLU and the KKK, agreeing to pay all legal costs incurred by the ACLU.[167]

The African American community was incensed by the entire episode, but whether shutting down the public access channel was a matter of black interests is subject to debate. Regulating speech, even the despicable, malicious, and stark-raving mad racist ranting of the KKK, has rarely proven beneficial for African Americans and proponents of civil rights, who have invariably found themselves labeled as dangerous "radicals" who threaten the social order. Painful as it might have been, protecting the right of free speech was, in the long run, probably more useful for black interests than keeping the hate-consumed maniacs of the KKK off the air.

The period from 1980 to 1991 saw significant satisfaction of some black demands on the system. Progress was made in the community's relationship with the KCPD, though this progress was modest and the relationship remained tension-fraught. Considerable improvement was made to the city's policy on minority contracting and in establishing a diverse municipal workforce, including at the highest ranks. Neighborhoods in the urban core continued to suffer decline, but this was attributable primarily to national and global economic conditions, as black elected officials secured more funds and projects for these areas than ever before. These successes were tempered, though, by the failure on questions regarding the city's electoral structure and the ambivalent outcome on free speech issues. Black Kansas Citians had much to be proud of in this period, not least because their elected leaders were essentially excluded from positions of formal power from 1979 to 1987 and still managed to drive the agenda at City Hall. Although Freedom itself withdrew as a special interest group during this period, it is owed a considerable portion of the credit for these victories. Were it not for its endorsement, the actors who produced these outcomes would not have been in office. Were it not for the electoral majorities Freedom commanded based on a relationship of trust and credibility, these elected officials would not have possessed the confidence and longevity they required to develop a mastery of the inner workings of City Hall.

During the period that stretched from 1980–1990, Freedom can be said to have travelled the distance between the political wilderness and significant power. Regardless of whether Freedom was incorporated by the municipal administration and its members occupied positions of formal power, the LPO succeeded in producing benefits for its African American constituency. Freedom produced those benefits by retaining its institutionalized character and by continuing to engage in effective strategic bargaining with nonblack political forces. Throughout the decade, the organization faced down rival claimants (including the black clergy and the Freedom Founders organization) to be the corporatist political voice of the community. Those competing claims to speak for the majority of the community produced complications for Freedom—and for delivering on black systemic demands—but did not ultimately compromise the LPO's position or prove substantively harmful to addressing black interests.

Although Freedom continued to be fully institutionalized during the 1980s, there was a change in its approach. The organization continued to use multiple tactics to achieve its goals, although it did withdraw from its traditional role as a lobbying group in the policy-making process. Instead, it more fully embraced its role as a standing campaign committee while occasionally using publicity and litigation to achieve its objectives. Freedom also persevered in utilizing a "black interests" organizing model even as the demise of Black Power and the failure of the 1984 Jesse Jackson presidential campaign caused that model to fall out of fashion. The use of this model was tempered by more pragmatism than ever before, but did not become so overwhelming as to shunt black interests aside; no amount of pragmatism could persuade Freedom to support some candidates who were relentlessly hostile to African Americans.

Most important, though, the 1980s saw a transition in Freedom's organizational orientation. It became less mass-oriented and more professionalized, which changed its relationship with its constituency. Throughout the 1960s and 1970s, and especially in 1979, the black community in Kansas City had extremely high levels of mobilization, not just at election time but in the intervening months as well. As a direct result of Freedom's organizational transition away from being mass-oriented in the 1980s, these high levels of mobilization came to an end. Indeed, in many respects the Freedom transition brought about the demobilization of the city's black community, just as the decade brought a similar fate to black populations throughout the nation. As the theory of black political efficacy outlined in this book would predict, this gradual transition first had effects on Freedom's organizational efficacy and subsequently on the black community's political efficacy.

Despite the decline in mobilization, Freedom was strong enough, and its elected officials at City Hall savvy enough, that Kansas City's black community achieved remarkably high levels of political efficacy during the 1980s. But, in keeping with the theory of rising expectations, it served to whet the appetite of black Kansas Citians, causing them to ponder what might be accomplished if an African American wielded real power at City Hall. The next chapter will consider that question, examining how Emanuel Cleaver worked with the more professionalized, less mass-oriented incarnation of Freedom to rise to the pinnacle of local power and what Cleaver and Freedom did with that power once they possessed it.

CHAPTER 5

At the Pinnacle of Power?
Freedom, Inc. in the Cleaver Years and Beyond
(1991–2007)

Freedom's transition during the 1980s would have lasting impact in the 1990s and beyond. This became most immediately obvious in the 1991 election, when Freedom was instrumental in electing Emanuel Cleaver as Kansas City's first black mayor, but played a much less significant role in his campaign than it had in previous citywide bids by black candidates. Despite having ostensibly arrived at the pinnacle of power, in the years immediately after Cleaver's election, the LPO went into rapid decline. It ceased to be effective because it lacked the key attributes of effective LPOs argued for throughout this book: institutionalization; a singular, corporatist nature; high levels of grassroots mobilization; and effective bargaining with nonblack allies. Instead of creating elected officials by throwing its strength into battle for them, Freedom was, in the words of one longtime activist, "no stronger than the candidates it runs. But the true measure of an organization like Freedom should be whether it can succeed at electing anyone it chooses, rather than relying on strong candidates to carry the day."[1]

In the absence of a strong, effective black LPO during the 1990s, black interests were not optimally served, despite the Cleaver mayoralty. There were many accomplishments of which to be proud, but some African Americans felt disappointment that Cleaver and his successors did not accomplish more. Black interests were not advanced to the extent that they might have been because Freedom was no longer able to supply the agitation or pressure that would have resulted in the satisfaction of additional demands.

Reaching the Pinnacle of Power
Freedom and the 1991 Municipal Elections

Productive as the period from 1980 to 1990 was in advancing some black interests, there was still much to be done. African Americans remained in a subordinate economic position, institutional racism continued to be a serious problem, and struggling urban core neighborhoods still did not receive a share of municipal resources equivalent to the level of their need, despite the clout that African American council members held in city government. As it had been in 1979, the logical solution to these problems for many seemed to be the election of an African American mayor. Emanuel Cleaver had been mulling a run for the city's top office for years. With Berkley retiring and running for his City Council seat again forbidden by the newly established term limits, Cleaver decided that 1991 was his year. Sending Cleaver to the 29th floor of City Hall naturally became Freedom's top priority in 1991 and would be used as an indicator of its relevance for the 1990s, a sign of whether its victory in 1987 was a fluke or a return to form. According to some politicos active at the time, Cleaver's race "was the only one [Freedom] really cared about."[2] But with the entire African American delegation to the City Council departing due to term limits, Freedom also knew the importance of the council races.

The Cleaver Campaign

Emanuel Cleaver's candidacy for mayor was a foregone conclusion by the summer of 1990, but he did not officially declare until the late fall.[3] His service as the mayor *pro tem*, high citywide profile, charismatic personality, popularity with African American residents, and solid legislative record should, by any reasonable standard, have made him the front-runner. Until shortly before the February 26 primary election, though, many local political observers treated his candidacy as an afterthought.[4] Public attention, at least that of the white majority and the daily press, was instead focused on two lavishly funded rivals: Dick King and Brice Harris.

King was the managing partner at one of the city's most powerful law firms. Decades earlier, King had been regarded as one of Missouri's rising political stars. At age 29, he was elected mayor of the neighboring city of Independence. He served one term before his career was overtaken by alcoholism (including an embarrassing public incident where, intoxicated, he stole six coats from the cloakroom of a restaurant). Several years later, with his addiction under control, King became the state's commissioner of revenue under Republican Governor Kit Bond. King moved from Independence to Kansas City, switched his party registration to Democrat, and became a favorite of organized labor.[5] Financially backing a group called Kansas City Progress that achieved success in 1990 in electing a school board slate, King believed the city was "dying on the vine" and only he could salvage it.[6] Backed by organized labor and some of his wealthy friends and clients, King was thought certain to advance to the general election.[7]

The other candidate thought to be assured of advancing to the general election was Harris, an administrator at the Metropolitan Community Colleges with no elective office experience. Harris was the chair of the Public Improvements Advisory Commission (PIAC), an important city commission that provided recommendations on infrastructure expenditures. Harris started the campaign with zero name recognition and owed his front-runner status to the fact that he was literally handpicked by a group of corporate elites to run for mayor. These corporate executives, led by the chief executives of United Telecommunications (now Sprint), Hallmark Cards, and the local utility, feared that a contentious election would result in the city turning away from the business-friendly policies of Dick Berkley. To stave off that prospect, they sought to use their collective resources to designate a successor early in the process. The group of executives met weekly and interviewed potential candidates over the course of a year. Dissatisfied with the crop of announced candidates (especially Cleaver, who had in 1989 opposed their pet proposal for $1.3 billion in capital improvements), the executives, most of whom lived in suburban Johnson County, Kansas, set out to recruit a candidate of their own. An outsider whose political identity could be built entirely from scratch, Harris fit their bill.[8] He became the candidate of the CA, due purely to his support from the civic elites who comprised the barely skeletal remnants of the once-proud LPO. The corporate executives pledged hundreds of thousands of dollars to his campaign, giving Harris more money to spend than any of his rivals, with King a close second.[9]

Also in the race were two City Council members, Bob Lewellen and Joanne Collins. Collins we have already encountered repeatedly. Lewellen was a successful businessman and two-term councilman, best known for being a Berkley ally who frequently made off-color jokes. Neither Lewellen nor Collins was expected to make much of a showing in the primary, as they lacked resources or significant organizational support.[10] Moreover, Collins and Lewellen were in the race primarily because they wanted to ensure that the general election featured at least one candidate who supported the council-manager system;[11] both King and Harris were reputed to favor a transition to the strong mayor form of government.

Through January and early February 1991, the media focus was squarely on Harris and King. This permitted Cleaver to quietly go about the work of consolidating his base in the black community. Cleaver was in a strong position with

African American voters before the campaign began, but there was some tension with other black community leaders over Cleaver's support of the 1990 zoo tax and the councilman's push to engage in redistricting before the 1991 election. This last initiative earned him a scathing indictment from former Freedom chairman James Tindall, who characterized it as a craven sell-out, saying:

> Can a leopard change his spots, or the Ethiopian his skin? It seems in the case of Rev. Cleaver that it is almost possible. It was Rev. Cleaver who stood so passionately against the Klan on the matter of racial injustice, and it has been Rev. Cleaver on the forefront of Civil Rights issues in the past. Yet he seems blind to this potential racial injustice, and the welfare of his own constituency. Does [sic] greater political aspirations mean that much?[12]

Cleaver set about easing this tension. Press observers criticized Cleaver for running a low-key campaign, but if they had bothered to venture into the black community they would have seen it bustling with Cleaver activity. Cleaver visited dozens of African American churches, social clubs, and neighborhood organizations every week, broadcasting a message that the city was in good shape but could become even better.[13] Cleaver's campaign inundated African Americans with the optimistic slogan, "You've got to believe!," aided by a gospel theme song of the same title, written by the music minister at Cleaver's church, and frequent glowing coverage from *The Call*.[14] The optimistic tone of it all was in marked contrast to what voters were hearing from Harris and King, who seemed to compete with one another to paint the more apocalyptic vision of the state of the city. Although it screened all of the major candidates and the outcome was foreordained, Freedom officially endorsed Cleaver in mid-January.[15] The LPO then immediately sprang into action on Cleaver's behalf, canvassing its wards, beginning an aggressive phone-banking operation that contacted each voter in the Freedom wards on three separate occasions, mailing literature to voters in the Freedom wards three times before the election, sponsoring radio advertisements, and reaching out to its community partners like the Baptist Ministers Union and the AME Ministerial Alliance.[16] This general strategy would form the scaffolding of all subsequent Freedom campaigns through the time of this writing.

An aggressive effort was essential, because Cleaver and his strategists, particularly an advisor named Luther Washington, were well aware that the candidate could advance to the general election only with a unified black vote. Some white observers, badly out of touch with the African American community, expected

Collins to draw a substantial share of the vote in the Freedom wards, especially after she received the endorsement of a leading black minister.[17] Neither Cleaver nor Freedom anticipated that, but there was some unease that even a few hundred extra votes for Collins might deny Cleaver a place in the general election.[18]

Although Cleaver and Freedom worked closely together in 1991, there was a major difference between the Cleaver campaign and Watkins's effort in 1979. Watkins's campaign was totally intertwined with Freedom's; there was no distinction between the two, as they shared staff and decision-makers. The overall Freedom effort, including strategic choices, endorsements in down-ballot races, and its interaction with other LPOs, was shaped purely by how decisions would affect "Bruce's chances." Not so in 1991, when a clear separation existed between Cleaver and Freedom. Freedom supplied ground troops and support for Cleaver's bid, and some of its members were key parts of Cleaver's inner circle and campaign team.[19] But the LPO did not make decisions in other races based on how they would impact Cleaver, nor were his personal preferences taken into account. Cleaver even declined to endorse (or oppose) other candidates featured on the Freedom ballot.[20] Eager to win, Cleaver was unwilling to place the entire machinery that would determine his political future in Freedom's hands. The stigma that was attached to Freedom among white voters at this time also meant that Cleaver felt the need to put some distance between himself and the LPO; this required a delicate balance that only Cleaver's prodigious political gifts could manage, because creating too much distance with Freedom would have deprived him of its electoral machinery and peeved his most important constituency. In addition, Freedom's formal leadership was in flux, leaving a power vacuum and complicating decision-making processes. As a candidate in the 1991 elections remembered it, "It never was clear to me who was really in charge."[21]

Although Cleaver focused on consolidating his base, he reached out to voters outside of the African American community. He made frequent appearances in front of white voters, stressing his theme that the city was in good shape that he alone could unify the city to make even more progress. These presentations attracted little attention while the media was fixated on Harris and King. In the middle of January, those two candidates suddenly realized what should have been obvious to anyone who analyzed the local political map: if Cleaver had the unified support of the black community, he would advance to the general election, leaving only one other spot available for the supposed front-runners.[22] Harris and King thus became engaged in an increasingly nasty battle with one another, each attempting to knock the other out of contention in order to secure the coveted general election slot. Together, the two spent an unprecedented one million dollars on television advertisements that made vicious personal attacks on one another. Harris slammed King for his alcoholism and living in a tax-abated mansion, while King denounced Harris for being handpicked by suburban corporate tycoons and a doctoral degree of questionable provenance.[23] Coupled with their doom-and-gloom messages of a city teetering on the verge of collapse and personalities that lacked the warmth to soften these rough edges (interview subjects recalled that Harris, in particular, was dismal on the stump and reeked of indecision when asked questions), the attack strategy ensured that the two front-runners engaged in a war of mutual destruction. The other three candidates in the race abstained from negative campaigning and were upbeat about the city's future. Nor did the other three candidates receive negative attention from the media, with the slight exception of Cleaver, who was drawn into—and skillfully exited—a racially tinged fiasco at the school district.[24]

On primary day, the Cleaver strategy proved successful. The mayor *pro tem* waltzed away with a victory, receiving 27,832 votes (37 percent). More than half of those votes came from the ten Freedom wards, where turnout was only slightly lower than elsewhere in the city, and where Cleaver received more than three quarters of the ballots cast (See Table 7). The great shock was that he would be faced in the general election not by Brice Harris or Dick King, but by Bob Lewellen. The two "front-running" candidates destroyed one another, allowing the low-key and low-budget but high-on-Kansas-City Lewellen campaign to finish a distant second with 12,951 votes. Lewellen edged Harris out by 411 votes. The implosion of Harris and King was taken as a sign to the civic elite that they could not dictate to the voters, and the corporate executives who recruited Harris were chastened (albeit temporarily) by their rejection.[25]

Unlike Bruce Watkins in 1979, Cleaver entered the general election the front-runner. He led Lewellen by a whopping 14,881 votes in the primary (compared to the roughly thousand votes by which Watkins led Berkley in 1979), had a higher profile, more institutional backing, considerably more personality, and exhibited stronger leadership. With King out of the race, Cleaver received the backing of organized labor.[26] He also received the informal support of many of the city's white liberals, with whom he had cultivated ties for years, and some of the corporate executives who originally backed Harris (although most remained neutral, having been humiliated by that experience).[27] Lewellen, by contrast, now became the choice of the humbled CA and some representatives of big business.[28] Cleaver remained the choice of Freedom and black voters, who redoubled

Table 7. Emanuel Cleaver's Electoral Performances and Voter Turnout in Predominantly African American Wards, 1991 City Primary

Ward	Cleaver Votes	Cleaver Percentage	Voter Turnout
2	1,218	87.8%	33.2%
3	1,432	90.3%	27.6%
14	1,647	86.6%	36.7%
16	1,280	78.3%	31.3%
17	1,852	89.6%	34.3%
18	1,375	67.4%	37.4%
27	1,629	76.3%	35.4%
28	1,036	77.8%	29.9%
29	1,631	87.5%	33.1%
30	1,408	69.8%	36.0%
Total in Predominantly African American Wards	14,508	78.3%	33.6%
Total in All Other Wards	13,324	17.6%	37.8%
Citywide Total	27,832	36.7%	36.7%

Source: Kansas City Election Board

their efforts. Buoyed by greater financial support than was available in the primary, Freedom's general election activities were more extensive in scope. The goal was to ensure that black voter turnout was equal to or higher than white voter turnout, something to be accomplished through the traditional means of distributing the Freedom ballot, mailing literature to African American households, telephoning voters repeatedly, having credible community figures inveigh on the need to vote, having those same figures loudly proclaim Cleaver's virtues, and, of course, using the raw enthusiasm stemming from the potential to make history.[29] Freedom and the Cleaver campaign took great care to stress "Rev's" long involvement with African American causes and his record of accomplishment on the council, while avoiding specifics on policy that might compromise his standing among whites. Again, Cleaver did not rely exclusively on Freedom to carry his message to African American voters. He made great use of the organization, but Freedom operated more like a parallel, supplementary campaign for Cleaver than as the entirety of his campaign (as it did for Watkins).

The Cleaver/Freedom efforts were abetted by the accidental nature of Lewellen's candidacy. Lewellen voted with Cleaver on most of the important issues during their shared council tenure, so he lacked any issue with which to distinguish himself from the mayor pro tem. Lewellen also lacked the attack instinct that might have allowed him to damage Cleaver with white voters. One longtime strategist maintains that Cleaver

> probably would have lost, if Lewellen had ever really run a negative ad against him. He did something about overuse of a car phone by Cleaver, but there was other material out there to go negative and he didn't use it. He listened to the folks, like the *Star*, who said that people were turned off by the negativity between Harris and King. They really weren't, but the political people were still in shock about that whole thing.[30]

The closest Lewellen came to an attack was to allege that Cleaver used his city-issued mobile phone a bit too often and could be a waffler.[31] Lewellen lacked the money or personality to make even these pitiful criticisms resonate and while he privately griped about reverse racism when his black "friends" declined to endorse him, he refused to trade in racist attacks.[32] Harris and King would not have had any of these problems, meaning that Cleaver was blessed by destiny to face the weakest possible general election candidate.

Polls taken during the heat of the general election campaign showed Cleaver walking away with an easy victory.[33] Speculation still abounded that these polls might suffer from the infamous Bradley effect, wherein white voters are theorized to tell pollsters that they would support a black candidate at rates higher than proved to actually be the case, and that Cleaver would go down to defeat due to weak support from whites. These fears proved unfounded, though the voting was racialized and highly polarized. Cleaver defeated Lewellen by the solid margin of 50,204 (53 percent) to 43,989 (47 percent), far narrower than the polls suggested, lending credence to the Bradley effect theory.[34] In later years, a mythology would take hold that Cleaver swept into office because of his unique ability to reach out to and reassure white voters. In fact, the new mayor received only 35 percent of the white vote; much of it likely owed more to the *Star*'s endorsement than

Table 8. Emanuel Cleaver's Electoral Performance and Voter Turnout in Predominantly African American Wards, 1991 City General Election

Ward	Cleaver Votes	Cleaver Percentage	Voter Turnout
2	2,020	96.5%	48.9%
3	2,760	97.6%	48.0%
14	2,542	94.0%	50.8%
16	2,227	89.7%	47.0%
17	2,963	97.0%	49.9%
18	2,193	76.8%	51.2%
27	2,626	83.6%	50.7%
28	1,801	90.1%	43.9%
29	2,665	95.7%	48.3%
30	2,280	81.0%	50.5%
Total in Predominantly African American Wards	24,077	88.1%	49.0%
Total in All Other Wards	26,127	39.1%	42.2%
Citywide Total	50,204	53.3%	44.0%

Source: Kansas City Election Board

any "Cleaver magic" with white voters.[35] The Northland, whose population was practically lily-white, gave Lewellen 70 percent of its votes. Many whites recalled the Cleaver of an earlier era when he was, in the words of a Cleaver-phobic *Star* letter-writer, a "young loudmouth militant" who was "not the type of person I want running this city" and remained distinctly uncomfortable with the man.[36]

The new mayor did not owe his office to an outpouring of support from newly color-blind white voters, but to Freedom and black voter support. For one thing, the size of Kansas City's black electorate had increased by nearly 3 percentage points since 1980.[37] Even a weakened Freedom, held at some distance from the

Cleaver campaign, possessed an excellent electioneering apparatus that knew how and where to reach that African American electorate. The Freedom machine mobilized black voters, causing the ten black-majority wards to have higher turnout than almost all wards with white majorities. Cleaver benefitted from almost unanimous support in the ten predominantly black wards, with nearly half of his total vote supplied by them (see Table 8). The minister-politician's charisma and ability to connect with audiences certainly helped, but his victory would have been impossible were it not for the infrastructure that Freedom put in place.

A Record of Mixed Success

Freedom activists were rightly elated by Cleaver's historic election. At the same time, the 1991 elections were not an unalloyed triumph for the LPO. Due to term limits, both of the council districts with African American majorities, the Third and the Fifth, would receive new representation. Throughout its history, Freedom's candidate had never lost an election for an in-district council seat in a black majority district. In 1991, despite an emotional appeal to voters that called on them to remember history and "Support the Bridge that brought us across," that claim ceased to be true.[38]

In the Third District, the traditional heartland of Freedom, Inc., Charles Hazley briefly considered waging a write-in campaign to keep his seat. Freedom activists convinced him that a write-in bid would be a waste of precious resources.[39] With Hazley out of the picture, two other candidates emerged: Carol Coe and Kit Carson Roque.

We have already briefly encountered the controversial Coe, who lost her 1990 campaign for reelection to the county legislature owing to her enormous unpopularity with white voters. She retained a constituency within the black community who appreciated what they perceived to be her fearlessness in defending black interests and were appalled by the shoddy treatment meted out to her by the *Star*.[40] Roque was Coe's polar opposite, a quiet and reserved attorney who favored reasoned negotiation over brazen confrontation. Roque also had what one would think of as an advantage in 1991, in that he was one of Emanuel Cleaver's closest personal friends and before declaring his own candidacy served as treasurer of Cleaver's mayoral campaign.[41]

Demonstrating that Freedom was not an extension of the Cleaver campaign and highlighting the limits of "Rev's" influence, the Freedom board overwhelmingly endorsed Coe over Roque.[42] Coe had long been a thorn in Cleaver's side, dating back to negative comments she made about him on a television talk show in 1987;[43] although she apologized for the comments, Cleaver allies were known to nurture a lingering distaste for Coe. Furthermore, the Coe endorsement was considered a liability for Cleaver since the former legislator was known to be unpopular with white voters. White voters would generally not have the opportunity to cast ballots for or against Coe since the Third District was overwhelmingly African American, but it was argued that her presence on the same slate as Cleaver would result in white voters identifying the mayoral candidate with Coe's brand of politics.[44] Some recall that the endorsement was made after an internal discussion to the effect that Coe's high name recognition and grassroots ties would lead her to victory, with or without Freedom on board. Publicly, Coe's endorsement was attributed to the women of Freedom, who felt taken for granted by the organization's male leadership.[45] Coe's campaign materials in the race also frequently emphasized her gender and empowerment for black women, featuring her in pictures with the city's other black women elected officials or comparing her to Harriet Tubman and Sojourner Truth.[46]

Roque was certain that he needed to go on the offensive to have the slightest chance of becoming a councilman. The race between the two thus quickly became as negative and personal as the Harris-King feud. Accusations of nonresidency, race traitorousness, treachery, and buffoonery flew back and forth while both candidates tried to portray themselves as the more proximate to Cleaver.[47] Roque further isolated himself from Freedom when, in a desperate last-minute gamble, his supporters printed a ballot that resembled the official Freedom ballot. Roque's "Freedom Now" ballot approximated Freedom, Inc.'s in design, style, and language and featured most of the same candidates, but substituted Roque's name for Coe's.[48] These tactics backfired and Coe won a convincing victory, reaffirming Freedom's position in the Third District.

Not so in the Fifth District, where longtime political insider Jim Wilson faced Freedom committeewoman and pharmaceutical company employee D. Jeanne Robinson. Wilson had an extensive history of political involvement, including serving in high-ranking administrative posts for Jackson County, a short stint as the executive director of the Housing Authority of Kansas City, and as right-hand man to barbecue baron Ollie Gates. Wilson was one of the grand old men of Freedom, so his endorsement was expected. What was not expected was that Robinson would campaign with such verve and vigor, using her relative inexperience to wage an effective door-to-door campaign as an outsider. What was certainly not expected was that former Freedom chairman James Tindall, who was related to Robinson, would lend his considerable political expertise and base to her campaign. Tindall attempted to deliver the Freedom endorsement to Robinson in the first place, but found Wilson's supply of old favors inexhaustible. The Jackson County legislator and clergyman then used his knowledge of how to win elections on Robinson's behalf. Robinson was endorsed by the CA, which helped with the 35 percent of the district's voters who were white. Robinson successfully painted Wilson as a member of an old guard, whose experience was really a synonym for outdated thinking when new ideas were needed.[49]

With the Freedom endorsement in hand, Wilson took the race for granted. Freedom campaigned for the council candidates featured on its ballot but devoted most of its energy to the Cleaver race, believing that his coattails would carry along the rest of the LPO's candidates. This resulted in Wilson's defeat, by the large margin of 8,453 (55 percent) to 7,022 (45 percent).[50] Robinson beat Wilson in ten of the twelve wards in the district, including most of the Freedom wards. The results of this race were widely interpreted as a sign that Freedom's political dominance in black majority districts was not absolute. Freedom's leadership chose to paint the election, after the fact, as an intra-family feud rather than a genuine defeat. One defeat does not make for irreversible decline, but the contrast between Cleaver's victory and Wilson's defeat seemed to suggest that Freedom efforts *alone* were no longer sufficient to win overwhelming black voter support.[51]

In the at-large races, too, Freedom's success was mixed. The LPO's candidate for the Third District At-Large seat, Majeeda Baheyadeen, lost overwhelmingly, unable to effectively compete with the large fundraising advantage and CA support of Ron Finley, a former NAACP branch president. Finley was a Freedom member, but lacked the internal base that Baheyadeen, whose husband was elected to the school board in 1990 and who was a co-founder of the Ad Hoc Group Against Crime, had.[52] Baheyadeen carried the Freedom wards, but only by modest margins, while Finley romped to victory in wards with white majorities. As a result, just as in the early years of Collins's service, the at-large seat in the heart of the black community would be held by someone with an ambivalent relationship with the LPO. In the Fifth District At-Large seat, the LPO was successful at electing an African American urban planner, Ken Bacchus. Bacchus defeated his white opponent, a wealthy doctor who self-financed his campaign and carried the CA's endorsement, by focusing on neighborhood issues.[53]

Perhaps the most controversial move made by Freedom during the 1991 elections was to decline to endorse two white incumbents, Chuck Weber and

Katheryn Shields. Weber and Shields were favorites of labor unions and were endorsed by Freedom in 1987.[54] Weber quickly lost whatever affection Freedom might have once had for him because, in the words of one person familiar with the group's thinking at the time, "Freedom thought Chuck was racist."[55] Both repeatedly clashed with Bryant, Cleaver, and Hazley. As a result of this repeated spurning and because labor had already cast its lot with Dick King over Cleaver, Freedom endorsed the opponents of Weber and Shields. The incumbents and their labor supporters were irate and made a series of comments that appeared to dictate to Freedom and the black community, only solidifying the organization's opposition to the duo.[56] Weber went on to use campaign materials that many observers felt were tinged with racism.[57] Freedom in turn distributed a flier that said:

> Stop the racist attacks on our community. Do not vote for Chuck Weber or Katheryn Shields. These people voted for the Ku Klux Klan to be on television, voted against having a black judge twice, they voted against the Cleaver plan and they believe a black man should not be mayor. Send them a message, we don't support the Klan or their friends, Weber and Shields.[58]

Weber and Shields won reelection, though Weber did so by a tight margin. They thus reentered office hostile to Freedom, its aspirations, and its elected members. Many other candidates featured on the Freedom ballot did win their races, though most of the margins were so lop-sided that Freedom could not be given much of the credit.

In short, there was much in the 1991 election results for African Americans and Freedom to celebrate. The new City Council would have five African American members (Cleaver, Bacchus, Coe, Finley, and Robinson), all of them current or lapsed members of Freedom. The lapsed members (Finley and Robinson) quickly made amends and were taken back into the fold. Most important, the euphoria over the election of the city's first African American mayor far surpassed any frustration that accompanied losses in the City Council races. The long-cherished goal of an African American occupying the 29th Floor of City Hall had been achieved.

Freedom was the lone LPO to mount a significant or effective effort for its candidates. Through the 1980s the CA had been coasting by, barely surviving. By 1991, it ceased to exist as a genuine organization; it met only in the few months directly surrounding the municipal elections, its officers were unknown to the general public, and it lacked any sort of volunteer or membership base. Its efforts in 1991 consisted of nothing except sending out mailings on its candidates' behalf, with the scope of the mailing determined by the largesse of the mayoral candidate funding it. Although the CA won ten races in 1991 (losing the biggest prize of all, the mayoralty), the organization's inactivity meant that the kindest remark even the most sympathetic *Star* columnist could make about the once-vaunted Association was "maybe the Citizens Association isn't as dead as people thought."[59] The CA's effective departure from the political scene brought a conclusive end to the organizational model which had long dominated Kansas City politics. The fact that Freedom stood alone among the city's LPOs as a living, breathing, and moderately efficacious organization seemed to promise that even better days were ahead for the organization and the African American community. Black Kansas Citians believed that they had reached the pinnacle of local power.

More of the Same: The 1995 Municipal Election

During his first term, Cleaver did little to stir up controversy or instill hostility toward him on the part of voters. A trip to Disney World that the mayor mistakenly billed to the city briefly enticed the scandal-minded members of the press, but it soon became clear that the so-called scandal was much ado about nothing.[60] Voters did reject Cleaver's pet proposal for a sales tax to fund a wide variety of capital improvements, improved city services, and housing rehabilitation in 1993.[61] Ridiculously and opaquely named Odyssey 2000, the rejection of that proposal was nevertheless followed by approval of subsequent ballot measures, indicating the failure of the earlier proposal did not reflect dissatisfaction with the mayor himself. Northlanders who overwhelmingly opposed Cleaver's candidacy in the first place continued to be unmoved by his charms, despite the fact that he appointed Northland councilwoman Sally Johnson as his mayor *pro tem.* The Disney World incident, the failure of Odyssey 2000, weak support in the Northland, and occasional criticism that the mayor was prone to changing his mind constituted the entirety of Cleaver's liabilities going into his reelection campaign in 1995. His charisma continued to win him admirers, as did his strong leadership of the City, his visible championing of improved race relations, and the fact that several important economic development projects began under his watch.

The odds favored Cleaver so strongly that few serious challengers emerged. The councilman for the prosperous Fourth District, Dan Cofran, declared his candidacy in the fall of 1994.[62] Cofran was regarded as a budget expert, but lacked much in the way of personality or a citywide profile. If anything, he was best known to voters for his luxurious mustache. His candidacy was hampered by the sense that he was challenging Cleaver out of pique, angered that the mayor removed him as chairman of the Finance Committee.[63] Also in the race was mass transit activist Clay Chastain, a figure widely known (and widely ridiculed) for his unflagging advocacy of failed ballot initiatives to construct a light rail system.[64] Chastain was eliminated after the primary.

Still wildly popular among African Americans, Cleaver was endorsed by Freedom in early February 1995. Cofran offered urban core and African American voters absolutely no reason to support him. The still-moribund CA self-destructively endorsed Cofran,[65] but Cleaver otherwise won most endorsements, including the Star's, and raised significantly more money than Cofran. In the primary alone, Cleaver out-raised Cofran by a ratio of six to one. Cofran never got any traction, despite using increasingly personal attacks on the mayor as a waffler, a showman, and fundamentally dishonest. Cleaver ran a positive campaign emphasizing the city's progress and only in the campaign's waning days did he deign to respond to Cofran's attacks, labeling him a "do-nothing" councilman.[66]

Freedom launched an aggressive drive to turn out black voters for Cleaver. Funded by contributions from the candidates on its slate as well as the candidates' financial backers, Freedom distributed thousands of pieces of literature, launched its most extensive telephone banking operation yet, canvassed neighborhoods, manned the polls on election day, aired ads on radio stations targeted toward African Americans, and provided free transportation to the polls.[67] Turnout was significantly lower in 1995 than it had been in the historic 1991 election, but black turnout still exceeded that of white turnout by several percentage points (see Table 9). Buoyed by near-unanimous African American support and a freak election day storm that affected only the Northland (thereby keeping his most determined detractors away from the polls), the incumbent mayor won decisively, collecting 51,057 votes (55 percent) to Cofran's 41,024 votes (45 percent). As in 1991, voting was racially polarized though Cleaver benefited from deeper white support than he had four years earlier. Cleaver received over 40 percent of the white vote in 1995.[68] Nevertheless, were it not for high black turnout and support for Cleaver, the mayor would have lost. With the host of institutional advantages that accompany incumbency, a strong record, and a pitifully weak challenger, Emanuel Cleaver's reelection was never much in doubt. Freedom did not therefore accrue much credit for it.

Table 9. Emanuel Cleaver's Electoral Performances and Voter Turnout in Predominantly African American Wards, 1995 City General Election

Ward	Cleaver Votes	Cleaver Percentage	Voter Turnout
2	2,311	89.3%	37.5%
3	3,089	96.8%	40.5%
7	2,725	95.4%	40.3%
14	2,384	90.2%	39.4%
15	3,056	92.5%	41.4%
16	2,920	92.3%	42.5%
17	3,069	91.4%	42.8%
18	3,056	92.5%	44.1%
Total in Predominantly African American Wards	22,610	93.2%	41.1%
Total in All Other Wards	28,447	41.9%	37.3%
Total	51,057	55.4%	38.0%

Source: Kansas City Election Board

Not so in the city council races, where Freedom proved itself to be the only LPO still capable of influencing electoral outcomes. Only Freedom activated a sizable army of campaign workers, effectively communicated on multiple occasions with its constituency by mail and telephone, presented a reasonably effective message (even if it consisted of little more than asserting that selected candidates would be the most supportive of Cleaver), and transported voters to the polls. The once-dominant CA's activity was reduced to little more than mailing a ballot to likely voters, wishing and hoping and praying that its proud history would still count for something with someone. It did not. When the CA and Freedom were not in agreement on a candidate, Freedom's candidate invariably defeated the one backed by the CA.[69]

For Freedom, the most important council race was in its Third District base. There, incumbent Carol Coe sought a second term. Coe was elected in 1991 with

Freedom's ardent backing, but by 1995 the councilwoman and the LPO were engaged in another one of their periodic feuds. She had stridently denounced a number of Freedom candidates and the organization itself as only "out for money" during the 1994 election cycle. Freedom's president at the time, Jackson County Legislator James Tindall, had not forgotten that Coe cast the deciding vote that denied him the chairmanship of the Legislature in 1987 and used this opportunity for reprisal.[70] Cleaver allies felt that Coe antagonized the mayor, either by attacking his policies directly or by forcing him to expend political capital to tamp down controversies she initiated.[71] A neighborhood activist, Mary Williams-Neal, was recruited by some Freedom insiders to make the race and received the LPO's endorsement.[72] Primarily to demonstrate its disdain for Freedom, the CA then chose to endorse Coe, despite the fact that her political orientation could not have diverged more widely from the CA's typical approach.[73]

Freedom exerted considerable effort on behalf of the little-known Williams-Neal, blanketing the Third District with literature and telephone calls. They found a receptive audience for their message that Williams-Neal would better advance the interests of the district's neighborhoods by being a reliable ally for Cleaver. Coe nevertheless won the primary on the strength of her years of involvement and undeniable political savvy. On primary day, though, Coe made a mistake that would haunt her for years to come. She justifiably denounced Kit Carson Roque for printing fake Freedom ballots four years earlier, but in 1995 Coe's workers distributed a ballot for "The Real Freedom, Inc." which closely resembled that of the real Freedom, Inc. in everything except the names listed on its slate. Freedom reacted furiously. The incident also provoked an investigation into her campaign's finances; before the general election, Jackson County Prosecutor Claire McCaskill (later a U.S. Senator) charged Coe with 20 violations of the campaign finance law, including converting some contributions into cash for personal use.[74] The maelstrom of negative publicity was overwhelming even by the singular standard one must apply to the career of Carol Coe. Aided by these factors and the high black turnout for Cleaver, whose supporters took the Freedom ballot at the polls as a matter of habit, Williams-Neal won the general election with 6,822 votes (54 percent) to Coe's 5,722 votes (46 percent).[75]

Freedom played a significant role in several other council races, though none so important as the Third District's. Freedom incumbent Ken Bacchus faced no serious challenge. Ron Finley and D. Jeanne Robinson were both elected over Freedom's opposition in 1991, but had since reconciled with the organization and found their way on to the Freedom ballot. Robinson was safe, but Finley faced stiff competition from AME clergywoman Saundra McFadden-Weaver. As a council member, Finley was irascible and known for haranguing city staff, but regarded as knowledgeable. McFadden-Weaver was an accomplished orator with something of a base among clergy, but her biggest support surprisingly came from white voters and Northlanders. Insiders speculate that these voters knew that Finley was African American but thought that McFadden-Weaver, who lacked the resources to blanket the city with campaign materials, was white; Northlanders supported her in large numbers during the primary, apparently thinking she was related to a popular Clay County activist named Gene McFadin. Finley then earned the reproach of the *Star* for a "sleazy" mailer that featured McFadden-Weaver's picture, but not his own, and read, "Saundra McFadden-Weaver is not related to Atty. Gene McFadin. She is an African Methodist Episcopal Minister who has no ties to the Northland."[76] Finley squeaked by to an 829-vote victory, and did so entirely on his margins in the Freedom wards.[77] Even in those wards, his margin was not overwhelming because of the support that McFadden-Weaver garnered from the black clergy. This demonstrated once again that Freedom was strongest when in firm alliance with the clergy and weakened, though not fatally so, when an alliance was absent.

The 1995 municipal elections resulted in some new faces at City Hall, but did nothing to change the fundamental dynamics of municipal politics. Emanuel Cleaver was reelected as mayor, showing that his political combination of tending to some African American interests while promoting the growth agenda that preoccupied civic elites was a popular one. Freedom proved itself to be the only LPO still worthy of the name, with the CA and most of the other political clubs exposed as organizations in name only. Political observers unanimously agreed that Freedom was the driving force behind the winners of the 1995 elections. Yet, Freedom itself was experiencing internal decay, a process that would soon accelerate. This would be clearly demonstrated in subsequent municipal elections, when conditions were different from those that prevailed in 1995. In the meantime, Freedom's reign inspired a confidence in the organization's ability to retain its allies in positions of power indefinitely. It also seemed to suggest, wrongly, that the potential for progress on African American issues was without limit.

The Internal Politics of Freedom, 1991–1999

When Emanuel Cleaver became mayor in 1991, African Americans took possession of an unprecedented amount of political power in Kansas City. African Americans occupied the mayor's office, four seats on the City Council, the local congressional seat, three school board seats (including the board presidency), five state legislative seats, and a seat in the county legislature (whose occupant, James Tindall, was frequently elected to serve as the body's chair). Every one of these officials was a member of Freedom. With this unprecedented power, one might think that Freedom would be able to coast along, using the institutional perquisites of incumbency to ensure its continued influence. One might think that such success would bring confidence in the leadership and the organization as a whole. Both suspicions would be false. Throughout the 1990s, Freedom was constantly buffeted by storms, some of them of its own making. By 1999—even as the organization remained an important part of the black community—it was clear that the constant drama, a never-ceasing campaign of scurrilous slander against it, continuing demobilization of the masses, and the problems of corruption and cliquishness left Freedom weaker than ever before. Freedom was also a victim of its own success; the fulfillment of the long-cherished goal of electing a black mayor, through no design of the occupant of that office, weakened the organization by creating a rival power center.

Changing Leadership, Confronting Fragmentation

In 1990, an internal coup ended the Freedom presidency and chairmanship of Archie Welch and the Rev. James Tindall, respectively. Welch was replaced on an interim basis by state senator Phil Curls, who previously served as president in the 1980s. Curls was nominally "in charge" of Freedom during the crucial 1991 elections, but his interim status denied him the imprimatur he needed to be decisively in control. Other elected officials, activists, and former leaders all made claims to being able to steer the organization in a particular way the 1991 elections. This muddied the waters considerably for others and led to a widespread perception that, crucial as Freedom was to Cleaver, the organization did not run the best campaign possible.[78]

In response to recognition that this leadership vacuum was a liability, soon after the 1991 municipal elections, Curls's interim status was dropped. Curls was selected on a permanent basis not just because he possessed the requisite political skills and connections (which he did, in abundance) but also because he was acceptable to all of the subgroups within Freedom. Starting in the 1990s, the interplay between these subgroups became an important factor in the governance and decision-making of the organization. Although subgroups had always existed in the organization, Freedom leaders found it increasingly difficult to maintain a united front amongst them at all times, with "infighting" and "fragmentation" increasingly dominating the group's internal politics.[79] One former Freedom leader described attempting to guide the organization's direction and membership as "kind of like herding, not cats, but snakes, because they'd turn around and bite you. They had their own agendas. It was very difficult [. . .] And it [had] the effect of tearing the organization asunder."[80] Every organization of any appreciable size *always* has subgroups, whose competing priorities and aspirants for leadership must be balanced in order to maintain peace. Nor is it perhaps even accurate to label the phenomenon being discussed here as concerning "subgroups," because that suggests that these groupings were relatively fixed and motivated by some definite set of goals. Instead, Freedom's subgroups were generally fluid in membership and defined by personality or tactical concerns. For example, some Freedom members clustered around Cleaver, others around Tindall, others around Curls and his family, a frequently renegade group around state representative Jackie McGee and councilwoman Carol Coe, and on and on. Curls was able to dispense with his interim status because he was on reasonably good terms with all of these subgroups and the leader most capable of coping with internal fragmentation.

To complete the leadership team in the largely honorific job of chairman of the board, Freedom members first elected Charles Hazley, who served from 1992 to 1993. Hazley then resigned the post, which was reclaimed by erstwhile occupant James Tindall. Although the Curls-Hazley and Curls-Tindall teams both had many positive attributes—including undeniable political savvy, experience in winning elections, and solid relationships with all Freedom subgroups—freshness and youth were not among them. All of these officers had already served previous terms in the Freedom leadership, their combined service in elective office approached half a century, and none could be said to represent a youthful perspective. None of these are necessarily liabilities, but they did represent a marked change from the days when "Doc" Holliday or even Curls and Hazley first claimed leadership roles in Freedom, when youth and freshness were regarded as salutary. It was also problematic that the leadership remained exclusively male. The LPO depended on the labor and commitment of African American women, including female elected officials, but seemed to have little room for them in the formal leadership. Moreover, the subgroup centered on McGee and Coe, who, as we shall see, frequently clashed with Freedom in very public ways, long clamored for the LPO to do a better job of empowering black women and, when it did not, used it as a rationale for their many ruptures from the organization.

The issue was resolved in 1994, when Freedom's leadership changed again. Demonstrating that he understood that the LPO's leadership should change with some regularity, Curls left the post voluntarily. Following a long tradition that saw board chairs replace retiring presidents, Curls's successor was Tindall. Tindall was, in turn, replaced as chair of the board by Mary Groves Bland, a long-serving and feisty state representative.[81] Tindall and Bland served through the devastating 1994 elections, which saw Freedom's candidate for county executive lose the primary by a few hundred votes and the crushing of Alan Wheat's senatorial ambitions. Since both leaders adopted a more consultative approach and wielded independent influence as elected officials, there was no move to replace them as there had been when Welch faced similarly devastating results four years earlier. Tindall and Bland were both at the center of subgroups, giving them leverage in Freedom's internal politics.

Tindall and Bland served in their respective positions until September 1996, when Tindall simultaneously resigned his positions as Jackson County Legislature chairman, Jackson County legislator, and Freedom president, because the bishop of his denomination ordered him to exit politics.[82] As Tindall was later charged, not long after he was consecrated as a bishop, with multiple counts of bribery, embezzlement, and filing false tax returns in a scandal that involved councilwoman D. Jeanne Robinson and the head of the Port Authority, one may wonder whether other factors were also involved. In 1999, Tindall was acquitted of all of the charges filed against him, except for one count of filing a false tax return.[83] Freedom went months without even an interim president, instead appointing a leadership team consisting of Bland, Curls, Welch, and "Doc" Holliday. Tindall and his allies attempted to install Lisa Hughes, a county employee and part of the Hughes family whose members have featured prominently in preceding pages, as president. Many members were clamoring for a woman to ascend to the presidency because, in the words of one Hughes supporter, "Women do all the work in this organization." Hughes had some support, but her candidacy foundered on the rocks of subgroup tension. Hughes's proximity to Tindall was a concern to his opponents within the organization, as was her embroilment in a miniature scandal of her own and her endorsement of a candidate in the race for a City Council vacancy.

Freedom member, Fifth District councilwoman, and Tindall relative D. Jeanne Robinson resigned her seat on the City Council after pleading guilty to extortion and mail fraud in a case unrelated to her official duties. (It was also unrelated to the aforementioned case involving Tindall, though her plea bargain with prosecutors led her to testify against the former county legislator.) A special election was called to fill the vacancy, with the two major candidates being Byther Williams, a longtime Freedom committeewoman, and Kelvin Simmons, a former Cleaver aide and director of the 1996 Missouri Democratic coordinated campaign. At the time of the succession drama, Simmons seemed to be the choice of most Freedom members, but Hughes backed Williams.[84]

Freedom operated with the "leadership transition team" called the Council of Presidents for nearly seven months, as jockeying for position raged on and the membership engaged in a heated debate. In June 1997, after receiving the blessing of the LPO's nominating committee, Mary Groves Bland defeated Hughes for the presidency in an open vote of 44 to 31.[85] Winning election based on her decades of service and experience in winning elections,[86] Bland became the first female president of Freedom. She would serve until 2000. Bland's replacement as board chair was Keith Thomas, a political functionary who served on the Jackson County Democratic Committee. Thomas defeated Bruce Watkins Jr. for the post, a tentative positive sign to those who criticized Freedom for recycling old faces.[87] Cleaver stayed out of the entire fracas. This was not surprising, as Cleaver generally excused himself from overt involvement in Freedom internal affairs during his mayoralty owing to the demands of the office, an understandable desire to distance himself from the LPO's more controversial decisions, and the nonexistent benefits to be gained from participating in the in-fighting. Cleaver was by no means apathetic about Freedom, but recognized that his own interests (and perhaps the organization's, to avoid conflation of its views with his) were better served by working through surrogates.

More than anything else, the prolonged drama demonstrated how rife with internal division and fragmentation the organization had become. Of course, since the very day of its founding Freedom members had disagreed with one another in public and behind closed doors. Uniformity was never expected, much less achieved. But in prior years, a six-month vacuum in and contest over leadership would not have occurred. That this sort of low-intensity conflict was permitted to endure so long, or that the decade contained more changes in leadership than any preceding one, was a mark of Freedom's declining organizational efficacy.

Accelerating the Demobilization of the Grassroots

The contest over leadership was not the only change in the organization during the Cleaver years. Even more than in previous decades, the LPO embraced professionalization at the expense of mass orientation and mobilization. Few of the activities that contributed to Freedom's grassroots base during the 1970s or even the 1980s continued into the 1990s. Occasional events were held that melded food, entertainment, and politics, like a significant voter registration drive.[88] These were open to the general public, but in practice catered mostly to Freedom members and the politically active. None of the subjects interviewed for this research could recall a single fundraiser Freedom held for itself during the Cleaver years, as the organization came to rely almost exclusively on contributions from candidates. Membership dues continued to be paid by several hundred people, but the total dollar amount was insignificant compared to the organization's fiscal needs. The most important events sponsored by the organization remained its preelection rally, sometimes accompanied by a parade through the Freedom wards. Although these events perhaps served to energize those already firmly committed to the candidates on the Freedom ballot, they did nothing to assuage the doubts of Freedom skeptics, bring new members into the fold, or build a mass movement for black interests.

During the 1990s, the last vestiges of the precinct captain network disappeared entirely. It is not fair to single Freedom out for the disappearance of a precinct captain network. Throughout the 1980s and 1990s, every other organization in the city that used such a system similarly saw its network evaporate. Still, no comparable replacement system for *two-way* communication was erected. Information typically flowed *from* Freedom *to* voters, rather than the other way around. Freedom publicized its activities and endorsements in *The Call* and *The Globe* (an organ of the black press founded in 1972), through direct contact with voters, and through civil society partners like professional organizations and churches, but did nothing to reproduce the information feedback loop that once existed. Many of Freedom's elected officials were in touch with the public mood, but they represented a fraction of the LPO's membership or board of directors, a body that grew to the remarkable size of 86 members. Relying on elected officials to pass along public sentiment was, moreover, certainly no solution on those occasions when the interests of the politicians differed from those of the masses. Freedom continued to hold regular meetings that were places of wide-ranging debate and open to the public, but even the monthly meeting went on hiatus during the leadership transition of 1996–1997.[89] Freedom was harmed by the fact that increasing numbers of urban core residents were departing the wards in which Freedom historically operated. The LPO struggled with ways to reach out to these voters, especially as many relocated in neighborhoods that were not predominantly African American.

Freedom became evermore, often exclusively, reliant on paid labor. Volunteers could sometimes be found for particularly popular candidates or because they believed deeply in Freedom's mission, but many of the LPO's workers were paid for their services. They were paid partly because of the great difficulty many of them had in taking time off work, partly to make the electoral machinery more reliable and consistent, and partly to provide economic opportunities to the community. For example, the phone banking operation typically hired several dozen unemployed African Americans for the duration of the campaign; although the work was short-term, its availability endeared the organization to those who received jobs and funneled some campaign dollars to those in the community who were desperately in need. Many interview subjects stressed that paid workers were no less committed to Freedom, its mission, or its candidates. Nevertheless, this did mean that professionalization became an even more dominant paradigm, which was by definition contrapuntal to a mass-oriented one. One sign that the LPO had become fully professionalized was the decision to name Bruce Watkins Jr. as its paid "executive director" in 1994. A paid executive was not a bad idea; indeed, it could easily be considered an important component of institutionalization. However, the executive director's tasks did not appear to include mobilizing a grassroots base or reaching out to new constituencies, like younger people who were not around or involved with Freedom in the days of Jordan and Watkins, Sr. Freedom's leadership readily conceded this point; during her presidency, Bland was vocal about the organization's failure at and need to reach out to younger people if Freedom was to survive. Although nearly everyone within Freedom agreed that something needed to be done to reconnect in a deeper fashion with the LPO's constituency, agreement was not reached on what form that action should take. Internal disagreement, lack of funds, and the more pressing problems of constant election cycles meant that even some simple steps, like building a website, were not taken. As a result, young people told media commentators that they felt isolated from Freedom and that they perceived themselves as having interests that diverged from the LPO's.[90] The perception reflected the false view that Freedom was primarily concerned about patronage and self-preservation. All of these factors—which can be placed under the heading "lack of effort"—contributed to the LPO becoming distant from its constituency and unable to mobilize it effectively, though it remained more connected to and concerned about that constituency than any other LPO in the city.

Charges of Corruption and Cliquishness

Arguably more damning still was the frequency with which Freedom came to be attacked as self-interested, corrupt, and cliquish. Similar criticisms had been made about Freedom almost since its founding, with the critics invariably asserting that the LPO had veered away from the example set in some earlier, more pristine era. Interview subjects who were highly critical of the 1990s incarnation of Freedom almost universally pointed to the 1960s or 1970s as periods when the LPO was free from corruption, cliquishness, or self-interest; yet, Freedom's opponents during those eras levied the same criticism as would be heard decades later. These circumstances, coupled with the fact that the evidence for corruption is not evidence at all but hearsay and rumor often promulgated by those who lost Freedom's endorsement, should cause us to be skeptical that the LPO became more self-interested and corrupt during the Cleaver years.

Nevertheless, it is absolutely true that *allegations* of unethical behavior became more frequent and polemical during the Cleaver years. Nearly every election came to feature a candidate (often an African American one) making the allegation that his or her candidacy was passed over by Freedom because career politicians inside the organization were out of touch and had sold out to white interests. In press conferences, interviews with the press, campaign literature, and paid advertisements, these candidates and their supporters—many of them members of Freedom—would allege that Freedom's endorsement was "for sale." It mattered not that those making this argument could never produce a shred of evidence to substantiate it. Given the LPO's method for selecting its candidates, where a screening/nominating committee made a recommendation to the full board of directors, even the idea seems absurd. The chances that any candidate could pay off enough people on a board of directors with dozens of members that made its decisions in public meetings that frequently featured heated debate and disagreement, and *not* leave a trail of evidence or have the facts of the pay off emerge, are nonexistent. As one longtime Freedom board member responded to this critique:

> If one or two people decided, I could say that. But the whole group votes on who they endorse, so that part wouldn't be true. To say that they just pick the one with the most money. What happens is, when they interview them, the committee votes on the one they going to endorse. Then they bring them to the group. And the group votes on them, and that's how it's done. So you can't say it's just for sale.[91]

What is clear, though, is that many candidates did not relish their screening experience. One African American candidate who did receive the endorsement vocalized this sentiment thus:

> I thought that a lot of the lines of questioning [were] unfair. I thought some of it was downright inappropriate, had nothing to do with my ability to serve. There was an emphasis on making contributions in order to promote my name and position on the ballot.[92]

An even more frequent narrative was that Freedom's endorsement decisions were made by a relatively small group of people and that the real decision was made far away from the formal process. The statement of one insider of a campaign that received Freedom's endorsement during this later period is representative. This insider said:

> The process was for us mainly finding someone who could get the endorsement. I was not especially, at the beginning, I was not aware how that happened. I thought it might have been as open as the *Star's* endorsement, where you just go and interview. But I saw pretty quickly that this is not how this process worked. That there was a much more intimate interview and there have to be people who believe in you who go to Freedom for you. So the job of the campaign was to find who that person could be, who would believe in the candidate and go on his behalf [. . .] I think it is four or five people in a restaurant making decisions and then disseminating them to people who rely on them to make decisions.[93]

Another political insider with experience in securing the Freedom endorsement concurred that the formal process was not as significant as the informal one with LPO elites. This insider commented, "There's this informal lobbying that sort of takes place with the board members, that you have to do to ensure that you are successful at the end of the process."[94]

The most intensive use of the deliberate strategy to discredit Freedom because of its endorsements came in 1994. In that spring's school board elections, the Freedom ballot included Darwin Curls (Phil Curls's brother) for a subdistrict seat, a black incumbent for an at-large seat, and a white incumbent for an at-large seat. Curls was challenged by Clinton Adams, while the two at-large incumbents were challenged by, among others, two additional African American candidates. Adams and one of the black challengers for the at-large seat assailed Freedom for endorsing a white incumbent and stated explicitly that the LPO's endorsements had been purchased by white people hostile to black interests for $30,000 (the source of this figure was never clear). In the process, the critics omitted the fact that they were largely bankrolled by white mortgage banker Jim Nutter (a key figure in Watkins's defeat in 1979 and Cleaver's victory in 1991), whose involvement was predicated on his views about the district's desegregation plan. Nutter's money granted his slate a victory, though Freedom succeeded in electing Curls over Adams.

The critique of Freedom as for sale became even more demagogic and brutal in that summer's Democratic primary. Alan Wheat gave up his House seat in a historic but ultimately futile bid for the United States Senate, setting up a crowded primary to replace him. Among the eleven candidates in the race were white state representative Karen McCarthy and African American state representative Jackie McGee. McGee believed that the 1994 primary would be a reenactment of the 1982 primary won by Wheat, where the white vote would be so fractured that a black candidate could win with a quarter of the ballots. This analysis was mistaken, as the liberal McCarthy proved effective at neutralizing the other white candidates in the race. Cleaver and Freedom endorsed McCarthy. McGee's relationship with Cleaver and Freedom had always been strained, so the fact that she was passed over was not surprising to anyone except for McGee. McGee and her supporters vociferously denounced Freedom week after week. They held press conferences, published ads, distributed literature labeling Freedom a bunch of "Uncle Toms," and granted interviews attacking the LPO as an unrepresentative clique, for sale, and insensitive to the needs of black women. McCarthy was called a "princess special interest" who was able to purchase Freedom's endorsement because the LPO's leaders were "clearly out of touch, out of their minds, or out for money."[95] These personal and vicious attacks may have won McGee some votes, but not enough to come remotely close to McCarthy or the second-place finisher. In a sign that Freedom remained relevant for all its travails and the abuse heaped at it during the campaign, McCarthy edged out McGee in the Freedom wards. Lest one think that Freedom's endorsement deprived the district of the potential for an African American representative, it bears noting that even if every last one of McCarthy's votes in the Freedom wards had instead gone to third-place finisher McGee, the latter still would have lost by a large margin.

Although the allegations of Freedom's endorsement being for sale appear to be false, the LPO is not blameless. The organization did little to counter this narrative, either by positively promoting itself or altering its behavior to make these allegations less viable. The potential for adopting a different fundraising approach seems to have been ignored. One African American member of the civic elite attributed many of Freedom's credibility and corruption problems to its fundraising methods:

> because in many ways they are under-funded. And I have had conversations with some of the leadership of Freedom, Inc. to say, why don't you host fundraisers so that you can have a pool of operational dollars to be independent and not really waiting on which candidate can make the greatest contribution to your organization, to get and have that decide things, not whether they're the most qualified person or not. Have your own independent source of funding so that you can truly look at each candidate irrespective of how much money they have in their campaign, in their coffers.[96]

Other allegations were also consistently made against Freedom. These included, as in the 1980s, that the LPO was tolerant of corruption and unethical behavior. Critics pointed to Freedom's occasional embrace of Carol Coe, who experienced many legal problems during her time in the public eye (though, it should be emphasized, Coe was cleared of wrong-doing in most of the allegations made against her). They pointed to Fifth District councilperson D. Jeanne Robinson, who resigned in 1996 after pleading guilty to mail fraud and extortion charges unrelated to her council office.[97] James Tindall, too, experienced legal difficulties; after stepping down from the Jackson County Legislature and the presidency of Freedom, he was convicted in 1999 on one count of filing false federal income tax returns but acquitted on multiple other counts.[98] Blaming Freedom for any of these events was absurd, especially since Robinson's most avid cheerleader during her initial election and her time in office was not Freedom but the *Star* and its city columnist, Yael Abouhalkah. Even more absurdly, the corruption of other municipal officials was somehow laid at the feet of Cleaver and, by extension, Freedom. Two additional members of the 1991–1995 City Council, Michael Hernandez and Chuck Weber, admitted to taking tens of thousands of dollars in bribes in exchange for providing assistance on development deals.[99] Neither Cleaver nor Freedom were remotely involved in that scheme; indeed, Freedom actively campaigned against both men.[100] The only case that could be said to include Cleaver even at the periphery was that of Elbert Anderson, and that only because he was the recipient of a mayoral appointment to the

Port Authority. Anderson was convicted in a bribery case related to casino development along on the Missouri River; it later emerged that he was a participant in bribes passed to Robinson and, he claimed, though a jury disagreed, Tindall.[101] It should be noted that the cases of Hernandez, Weber, Anderson, Tindall, and Robinson joined a spate of other corruption cases then being prosecuted in Missouri. This public integrity probe resulted in the downfall of the state's powerful House speaker and a host of other politicos, most of them white. Cleaver and Freedom were unjustly tarred by Dan Cofran and others as "tolerant" of corruption because fully one third of the 1991–1995 City Council pled guilty to illegal conduct.

Finally, Freedom was accused by its critics of becoming insular and cliquish. Critics claimed that the organization was effectively dominated by a "*very* small group of people—a very, very small group of people" who acted primarily to protect their own interests.[102] The notion that Freedom was self-serving and cliquish dated back at least to the 1971 municipal elections, but was now increasingly accompanied by allegations against specific individuals and families. One subject interviewed for this research asserted that, from the 1990s forward, Freedom was dominated by just four families, whose members occupied a huge percentage of the black community's elective offices, appointive offices, and Freedom leadership posts. There is no small amount of truth to the assertion; to take just one example, seven out of 28 candidates on Freedom's primary ballot in 1996 were members of those four families.[103] However, this may not be the product of cliquishness. Instead, it appears to be tied to the common tendency to vote for well-known names (Bush and Kennedy spring to mind) or to follow in the family business. Many within the organization conceded that Freedom put a high value on loyalty. Those who remained loyal to the organization the longest were the most likely to gain power and, as a practical matter, those who have been unswervingly loyal to the organization for the longest periods of time *do* belong to a relatively small circle.

The assertion of insularity should not be uncritically accepted. Numerous interview subjects pointed out that the people making this claim are usually those who have not bothered to try to become part of the organization in the first place. One longtime Freedom activist responded to the criticism in this way:

> To become a member of the Board, you just pay your dues and come to meetings. You just come through the door and pay $50. The idea that Freedom is closed, that's a perception, just a perception. That doesn't make a lot

of sense. Every person that is a member is a board member and has a say in how the organization is run. It is not a closed organization. You don't have to be invited to participate.[104]

However, these sensible defenses are less relevant than the fact that the demobilization of the black community during the 1980s and 1990s contributed to the ill feelings of those who held the view that the group had become insular and cliquish. One prominent and well-respected older community activist expressed a view that the organization's insularity closed off opportunities for cooperation, saying of Freedom:

> Far too often these days, it seems to me, there's a core group of people in the community who get involved in things, from my perspective, more for the notoriety that comes from that rather than for the purpose that the organization has. So obviously since I've never actually belonged to Freedom and don't attend the meetings, I must not consider what they're doing the most important thing, otherwise I'd probably make some time for it. But I don't. . . I'm not feeling that I would necessarily fit in, because I'm very mission-oriented.[105]

Still others point out that, even if one does accept the notion that Freedom became insular, the organization was not solely to blame. Members of the clergy interviewed for this book expressed the view that Freedom did not reach out to them as much as it could or did in prior years, but conceded that it was "a two way direction," with the black clergy failing to engage Freedom as it had in the 1970s and 1980s.[106]

A similar problem was the contention that the LPO was resistant to criticism and attempted to dictatorially impose the views of the leadership clique on the whole membership. Perhaps the best example of this came in 1997, when several board members were called before an "ethics committee" to discuss their flouting of the LPO's policy that board members should not publicly criticize the organization or dissent from its endorsements. Several of these members had criticized Freedom in print for being cliquish or had dissented from the LPO's endorsement of Kelvin Simmons for a vacant seat on the City Council. None were punished in any way, though one of the members so chastised, state representative Lloyd Daniel, claimed that he had been "kicked out" of Freedom. In reality, he resigned from the LPO, claiming that Freedom was motivated by self-preservation and not the pressing needs of "working people." Daniel was always to the left of the local mainstream and wanted Freedom to be something it was never intended to be, a broad church interracial movement of the working class that would take on a political system he regarded as "a criminal conspiracy."[107]

All of these criticisms became more common, powerful, and even self-fulfilling during the Cleaver years. It cannot be stated often enough that the objective truth of most of these allegations is debatable, while some are simply false or sour grapes. Nevertheless, the fact that these attacks were so frequently made suggests that their articulators were tapping into a view held by some contingent of the black population. Moreover, the constant repetition of the same attacks year in and year out eventually had an effect, as was intended. As one interview subject said, by the late 1990s and early 2000s, entanglement with Freedom was something that municipal candidates did not relish but instead, for many, became "a cross that you must bear."[108] Freedom accumulated a huge store of credibility from its activities in the 1960s, 1970s, and even 1980s, but those who knew and cared about its triumphs in those decades were a shrinking group. Even among those who were grateful for Freedom's history-making role, the never-ending assault on the LPO caused some to question its credibility. At the time of the 1997 leadership transition, for example, *The Call,* which had morphed over the years from ambivalent to hostile to generally supportive in its feelings toward Freedom, published a scathing, damning-with-faint-praise editorial about the LPO. It read in part:

At this point in its history, Freedom, Inc., needs new, vigorous leadership. Its new president should be young, energetic with a winning personality, unquestioned integrity, the ability to get along with and cooperate with all kinds of people and be knowledgeable about local, state and national politics. Freedom needs a new approach. Its new leaders should put the community first as it did when it was started by Jordan and Watkins back in the 1960's [*sic*]. The personal interests of the officers or Freedom should take a back seat with the interests and the welfare of the people in the community as the major focus. There are people within Freedom's membership who can provide the new, fresh approach that is now needed. As was the case in the past, Freedom, Inc. should conduct a wide membership campaign so that it will have a solid core of people who believe in and will support a strong organization and will pay dues so that the organization can support itself and not depend upon financial contributions from candidates and outside agencies. Freedom should stand on its own feet and develop the responsibility that an independent political organization should have.[109]

Freedom, Emanuel Cleaver, and the Role of Intermediary

The most significant change in Freedom's internal politics and structure, though, was not one entirely within the LPO's control. One of Freedom's major tasks over the years was to serve as an intermediary between the African American community and white civic and political elites. When these elites sought support for pet projects or favored candidates, it was Freedom that they approached to rally African Americans on their behalf. In exchange, Freedom bargained with those elites and demanded a wide variety of concessions to black interests. Freedom intentionally sought out this role; indeed, the ability to serve as an effective representative of the majority of black Kansas Citians, to negotiate from a position of strength on the community's behalf, to influence African Americans to uphold the community's end of whatever bargains were struck, and to then deliver visible benefits to the community were absolutely central to Freedom's self-conception and its path to success. For its first thirty years, white elites invariably turned to Freedom (even when they did not want to) because it was perceived to be the single, corporatist political voice of the community, unrivaled in its ability to perform this role on a sustained basis. Other figures and organizations outside of Freedom were certainly approached (particularly if those seeking an intermediary met with failure in their discussions with Freedom) to fill this role. But until 1991, Freedom was unmatched in its ability to convene relevant political actors in the black community, to create something approximating a united front, to effectively enter into short-term bargains with white elites, or to ensure that the bargain was upheld on both ends.

Emanuel Cleaver's election as mayor ruptured this dynamic. By virtue of his office, unsurpassed public profile, and the strong sense of pride that black Kansas Citians took in him, Cleaver effectively supplanted Freedom as the most important African American political actor in town. Cleaver remained a loyal member of the LPO and did nothing to consciously harm the organization, but his mere presence at the pinnacle of power was sufficient to cause many to consider whether Freedom remained necessary or to disregard it entirely. Candidates seeking public office or advocates of ballot initiatives went to Cleaver first and only afterwards did they approach Freedom for public support. As one former Freedom leader assessed it, this "tied the organization's hands on ballot issues. If Rev. [Cleaver's nickname—ed.] wanted a proposition to fund the zoo or the airport or the sewers, the organization invariably supported those things."[110] The mayor was presumed to be able to deliver the African American vote almost single-handedly and candidates coveted a picture of themselves shaking hands with Cleaver or permission to use a friendly word in the same way that they once coveted a spot on the Freedom ballot. Most white elites simply assumed that, if need be, Cleaver could dictate to Freedom; they failed to understand that the LPO was not the mayor's personal fiefdom and that the reins of leadership were held by others, who had different political priorities. To his credit, Cleaver did not encourage anyone to think in this way and refrained from overt intervention in the LPO's internal affairs. At the same time, the margins which Freedom could deliver to Cleaver's favored causes gave the mayor clout with white elites he might not have otherwise had.[111]

During his mayoralty, Freedom members were reluctant to express any disapproval of or disagreement with the mayor. It was felt that he was, in general, doing a good job, had a concrete vision of where he wished to lead the city, and that any criticism would only be used by enemies of the black community. As a result, Freedom often found itself following the mayor's lead, ceding its intermediary and agenda-setting roles to him. The LPO, too, relied on the "Cleaver magic" to move its voters to the polls and to encourage specific outcomes. Freedom materials from this period are replete with photos of and testimonials from the mayor—far more than had been the case with any previous Freedom member, leader, or candidate—and entreaties that the way to support the mayor was by voting the Freedom-recommended position. Cleaver possessed a greater ability than Freedom did to deliver the benefits he promised during bargaining; he had control over patronage and policy, while Freedom could only promise to agitate or turn out voters. Finally, elites of all kinds naturally prefer to engage in bargaining with a singular intermediary, one person, than to grapple with the diverse, ever-changing positions of Freedom's 86-member board. As one Cleaver confidante noted, "A lot of folks in the majority community felt that they could go to Cleaver because he was a much more palatable alternative than the folks over at Freedom, who some considered, by their standards, to be a little more radical."[112]

At the same time, the African American members of the City Council frequently disagreed quite vigorously with Cleaver and some of his policies. These disputes were not always publicly aired, but "behind the scenes" the African American council people were not a united front. Longtime observers were puzzled by the fact that Freedom seemed unable to create the same sort of discipline that it had in the past. One political insider who arrived at City Hall for the first time during Cleaver's second term said:

One of the things that shocked me, and this probably shows my ignorance, when I first [came to City Hall] in 1995, I couldn't understand why the various elected black officials weren't on the same page. You had the first elected African American mayor, who was having problems with Ken Bacchus on issues. [. . .] There seemed to be as much division in the African American community in the Caucasian community, and for whatever reason that surprised me. I just figured they'd be all on the same page, because they're all Democrats and they all believe in the same things, but you wouldn't have known it. And I did not see Freedom being actively involved in trying to sort that out.[113]

With all of these conditions, it is not at all surprising that Cleaver effectively and unintentionally displaced Freedom as a rival power center, weakening Freedom's claim to be the corporatist political voice of the community, and better positioned to bargain with nonblack political forces. Deprived of these major sources of power, Freedom was weakened. This decline in organizational efficacy was self-reproducing. If voters' affection was now transferred to the personage of Cleaver, civic elites had no reason to promise Freedom anything in exchange for its support; if Freedom could not offer anything concrete to its constituents in exchange for their support, voters had no reason to give it to the LPO. To be clear, the LPO continued to be consulted and its endorsement still sought by nearly every candidate or ballot initiative imaginable. What changed was the intensity with which this support was sought, the extent to which others were willing to bargain to receive it, the priority ascribed to earning it, and the availability of "alternatives." This is the sort of power that, once lost, is difficult to reclaim. That Cleaver became less prominent on the political scene from 1999 until his successful congressional campaign in 2004 did not result in Freedom's erstwhile status being transferred back to it. It was simply lost.

Freedom, Inc. at the End of the 1990s

In short, the Cleaver years were not the paradise for Freedom that was expected when the city's first African American mayor took office in 1991. Quite the contrary, Freedom was internally weaker at the end of the 1990s than it had been at the beginning of the decade. Freedom, Inc. weakened in the 1990s because it was a living, breathing organization, with its own internal politics and sometimes unpredictable responses to external stimuli. This is what accounts for the seemingly paradoxical fact that Freedom's internal strength declined at the same time that it achieved its long-cherished goal of electing an African American mayor.

For all this litany of ways in which Freedom declined over the course of the 1990s, it is important to remember that it remained the dominant LPO in the black community and in the entire city. Freedom alone among the city's LPOs retained any sort of standing electioneering apparatus, the loyalty of members, or a clear mission. Even those who were willing to denounce Freedom to the press came calling, replacing their criticism with deference at least for the few minutes when they were in the presence of the membership. As Mary Bland said, "'It's amazing how everyone talks about how terrible Freedom is, but they always want to be part of the organization."[114]

Unfortunately, simply being the dominant political organization in Kansas City was not enough. The gradual decline in Freedom's potency impaired the ability of African Americans to make demands on the system or to elect candidates of their choice. Quite contrary to the assertions of its harshest critics, Freedom's decline impacted more than just a few families or an insular band of black elites. It had consequences for the entire African American community.

Does Black Power Mean Black Interests Are Served? Municipal Policy-Making in the Cleaver Years

When Emanuel Cleaver was inaugurated as mayor of Kansas City, Missouri in April 1991, African Americans held an unprecedented amount of formal political power in the region. Black Kansas Citians were eager and excited about what the future would hold, believing that arrival at the pinnacle of power would finally produce the sort of radical change for which they had long been clamoring. Through a combination of unrealistic expectations, the need for Cleaver and black council members elected at-large to avoid angering whites, and, most importantly, the withering of Freedom, radical change did not come for black Kansas Citians. This does *not* mean that Cleaver's tenure in office was unsuccessful. Quite the contrary, Emanuel Cleaver ranks among the best mayors that Kansas City has known. Nor does it mean that the Cleaver administration failed to advance black interests. It did—but not to the extent that it might have, if the administration had faced a more organized campaign of agitation and pressure from Freedom. Kansas City's experience with an African American mayor was similar to that of other major American cities: Progress for black residents was real but limited, breeding disillusionment.

During this time, Freedom ceased intervening in the municipal policy-making process at all, consciously deciding, as one key Freedom strategist put it, that electoral "politics is our only business."[115] This was a continuation of the path the LPO chose in the preceding decade. During the Cleaver years, Freedom took formal positions on policy only when a ballot initiative was involved. The organization almost never formally lobbied on behalf of policies, issued reports, or sought to act as a special interest group, as it had in the 1960s and 1970s. Interview subjects familiar with the policy-making process at City Hall during this time could recall only a handful of occasions, and some not even that, when Freedom contacted policy-makers with an "official position" from the organization. These informants could recollect dozens of occasions when *members* of Freedom contacted them on policy matters, often claiming to represent the "community" at large, while holding a position diametrically opposed to others claiming they represented the "community," but lamented the fact that it was difficult to sort out where Freedom itself stood. Indeed, one municipal policy-maker had this to say:

> The one thing I don't think they've done as well as Citizens or Forward [Forward Kansas City, an LPO that advocates for Northland regional interests—ed.], if there is an important issue, their boards will meet and take a position and communicate that as a board. I haven't seen that out of Freedom. If they would come to me and say how could we be more effective at City Hall, I think that would be one of my suggestions. That you take a vote and that this is the official position, or that you've been authorized by Freedom, Inc. to advocate on behalf of this candidate or position.[116]

The regular monthly meeting of Freedom remained an open forum where policy could be discussed. The threat that the LPO would withdraw its support at the next election remained present. However, the approval of term limits diminished the potency of the threat, as, for many council members, there would not be a next election. Leveraging electoral support for particular policy outcomes was increasingly restricted only to the biggest, most important issues of all. As a result, it is fair to say that Freedom completely divorced itself from the policy-making process. The withdrawal of the black LPO from the unifying or pressure-applying role that it could play meant that less was accomplished than might otherwise have been. This came a time when there were four major recurring issues areas for black Kansas Citians: crime and policing, diversity in municipal government, redevelopment of the famed Jazz District, and neighborhood revitalization and economic development.

Crime and Policing

The major preoccupation of the African American community during Cleaver's first three years in office was the shocking prevalence of crime, especially murder and gang-related crime. These types of crime reached record levels for several consecutive years in the early 1990s, with a string of years with record-breaking numbers of homicides: 150 in 1992, 153 in 1993, and 142 in 1994.[117] The increase in crime was consistent with national patterns, but the city had one of the highest crime rates in the country, especially for young African American males. The local outcry for action to be taken was justifiably immense, with *The Call*, the Ad Hoc Group Against Crime, and the faith community all entreating the mayor and council to do *something*. One Baptist church at 27th Street and Prospect Avenue, near the epicenter of the crime wave, even built a mock cemetery, adding a cross for each murder victim, to draw attention to the problem. The outcry against crime was largely contained to the urban core. This was because the explosive increase in murders and gang-related crime was contained to a narrow corridor within the urban core; residents of the southwest corridor or the quasi-suburban Northland were untouched by, even blissfully unaware of, the situation.

As has been noted previously, the Kansas City Police Department is funded by but not under the control of the City. The extent to which municipal policymakers could effect change in the KCPD's response to violent crime was limited. Nevertheless, Cleaver used public relations and personal charisma to bring greater attention to the victims of crime. He would visit crime scenes, interacting with family members and neighbors. A "gang summit," organized by national groups and figures like Ben Chavis, attracted antigang crusaders from around the country, bringing attention to the problem and producing a handful of ideas that would be used by the KCPD.[118] Although these events were more symbolic than substantive, they at least seemed to suggest that the issue was a priority for the mayor (an ex officio member of the Police Board) and his administration. Action of a more substantive nature came when Cleaver successfully shepherded through the City Council and the Police Board a proposal for "Community Action Teams," a form of community policing. Acting under intense pressure from the black community, the KCPD resumed foot patrols in high-crime areas. These initiatives, continually developing partnerships with civil society groups, and an improving economy succeeded in reversing the trend towards higher crime by 1995.[119]

Unlike in previous decades, police brutality was not a burning issue. There were incidents of brutality that received attention, but they seemed to be less patently outrageous, less publicized, and less frequent than in the past. Alas, even when incidents of brutality did arise, Cleaver did little about them. Instead, the mayor stayed far away from these situations. None of the African American members of the council were vocal when cases of police brutality arose, with the exception of Carol Coe, whose own run-ins with the police made her a less-than-ideal messenger. During one of the most troubling incidents of the 1990s, when neighbors reacted violently to a police killing of a drug-crime suspect, all five black council members hastened to condemn the violence, denounce the "thugs" involved, and deny that a "riot" or "racial incident" had taken place.[120] The facts that the police officer and the suspect/victim were both African American and that the suspect/victim reportedly drew a firearm were certainly relevant and perhaps mitigated the social implications of the situation. Still, it was disturbing to see the speed and intensity with which elected officials denied even the faintest possibility that the subsequent actions of the neighbors (which included setting cars ablaze) were a reaction to systemic issues rather than mindless destruction. The notions that the incident might have been triggered by decades of insensitive police behavior in black neighborhoods, frustration with the blatant racism of the criminal justice system, distrust of legal authority, or anger at the increasingly militaristic approaches that worked silently behind the friendly face of community policing were never entertained. These potentialities were dismissed because the circumstances of the incident that created the furor lacked the noble, easily martyred victim that public opinion demands and reality so rarely supplies. Those hoping that an unprecedented presence for African Americans in the corridors of municipal power would result in systemic changes to the city's method of policing, particularly in predominantly black neighborhoods, would be sorely disappointed.

Diversity in Municipal Government

Another issue from past decades that carried over into the Cleaver years was that of diversity in municipal government, through employment, contracting, and appointed office. Remarkable progress was made on this issue over the twenty year period from 1971 to 1991, but more remained to be done. There was some notable progress on this front during the Cleaver administration, starting with the fact that the new mayor appointed more African Americans and Latinos to municipal boards and commissions than any of his predecessors.[121] African Americans and Latinos remained underrepresented on these bodies, compared to their share of the population, but the disparity was dramatically reduced. African Americans or Latinos were named to all of the most important municipal boards, and many were made chairs. Similarly, the number of African American department heads and senior managers increased over time, although it was still not fully representative of the population or the municipal workforce. For several years in the mid-1990s, two of three assistant city managers were African American and were considered more influential than the actual city manager.

Of course, these were largely symbolic accomplishments that cost little and did not necessarily result in a government that was more responsive to its black citizens.[122] On a more substantive note, the city became more committed than ever to its affirmative action policies in employment and contracting. After courts struck down affirmative action and supplier diversity policies similar to Kansas City's, many municipalities threw up their hands in despair. Under the leadership of Cleaver and several African American members of the City Council, Kansas City followed a different route. It revised its municipal ordinances to make its diversity programs withstand legal scrutiny, including commissioning an expensive disparity study to document the effects of historic and contemporary discrimination against and exclusion of African Americans, Latinos, women, and other "disadvantaged" groups. The city retained its MBE (minority business enterprise) and WBE (woman-owned business enterprise) designations for contracting, but added one for disadvantaged business enterprises (DBE), which could be granted to businesses that could prove they had been socially disadvantaged, and set numerical goals for participation by all of these business types on municipal projects. A Fairness in Construction Board was created to implement, monitor, and improve upon the process by which MBEs, WBEs, and DBEs received work from the city.[123] Although problems would persist, this system represented a distinct improvement over the past and resulted in hundreds of millions of dollars in contracts being let to African American-owned companies.

Achieving progress on diversity in employment, contracting, and appointive office was not an unvarnished success. The city lost an opportunity to appoint its first African American and female city manager, something for which Cleaver is partly to blame. Under the council-manager system, the city manager is the chief executive of the city. The city manager wields enormous power and is capable of subverting the will of the mayor and council. Implementing policy is often more important than making it, and this is particularly true for populations that have been historically disadvantaged by the policy process and bureaucracies. Appointing a city manager sensitive to the aspirations of African Americans is thus crucial to the advancement of black interests, though phenotype is by no means the determinant of such sensitivity.

In 1993, the City Council unceremoniously dumped the incumbent city manager. The director of the Neighborhood and Community Services Department, Mary Vaughn, was named as the acting city manager. Vaughn, an African American woman, had worked for the city for nearly three decades, was regarded as highly competent, and was well liked by neighborhood leaders at a time when the council professed to be making neighborhood issues its priority. Vaughn and her husband were also believed to be personal friends of Cleaver. A national search for a new city manager produced three finalists: Vaughn and two white males. The council became deadlocked over whom to select as the new manager, particularly because all involved agreed that the selection should be made with a super-majority of ten and not the mandatory majority of seven. Vaughn, who had by then been acting city manager for six months, claimed the support of four council members: Bacchus, Coe, Robinson, and the Northland's Sally Johnson. Larry Brown, a highly mobile city manager then working in Ann Arbor, Michigan, had the support of seven council members who insisted that his finance background was more relevant than Vaughn's front-line service delivery experience. Three nonwhite members—Cleaver, Finley, and Michael Hernandez—were said to be in Brown's camp. After a lengthy standoff, Vaughn was summoned to Cleaver's office where he informed her that he would not support her and that her selection was impossible. Vaughn withdrew the very next day, much to the consternation of the black press, black clergy, and neighborhood leaders throughout the city.[124] There is no doubt whatever that Cleaver's lack of support for Vaughn was the major impediment to her selection. At the time, Cleaver possessed enormous influence with his colleagues and could rally a majority for anything that took his fancy. Historical norms dictated that the mayor was given the central role in choosing a new city manager, a norm that did not apply to decisions about whether incumbent managers should be retained.[125] It is not to indulge in the fantasy of the omnipotent executive to contend that Vaughn would have become the city manager if Cleaver had thrown her his support.

Given the fact that Vaughn was eminently qualified and her brief interim tenure was regarded as a success, one can only speculate as to why Cleaver did not support her. It is well within the realm of possibility that the mayor feared that he would be regarded (even more than racism already caused him to be) as a mayor exclusively by, for, and of black Kansas Citians. The black political actors that would normally have sprung into action to defend Vaughn—Freedom, Inc. chief among them—were conspicuously absent from the debate. Although Freedom members spoke up for Vaughn in their personal capacities, the organization itself did not. Nor did Freedom threaten repercussions if Vaughn was not selected, as it had under previous mayors. Freedom and other African American political actors restrained themselves out of fear that opposing Cleaver would weaken his standing with white voters and harm their own standing among black voters, whose loyalty to the mayor was remarkable. It would be more than a decade before Kansas City selected its first African American city manager; a female manager has yet to be selected. Brown, incidentally, proved to be an unmitigated disaster and quit under imminent threat of termination less than three years after being hired.

Jazz District Redevelopment

During the Cleaver years, African Americans were keenly interested in the redevelopment of the historic Jazz District. While a councilman, Cleaver devised an innovative plan to fund a variety of neighborhood improvements, including the Jazz District. The plan called for expending $20 million at 18th and Vine to build the International Jazz Hall of Fame, a Negro Leagues Baseball Museum, and catalyze development in the District. This initiative was important for the bricks-and-mortar construction it would bring to a supposedly blighted neighborhood, but also because of the District's symbolic importance as the historic heart of the African American community.

The redevelopment of the Jazz District was plagued by controversy, problems, and lengthy delays. Other components of the Cleaver Plan—like improvements in the Brush Creek corridor and a new arena for the American Royal rodeo—were open to the public long before the Jazz District project had so much as a definite plan.[126] When one of the original partners, the Charlie Parker Foundation which was to operate the International Jazz Hall of Fame, abandoned the project and the Negro Leagues Baseball Museum suggested that it would only operate a limited, satellite facility at 18th and Vine, it was Cleaver's intervention that salvaged the project.[127] Cleaver made the revitalization of 18th and Vine the

centerpiece of his legacy in the African American community and the dogged-
ness with which he pursued the project eventually succeeded. The revitalized
Jazz District finally opened in 1997, eight years after the Cleaver Plan made construction possible.[128] What was once a desolate area became one of Kansas City's
showpieces, with the American Jazz Museum, the Negro Leagues Baseball Museum, the Gem Theater, and the Blue Room jazz club all winning rave reviews. The
city's expenditures in the district exceeded the planned budget, leading to intense
criticism from those who were not excited about the project in the first place.[129]
Further criticism was leveled because the other development to be catalyzed by
the cultural attractions, like service businesses and new housing, did not immediately materialize and the Jazz District was often vacant after dark. New housing
and a handful of businesses did eventually come to 18th and Vine, though not on
the scale anticipated and only after Cleaver's tenure in office ended.

For all this criticism, there can be no denying that the revitalization of the
Jazz District was an important accomplishment. It was important because of
the District's historical and cultural significance, because it represented a significant investment in a predominantly African American neighborhood, and
because it was an attempt by the city to create a cultural attraction in the black
community. The District was among the first Tax Increment Financing (TIF)
districts in the city. The TIF designation was intended to capture incremental
tax revenue to fund revitalization. This plan was unsuccessful, but the effort
to use new tools to stimulate economic development in underserved areas was
praiseworthy. A TIF plan was established at the express direction of African
American council members, who made it known that they would be reluctant
to use the tool in other areas of the city (where it was eagerly sought and would
eventually become common to the point of abuse) unless 18th and Vine received the designation.

Neighborhood Revitalization

The Jazz District was not the only project designed to revitalize a predominantly African American neighborhood during the Cleaver years, but it was the
largest. Also notable was the Mt. Cleveland Initiative, spearheaded by a group of
nonprofits that later became known as Swope Community Enterprises (SCE),
in the heart of the urban core. SCE's member entities built a $18 million com-
munity health center, new housing for low-income residents, an office building,
and participated in the development of a major customer service center for H&R
Block. Municipal government provided a variety of tax incentive and financing
tools to these projects.

Although funds were expended on a number of other neighborhood revitalization projects in the African American community, frequently using federal
grant funds, none approached the size and scale of those found in the Jazz District and Mt. Cleveland. City government continued to spend modest amounts
on new infrastructure, housing, and amenities in urban neighborhoods, sometimes through CDCs, on the theory that these small-scale investments would
metastasize. During the 1995–1999 council term, many CDCs saw their appro-
priations from city government decline or terminated altogether. The leader of
this drive to defund CDCs was Third District councilwoman Mary Williams-
Neal, who grew frustrated with the lack of production by and corruption within
some CDCs.[130] This was a sore point for many African American activists. They
saw their neighborhoods declining, largely because of broader social forces, and
little or no response from black elected officials. Private capital was not eager to
invest in these communities, making it difficult for the city to do much, and federal funding cuts meant that the city could not distribute the same largesse that
it had in the 1970s and 1980s.

Out of political expediency, some resources were deployed in low-need areas
that might have otherwise been used to improve high-need, predominantly African American neighborhoods. In contests for shares of an ever-shrinking pot
of dedicated neighborhood funding, African American elected officials in the
1990s found themselves out-flanked or out-voted when seeking to direct more
money to the neighborhoods they represented. Sometimes, in order to keep
peace on the council, they opted not to fight, but permitted other areas of the
city to take larger shares of the funds than need or population would dictate.
Freedom, which in earlier years might have intervened by making its future endorsement contingent on support for a particular project or level of investment,
refrained from any involvement in the issue.

Cleaver and his allies did attempt to increase the funds available for revitalization of African American neighborhoods. The Odyssey 2000 proposal, for
example, would have created a sales tax to fund neighborhood and housing improvements. It was rejected by the voters despite Cleaver's strong support.[131] TIF
and an assortment of other innovative economic development tools were introduced or enhanced during the Cleaver administration. These tools were generally intended to benefit neglected neighborhoods, those where development
would not take place but for the incentive or some other public intervention
into the market. In practice, the municipal growth machine hijacked these programs and ensured that even the most prosperous and thriving of neighborhoods could access these tools.[132] With prosperous neighborhoods able to use

these incentive programs, neglected African American neighborhoods were deprived of the competitive advantage the programs might have provided them. As a result, the very tools designed to revitalize the least-advantaged neighborhoods instead reproduced the divide between the city's rich and poor areas. The under-concentration of incentives in high-need areas would grow worse after Cleaver left office, but the permissive tone creating that pattern was set in his administration.[133]

Criticism of Cleaver's Approach to Black Interests

The efforts of Emanuel Cleaver, African American members of the City Council, and sympathetic white allies produced some concessions to black demands on the system. African Americans interviewed for this book universally professed gratitude for and pride in Cleaver's service as mayor. However, a divide existed in views about the extent to which his mayoralty made a difference in the lives of black Kansas Citians. Some interview subjects pointed to infrastructure, capital improvements, and housing as tangible evidence of the difference his administration wrought. One longtime neighborhood activist was representative of this view, stating "When you look at the things that happened around 12th Street, [that is] one difference that he made [. . .] I think he made a difference." This activist also believed that expectations of Cleaver were too high, saying "I have never been under the illusion that having a person of any particular race will solve the problem of the whole race when they're in office."[134]

Others, though, expressed a profound disappointment in what Cleaver was able to accomplish. These interview subjects criticized Cleaver for not demonstrating stronger leadership on black issues. As mayor, they maintained, Cleaver strayed far from his radical and revolutionary roots to adopt a managerial approach. Cleaver heavily promoted several municipal job creation programs, but did little to address chronic racial, class, or spatial disparities in employment patterns. Some critics wondered why Cleaver was not more outspoken on the many travails of the Kansas City, Missouri School District, although the district's complete independence from local government ought to absolve him of responsibility on that count. Others questioned why the Housing Authority of Kansas City, which served primarily African American clients, was allowed to wallow in poor management to the point that a federal court ordered it into receivership; Cleaver installed his top aide at the authority to resolve its manifold issues shortly before the court order, but the dysfunction was too deeply entrenched and too long-standing for that appointment to make any difference.[135]

More than anything else, critics of local government's responsiveness to African American interests during the Cleaver years wanted a bolder mayor. Criticisms of this sort are far more subjective than any other kind; they ask for a different but vaguely defined tone. Vague as they may be, there is an element of truth to these critiques. Cleaver was frequently reluctant to appear as though he were showing favoritism to the black community or to be pigeon-holed as concerned only about black issues. A good example of this came at the end of his term, when Cleaver effectively disowned his excellent record of appointing African Americans to important positions. When asked during an interview with *The Call* whether he set out to appoint a large number of African Americans to boards and commissions, the mayor responded, "No, I really didn't. I simply wanted to have an open administration where people of color would play prominent roles in the evolution of my vision."[136] Cleaver and his advisers were deeply aware of the mayor's tenuous hold on white support; he never won a majority of the white vote and a significant portion of the white electorate persisted, all evidence to the contrary, in believing that Cleaver was a dangerous black militant. African American critics sometimes seemed to ignore the structural realities of local politics, which demanded support from a share of these very same white voters. These critics allowed their expectations to outpace what was objectively possible.

In short, Cleaver was subject to what Thompson has called "double trouble," a phenomenon whereby black mayors are criticized by white voters for being excessively race-conscious while they are simultaneously criticized by black voters for being insufficiently race-conscious.[137] Unlike Thompson's prime example of this phenomenon, former New York City mayor David Dinkins, Cleaver suffered no electoral consequences from his double trouble; he was later elected to Congress from a white majority district and his black critics were reluctant to publicly say an unkind word about the man. The low intensity of the criticism faced by Cleaver is a testament to his prodigious political gifts and genuine accomplishments, but does not eradicate the reality that some African Americans expected the election of a black mayor to accomplish more than it did.

Critics tend to wrongly focus their dissatisfaction on Cleaver or his black council colleagues. This causes them to ignore the total absence of pressure placed on these individuals by Freedom during the 1990s. Policy makers respond to agitation and pressure. The approach taken by Freedom during the Cleaver years was to put boundless confidence in the mayor, to let him, in the words of one interview subject, "rule the roost."[138] Freedom gave the mayor unwavering support rather than publicly challenging him, even though some interviewees acknowledged that Cleaver's administration and its approach to black issues "irritated some in Freedom."[139] Past mayors, even those with whom Freedom maintained a warm relationship, could rely on constant confrontation, challenges, and negotiation from Freedom. Not all of those confrontations were successful, but their simple existence was sufficient to worry successive administrations. In the absence of any similar pressure from Freedom from 1991 to 1999, it is unsurprising that less was accomplished in transforming black Kansas City than some of the most ardent advocates of a black mayor hoped. Similarly, with black elected officials and Freedom unable to produce the benefits expected by the black community from its moment of greatest triumph, the Cleaver election, it is hardly surprising that African American voter turnout subsequently plummeted; with the disillusionment that comes from experience, African American voters no longer found Freedom's entreaties about the importance of a particular election so credible.

Freedom in Decline
Municipal Elections After Cleaver

Actions have consequences. The consequences may be delayed, unpredictable, and reversible, but they exist. By the end of the 1990s, Freedom's actions over the previous fifteen years—the embrace of professionalization at the expense of mobilization and mass orientation, the constant criticism of self-interest and insularity, the internal fragmentation, the ceding of the power to bargain with non-black political forces to Cleaver, the abandonment of the policy-making process, and the disappointment over the extent to which arriving at the pinnacle of power actually improved the lives of black Kansas Citians—had consequences. What these consequences were would become known after Freedom suffered losses in three consecutive municipal elections: 1999, 2003, and 2007.

The 1999 Elections

As Emanuel Cleaver prepared to leave office in 1999, having run up against the city's two-term limit, it was unclear what Freedom's role in city politics would be. Some expected Freedom to rally its forces in order to retain some degree of control at City Hall, others seemed to believe that such a high level of black representation in municipal government was now a naturally occurring phenomenon that required no effort, and still others expected Freedom to reduce its involvement since it had achieved the goal of electing a black mayor. Freedom opted for the first route, but the 1999 elections proved to be an embarrassing rout for the organization.

One trouble was that the organization was remarkably divided on what action it should take in the mayor's race. Four major candidates were in the running. Kay Waldo Barnes, a former one-term Jackson County legislator and one-term Kansas City councilwoman, was considered the front-runner. Barnes was appointed by Cleaver to chair the powerful TIF Commission, where her leadership impressed many and garnered the endorsement of the remnants of the CA. By investing her own money in her campaign, Barnes held a significant fundraising advantage. Although she treated the organization with respect, Barnes did not anticipate winning the Freedom endorsement. George Blackwood was a two-term incumbent councilman holding the at-large seat for the city's far southern district. Blackwood was mayor pro tem in Cleaver's second term and the incumbent mayor made no secret of the fact that he'd like to see Blackwood as his successor. Jim Glover was a two-term incumbent councilman known for his commitment to neighborhood issues, but not regarded as having an abundance of charisma. The only African American candidate in the race was Janice Ellis, a successful businesswoman, columnist for the local black press, and former high-ranking city staffer in Milwaukee.[140] The politically unknown Ellis entered the race only after better-known African American politicians declined to run.

Freedom dithered longer than normal in deciding whom to endorse. Although she began the race without a political base, Ellis won the support of some of the most prominent members of the black clergy (owing to the influence of her own pastor, the widely revered Wallace Hartsfield Sr., and a long record of philanthropy that she shared with her husband, the head of Swope Community Enterprises, the city's largest community health center and community development corporation). A significant investment of her own money funded name recognition-boosting efforts in the black community; with Ellis's face plastered on billboards throughout the urban core, many "average" voters became aware that a black candidate was in the race.[141] These factors, coupled with the appeal of Ellis's promise to bring a more business-like and sensitive approach to city services, made her a serious candidate. Ellis was not particularly favored by Freedom "insiders," largely because she was an enigma to them (at least on a political level, though they knew her socially). She was "an African American candidate that had not grown up in the traditional elected offices and [did not have] an intimate relationship with the older African American political organizations," while "Emanuel Cleaver, who came up out of that tradition, was behind a white candidate." The organization was thus "caught between this 'traditional' behavior [supporting those who came up through traditional elected offices and the organization itself—ed.] or whether to support the black candidate."[142] The influence of the black ministers, and an awareness that it would look bad for the LPO to pass over a qualified black candidate in favor of a white one, prevailed. The Freedom nominating committee was led by veterans who recalled the damaging 1983 split with the ministers. Just weeks before the primary, the nominating committee recommended that Ellis head the Freedom ballot. Cleaver then made a rare overt intervention into Freedom affairs, writing a controversial memo to the board of directors urging them to spurn the committee recommendation and endorse Blackwood (despite the fact that Cleaver's wife was then an employee of the health center led by Ellis's husband). Angering Cleaver, the Freedom board declined to take his advice after what one person called a "rather contentious meeting."[143]

Hampered by a lack of money with which to run a campaign, Freedom's activities were limited, conventional, and late-starting. As one political insider said, "an organization whose power could have been felt very much in that race waited so late [. . .] that the power they could have, and affected the outcome of the primary, was compromised."[144] A great deal of distance existed between the command structures of the Ellis campaign and Freedom, with Ellis undertaking most of her efforts independent of the LPO. In previous years, even a lackluster Freedom campaign could have produced sufficient unity and turnout among African Americans to guarantee Ellis a spot in the general election. Not so in 1999, when Ellis placed a close third. On her own merits and with Freedom's blessing, she did emerge as the favorite of a majority of African Americans. In the city's eight predominantly black wards, Ellis collected roughly 57 percent of the vote. Blackwood collected less than a quarter of the black vote, purely on the basis of Cleaver's support for him. Ellis's real problem was that turnout in the African American wards was dismal—just 19.5 percent (see Table 10). Perhaps most striking is the fact that Freedom did nothing special to appeal to black women, when Ellis could have been Kansas City's first woman mayor and one of only a handful of black women elected to a mayoralty anywhere in the country. Had turnout in the predominantly black wards risen by only 5 percentage points and still given Ellis the same percentage of their votes, she would have easily bested Blackwood for a spot in the general election. Those who participated in the campaign still believe that if Freedom had made its endorsement a bit earlier in the

Table 10. Janice Ellis's Electoral Performance and Voter Turnout in
Predominantly African American Wards, 1999 City Primary

Ward	Ellis Votes	Ellis Percentage	Voter Turnout
2	599	50.9%	23.6%
3	848	58.6%	21.3%
7	844	61.9%	19.2%
14	710	57.1%	18.9%
15	870	59.7%	20.4%
16	801	55.8%	20.0%
17	864	53.3%	21.0%
18	861	56.7%	20.0%
Total in Predominantly African American Wards	6,397	56.8%	19.5%
Total in All Other Wards	4,809	11.5%	20.2%
Citywide Total	11,206	21.2%	20.1%

Source: Kansas City Election Board

cycle, Ellis would have beaten Blackwood and set up the first all-female field in a
Kansas City mayoral election.

With its first choice eliminated from the contest, Freedom followed Cleaver's
advice and turned to George Blackwood as its candidate. The campaign did not
go well. Blackwood attempted to cast himself as the pseudo-incumbent, claiming
that he would continue Cleaver's legacy. Blackwood's style failed to energize anyone and his campaign was badly damaged when the media reported that he had
been stopped by police for driving while intoxicated. Barnes sailed through the
general election campaign, aided by a command of the issues, a dignified style
that appealed to voters, her self-financing of the campaign, and the support of
the *Star*. Barnes did not make a particularly vigorous effort with African American voters but was nonetheless helped by endorsements from Alan Wheat's

father, a dozen prominent black ministers, and *The Call*. Cleaver refrained from making a formal endorsement of Blackwood, though he did everything imaginable to convey his feelings in informal fashion. Barnes became the first woman to serve as Kansas City's mayor, swamping Blackwood with 58 percent of the vote.[145] Blackwood benefited from a fairly united vote in the largely black wards. In the eight Freedom wards, Blackwood won 9,568 votes (66 percent) to Barnes's 4,955 votes (34 percent). This unity did less good than it might have because turnout remained pitiful, just 25 percent of voters in the Freedom wards came to the polls, compared to approximately 30 percent in the rest of the city. For all his attempts to portray himself as the second coming of Emanuel Cleaver, George Blackwood did not mobilize black voters. Freedom engaged in its conventional tactics—dispatching paid canvassers and poll workers, distributing ballots and literature, running a phone bank, and printing newspaper advertisements—but these tactics lacked the urgency or the power to persuade voters to turn out that they once possessed. Even significant improvement in black voter turnout would not have carried Blackwood to victory.

Freedom's showing in the City Council races was worse. Only six of the twelve races were contested and Freedom endorsed a candidate in just five of them. In four of those five contests, the Freedom-endorsed candidate lost, not least because the organization did little to engage in strategic bargaining with other organizations and political actors. Although the CA was, by consensus, near-impotent, Freedom might have been able to influence more election outcomes had it made bargains with that organization (and others) as it had done in previous years. But, in the words of one key Freedom strategist, "We just [didn't] put in much effort in working with Citizens."[146] Only Troy Nash in the Third District's at-large race emerged victorious over clergywoman Saundra McFadden-Weaver; while Freedom's efforts on his behalf helped, his success was also attributed to an overwhelming fundraising advantage and a compelling personal story.[147] Freedom proved unable to influence the endorsements of other organizations or to engage in the sort of pragmatic bargaining that resulted in cross-endorsements. Throughout the black community, Freedom candidates did win strong support from African American voters, demonstrating the continued influence of the LPO. But as has already been noted, turnout was abysmal. In most cases, even improved turnout would not have reversed the outcomes. Nevertheless, the low turnout could be—and was, by some—interpreted as a vote of little confidence in Freedom's political leadership. There was ample room for criticism of the Freedom council ballot. Those who maintained that the LPO was dominated by a handful of families found evidence for their claim in the 1999 Freedom ballot, where two out of five candidates in contested council races were members of those families. In a historic omission, the LPO refrained from endorsing *any* candidate in the Third District, Freedom's traditional heartland. Incumbent Mary Williams-Neal was locked in a rematch with Carol Coe. Both candidates had serious detractors: Williams-Neal's critics called her ineffective and nonresponsive, while Coe's cited the candidate's legal problems and past run-ins with Freedom. Williams-Neal resigned from Freedom and even had the nerve to ask that her membership dues be refunded as she denounced the LPO as "unethical" for reasons she did not explain.[148] Both had supporters within Freedom, with Cleaver calling himself a "flag-waving Mary Williams-Neal supporter" and a host of Freedom activists endorsing Coe. The group was unable to agree on a candidate, a reflection of the extent to which fragmentation had consumed the organization. Williams-Neal won handily, but indecision in the race hardly helped Freedom's reputation.

In short, the 1999 municipal elections were disastrous for Freedom. Only one of its candidates who faced a contested race won, despite the relatively broad support that the black community gave to Freedom candidates. In one of the most devastating blows of all, the predominantly African American Fifth District saw its at-large seat filled by a white councilperson for the first time in sixteen years. That election demonstrated that, without high black turnout to support a black candidate, the seat could easily be filled by whites for the foreseeable future. The City Council continued to have four African American members, but only because Alvin Brooks, the first black municipal department head and founder of the Ad Hoc Group Against Crime, won an at-large seat from the Sixth District. This marked the first time that an African American won a seat outside of the urban core, but Brooks had no opponent. His name was almost universally known citywide, scaring off potential opposition. A week after the municipal elections, Freedom lost a special election for a state representative seat in the heart of the urban core. A Freedom "insider" was selected by the LPO instead of Freedom member and school board member Terry Riley; Riley won in a romp.[149] With such monumental failures in such quick succession, Freedom was held to be in decline, unable to mobilize its constituency to go to the polls or to believe that the community's future was at stake.

Changing Leadership, Similar Outcomes

Just one year later, Mary Groves Bland decided to step down as president of Freedom. The widely respected Bland sought to concentrate her energies on her service as a state senator, a post to which she had just been elected (to fill a seat left vacant by Phil Curls, who resigned due to poor health). The battle for the presidency was a pitched one, between former councilmen Mark Bryant and Charles Hazley. Although both men served on the City Council a decade earlier, one Freedom board member explained that Bryant "represented sort of a fresh face, a new voice, more mainstream fella that could bridge the gap between the Troost divide."[150] Bryant won on a vote of 35 to 23, promising to reinvigorate Freedom. Like those before him, Bryant realized that Freedom's base was increasingly restricted to senior citizens who fondly remembered Leon Jordan and Bruce Watkins. Upon his election, Bryant told the press, "There is a perception that Freedom is a closed club, and I would like to dispel that perception. For many years a small group of individuals have been consistently vigilant in maintaining and operating this organization. I think we have reached a point in our history where our constituents would welcome seeing someone else assume leadership." To counter the perception that Freedom was a "closed" group, Bryant initiated a policy that automatically gave all dues-paying members seats on the board of directors.

The new president pledged to expand Freedom's demographic and geographic reach. This vision was well received by local commentators, even those who questioned whether Freedom remained necessary. One journalist covering Bryant's ascension to the presidency said—not entirely correctly—of the organization that, "Freedom remains a child of the civil rights movement, yet to move into the 21st century. The practice of sit-in-style political tactics and guilt trips does not work in an age of high-dollar lobbyists, multimillion-dollar campaigns, and the Internet. The organization's biggest problem is its difficulty in connecting with African-Americans under 40."[151]

Unlike in previous elections, no new chairperson of the board was elected. From 2000 until the time of writing, the organization has not elected a board chair. The position has not been formally eliminated, but no effort has been made to resuscitate it. Some members felt that the dual positions of president and board chair unnecessarily muddled the leadership structure and chain of command. Others felt that past presidents and board chairs too frequently came into conflict with one another, with board chairs sometimes using their positions to undermine the president's authority or to plan campaigns for the presidency. Still others lament that the organization lacks a board chair; calling it "crazy" that a chair has not been elected, one longtime Freedom member recalled that, in the past, the strengths and weaknesses of respective presidents and chairs balanced one another and allowed them to play a version of the classic "good cop/bad cop" game with outsiders. Without a chair, this member said, more was expected of the president than any one person could possibly deliver.[152]

Despite his sensible promises, Bryant was largely unable to execute his vision. Quite aside from fulfilling grand strategy imperatives like appealing to younger people, basic organizational tasks went unperformed. Well into the Internet age, for example, the LPO lacked a rudimentary website or a comprehensive e-mail marketing list. (Freedom did not establish an Internet presence until 2010.) Attempts to mobilize the grassroots connection, resume providing social services, engage more deeply in the policymaking process, or host many more social activities proved difficult to realize. To many in and outside of the organization, it seemed to do little in the years in between elections. Indeed, one younger Freedom activist interviewed for this book described the organization's "relationship" with the community as a short-term one devoid of real meaning and driven by temporary needs, instead of one where it was "there in the beginning, there in the middle, and there at the end."[153] Bryant does not deserve the blame for this, as the constant increase in tension between subgroups made it ever more difficult to reach consensus on the path forward. Bryant deserves credit for improving the organization's reputation after the spate of indictments in the 1990s; as one white former elected official put it, "He gave them credibility again."[154]

A lack of progress in resuscitating Freedom became evident in 2003. With many policy triumphs during her first term, Mayor Kay Barnes faced only token opposition and most council incumbents faced no opposition at all. Freedom devoted its energies to three at-large council races and the in-district race for the Third District. All four of its priority candidates lost. In the Third District, Freedom endorsed councilman-turned-county legislator Ron Finley over Saundra McFadden-Weaver. This move rankled those already prone to viewing Freedom as a "closed group" that continually recycled the same faces.[155] Aided by the endorsement of many clergy, McFadden-Weaver won with 59 percent of the vote.[156] It marked only the second time that an in-district council candidate with Freedom's blessing lost in a district with an African American majority.

Freedom's win-loss ratio was better in 2007, but the LPO nonetheless lost the two races about which it cared most deeply. Alvin Brooks entered a field of twelve candidates in a quest to become the city's second African American mayor. With Freedom's strong endorsement, Brooks advanced to the general election on the strength of his support among African American voters (although Janice

Ellis, making her second bid for the job, received 20 percent of the black vote). He faced former city auditor Mark Funkhouser, a favorite of liberals and conservatives alike for his opposition to economic development tax incentives. The *Star* had long been enamored with Funkhouser and unleashed a propaganda effort on his behalf the likes of which had not been seen since the paper's 1963 crusade against Dutton Brookfield.

Freedom's efforts were restricted because the organization had less money than ever before. The LPO, registered only as a Missouri state political committee, spent money and manpower to elect Emanuel Cleaver to Congress in 2004. Doing so violated federal election law and resulted in the Federal Election Commission levying a $45,000 fine against Freedom.[157] The organization's ability to pay for election workers and literature in the 2007 campaign was limited. Freedom campaigned on Brooks's behalf, but its efforts failed to inspire African American voters to turn out in substantial numbers. Funkhouser bested Brooks by 850 votes out of 84,000 cast, but Brooks garnered over 90 percent of the vote in the Freedom wards (see Table 11). Funkhouser was almost as popular in the rapidly growing Northland and in the southwest corridor, and turnout in the Funkhouser strongholds was considerably higher than in Brooks's bastions. A similar situation prevailed in the Fifth District at-large race, where Freedom tried to elect an African American to represent the black majority district. The effort failed. Freedom succeeded in ousting Saundra McFadden Weaver in the Third District, but its success in doing so was attributed to the incumbent councilwoman's legal troubles (she was convicted of mortgage fraud in a scandal unrelated to her council office) rather than anything the LPO did on her opponent's behalf.[158]

While the individual candidates could have made adjustments to their campaigns that might have altered the outcome, Freedom's inability to mobilize voters to the same extent that it once had was universally considered a major factor in these losses. The organization retained a constituency, but, in the words of one longtime member, "The people that supported Freedom for a number of years are dead or dying."[159] It continued to be courted by candidates (because one would rather have the endorsement than not have it), could claim most of the city's black elected officials as members, and remained a forum for discussing black interests, but not even Freedom's most loyal partisans contended that it was the powerful machine it once was. As one interviewee said, Freedom was "no stronger than the candidates it [ran]."[160] The organization suffered from a negative reputation, but, as one interviewee pointed out:

Table 11. Alvin Brooks's Electoral Performance and Voter Turnout in Predominantly African American Wards, 2007 City General Election

Ward	Brooks Votes	Brooks Percentage	Voter Turnout
2	1,845	92.2%	23.4%
3	2,270	93.2%	23%
7	2,041	91.4%	23.7%
14	1,900	91.6%	24%
15	1,867	88.6%	24.8%
16	2,392	92%	26.5%
17	2,407	84.3%	29.3%
18	2,568	91.7%	27.4%
Total in Predominantly African American Wards	17,290	90.5%	25.3%
Total in All Other Wards	24,659	36.5%	26.2%
Citywide Total	41,949	49.3%	26.1%

Source: Clay County, Kansas City, and Platte County Election Boards

People criticize Freedom and talk bad about Freedom and claim that Freedom is corrupt and Freedom is that or Freedom is that. Every single one of them seeks the endorsement. And it seems to me that if you believe the words coming out of your mouth, you would not be seeking an endorsement or perceive the endorsement to be such a prize.[161]

The organization seemed to have lost what little ability it once had to compel unity among African American politicos; many interview subjects felt that even though "Freedom *could* be the group that brings folks together, I don't know whether that is realistic [. . .]. Just because something that happened ten, fifteen, twenty years ago that somebody can't turn the page [. . .]. Because of whatever they may have done here or there, there may be some people that will never work with them because of whatever. . ."[162] Similarly, the organization no longer seemed capable of scaring or bargaining with white politicians into modifying their behavior. Many African Americans lamented this development, claiming that "even if their power was marginalized in their own African American community, [Freedom] was still perceived as a force in the majority community" but failed to use that perception to achieve any observable goals.[163]

Even with these liabilities, Freedom did not face serious competition from any other black political organization, or from any other LPO, in the city. The CA won many races lost by Freedom, but its role in those victories was tangential to the point of irrelevance. A former elected official from the CA's supposed base in the southwest corridor said, "I don't think Citizens even exists any more. It's just a few people that gather together at election time to try and drive their particular candidate and whoever has the largest faction within Citizens wins."[164] The organization-based paradigm of local politics, which had long dominated local political life, was dead; one savvy former elected official held the impact of all of the city's LPOs (with the exception of Freedom) to be "bordering on meaningless" in an era of the Internet, social media, and easy access to information.[165]

The broader African American community, too, saw its political influence at a low point. With the exception of a handful of redevelopment projects in the Third and Fifth Districts and the appointment of the first African American city manager in 2003, few could point to any serious attempt to advance black interests during this time, even though a number of officials (including especially Barnes herself) were sympathetic to the concerns of the black community. Freedom itself was more disengaged from the policy process than ever before; one interview subject sounded a representative note by commenting of this period, "I don't know *what* their [policy] agenda is."[166] Even the baseline level of symbolic representation experienced deterioration. After the 2007 elections, the City Council had just three African American members. Black symbolic representation thus actually regressed to where it was between 1975 and 1983. By a wide variety of measures, the ability of African American Kansas Citians to successfully press demands on the system was weaker than at any time since the 1960s.

Beyond 2007: The Future of Freedom

Freedom's members and leadership were cognizant that change was required. Truly committed to the causes of freedom and equality, they recognized that Freedom's ability to produce the sort of systemic change for which it was created tapered off over the past decade. Shortly after the 2007 elections, Mark Bryant resigned as president of Freedom. He was replaced by state representative Craig Bland, the son of former Freedom president Mary Groves Bland, who pledged to revitalize the LPO by appealing to young people, using new technology, and reconnecting with the grassroots.[167] There were some who criticized his succession to the presidency on the grounds that it made Freedom more insular, but Bland met with some modest success in fulfilling his promises to make the organization more open, accessible, youth-oriented, credible, and efficacious. Some interviewees felt that the organization was on the upswing under Bland's leadership, running effective campaigns and engaging in more grassroots activities. Said one interviewee:

> I think the way Freedom has handled their screening in the [2007 and 2011] elections is as good as any of the other organizations. I think they are trying to support the best candidates and then ask for money, rather than what I think was maybe the way they operated earlier [. . .] I think they've grown as an organization. There was no organization that worked harder than Freedom. I mean, they were ten times better than Forward and Citizens put together.[168]

Others disagreed, saying that Bland lacked the ability to "make deals" or to raise the roughly $100,000 required to run a Freedom campaign, particularly after changes to Missouri law prohibited candidates from making direct contribution to organizations like Freedom.[169] In January 2012, Bland resigned the presidency of Freedom. He was replaced in the interim by a troika consisting of Gayle Holliday (ex-wife of Harold Holliday and a longtime political insider), Charles Hazley (until his passing in 2013), and Shalonn "Kiki" Curls (a state senator and niece of Phil Curls). In March 2012, the Missouri Ethics Commission (the state's campaign finance and lobbying regulatory body) fined Bland and two other former officials of the LPO for ethics violations, including keeping inaccurate records and converting organizational funds to personal use.[170] These events once again raised the questions of whether Freedom could regain what it had lost over the course of the 1980s and 1990s: its status as a fully institutionalized LPO that engaged in multiple tactics, its corporatist status as the voice of the black community, its ability to mobilize the city's black population, and its mastery of political bargaining to wrest concessions from the system. If those characteristics could be regained, the organization's glory days might be reclaimed. Hope that such a return can be achieved remains because, as one interviewee expressed it, "Just when you count them out, [think] that it's over, that Freedom is dead, they'll come back and surprise you!"[171]

CHAPTER 6

"We Didn't Expect You to Be So Good at It"
Local Political Organizations, Institutionalization, and Black Political Efficacy in Kansas City

The story of Freedom, Inc. is one of its unanticipated rise to preeminence within the political ecosystem of Kansas City, Missouri. White elites—and many African American residents and politicos—were shocked at Freedom's ability to unify the black community, to win elections, and to use this newfound power to secure the advancement of black interests. As *Kansas City Star* political cartoonist Lee Judge put it, when white elites told African American Kansas Citians to put their faith in the political process, "we didn't expect you to be so good at it."[1] Freedom's multitude of successes include electing the first African American member to the City Council, beating segregationists at the ballot box to pass a public accommodations ordinance, salvaging a fair housing ordinance, eradicating the influence of the factional "plantation bosses," expanding black symbolic representation on the City Council and in municipal managerial posts, proving essential to seven mayoral victories, expending additional resources on neighborhood development in the urban core, electing Emanuel Cleaver the city's first African American mayor, forcing white elites to treat the black community with respect in political matters, and (to varying degrees) politically uniting and mobilizing the black community. Although Freedom suffered defeats, including Bruce Watkins's loss and the damage done by a decade of corruption scandals beginning in the mid-1980s, and saw its influence wane, Freedom served for decades as the embodiment of the collective agency of Kansas City's black community and as its preeminent political voice.

It is no overstatement to say that, aside from the black church, Freedom, Inc. has been more meaningful for and important to Kansas City's African American community than any other local institution. Freedom, Inc.'s impact has been truly revolutionary, a fact that is reflected in the esteem in which the organization was long held and continues to be held, even in its currently chastened state, by many African American Kansas Citians. As one former elected official put it in an interview, "I would hate to think what life in Kansas City would have been like, certainly in the '60s and '70s and even early '80s, had Freedom not been around."[2] Although Freedom has made missteps along the way, the LPO's overall record is one of which its members can be proud.

Testing the Theory of Black Political Efficacy in Kansas City

The story of Freedom, Inc. provides strong support for the theory of black political efficacy articulated throughout this book. That theory holds that, in advancing black interests and achieving a high level of black political efficacy in urban political systems, the existence of strong, institutionalized local political organizations matters. Institutionalized organizations are ones that are formal, independent, use multiple tactics, especially electoral politics, to influence political outcomes, and utilize a black interests organizing model. These institutionalized organizations then aggressively press for black demands on the system to be satisfied in tangible ways. Moreover, the theory holds that institutionalized LPOs are most effective when they are the single, corporatist voice of the black community, when they achieve high levels of mobilization in the black community, and when they enter into effective, strategic bargaining with nonblack political actors. In the absence of institutionalized LPOs or in the presence of LPOs that do not effectively unite the community, mobilize, or bargain, African American demands on the system are more likely to go ignored and unmet.

The preceding chapters are rife with evidence to support this theory. To further amplify this evidence, two indices were created to measure the strength of the relationship between a strong black LPO and the advancement of black interests. Both of these indices are designed to measure efficacy, which is the power of a group to collectively shape political events and outcomes. However, black political efficacy and the organizational efficacy of a black LPO are decidedly not the same thing. It is, for example, possible for a highly efficacious black LPO to exist and secure its own program, but utterly fail in delivering gains for the broader African American community.

The first of these indices, the Black Political Efficacy Index (BPEI), is intended to measure the extent to which an African American community itself is efficacious at securing tangible political goals, independent of the agenda of any particular LPO. The BPEI ranges from 0 (Very Low) to 60 (Very High) and measures six components: symbolic representation among elected officials, public employment, elite legitimation and bargaining, electoral success, policy responsiveness, and self-determination. Full details on the index can be found in Appendix 1.

The companion index, the Organizational Efficacy Index (OEI) is intended to measure the extent to which a black LPO is an efficacious and influential actor *within* its political system; it measures the strength of the organization itself, including its ability to unite black voters, mobilize the community, and bargain with external actors. The OEI ranges from 0 (Very Low) to 60 (Very High), and measures four aspects of an LPO's success: elite legitimation and bargaining, electoral success in predominantly African American districts, electoral success in at-large elections, and policy responsiveness. Full details of the index are found in Appendix 2.

The BPEI and the OEI were used to assess the efficacy of Kansas City's African American community and Freedom, Inc. at various intervals between 1962 and 2007. Tables 12 and 13 provide detail on Freedom's OEI and Kansas City's BPEI scores at regular intervals during the period covered by this book. These scores are intended to give readers a sense of where the LPO and the African American community are at a particular moment in time and to track how efficacy changes

Table 12. Freedom, Inc.'s Organizational Efficacy Index Scores by Component, 1962–2007

Year	1962/ 1963	1968	1971/ 1975	1979	1983	1987	1991	1999	2007
Elite Legitimation	Low (2)	High-Mod. (6)	High (8)	High (8)	High-Mod. (6)	High (8)	High-Mod. (6)	High-Mod. (6)	Low-Mod. (4)
Electoral Success— Black Districts	High (8)	Very High (10)	Very High (10)	Very High (10)	High (8)	High (8)	High-Mod. (6)	High (8)	High (8)
Electoral Success—At-large Elections	Low (3)	High (12)	High (12)	Low-Mod. (6)	High (12)	High (12)	Very High (15)	Low-Mod. (6)	High-Mod. (9)
Policy Responsiveness	Low-Mod. (10)	High (20)	Very High (25)	High-Mod. (15)	Low (5)	Low-Mod. (10)	Low-Mod. (10)	Low (5)	Low (5)
Total	Low (23)	High (48)	High (55)	High-Mod. (39)	Low-Mod. (31)	High-Mod. (38)	High-Mod. (37)	Low-Mod (25)	Low-Mod. (26)

Table 13. Kansas City's Black Political Efficacy Index Scores by Component, 1962–2007

Year	1962/ 1963	1968	1971/ 1975	1979	1983	1987	1991	1999	2007
Symbolic Representation	Low (1)	High-Mod. (3)	High (4)	High (4)	High (4)	High (4)	Very High (5)	High (4)	High-Mod. (3)
Public Employment	Low (1)	Low-Mod. (2)	High-Mod. (3)	High-Mod. (3)	High-Mod. (3)	High-Mod. (3)	High-Mod. (3)	High (4)	Very High (5)
Elite Legitimation	Low (1)	High-Mod. (3)	High (4)	Very High (5)	High (4)	High (4)	Very High (5)	High-Mod. (3)	High-Mod. (3)
Electoral Success	Very Low (0)	High-Mod. (6)	High (8)	Low (2)	Low (2)	High-Mod. (6)	Very High (10)	Low (2)	Very Low (0)
Policy Responsiveness	Very Low (0)	High-Mod. (15)	High (20)	High-Mod. (15)	High (20)	Very High (25)	High (20)	Low-Mod (10)	Low (5)
Self-Determination	Very Low (0)	High-Mod. (6)	High (8)	High (8)	High-Mod. (6)	High-Mod. (6)	High-Mod. (6)	Low-Mod. (4)	Low-Mod. (4)
Total	Very Low (3)	Low-Mod. (35)	High-Mod. (47)	High-Mod. (37)	High-Mod. (39)	High (48)	High (49)	Low-Mod. (27)	Low (20)

over time; they are not intended to be exhaustive or to be interpreted without the benefit of the substantiating detail provided in the preceding chapters. Figure 3 presents a graphic rendering of change in Freedom's OEI score and Kansas City's BPEI score between 1962 and 2007.

When Freedom was founded in 1962, Kansas City's African American community was deeply inefficacious. African American residents had minimal political power, with few representatives of even the symbolic variety, no ability to influence public policy, and little control over their own political destinies. Freedom was not terribly efficacious at its founding, when it was but one of many political organizations serving the black community and was attempting to end the stranglehold of the old-line Democratic factions. Through a confluence of circumstance, personality, and smart politics—especially positioning itself as the corporatist political voice of the community, working hard at mobilizing the community, and engaging in strategic bargaining with nonblack political forces—the organization rapidly grew and became an important actor in local politics. The organization was fully institutionalized by the early 1970s and its ascent in power and efficacy in local politics continued until 1979, when Bruce Watkins's loss and its effects proved devastating to Freedom. This decline persisted through most of the 1980s before a canny political strategy resuscitated the organization's reputation and modestly improved its efficacy. Freedom achieved its greatest municipal triumph when it elected Emanuel Cleaver mayor in 1991, despite the fact that the organization's efficacy was lower than in its previous attempt at electing a black mayor. Paradoxically, the election of an African American mayor diminished Freedom's efficacy rather than enhancing it, through the creation of a rival power center and the dilution of the LPO's claim to being the single, corporatist political voice of the black community. Freedom's organizational efficacy steadily declined after 1991, especially as demobilization became endemic and strategic bargaining with nonblack political forces became more difficult, to the point that the organization gradually became deinstitutionalized.

Figure 3. Freedom, Inc.'s OEI Scores and Kansas City's BPEI Scores, 1962–2007.

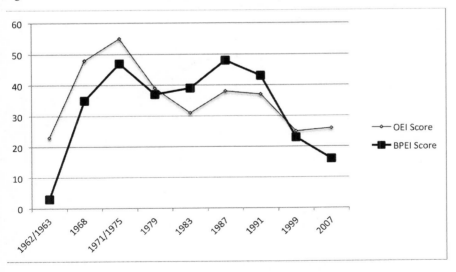

These findings are consistent with the views of interview subjects, who invariably described the 1970s as Freedom's glory days and the period from the mid-1990s onward as one of decay.

As Figure 7.1 demonstrates, Kansas City's black community followed a similar trajectory in its political efficacy. Before the founding of Freedom, the community hovered near absolute inefficacy, with no meaningful voice in elections or policy-making and minimal symbolic representation. Within a few years of Freedom's founding, the African American community became reasonably efficacious, able to claim victories like the public accommodations ordinance, fair housing ordinance, Model Cities spending, and the appointment of several African American department directors in municipal government. In the 1980s, the community experienced higher efficacy than Freedom did, but generally followed the pattern set by the LPO. The high level of political efficacy attained by the African American community during the 1980s is directly attributable to the considerable power wielded by several black and Latino members of the City Council. Contrary to the predictions of some who championed his election, Emanuel Cleaver's mayoralty did not usher in an era of unprecedented advancement of black interests. Cleaver's administration did have notable achievements for African Americans, but black political efficacy was higher during the 1970s than at any point during or after the Cleaver years.

Based on the analysis of these indices, there is ample reason to believe that black political efficacy is directly linked to the existence of strong, institutionalized LPOs. As Freedom became more institutionalized, its organizational efficacy increased. When Freedom effectively served as the single political voice of the community, achieved high levels of mass mobilization, and entered into strategic bargaining with partners, its organizational efficacy was enhanced further. As Freedom's organizational efficacy increased, the black community's political efficacy also rose. Declines in Freedom's efficacy were accompanied by similar falls in the efficacy of the broader community. This relationship was not absolute. Organizational success by Freedom usually preceded policy victories by the broader community, while the community managed to maintain some level of efficacy even during the dark days of the early 1980s. Even then, though, a relationship existed. For example, the black community's ability to extract policy concessions during the 1980s is directly attributable to the seniority accrued by Freedom elected officials.

Aside from the results found in the analysis of the BPEI and OEI scores, the story of Freedom provides many reasons to support the theory of black political efficacy argued for by this book. The most important element of that theory holds that black political efficacy is best served when an institutionalized black LPO exists to press for the community's demands. Freedom was Kansas City's first local political organization to adopt any of the components of institutionalization, but it was not until the early 1970s that Freedom became fully institutionalized. The era of full institutionalization lingered through the 1980s, but gradually diminished in the 1990s. As Figure 7.1 shows, Kansas City's black community experienced extremely low levels of political efficacy until *after* the emergence of Freedom and community-wide efficacy moved in concert with Freedom's development as an institutionalized organization. The lone exception comes in the 1980s, when community-wide political efficacy thrived despite the weakening of Freedom. Even this exception owes itself to Freedom's political hegemony within the black community, which permitted a group of Freedom members to accrue seniority and legislative knowledge they used to steer public policy in ways favored by African American residents. When Freedom's institutional character declined—especially through its retreat from the policy-making process—and organizational efficacy suffered, so did community-wide political efficacy. This is especially apparent in the late 1990s and 2000s, when the absence of a strong organization making policy demands and *credible* political threats on behalf of African Americans meant that black interests went largely untended.

The model argued for by this book further holds that black political efficacy is highest when there is a single, corporatist LPO that serves as the primary locus of African American political activity. This contention, too, is supported by the story of Freedom, Inc. For the first decade of its existence, Freedom was only one of many African American political organizations in Kansas City, although since most of the rival organizations were designed to serve white factional interests, using the nomenclature of "black political organization" is misleading. Nevertheless, black political efficacy increased considerably as African American political activity was increasingly concentrated within Freedom in the late 1960s. The longest sustained period of high political efficacy (roughly from 1971 to 1978) came when local black politics was conducted almost exclusively through Freedom. Similarly, black political efficacy was harmed when some clergy broke away from Freedom in the 1983 mayoral race, when some black politicians broke away from Freedom in the 1987 mayoral race, and, most substantially, when Emanuel Cleaver constituted a rival power center in the 1990s. This is not to pass judgment on whether any of these breaks were justified or whether Freedom was/is the most appropriate vehicle for a single corporatist body; it is only to state that the division and confusion which resulted was not conducive to African American political empowerment. In some cases, black political efficacy was high despite the division, but the story of Freedom makes it clear that the community's clout could have been even greater in the absence of this dissension.

This finding should not be surprising. Serious scholars and polemicists alike dating back at least to David Walker have asserted that operational unity is vital to the success of any African American political project. The case of Freedom provides support for averring that unity alone provides the strength required to wrest concessions to black interests from the hands of the power structure. The frequent internal debate within Freedom, over strategy, candidates, and policy itself, also suggests that concerns about corporatist groups, like those expressed by Reed[3] and Shelby,[4] may be alarmist. Little in the case study suggests that these fears that black politics practiced through a corporatist group leads to stifled debate, the stripping away of liberty, or the regulation of blackness are well founded.

The next major contention made by the theory is that black political efficacy is best served when an institutionalized LPO cultivates and sustains a high level of grassroots mobilization. Support for this contention is overwhelming. Freedom's glory days occurred during the 1970s, when the organization relentlessly pursued a grassroots base and undertook a wide variety of activities explicitly designed to mobilize the masses of the city's black community. Freedom used its precinct captain network, reciprocal information and feedback loops, social activities, and an army of volunteers to ensure that it was connected to its constituents and able to move them into political action. The most significant declines in Freedom's efficacy came when the LPO shifted its orientation to a professionalized one and began the slow process of demobilization. As the LPO became more professionalized and less mass-oriented in the 1990s and 2000s, its efficacy sunk further. Moreover, as Freedom increasingly restricted its activities to electioneering and refrained from addressing pressing community needs outside of its endorsements, it effectively demobilized the population, its credibility waned, and its effectiveness dissipated.

The final major contention made by the theory is that black political efficacy is best served when an institutionalized LPO engages in strategic, short-term bargaining with nonblack political forces. These nonblack political forces are willing to engage in bargaining, trading concessions for the LPO's support, because the LPO is believed to have credibility and clout within the African American community. Here, too, the story of Freedom provides support for the argument. Freedom's efficacy grew in the 1960s as it demonstrated that it had a genuine constituency among African American voters. Indeed, in its first municipal election, the 1963 primary, Freedom was largely ignored by white elites and the press. After Bruce Watkins won the primary on the strength of his support from Freedom members, the LPO suddenly became attractive to white elites in need of entry to the black community. The Citizens Association made concessions to Freedom in recognition of the fact that the LPO could win votes for the reform slate in the African American community. This permitted Freedom to present certain concrete accomplishments, like the public accommodations ordinance, to African American voters, enhancing its support with those voters and reifying its importance as the CA's intermediary with the black community. So long as Freedom could produce overwhelming margins for its candidates among African Americans, it was very much in demand by white elites as an intermediary and thus able to successfully press African American demands on the system. When this was the case, as in the 1970s, Freedom's efficacy was high indeed. When Freedom was unable to muster strong support for its candidates, as in the 1983 primary or from the mid-1990s onward, the LPO was not as heavily wooed for bargaining purposes by white elites and was able to produce fewer tangible benefits for its constituency. These periods correspond with times when Freedom's organizational efficacy was comparatively low. Similarly, when white elites considered Emanuel Cleaver to possess greater credibility among African American voters than Freedom itself (and to be an easier force to bargain with), Freedom's efficacy suffered.

Throughout its history, Freedom always sought to craft interracial alliances through bargaining. Freedom's most efficacious period in municipal politics came in the 1970s, when the LPO consciously pursued a balance of power strategy that focused on satisfying short-term objectives. During the balance of power years, Freedom broke from its former coalition partner, the CA, when that organization refused to grant concessions that were important to African American voters. No counter-example exists to demonstrate what Freedom's efficacy would have been like had it been unwilling to engage in interracial bargaining, though the organization exerted less effort at this from the mid-1990s onward, a time of lower efficacy. However, it only stands to reason that in a city where African Americans comprise just one third of the population that ruling out interracial bargaining would doom a black LPO to inefficacy. Moreover, the militant organizations that arose in the city during the late 1960s and early 1970s frequently ruled out these alliances. They all failed, though not necessarily because of their position toward interracial entanglements.

It should be stressed that the sort of strategic bargaining Freedom engaged in was *not* of the ideological sort described by Sonenshein.[5] Instead, interracial alliances were almost always built around immediate-term interests, such as a single issue, candidate, or shared enemy. As a result, these alliances were short-lived. It also bears noting that almost no effort was placed into cultivating political alliances with the city's Latino community. Although the Latino population remains only one third of the size of the African American population, it is growing and the lack of a functional "black-brown" alliance may prove a serious liability in the future.

What Freedom, Inc. Means for Black Politics

The story of Freedom, Inc. is an enthralling one, full of intriguing twists and turns. We should be careful not to read *too* much into this story of one organization in one city; Kansas City and Freedom may indeed prove to be singular, extraordinary, and inapplicable across the country. The record of LPOs in cities like Birmingham, Detroit, and New Orleans suggests that there is nothing at all sui generis about Freedom, and Kansas City's status as perhaps the most average of all American cities implies that the lessons it has to teach are quite transferrable.[6] With that in mind, the story of Freedom, Inc. carries two major implications for a broader black politics.

The first is that local African American communities see their interests—however one chooses to define those interests—best served when strong, institutionalized organizations exist to advocate for them. The *best* route to transforming conditions does not lie in the traditional fixation on electing an African American mayor or City Council majority, because it is not enough for African American communities to have sympathetic "black faces in high places." Instead, organizations must exist which are formal, independent, pursue multiple tactics including electioneering, and are organized around black interests. These organizations should be transparent, democratic, and accountable. Doing this work of institution-building will grant the African American community the leverage that it requires to successfully press its demands on the system, gain political empowerment, and achieve high levels of political efficacy.

Moreover, institutionalized organizations themselves can be more or less effective. When institutionalized organizations take great pains to serve as a broad church movement, capable of effectively being the single, corporatist voice of African American politics without stifling subgroup interests, black interests are even better served. When institutionalized organizations do what it takes in order to achieve high, sustained levels of mobilizations, black interests are still better served. And when institutionalized organizations are able to engage in effective, strategic bargaining that wrests immediate-term concessions as the price of interracial alliance, African American interests are better served. When all of these conditions are present at once, African American demands on political systems will be well satisfied, indeed. It is readily acknowledged that it is far easier to identify these characteristics in an academic environment than it is to practice them in the hardscrabble world of politics. Still, it is hoped that this finding can be used by African American LPOs to guide them in their quests for equality and justice.

The second implication of the story of Freedom pertains to the national political discussion. As scholars like Smith[7] and Walters[8] have argued, the past three decades have not been kind to African Americans at the national level. This dearth of progress is attributable to the fact that African American politics at the national level (and in many localities, for that matter) has not been institutionalized. Although Barack Obama was elected the nation's first African American president in 2008, he made it clear, in his campaigns and while governing, that he was not interested in pursuing particularistic policies to address racial disparities. Even with an African American elected to the nation's highest office, there is today not even one national organization dedicated to promoting African American interests that might be regarded as fully institutionalized. There are number of organizations that are independent, or organized around black interests, or that engage in multiple tactics to influence outcomes. There is no strong national African American organization that does all of those things, or that consistently and effectively uses electoral politics to influence outcomes. This is important because, as this book has made clear, individual and personal political organizations are neither as sustainable nor as effective in the long-term as are institutional ones. As such, the best way to advance African American interests in the twenty first century is by concentrating our collective energies on institutionalizing African American politics and building efficacious black political organizations. This would end the trend of regression on African American interests that has been amply demonstrated at the national level in recent years, allowing African American communities to have their interests attended to more regularly.

This is a tall order, but it is not impossible. After all, when Freedom was founded in 1962 there were very few who anticipated that the organization would prove to be the "bridge that brought us across" that generations of African American

Kansas Citians consider it to be. There were few who thought the organization would survive so much as a year, much less become the nation's oldest still-existing black LPO, very much alive after half a century. There were few who believed that the LPO could achieve the many remarkable feats that dot its history, including the election of a host of African American elected officials and some real improvement in the lives of African American Kansas Citians. Even though the organization has fallen on harder times—though only a fool would rule out a comeback, given the many resurgences that sprinkle the organization's history—Freedom, Inc. has a proud history that shows just how much is possible for African American communities when they band together and pursue common interests. The story of Kansas City, Missouri's Freedom, Inc. should give us hope that "dignity, equality, freedom" are indeed possible, "thru unity."

The Black Political Efficacy Index (Index Points)

Component	Very Low	Low	Low-Moderate	High-Moderate	High	Very High
Symbolic Representation	Jurisdiction has no black elected officials (BEOs).	Jurisdiction has BEOs, but all are elected from districts with African American majorities and the African American population is numerically underrepresented.	Jurisdiction has BEOs proportionate to the share of the African American population, but all are elected from districts with African American majorities.	Jurisdiction has BEOs elected both from districts and at-large, but the African American population is numerically underrepresented.	Jurisdiction has BEOs proportionate to the share of the African American population elected both from districts and at-large.	Same as high, but the jurisdiction's top elected executive is also African American.
	(0)	(1)	(2)	(3)	(4)	(5)
Public Employment	African American are employed only in menial jobs, in disproportionately low numbers, and are not appointed to offices.	African Americans are not appointed to offices. African Americans are employed only in menial jobs, but in numbers proportionate to their share of the population.	African Americans are appointed to a small number of offices and hold some managerial jobs, primarily in "black-oriented" departments (e.g., urban affairs or human relations).	African Americans are appointed to offices and hold managerial jobs across government, but in disproportionately low numbers.	African Americans are appointed to offices and hold managerial jobs, in numbers proportionate to their share of the population.	Same as high, but the jurisdiction's top appointed official and manager is also African American.
	(0)	(1)	(2)	(3)	(4)	(5)

Appendix 1 (continued)

Component	Very Low	Low	Low-Moderate	High-Moderate	High	Very High
Elite legitimation and bargaining	Non-black elites frequently engage in open race-baiting and overtly white supremacist rhetoric.	Non-black elites generally ignore African American leaders and organizations. Some reactive bargaining takes place, but only on low-impact issues.	Many non-black elites proactively seek bargaining and alliance-building with African American leaders and organizations, but only on low-impact issues.	Many non-black elites engage in reactive bargaining and alliance-building with African American leaders and organizations, but on high-impact issues.	Many non-black elites engage in proactive bargaining and alliance-building with African American leaders and organizations, on high-impact issues.	Most non-black elites engage in proactive bargaining and alliance-building with African American leaders and organizations, on high-impact issues.
	(0)	(1)	(2)	(3)	(4)	(5)
Electoral success	Candidates win office despite—and often because of—the overwhelming opposition of African American voters. African American voter turnout is exceptionally low.	Candidates win office despite the opposition of African American voters.	The African American vote is divided nearly equally among winning and losing candidates.	African American voters give a majority of their votes to the winning candidate, but the margin of victory is larger than the number of African American votes.	African American voters give a strong majority to the winning candidate, supplying the candidate's margin of victory.	African American voters give a strong majority to the winning candidate, supplying the margin of victory. African American voter turnout is crucial to the winning.
	(0)	(2)	(4)	(6)	(8)	(10)

Appendix 1 (continued)

Component	Very Low	Low	Low-Moderate	High-Moderate	High	Very High
Policy responsiveness	Black interests are ignored or actively harmed. Any mention of African American demands is met with overtly white supremacist rhetoric and open race-baiting. (0)	Black interests are largely ignored, but some symbolic steps may be taken. African American participation in the policy process is met with antagonism and harms the cause. (5)	Symbolic action is regularly taken on black interests, in direct response to African American participation in the policy process. (10)	When an interracial coalition is built, substantive action on black interests is sometimes taken. African American participation in the process and explicit advocacy for black interests is met with antagonism. (15)	When an interracial coalition is built, substantive action on black interests is regularly taken. Action is taken in direct response to African American participation in the process and explicit advocacy for black interests. (20)	Policymakers frequently take substantive action to further black interests. African American participation in the process and explicit advocacy for black interests is by itself sufficient to produce this response; interracial alliances are unnecessary, though not undesirable. (25)
Self-determination	African American leaders, black issue agendas, and the financial resources for community programs are provided by external parties without consulting the black community. (0)	African American leaders, black issue agendas, and financial resources for community programs are provided by external parties after minimal consultation with the black community. (2)	African American leaders are selected by the black community, but issue agendas are still driven by external parties after minimal consultation with those leaders. Financial resources for community programs are largely, but not entirely, derived from external parties. (4)	African American leaders are selected by the black community, but issue agendas are still driven by external parties after significant consultation with those leaders and some community-wide involvement. Financial resources for community programs are largely derived from external parties. (6)	African American leaders and issue agendas are selected by and accountable to the black community, without the intrusion of external parties. Financial resources for community programs are derived in nearly equal measure from external parties and the community itself. (8)	African American leaders and issue agendas are selected by and accountable to the black community, without the intrusion of external parties. Financial resources for community programs are largely supplied by the community itself. (10)
Total Index Score	0 - 11	12 - 23	24 - 35	36 - 47	48 - 59	60

Appendix 2

The Organizational Efficacy Index (Index Points)

Component	Very Low	Low	Low-Moderate	High-Moderate	High	Very High
Elite legitimation and bargaining	Elites unanimously attack the LPO, refuse its endorsement, and do not engage in bargaining. White elites may race-bait and use overtly white supremacist rhetoric to denounce the LPO.	Elites generally ignore the LPO and its leaders. Some reactive bargaining may take place, but only on low-impact issues, and the LPO's endorsement is not actively sought.	Elites proactively seek to bargain and build alliances with the LPO, but only on low-impact issues. The LPO's endorsement is sought, but not regarded as a high priority.	Elites reactively bargain and build alliances with the LPO, but on high-impact issues. The LPO's endorsement is sought and regarded as being of middling importance.	Elites proactively bargain and build alliances with the LPO, including on high-impact issues. The LPO's endorsement is sought and highly prized.	Elites proactively bargain and build alliances with the LPO, including on high-impact issues. Elite behavior conforms to the LPO's demands. The LPO's endorsement is actively sought and considered crucial.
	(0)	(2)	(4)	(6)	(8)	(10)
Electoral success – predominantly black districts	A majority of candidates endorsed by the LPO lose (or equally divide) the African American vote and the election, African American voter turnout is poor, and LPO efforts have minimal impact on the outcome.	A majority of candidates endorsed by the LPO lose the African American vote but win the election. LPO efforts are responsible for increasing the candidates' share of the African American vote.	A majority of the candidates endorsed by the LPO win the African American vote but lose the election. LPO efforts are responsible for increasing the candidates' share of the African American vote or for stimulating African American voter turnout.	The number of candidates endorsed by the LPO that win the Black vote and the election is equal to the number that lose the African American vote and the election. LPO efforts are responsible for increasing candidates' shares of the African American vote or for stimulating African American voter turnout.	A majority of the candidates endorsed by the LPO win the African American vote and the election, but their victory margin is larger than the number of votes influenced by the LPO. LPO efforts are responsible for increasing the candidates' share of the African American vote or for stimulating African American voter turnout.	A majority of the candidates endorsed by the LPO win the African American vote and the election, with the margin of victory supplied by votes influenced by the LPO. LPO efforts are responsible for increasing the candidates' share of the African American vote and for stimulating African American voter turnout.
	(0)	(2)	(4)	(6)	(8)	(10)

Appendix 2 (continued)

Component	Very Low	Low	Low-Moderate	High-Moderate	High	Very High
Electoral success – at-large elections	A majority of the candidates endorsed by the LPO lose the election (or equally divide) the African American vote and the election, African American voter turnout is poor, and LPO efforts have minimal impact on the outcome.	A majority of the candidates endorsed by the LPO lose the African American vote but win the election. LPO efforts are responsible for increasing the candidates' share of the African American vote.	A majority of the candidates endorsed by the LPO win the African American vote, but lose the election. LPO efforts are responsible for increasing the candidates' share of the African American vote or for stimulating African American voter turnout.	The number of candidates endorsed by the LPO that win the African American vote and the election is equal to the number that lose the African American vote and the election. LPO efforts are responsible for increasing candidates' shares of the African American vote or for stimulating African American voter turnout.	A majority of the candidates endorsed by the LPO win the African American vote and the election, but their victory margin is larger than the number of votes influenced by the LPO. LPO efforts are responsible for increasing the candidates' share of the African American vote or for stimulating African American voter turnout.	A majority of the candidates endorsed by the LPO win the African American vote and the election, with the margin of victory supplied by the African American votes influenced by the LPO. LPO efforts are responsible for increasing the candidates' share of the African American vote and for stimulating African American voter turnout.
	(0)	(3)	(6)	(9)	(12)	(15)

Appendix 2 (continued)

Component	Very Low	Low	Low-Moderate	High-Moderate	High	Very High
Policy Responsiveness	The LPO's policy positions are ignored or actively opposed. Advocacy by the LPO in the policy process is met with hostility and attacks, up to and including overtly white supremacist rhetoric and race-baiting. Alternatively, the LPO does not become involved in the policy process at all.	The LPO's policy positions are largely ignored, but some symbolic steps may be taken. Alternatively, the LPO does not formally involve itself in the policy-making process but seeks to informally influence the positions of public officials through its candidate endorsement process. Advocacy by the LPO in the policy process is met with hostility and is frequently counterproductive.	The LPO's policy positions are regularly attended to through symbolic action, or the LPO does not formally involve itself in the policy-making process but seeks to informally influence the positions of public officials through its candidate endorsement process.	The LPO's policy positions are sometimes attended to with substantive action, but only when the LPO is part of an interracial coalition. Participation by the LPO itself is regarded with some hostility, but this hostility is not enough to derail substantive action.	The LPO's policy positions are regularly attended to with substantive action. This action is taken in direct response to the LPO taking a leading advocacy role in the policy process, but with the support of an interracial coalition.	The LPO's policy positions are almost always attended to with substantive action. Advocacy by the LPO in the policy process is both a necessary and sufficient condition for this substantive action. Interracial coalitions are unnecessary, though not undesirable.
	(0)	(5)	(10)	(15)	(20)	(25)
Total Index Score	0 - 11	12 - 23	24 - 35	36 - 47	48 - 59	60

Appendix 3

Freedom, Inc. Leadership

PRESIDENT	CHAIR	DATES
Leon Jordan	Bruce Watkins	1962–1970
Bruce Watkins	Harold Holliday, Sr.	1970–1972
Bruce Watkins	Harold Holliday, Jr.	1972–1975
Harold Holliday, Jr.	Charles Hazley	1975–1978
Bruce Watkins	Harold Holliday, Jr.	1978–1979
Phil Curls	Emanuel Cleaver	1980–1984
Archie Welch	James Tindall	1984–1990
Phil Curls	Charles Hazley	1990–1992
Phil Curls	James Tindall	1992–1994
James Tindall	Mary Groves Bland	1994–1996
Council of Presidents Transition Team (Mary Groves Bland, Harold Holliday, Jr., Phil Curls, Archie Welch)	Mary Groves Bland	1996–1997
Mary Groves Bland	Keith Thomas	1997–2000
Mark Bryant	None	2000–2007
Craig Bland	None	2007–2012
Transition Team (Craig Bland, Shalonn "Kiki" Curls, Charles Hazley [2012-2013], Gail Holliday)	None	2012–present

Appendix 4

African American Municipal Elected Officials in Kansas City, Missouri

ELECTED OFFICIAL	OFFICE	IN OFFICE	ENDORSED BY FREEDOM
Bruce Watkins, Sr.	Third District Councilmember Fifth District Councilmember	1963–1966 1975–1979	1963 1975
Dr. Earl Thomas	Third District At-Large Councilmember	1963–1971	1967
G. Lawrence Blankinship	Third District Councilmember	1966–1971	1966, 1967
Charles Hazley	Third District Councilmember	1971–1991	1971, 1975, 1979, 1983, 1987
Richard Tolbert	Third District At-Large Councilmember	1971–1973	1971
Joanne Collins	Third District At-Large Councilmember	1973–1991	1983, 1987
Rev. Emanuel Cleaver, II	Fifth District Councilmember Mayor	1979–1991 1991–1999	1979, 1983, 1987 1991, 1995
Mark Bryant	Fifth District At-Large Councilmember	1983–1991	1983, 1987
Carol Coe	Third District Councilmember	1991–1995	1991
Ronald Finley	Third District At-Large Councilmember	1991–1999	1995
D. Jeanne Robinson	Fifth District Councilmember	1991–1996	1995
Kenneth T. Bacchus	Fifth District At-Large Councilmember	1991–1999	1991, 1995
Mary Williams-Neal	Third District Councilmember	1995–2003	1995
Kelvin Simmons	Fifth District Councilmember	1997–2000	1997, 1999

Appendix 4 (continued)

ELECTED OFFICIAL	OFFICE	IN OFFICE	ENDORSED BY FREEDOM
Troy Nash	Third District At-Large Councilmember	1999–2007	1999, 2003
Alvin Brooks	Sixth District At-Large Councilmember	1999–2007	1999, 2003
Terry Riley	Fifth District Councilmember	2000–2011	2000, 2003, 2007
Saundra McFadden-Weaver	Third District Councilmember	2003–2007	—
Sharon Sanders-Brooks	Third District Councilmember	2007–2011	2007
Melba Curls	Third District At-Large Councilmember	2007–present	2007, 2011
Jermaine Reed	Third District Councilmember	2011–present	2011
Rev. Michael Brooks	Fifth District Councilmember	2011–2014	—
Sylvester James	Mayor	2011–present	2011

Appendix 5

Predominantly African American Wards ("Freedom Wards") in
Selected Municipal Election Years

Election Year	Number of Predominantly African American Wards	Wards
1963	5	2, 3, 14, 16, 17
1971 and 1975	7	2, 3, 14, 16, 17, 18, 19
1979 and 1983	6	2, 3, 14, 16, 17, 18
1987 and 1991	10	2, 3, 14, 16, 17, 18, 27, 28, 29, 30
1995, 1999, 2003, and 2007	8	2, 3, 7, 14, 15, 16, 17, 18

Appendix 6

Support for Freedom, Inc.-Endorsed
Candidates in Selected Mayoral Elections

Year	Freedom Candidate	Votes (%) in Wards with African American Majorities	Citywide Votes (%)
1963 General	Ilus Davis	7,743 (42.7%)	54,717 (51.1%)
1971 General	Dr. Charles Wheeler	12,033 (64%)	57,870 (55.5%)
1975 General	Dr. Charles Wheeler	12,354 (75%)	45,110 (58.7%)
1979 General	Bruce Watkins, Sr.	27,949 (89%)	52,796 (41.9%)
1983 Primary*	Joe Serviss	——	11,153 (17%)
1983 General*	Dr. Charles Wheeler	——	36,180 (40.6%)
1987 General	Richard Berkley	11,556 (60.7%)	50,992 (62.3%)
1991 General	Rev. Emanuel Cleaver	24,077 (88.1%)	50,204 (53.3%)
1995 General	Rev. Emanuel Cleaver	22,610 (93.2%)	51, 057 (55.4%)
1999 Primary	Dr. Janice Ellis	6,397 (56.8%)	11,206 (21.2%)
1999 General	George Blackwood	9,568 (65.9%)	31,319 (41%)
2007 General	Alvin Brooks	17,290 (90.5%)	41,949 (49.3%)

* Ward and precinct level data is not available for the 1983 municipal elections.

Notes

Introduction

1 These organizations are sometimes called slating groups or political clubs. The term local political organization is used here to refer to these entities because it is inclusive of the wide range of activities they may undertake (extending far beyond assembling slates), is appropriate in both partisan and nonpartisan electoral systems, and better conveys the long-lasting nature of these groups. The term also implies a higher level of structural complexity and the presence of a distinct organizational culture, both of which are to be found in the groups being described here.

2 Edward C. Banfield, *Big City Politics* (New York: Random House, 1965); Edward C. Banfield and James Q. Wilson, *City Politics* (Cambridge: Harvard University Press, 1967); James Q. Wilson, *Negro Politics: The Search for Leadership* (New York: Free Press, 1960).

3 Floyd Hunter, *Community Power Structure: A Study of Decision Makers* (Chapel Hill: University of North Carolina Press, 1953); Floyd Hunter, *Community Power Succession: Atlanta's Policy-Makers Revisited* (Chapel Hill: University of North Carolina Press, 1980); Jon C. Teaford, "New Life for an Old Subject: Investigating the Structure of Urban Rule," *American Quarterly* 34, no.3 (1985): 346–356.

4 Robert A. Dahl, *Who Governs? Democracy and Power in an American City* (New Haven: Yale University Press, 1961); Douglas Yates, *The Ungovernable City: The Politics of Urban Problems and Policy Making* (Cambridge: MIT Press, 1977).

5 Betty H. Zisk, *Local Interest Politics: A One-Way Street* (Indianapolis: The Bobbs-Merrill Company, 1973); Betty H. Zisk, Heinz Eulau, and Kenneth Prewitt, "City Councilmen and the Group Struggle: A Typology of Role Orientation," *The Journal of Politics* 27, no. 3 (1965): 618–646.

6 Harvey Molotch, "The City as Growth Machine," *American Journal of Sociology* 82 (1976): 309–332.

7 Clarence N. Stone, *Regime Politics: Governing Atlanta, 1946–1988* (Lawrence: University of Kansas Press, 1989).

8 Rufus P. Browning, Dale Rogers Marshall, and David H. Tabb, *Protest Is Not Enough: The Struggle of Blacks and Hispanics for Equality in Urban Politics* (Berkeley: University of California Press, 1984); Rufus P. Browning, Dale Rogers Marshall, and David H. Tabb, *Racial Politics in American Cities* (New York: Longman, 1990); Rufus P. Browning, Dale

Rogers Marshall, and David H. Tabb, *Racial Politics in American Cities, Third Edition* (New York: Longman, 2003).

9 Manning Marable, *Race, Reform, and Rebellion: The Second Reconstruction in Black America, 1945–1990 (Revised Second Edition)* (Jackson: University Press of Mississippi, 1991); Robert C. Smith, *We Have No Leaders: African-Americans in the Post-Civil Rights Era* (Albany: State University of New York Press, 1996).

10 Devin Bent, "Partisan Elections and Public Policy: Response to Black Demands in Large American Cities," *Journal of Black Studies* 12, no. 3 (1982): 291–314; Lawrence Bobo and Franklin D. Gilliam Jr., "Race, Sociopolitical Participation, and Empowerment," *American Political Science Review* 84, no. 2 (1990): 377–393; Zoltan L. Hajnal, "White Residents, Black Incumbents, and a Declining Racial Divide," *American Political Science Review* 95, no. 3 (2001): 603–617; Derek S. Hyra, "City Politics and Black Protest: The Economic Transformation of Harlem and Bronzeville," *Souls* 8, no. 3 (2006): 176–196; Karen M. Kaufmann, "Black and Latino Voters in Denver: Responses to Each Other's Political Leadership," *Political Science Quarterly* 118, no. 1 (2003): 107–125; Karen M. Kaufmann, *The Urban Voter: Group Conflict and Mayoral Voting Behavior in American Cities* (Ann Arbor: University of Michigan Press, 2004); Richard A. Keiser and Katherine Underwood, *Minority Politics at the Millennium* (New York: Garland Publishing, 2000); Kenneth R. Mladenka, "Blacks and Hispanics in Urban Politics," *American Political Science Review* 83, no. 1 (1989): 165–191; Raphael J. Sonenshein, "The Dynamics of Biracial Coalition: Crossover Politics in Los Angeles," *Western Political Quarterly* 42, no. 2 (1989): 333–353.

11 Abdul Alkalimat and Doug Gills, *Harold Washington and the Crisis of Black Power in Chicago* (Chicago: Twenty-First Century Books and Publications, 1989); Julian Bond, "Practical Politician: Julian Bond," *Black Politician* 1, no. 2 (1969): 28; Marcus D. Pohlmann and Michael P. Kirby, *Racial Politics at the Crossroads: Memphis Elects Dr. W.W. Herenton* (Knoxville: University of Tennessee Press, 1996); Alex Poinsett, *Black Power, Gary Style: The Making of Mayor Richard Gordon Hatcher* (Chicago: Johnson Publishing Company, 1970).

12 Banfield and Wilson, *City Politics*.

13 Banfield, *Big City Politics*.

14 Chandler Davidson and Luis Ricardo Fraga, "Slating Groups as Parties in a 'Nonpartisan' Setting," *Western Political Quarterly* 41, no. 2 (1988): 373–390.

15 Amy Bridges, *Morning Glories: Municipal Reform in the Southwest* (Princeton: Princeton University Press, 1997).

16 M. Margaret Conway, "Voter Information Sources in a Nonpartisan Local Election," *Western Political Quarterly* 21, no. 1 (1968): 69–77.

17 Jeanne Theoharis and Komozi Woodard, *Freedom North: Black Freedom Struggles Outside the South, 1940–1980* (New York: Palgrave Macmillan, 2003); Jeanne Theoharis and Komozi Woodard, *Groundwork: Local Black Freedom Movements in America* (New York: New York University Press, 2005).

18 James Jennings, *The Politics of Black Empowerment: The Transformation of Black Activism in Urban America* (Detroit: Wayne State University Press, 1992).

19 Charles D. Hadley, "The Transformation of the Role of Black Ministers and Black Political Organizations in Louisiana Politics," in *Blacks and Southern Politics,* ed. Laurence W. Moreland et al. (New York: Praeger, 1987), 133–148.

20 Ronald E. Brown and Carolyn Hartfield, "Black Churches and the Formation of Political Action Committees in Detroit," in *Black Churches and Local Politics: Clergy, Influence, Organizational Partnerships, and Civic Empowerment,* ed. R. Drew Smith and Fredrick C. Harris (Lanham: Rowman and Littlefield, 2005), 151–170.

21 Wilbur C. Rich, *Coleman Young and Detroit politics: From Social Activist to Power Broker* (Detroit: Wayne State University Press, 1989).

22 R. Drew Smith and Fredrick C. Harris, *Black Churches and Local Politics: Clergy Influence, Organizational Partnerships, and Civic Empowerment* (Lanham: Rowman and Littlefield, 2005).

23 M. Elaine Burgess, *Negro Leadership in a Southern City* (New Haven: College and University Press, 1961).

24 C.A. Bacote, "The Negro in Atlanta Politics," *Phylon* 16, no. 4 (1955): 335–350; Banfield, *Big City Politics;* Ronald H. Bayor, *Race and the Shaping of Twentieth-Century Atlanta* (Chapel Hill: University of North Carolina Press, 1996); Richard A. Keiser, *Subordination or Empowerment? African-American Leadership and the Struggle for Urban Political Power* (New York: Oxford University Press, 1997); Stone, *Regime Politics;* Jack L. Walker, "Protest and Negotiation: A Case Study of Negro Leadership in Atlanta, Georgia," *Midwest Journal of Political Science* 7, no 2. (1963): 99–124.

25 Leonard N. Moore, *Carl B. Stokes and the Rise of Black Political Power* (Urbana: University of Illinois Press, 2002); William E. Nelson Jr., "Cleveland: The Rise and Fall of the New Black Politics," in *The New Black Politics: The Search for Political Power,* ed. Michael B. Preston and Lenneal J. Henderson (New York: Longman, 1982), 187–208; William E. Nelson Jr. and Philip J. Meranto, *Electing Black Mayors: Political Action in the Black Community* (Columbus: Ohio State University Press, 1977).

26 Alkalimat and Gills, *Harold Washington and the Crisis of Black Power in Chicago.*

27 Josh Sides, "A Simple Quest for Dignity: African American Los Angeles Since World War II" in *City of Promise: Race and Historical Change in Los Angeles,* ed. Martin Schiesl and Mark M. Dodge (Claremont: Regina Books, 2006), 109–126; Raphael J. Sonenshein, *Politics in Black and White: Race and Power in Los Angeles* (Princeton: Princeton University Press, 1993), 60.

28 James Jennings and Mel King, *From Access to Power: Black Politics in Boston* (Cambridge: Schenkman Books, 1986).

29 Komozi Woodard, *A Nation Within A Nation: Amiri Baraka (LeRoi Jones) and Black Power Politics* (Chapel Hill: University of North Carolina Press, 1999).

30 Chandler Davidson, *Biracial Politics: Conflict and Coalition in the Metropolitan South* (Baton Rouge: Louisiana State University Press, 1972).

31 Richard Arrington, *There's Hope for the World: The Memoir of Birmingham, Alabama's First African American Mayor* (Tuscaloosa: University of Alabama Press, 2008); Andra Gillespie and Emma Tolbert, "Racial Authenticity and Redistricting: A Comparison of Artur Davis's 2000 and 2002 Congressional Campaigns," in *Whose Black Politics?*

Cases in Post-Racial Black Leadership, ed. Andra Gillespie (New York: Routledge, 2010), 45–66; Huey L. Perry, "The Evolution and Impact of Biracial Coalitions and Black Mayors in Birmingham and New Orleans," in *Racial Politics in American Cities, Third Edition,* ed. Rufus P. Browning, Dale Rogers Marshall, and David H. Tabb (New York: Longman, 2003), 227–254.

32 Baodong Liu and James M. Vanderleeuw, *Race Rules: Electoral Politics in New Orleans, 1965–2006* (Lanham: Lexington Books, 2007); Perry, "The Evolution and Impact of Biracial Coalitions and Black Mayors in Birmingham and New Orleans," 227–254; Alvin J. Schexnider, "Political Mobilization in the South: The Election of a Black Mayor in New Orleans," in *The New Black Politics: The Search for Political Power,* ed. Michael B. Preston, Lenneal J. Henderson Jr., and Paul Puryear (New York: Longman, 1982), 221–240.

33 Robert C. Smith, *We Have No Leaders: African Americans in the Post-Civil Rights Era* (Albany: State University of New York Press, 1996), 127–138; Adolph L. Reed, *Stirrings in the Jug: Black Politics in the Post-Segregation Era* (Minneapolis: University of Minnesota Press, 1999), 117–159.

34 Mack H. Jones, "Politics and Organizational Options: Comments on Essay VI: 'The Next Five Years: II. Organizational Options,'" *National Political Science Review* 8 (2001): 50–57.

35 Todd C. Shaw, *Now Is The Time! Detroit Black Politics and Grassroots Activism* (Durham: Duke University Press, 2009).

36 Dahl, *Who Governs?;* Mancur Olson, *The Logic of Collective Action: Public Goods and the Theory of Groups* (Cambridge: Harvard University Press, 1965); E.E. Schattschneider, *The Semisovereign People: A Realist's View of Democracy in America* (New York: Holt, Rinehart and Winston, 1960); Anne Schneider and Helen M. Ingram, *Deserving and Entitled: Social Constructions and Public Policy* (Albany: State University of New York Press, 2005); Stone, *Regime Politics.*

37 Kenneth T. Andrews and Bob Edwards, "Advocacy Organizations in the U.S. Political Process," *Annual Review of Sociology* 30 (2004): 479–506.

38 Allan J. Cigler and Burdett A. Loomis, *Interest Group Politics, Seventh Edition* (Washington: CQ Press, 2007); Richard A. Smith, "Interest Group Influence in the U.S. Congress," *Legislative Studies Quarterly* 20, no. 1 (1995): 89–139.

39 Michael T. Heaney, "Identity Crisis: How Interest Groups Struggle to Define Themselves in Washington," in *Interest Group Politics, Seventh Edition,* ed. Allan J. Cigler and Burdett C. Loomis (Washington: CQ Press, 2007), 279–300; John J. Mearsheimer and Stephen J. Walt, *The Israel Lobby and U.S. Foreign Policy* (New York: Farrar, Straus, and Giroux, 2007); Kelly D. Patterson and Matthew M. Singer, "Targeting Success: The Enduring Power of the NRA," in *Interest Group Politics, Seventh Edition,* ed. Allan J. Cigler and Burdett A. Loomis (Washington: CQ Press, 2007), 37–64.

40 Shaw, *Now Is The Time!,* 13–38.

41 Stokely Carmichael and Charles V. Hamilton, *Black Power: The Politics of Liberation in America* (New York: Vintage Books, 1967); William A. Clay, *Just Permanent Interests: Black Americans in Congress, 1870–1991* (New York: Amistad Press, 1992), 339–354;

Harry Holloway, "Negro Political Strategy: Coalition or Independent Power Politics," *Social Science Quarterly* 49 (1968): 534–547; Sonenshein, *Politics in Black and White,* 246–282.

42 Carmichael and Hamilton, *Black Power.*

43 Michael C. Dawson, *Behind the Mule: Race and Class in African-American Politics* (Princeton: Princeton University Press, 1994), 10–11; Michael C. Dawson, *Black Visions: The Roots of Contemporary African-American Political Ideologies* (Chicago: University of Chicago Press, 2001), 1–43.

44 Ronald W. Walters, *Black Presidential Politics in America: A Strategic Approach* (Albany: State University of New York Press, 1988), 1–26.

45 Reed, *Stirrings in the Jug,* 117–159.

46 Amy Hart, "The Founding of Freedom: A Kansas City Civil Rights Organization Since 1962" (MA thesis, Central Missouri State University, 2006).

Chapter 1

1 United States Census Bureau

2 A. Theodore Brown and Lyle W. Dorsett, *K.C.:A History of Kansas City* (Boulder: Pruett, 1978), 1–37; Tracy Thomas and Walt Bodine, *Right Here in River City: A Portrait of Kansas City* (Garden City: Doubleday, 1976).

3 Brown and Dorsett, *K.C.,* 1–67.

4 Sherry Lamb Schirmer, *A City Divided: The Racial Landscape of Kansas City* (Columbia: University of Missouri Press, 2002), 2–25.

5 Brown and Dorsett, *K.C.*

6 Lyle W. Dorsett, *The Pendergast Machine* (New York: Oxford University Press, 1968), 4; Lawrence H. Larsen and Nancy J. Hulston, *Pendergast!* (Columbia: University of Missouri Press, 1997), 24–43; William M. Reddig, *Tom's Town: Kansas City and the Pendergast Legend* (Philadelphia: J.B. Lippincott Company, 1947).

Prior to the enactment of "charter" government in 1925, the City Council was bicameral.

7 Brown and Dorsett, *K.C.,* 99–130.

8 Dorsett, *The Pendergast Machine,* 19–40; Larsen and Hulston, *Pendergast!,* 24–43; Reddig, *Tom's Town,* 37–48.

9 Ibid.

10 Merle Clayton, *Union Station Massacre: The Shootout that Started the FBI's War on Crime* (Indianapolis: Bobbs-Merrill, 1975).

11 Although the governor claimed only the noblest motivations, his actions were politically motivated. In 1938, he ran for the Democratic nomination for United States Senate against Harry Truman. Truman was linked to the Jackson County machine, to the point that he was sometimes called "the Senator from Pendergast." Despite that connection, even his critics were forced to concede that Truman was impeccably honest and never engaged in any of the activities for which the machine was infamous (David G. McCullough, *Truman* (New York: Simon and Schuster, 1992)).

12 Larsen and Hulston, *Pendergast!*, 152–187.

13 Edward C. Banfield and James Q. Wilson, *City Politics* (Cambridge: Harvard University Press, 1967), 134–136; A. Theodore Brown, *The Politics of Reform: Kansas City's Municipal Government* (Kansas City: Community Studies, Inc., 1958).

14 Brown and Dorsett, *K.C.*, 99–130.

15 Ibid; Schirmer, *A City Divided*, 124–126.

16 Larsen and Hulston, *Pendergast!*, 71–129.

17 Steve Kraske, "Kansas City needs a strong-mayor system of government," *Kansas City Star*, March 12, 2011.

18 "History," Citizens Association, accessed April 10, 2011, http://www.citizensassociation.com/history.

19 Brown, *The Politics of Reform*; Kenneth E. Gray, *A Report on Politics in Kansas City, Missouri* (Cambridge: Joint Center for Urban Studies, 1959).

20 Brown, *The Politics of Reform: Kansas City's Municipal Government.*

21 Amy Bridges, *Morning Glories: Municipal Reform in the Southwest* (Princeton: Princeton University Press, 1997).

22 Gray, *A Report on Politics in Kansas City, Missouri.*

23 Cookingham, the manager revered by reformers, resigned immediately after the Democratic Coalition claimed victory in 1959 and before its members took office. He did not go quietly, condemning what he saw as the Coalition's injection of partisanship, factionalism, and corruption into municipal government.

24 This sexist term is used advisedly; Kansas City had no women elected to municipal office or in high-ranking appointive office until 1963.

25 United States Census Bureau, "Table 26. Missouri—Race and Hispanic Origin for Selected Large Cities and Other Places: Earliest Census to 1990," *Historical Census Statistics on Population Totals by Race, 1790 to 1990, and by Hispanic Origin, 1970 to 1990, for Large Cities and Other Urban Places in the United States* (Washington: United States Census Bureau, 1991).

26 Lorenzo J. Greene, Gary R. Kremer, and Antonio F. Holland, *Missouri's Black Heritage, Revised Edition* (Columbia: University of Missouri Press, 1993), 8–87.

27 Charles E. Coulter, *Take Up the Black Man's Burden: Kansas City's African American Communities, 1865–1939*; Kevin Fox Gotham, *Race, Real Estate, and Uneven Development: The Kansas City Experience, 1900–2010, Second Edition* (Albany: State University of New York Press), 27–50; Schirmer, *A City Divided*, 73–119.

28 Gotham, *Race, Real Estate, and Uneven Development*, 27–50.

29 Schirmer, *A City Divided*, 73–119.

30 Gotham, *Race, Real Estate, and Uneven Development*, 13; Douglas S. Massey and Nancy M. Denton, *American Apartheid: Segregation and the Making of the Underclass* (Cambridge: Harvard University Press, 1993), 75–77.

31 Monte Piliawsky, "Black Political Empowerment in Kansas City," in *The State of Black Kansas City 1991*, ed. Sandra V. Walker (Kansas City: The Urban League of Greater Kansas City, 1991), 163–190; Schirmer, *A City Divided*, 181–189.

32 *Kansas City Star,* "Giant Step for Kansas City," March 29, 1991.

33 Piliawsky, "Black Political Empowerment in Kansas City;" Schirmer, *A City Divided,* 28–29, 64–66, 152–162.

34 Schirmer, *A City Divided,* 157–160.

35 Schirmer, *A City Divided,* 18–25, 124–126, 166–173.

36 Greene, Kremer, and Holland, *Missouri's Black Heritage,* 112, 148.

37 Schirmer, *A City Divided,* 64–65.

38 Schirmer, *A City Divided,* 154.

39 Piliawsky, "Black Political Empowerment in Kansas City," 163–190.

40 Kansas City Times, "Watkins Charges Ties with Wagner," March 6, 1963.

41 Gray, *A Report on Politics in Kansas City, Missouri;* Kansas City's Municipal Court uses the "Missouri Plan" for judicial appointments. A nominating committee comprised of citizens selects three nominees for a vacancy. The full City Council then selects a judge from among the nominees. The judge serves a four-year term, at which point he/she faces a retention election.

42 Armstead L. Robinson and Patricia Sullivan, *New Directions in Civil Rights Studies* (Charlottesville: University Press of Virginia, 1991), 1–7; Jeanne Theoharis and Komozi Woodard, *Freedom North: Black Freedom Struggles Outside the South* (New York: Palgrave Macmillan, 2003); J. Mills Thornton III, *Dividing Lines: Municipal Politics and the Struggle for Civil Rights in Montgomery, Birmingham, and Selma* (Tuscaloosa: University of Alabama Press, 2002), 1–19.

43 Gaines was the plaintiff in *Missouri ex. rel. Gaines v. Canada* (1938), a case that paved the way for *Brown*. Gaines sought admission to the law school at the University of Missouri, arguing that the state's university for African Americans (Lincoln University) did not offer a law degree. The United States Supreme Court agreed; it held that where "equal opportunities" did not exist for African American students at universities designated for blacks, those students must be admitted to programs at other public universities in the state. Gaines won admission to the University of Missouri but never attended; he disappeared under mysterious circumstances in 1939.

44 Amy Hart, "The Founding of Freedom: A Kansas City Civil Rights Organization Since 1962;" Schirmer, *A City Divided,* 222–224.

45 Hart, "The Founding of Freedom;" Schirmer, *A City Divided,* 214–217.

46 Gray, *A Report on Politics in Kansas City, Missouri.*

47 Hart, "The Founding of Freedom;" Schirmer, *A City Divided,* 219–221.

48 Interview with author.

49 Delia C. Gillis, *Kansas City* (Charleston: Acadia, 2007), 111.

Chapter 2

1 Harry Jones Jr., "A Dilemma in Council Plans," *Kansas City Star,* December 24, 1961. Prior to the adoption of charter government, there were a handful of unsuccessful black candidates for the bicameral Council. One such candidate was T.B. Watkins, who ran for alderman from Ward 8 in 1922. Watkins was active in Republican politics, but ran in

defiance of the Republican machine as an independent and a "race man." He was hurt and angered when blacks loyal to the Democratic and Republican machines put party above racial unity (Sherry Lamb Schirmer, *A City Divided: The Racial Landscape of Kansas City, 1900–1960* [Columbia: University of Missouri Press, 2002], 144, 149, 153). Watkins was the step-father of Bruce Watkins, one of Freedom's founders.

2 Harry Jones Jr., "Vote Fight Looms in a Council Shift," *Kansas City Star,* November 12, 1961.

3 Kansas City Times, "Rival Council Plans Offered," November 15, 1961.

4 *Kansas City Star,* "Politics Bid in City Districts," November 14, 1961; *Kansas City Times,* "Voting Reform Plan Advances," November 14, 1961.

5 *Kansas City Star,* "Politics Bid in City Districts," November 14, 1961.

6 William R. Graves, "O.K. 6–6 by Nearly 4–1," March 7, 1962.

7 Harry Jones Jr., *Kansas City Star,* "Vote Fight Looms in a Council Shift," November 12, 1961.

8 *Kansas City Star, Kansas City Times,* "Shute Resigns as CBAR Head," November 24, 1961.

9 *Kansas City Times,* "Civil Rights Stand Recalled by Davis," February 5, 1963.

10 Jones, "A Dilemma in Council Plans."

11 Amy Hart, "The Founding of Freedom: A Kansas City Civil Rights Organization Since 1962" (MA thesis, Central Missouri State University, 2006); Interview with author; *Kansas City Star,* "Bohannon View on Slaying," July 15, 1970; *Kansas City Star,* "Hunt for 3 Killers," July 15, 1970; Bill Moore, *Kansas City Star,* "Mission to Liberia, Acrimony at Home," July 15, 1970.

12 Interview with author.

13 Interview with author.

14 Interview with author.

15 Graves, "O.K. 6–6 by Nearly 4–1."

16 Jones, "A Dilemma in Council Plans."

17 Interview with author.

18 *Call,* "Holliday in Call for Debate with Watkins," March 15, 1963.

19 *Call,* "Bruce R. Watkins Files for State Legislature on Republican Ticket," April 16, 1956.

20 *Call,* "Holliday in Call for Debate with Watkins."

21 Interview with author.

22 Neither the *Times* nor the *Star,* which as a matter of course provided readers with the most minute details about the functioning of dozens of political and social clubs, saw fit to print anything about the founding of the new organization. Indeed, the first mention of Freedom in the daily papers seems to have come in the heat of the last three weeks of the 1963 municipal elections.

23 *Call,* "'Freedom, Inc.' Name of New Political Group," May 4, 1962.

24 Ibid.

25 Interview with author.

26 Johnson would later become affiliated with Freedom, serving several terms in the Missouri House of Representatives as a Freedom-supported candidate. In the 1970s, he broke with the organization before repairing the relationship again in the late 1980s.

27 Interview with author.

28 Interview with author.

29 Interview with author.

30 Louis Blue, *Call,* "Leon Jordan Takes Over 14th Ward From Moran," August 10, 1962.

31 *Kansas City Star,* "Third District to Place Two Negroes on Council," February 6, 1963.

Lincoln High School is also notable for being a launching place for the career of Aaron Douglas. Douglas, the leading visual artist of the Harlem Renaissance, spent several years as the school's art teacher (Susan Earle, *Aaron Douglas: African American Modernist* [New Haven: Yale University Press, 2007], 82).

32 *Call,* "Negroes Unopposed in Third," February 8, 1963; Interview with author; *Kansas City Star,* "Third District to Place Two Negroes on Council."

33 *Kansas City Times,* "Citizens Endorsed by Freedom Inc.," March 14, 1963.

34 *Kansas City Star,* "Holliday Denies Faction Control," March 7, 1963.

Holliday's supporters also insisted that a formal endorsement of Holliday for the district seat and Watkins for the at-large seat was made by Freedom in 1962. All other Freedom officials strongly denied this contention.

35 *Kansas City Times,* "Citizens Endorsed by Freedom Inc.," March 14, 1963.

36 *Kansas City Times,* "Freedom, Inc. President Scolds Council Candidate," March 9, 1963.

37 *Kansas City Star,* "Happy to Receive Wagner's Support," February 22, 1963.

38 Melba Marlow, *Call,* "Bruce Watkins Made History As Elected Official," September 19, 1980.

39 *Kansas City Times,* "The City Vote," February 27, 1963.

40 *Kansas City Star,* "Holliday Denies Faction Control."

41 *Kansas City Times,* "Citizens Endorsed by Freedom Inc."

42 *Kansas City Times,* "Freedom, Inc. President Scolds Council Candidate."

43 *Kansas City Star,* "Watkins Charges Ties with Wagner," March 6, 1963.

44 Harry Jones Jr., "Citizens Back Bruce Watkins," *Kansas City Times,* March 5, 1963.

45 Marlow, "Bruce Watkins Made History As Elected Official."

46 *Call,* "Endorsement," March 8, 1963; *Kansas City Star,* "Mayor and Councilmen for the Hard City Job," March 22, 1963.

47 Brookfield, the Republican owner of a large manufacturing concern, founded the IVA as a personal vehicle for his mayoral ambitions after he lost the CA endorsement to Davis, a Democratic former city councilman, attorney, and banker. The CA traditionally split its council endorsements equally between Democrats and Republicans, but slated a Democrat for the mayoralty. Brookfield objected to this custom and founded his own organization. The IVA presented a full slate of candidates in the municipal election, most

of whom ultimately drew support from the Democratic factions. The IVA ceased to exist immediately after the 1963 elections, never having been anything more than a vehicle for Brookfield.

48 *Kansas City Star,* "Call Support to Brookfield," March 15, 1963.

49 Rufus P. Browning, Dale Rogers Marshall, and David H. Tabb, *Protest Is Not Enough: The Struggle of Blacks and Hispanics for Equality in Urban Politics* (Berkeley: University of California Press, 1984).

50 Raphael J. Sonenshein, *Politics in Black and White: Race and Power in Los Angeles* (Princeton: Princeton University Press, 1993).

51 *Kansas City Times,* "Citizens Endorsed by Freedom Inc.," March 14, 1963.

52 *Kansas City Star,* "Watkins Charges Ties with Wagner;" *Kansas City Times,* "Freedom, Inc. President Scolds Council Candidate."

53 *Kansas City Star,* "Mayor and Councilmen for the Hard City Job."

54 Of course, the support for Brookfield, Davis's opponent, in the 14th Ward and other black majority areas was not only attributable to the factions. As noted earlier, Brookfield was endorsed by *The Call,* which maintained that Davis was not a supporter of civil rights.

55 William R. Graves, "Council Reins Won by Citizens," *Kansas City Times,* March 27, 1963; *Kansas City Star,* "The Election Results by Wards," March 27, 1963.

56 Harry Jones Jr., "Votes Realign Base of Power," *Kansas City Star,* March 27, 1963.

57 Marlow, "Bruce Watkins Made History As Elected Official."

58 Marlow, "Bruce Watkins Made History As Elected Official."

59 *Kansas City Times,* "Davis Asks OK on Rights Bill," March 10, 1964.

60 *Kansas City Star,* "The Moral and Economic Issues of Public Accommodations," March 19, 1964;" *Kansas City Star,* "Kansas City's Reputation on Civil Rights," March 26, 1964; *Kansas City Star,* "Both Sides Offer Rights Bill Views," April 3, 1964; *Kansas City Times,* "Rights Bill Given Citizens Support," March 13, 1964.

61 Harry Jones Jr., "Step Up Drives in Rights Vote," *Kansas City Star,* March 18, 1964; *Kansas City Times,* "Tavern Men Wage Their Own Battle," March 2, 1964.

62 Dennis Farney, "Good Marks Given the Outgoing Mayor," *Kansas City Star,* March 13, 1973.

63 *Kansas City Times,* "Named to Head Race Campaign," March 5, 1964.

64 *Kansas City Star,* "Both Parties for Rights Law," April 2, 1964; *Kansas City Times,* "Labor Council to Rights Bill," March 11, 1964; *Kansas City Times,* "Rights Bill Given Citizens Support," March 13, 1964.

65 *Kansas City Times,* "Davis Asks OK on Rights Bill," March 10, 1964.

66 *Kansas City Times,* "Urge Approval of Racial Bill," April 6, 1964.

67 Harry Jones Jr., "Step Up Drives in Rights Vote," *Kansas City Star,* March 27, 1963.

68 Watkins alleged that certain faction leaders were instructing their black patronage appointees to refrain from involvement in the pro-public accommodations campaign or lose their jobs. Although some of the specifics of Watkins's claims may have been inaccurate, there is no question that his general point—that the faction leaders were being less than vigorous on the issue—was correct.

69 Jim Brown, "Wide Support for Rights Bill," *Call,* July 10, 1964.

70 *Kansas City Star,* "Favor Racial Move in Poll," March 11, 1964.

71 *Kansas City Times,* "Tavern Men Wage Their Own Battle."

72 *Kansas City Star,* "An All-Out Effort by Tavern Owners," March 30, 1964.

73 *Kansas City Star,* "Ask No By Voters on Bias Ordinance," March 11, 1964.

74 *Kansas City Star,* "An All-Out Effort by Tavern Owners."

75 *Call,* "Civic Groups Gird for Fight," January 17, 1964.

76 Marlow, "Bruce Watkins Made History As Elected Official."

77 *Kansas City Star,* "A Heavy Vote on Racial Law," April 7, 1964.

78 Lena R. Smith, "Add 5,000 New Voters," *Call,* March 20, 1964. Importantly, many of the new registrants were in the 2nd Ward, Wagner's fiefdom. Discouraging voter registration among residents who could not be relied upon to provide solid support for the JDC slate had long been a technique used by Wagner and McKissick to retain control. The newly registered voters in the 2nd Ward were not Wagner loyalists, as later elections would soon demonstrate, which is one reason that Operation PA concentrated its efforts there.

79 William R. Graves, "Close Race Bill Victory," *Kansas City Times,* April 8, 1964.

80 Louis Blue, "Kansas City Passes Rights Bill," *Call,* April 17, 1964.

81 Jim Brown, "Slim Chance for 2nd Negro State Lawmaker," *Call,* July 10, 1964.

82 Phillips Committee for Congress, "Vote for Judge Hunter Phillips (Paid Political Advertisement)."

83 Although Phillips held the title of "judge," the Jackson County Court was the legislative body for the county. The judges held positions that in other jurisdictions were referred to as county commissioners or supervisors. Adoption of charter government in Jackson County during the 1970s eliminated the county court and replaced it with a legislature and elected county executive.

84 *Call,* "Negro Votes Cannot Desert Bolling," April 10, 1964; *Call,* "Lines Drawn for Political Battle," July 3, 1964; Steven A. Glorioso, "Fight Against the Factions: The 1964 and 1966 Democratic Primaries" (MA thesis, University of Missouri-Kansas City, 1974).

85 Glorioso, "The Fight Against the Factions."

86 Brown, "Slim Chance for 2nd Negro State Lawmaker;" *Call,* "Kansas City Will Send Three to Legislature," August 14, 1964.

87 This is because the CA and the "reform" movement depended on the votes of Republicans in the silk stocking district for victory in nonpartisan city elections. These Republicans could not cast ballots in the county's Democratic primaries, which were subsequently won by factional candidates. Even reform-minded Democrats were not willing to abandon the party to vote for Republican nominees in the partisan county elections.

88 Glorioso, "The Fight Against the Factions."

89 Interview with author.

90 Henry C. Gold, "Bolling Victory Easy: Gets Negro Aid," *Kansas City Times,* August 5, 1964.

91 Robert P. Sigman, "Factions Hold to Courthouse," *Kansas City Times,* August 5, 1964.

92 *Call,* "Kansas City Will Send Three to Legislature."

93 Glorioso, "The Fight Against the Factions."

94 Ibid.

95 Harry Jones Jr., "Sad, Stunned by Loss," *Kansas City Star,* March 18, 1964; Michael J. Kelley, "Curry Slate Sweeps 8 Offices," *Kansas City Times,* August 3, 1966; *Kansas City Times,* "Jackson County Election Results," August 3, 1966.

96 Kevin Fox Gotham, *Race, Real Estate, and Uneven Development: The Kansas City Experience, 1900–2010, Second Edition* (Albany: State University of New York Press, 2014), 75–94.

97 *Kansas City Star,* "A Racial Fear on Home Plan," December 6, 1966.

98 *Kansas City Times,* "Urban Renewal Funds Sought," March 24, 1967.

99 Gotham, *Race, Real Estate, and Uneven Development,* 95–126.

100 *Time,* "Chief Clarence Kelley: A Dick Tracy for the FBI," June 18, 1973.

101 Among those falling under this heading was Wayne Morse, a candidate for the seat once held by Bruce Watkins. Morse declared the John Birch Society too moderate for his tastes and frequently engaged in one-man pickets against civil rights. When told that many viewed him as a racist, he calmly replied that it was not true, because he was not a "Negro hater" but a "n——hater" (Michael J. Kelley, "Wide Contrast in Third District," *Kansas City Times,* March 24, 1967).

102 Charles Hammer, "Varied Ballot After Primary," *Kansas City Star,* March 5, 1967.

103 William R. Graves, "Citizens Name 2 for Council," *Kansas City Times,* December 8, 1966.

104 Michael J. Kelley, "Heat Builds in Council Race," *Kansas City Star,* March 15, 1967; *Kansas City Times,* "Apart on Role of Mrs. Hagan," February 14, 1967; *Kansas City Times,* "A Hard Fight on Mrs. Hagan," February 17, 1964.

105 William R. Graves, "Citizens Plan All-Out Drive," *Kansas City Times,* February 6, 1967; Michael J. Kelley, "Factions Shun City Elections," *Kansas City Times,* February 2, 1967.

106 William R. Graves, "Ten Citizens Candidates Elected," *Kansas City Times,* March 29, 1967.

107 *Kansas City Times,* "Moved by Tragedy," April 5, 1968.

108 *Kansas City Star,* "Youths in March Here," April 9, 1967.

109 Kansas City, Missouri Mayor's Commission on Civil Disorder, *Final Report* (1968), 32.

110 *Call,* "Kansas City Rioting Ends with 6 Dead: Many Questions on Police Action in Riots," April 19, 1968; Charles Hammer, "Rights Leader Hits Police Tactics," *Kansas City Times,* April 10, 1968; Commission on Civil Disorder, *Final Report;* Fred Kiewit, "Riot Tempo Mounted Quickly," *Kansas City Star,* April 14, 1968; *Kansas City Times,* "Disorder in City Wanes," April 10, 1968; *Kansas City Times,* "Guard in City Number 2,200," April 10, 1968; *Kansas City Times,* "Test Case Blamed in Disorder," April 19, 1968; *Kansas City Times,* "Few Breaks in Calm," April 12, 1968; *Kansas City Times,* "Order in City, Curfew Lifted," April 15, 1968.

111 *Kansas City Star,* "Take 2 Whites in Sniper Area," April 12, 1968.

112 Commission on Civil Disorder, *Final Report.*

113 Commission on Civil Disorder, *Final Report,* 32. Interestingly, the Commission occasionally referred to the disturbance by the more politically charged term "uprising." Use of that term—with its implication of conscious political intent—would seem to belie the claim that the "disturbance" was the product of shock to the psyche.

114 Commission on Civil Disorder, *Final Report,* 46.

115 Gotham, *Race, Real Estate, and Uneven Development,* 95–152.

116 Charles Hammer, "Davis Dispels Fair Housing Fear," *Kansas City Star,* April 7, 1967.

117 Gotham, *Race, Real Estate, and Uneven Development,* 127–139.

118 Kansas City Citizens Council, *Don't Be An April Fool!*

119 Commission on Civil Disorder, *Final Report.* Moreover, 33 percent of whites felt that the *primary* cause of the rebellion was "agitation" by "radical leaders" and 12 percent of whites felt the *primary* cause was that black citizens "just wanted to destroy." In contrast, 68 percent of blacks felt that the rebellion would *improve* conditions in the long run and just 19 percent of blacks felt that their treatment in Kansas City was fair.

120 John T. Dauner, "New Housing Step Seen," *Kansas City Times,* April 13, 1968.

121 For understandable reasons, it was important to Freedom that the local fair housing law not be regarded as having been mandated from Washington. If local black elected officials were regarded as having simply done as Washington ordered, they would not be able to claim much-deserved credit from their constituents for having taken action on an important issue.

122 *Kansas City Star,* "Cleaver on the Outside, Looking In," April 9, 1975. Only after Cleaver moderated his own views and sought to leave the world of community activism for electoral politics did he become involved with Freedom. Receiving a shellacking by Freedom in his 1970 campaign for state legislature and again when he ran against Bruce Watkins for a City Council seat in 1975 enhanced his respect for the organization.

123 *Call,* "Freedom-CCP Beat Factions," August 19, 1968.

124 Affiliated Democratic Club, "Vote for the True Negro Democratic Ballot (Paid Political Advertisement)."

125 *Call,* "Freedom-CCP Beat Factions."

126 Ibid.

127 Michael J. Kelley, "C.C.P. Unhurt by Ticket Splitting," *Kansas City Times,* November 6, 1968.

Chapter 3

1 Ronald W. Walters, *Black Presidential Politics in America: A Strategic Approach* (Albany: State University of New York Press, 1988), 112.

2 Vincent J. Cannato, *The Ungovernable City: John Lindsay and His Struggle to Save New York* (New York: Basic Books, 2001), 119–154, 301–374.

3 Ronald W. Walters, *Freedom Is Not Enough: Black Voters, Black Candidates, and American Presidential Politics* (Lanham: Rowman and Littlefield, 2005), 27–76.

4 Interview with author.

5 As though consciously striving to permanently seal off any hope of reconciliation between the old-line Democratic factions and African Americans, the most important of the former, the Democratic Good Government Association of state Rep. Will Royster (a city councilman on the tumultuous 1959–1963 council) endorsed George C. Wallace in his 1968 independent bid for president. The faction delivered a healthy majority for Wallace in the precincts in which it was active (Michael J. Kelley, "C.C.P. Unhurt by Ticket Splitting," *Kansas City Times,* November 6, 1968).

6 The local earnings tax is a tax on income paid by city residents and by nonresidents whose place of employment is within the city limits.

7 *Kansas City Times,* "Watkins Cites Black Needs," December 8, 1970.

8 The tax increase was ultimately narrowly adopted, even without Freedom's involvement.

9 John T. Dauner, "Council Vacancy Delay," *Kansas City Times,* March 2, 1974.

10 Louis Blue, "Kansas City to Send Two Blacks to Demo Convention for 1st Time," *Call,* May 26, 1972. As part of a compromise, Bruce Watkins was given ½ of a vote at the 1968 Democratic National Convention in Chicago. That marked the first time that black Kansas Citians had any official representation at a Democratic National Convention.

11 *Kansas City Star,* "Hunt for 3 Killers," July 15, 1970.

12 Indeed, the police investigation initially focused on Jordan's primary opponent, Lee Bohannon, who was regarded as a "militant" for his activism in the youth-oriented Social Action Committee of 20 (SAC-20). The police investigation file contained reams of material on Bohannon, describing him as an "agitator." Police also investigated the local Black Panthers, some of whose members Jordan had described to an investigator of the House Committee on Internal Security as "gangsters who preyed on the community" because of their tactics in collecting funds.

13 Until the early 1980s, Kansas City was home to one of the largest Mafia organizations in the country, usually ranking only below New York and Chicago in its size and scope. The Kansas City mob controlled one of the Teamsters' pension funds during this period, giving it substantial financial resources.

14 Mike McGraw and Glenn E. Rice, "Case Closed," *Kansas City Star,* June 21, 2011.

15 Melvin D. Lewis, "Neighbors Silent on Jordan Murder," *Kansas City Star,* July 15, 1970.

16 Mamie Hughes, interviewed by Horace Peterson.

17 *Kansas City Star,* "Bohannon View on Slaying," July 15, 1970.

18 Interview with author.

19 Harry Jones Jr., "Third District Races Pit Youth Vs. Experience," *Kansas City Star,* February 25, 1971.

20 Bruce R. Watkins, "Watkins Tells Why He Doesn't Want Blankinship Re-Elected," *Call,* February 19, 1971.

21 Jones, "Third District Races Pit Youth Vs. Experience;" *Kansas City Star,* "Charles Hazely (sic) Files for Council Seat," January 19, 1971.

22 Robert Sigman, "Council Races Warm up," *Kansas City Star,* March 21, 1971; *Kansas City Star,* "Blankinship Blasts 'Bossism' in City," March 29, 1971.

23 *Call,* "Blankinship Speaks out Where Its (*sic*) Counts," March 26, 1971; *Kansas City Star,* "Blankinship Cites Record of Projects," February 5, 1971.

24 Although Blankinship and Thomas cast the only dissenting votes on the 1970 redistricting proposal because of its dilution of the Fifth District's black vote, they did not aggressively oppose it. Their failure to do so was one of the many charges of ineffectiveness that Freedom would level against the incumbents during the 1971 campaign.

25 Mike Fancher, "Fifth District Has Option," *Kansas City Times,* March 23, 1971.

26 *Call,* "Freedom, Inc. Holds Rally," February 26, 1971.

27 *Call,* "Blankinship Asks Where Opponent Is," February 19, 1971; Sigman, "Council Races Warm up."

28 *Call,* "Says Blankinship Will Win Support of Black Community," January 29, 1971; *Call,* "Another Business Man Tells Why He Supports Lawrence Blankinship," February 5, 1971; *Call,* "Rev. Charles Briscoe Predicts G.L. Blankinship Re-election," February 12, 1971; *Call,* "Bernard Powell Says Young People Support Blankinship," February 19, 1971.

29 *Call,* "Brookfield, Thomas, and Blankinship," March 26, 1971.

30 William R. Graves and John T. Dauner, "Back Brookfield," *Kansas City Times,* January 8, 1971; Robert P. Sigman, "Citizens Association Ready to Chalk up Slate," *Kansas City Star,* January 3, 1971; Robert P. Sigman, "Blacks Bid for Backing," *Kansas City Star,* January 6, 1971.

31 These remarks were made by both African American and white CA members, although 18 of the CA's 21 black "governors" supported Hazley. Some individuals, primarily conservatives, veered close to using overtly racist language in denouncing the "bullying" of Freedom. The most notable of Blankinship's three black defenders in the CA was Everett O'Neal, the Freedom-endorsed candidate for the Third District at-large seat in 1963 (*Call,* "Another Business Man Tells Why He Supports Lawrence Blankinship"). In the intervening years, O'Neal had further improved his reputation with a segment of the business community by consistently denouncing any form of civil rights activism other than behind the scenes elite negotiations. He regularly criticized Dr. King and the southern movement, while insisting that a self-created educational deficit among African Americans was the primary cause of racial inequality. Despite his past endorsement by the organization, in 1971, he would be one of Freedom's most high-profile antagonists. Indeed, Freedom leaders would petition the Board of Elections to prohibit O'Neal from being an election judge because of his outspoken opposition to the Freedom slate (Stephen Nicely, "Voting Charges Fly," *Kansas City Star,* March 5, 1971).

32 Graves and Dauner, "Back Brookfield."

33 Robert M. Dye, "Wheeler Dodges Debate, Tags Citizens as G.O.P.," *Kansas City Times,* March 19, 1971.

34 John T. Dauner, "Wheeler, Brookfield Square off again," *Kansas City Times,* March 5, 1971.

35 John T. Dauner, "Freedom Backs Wheeler," *Kansas City Times,* April 13, 1968.

36 Robert P. Sigman, "Wheeler in Mayor's Race," *Kansas City Star,* January 12, 1971.

37 *Kansas City Star,* "The Factions Are A Major Issue in This City Campaign," March 26, 1971.

38 Indeed, the enmity between Wheeler and the newspaper would only grow over time. The mayor later published a book, consisting entirely of his diary entries, for the express purpose of exposing what he regarded as bias and mendacity by the *Star* (Charles B. Wheeler, *Doctor in Politics* [Kansas City: Inform, Inc., 1974]).

39 *Kansas City Times,* "The At-Large Candidates for City Council," February 26, 1971; *Kansas City Star,* "The District Candidates for City Council," February 26, 1971.

40 Michael J. Satchell, "Faction Support Debated by Mayor Candidates," *Kansas City Star,* March 14, 1971; Robert P. Sigman, "Faction Edge to Wheeler," *Kansas City Star,* March 3, 1971.

41 *Call,* "Brookfield Our Choice," March 19, 1971.

42 The paper's strong support for Dr. Earl Thomas is perhaps explained by the fact that its owner, Mrs. C.A. Franklin, was a good friend of the incumbent councilman. In addition, G. Lawrence Blankinship's charming wife, Opal, authored the newspaper's social column for many years prior to and after the campaign. These relationships do not explain the broader disconnect between the two institutions, however.

43 Dauner, "Freedom Backs Wheeler," Freedom, Inc., "Vote the Freedom, Inc. Democratic Ballot (Paid Political Advertisement);" Freedom, Inc., "Men Who Care (Paid Political Advertisement);" *Call,* "Watkins Charges 'Racism,'" February 26, 1971; The Committeemen and Women of the Inner City, "An Open Letter to the Public (Paid Political Advertisement)."

44 Sigman, "Wheeler in Mayor's Race."

45 The Committeemen and Women of the Inner City, "An Open Letter to the Public (Paid Political Advertisement)."

46 G.L. Blankinship, "Open Letter to Third District Voters (Paid Political Advertisement)."

47 *Kansas City Star,* "Blankinship Blasts 'Bossism' in City."

48 *Kansas City Star,* "Citizens Headquarters," February 16, 1971.

49 *Call,* "Mrs. Fannie Meek Speaks out against Tactics Used against Councilman Larry Blankinship," March 26, 1971; *Kansas City Star,* "Blankinship Blasts 'Bossism' in City."

50 Nicely, "Voting Charges Fly."

51 *Call,* "Third District Race 'Hottest' One in Town," March 19, 1971.

52 Robert M. Dye, "Watkins Charges Funds Offered for Black Vote," *Kansas City Times,* March 27, 1971.

53 *Kansas City Star,* "Brookfield Replies to Watkins Charge," March 28, 1971.

54 Robert P. Sigman, "Wheeler, 8 Citizens Victors," *Kansas City Times,* March 31, 1971.

55 Ibid.

56 *Call,* "Wheeler and Freedom Win City Election," April 2, 1971.

57 By City Charter, council vacancies occurring less than eighteen months before the expiration of the council term are filled by the council sitting as a committee of the whole. Vacancies occurring more than eighteen months before the expiration of the council term are filled by calling a special election.

58 Melba Marlow, "Tolbert Accuses Council and Press of 'Personal Vendetta' against Him," *Call*, July 20, 1973; Roger Moore, "Tolbert Gone. Puzzlement Lingers on," *Kansas City Star*, January 27, 1974; Roger Moore, "Tolbert Decides to Leave Council," *Kansas City Star*, January 25, 1974; *Call*, "Councilman Richard Tolbert Forms New Political Party," February 18, 1972; *Call*, "Freedom, Inc. Censures Councilman Tolbert," February 25, 1972; *Call*, "Tolbert Defies Council, Ignores Council Session," March 3, 1972; *Call*, "Tolbert Gets No Support on Resolution Calling for Own Impeachment," March 31, 1972; *Call*, "Tolbert to Run for Mayor," June 8, 1973; *Call*, "Tolbert in Squabble over City Car," July 13, 1973; *Call*, "Tolbert Gains Community Support through Friends," September 14, 1973.

59 Lois Leuellyn, "Council Candidates Backed," *Kansas City Star*, March 6, 1970; *Call*, "Five in Race for City Council Spot," February 1, 1974.

60 However, in 1971, the only vacancies in recent memory had occurred when CA-sponsored individuals had resigned during periods of CA dominance on the council. It is therefore not quite as clear as Freedom's allies claimed whether the procedural norm was one of allowing the sponsoring LPO to play the dominant role in selecting a replacement or one of enhancing the institutional power of the CA.

61 Interview with author.

62 Louis Blue, "Freedom Wins Despite Smears," *Call*, August 11, 1972.

63 The break between Freedom and Johnson would later become even more serious. In 1978 he chose to run for state representative against Orchid Jordan, the widow of Leon Jordan. The rift would later mend again, but the campaign against Jordan made Johnson persona non grata in Freedom circles for several years.

64 *Call*, "Five in Race for City Council Spot."

65 *Call*, "Three Groups Endorse Mrs. Joanne Collins," February 8, 1974.

66 *Call*, "Baptist Union Reaffirms Support of Michael Myers," February 8, 1974.

67 *Call*, "The Council Seat Vacancy," March 1, 1974.

68 *Call*, "Herman Johnson Top Choice of Citizens Assn.," February 15, 1974; *Kansas City Star*, "Citizens List 3 for Council," February 10, 1974.

69 *Kansas City Star*, "Suit on Secret Meeting," February 18, 1974.

70 Robert L. Carroll, "Myers Serving Probation," *Kansas City Star*, February 26, 1974.

71 Kate Lahey, "Third Ballot Ends Tension, Fills Vacant Council Seat," *Kansas City Star*, March 10, 1974.

72 Interview with author.

73 James C. Fitzpatrick, "Brownfield Explains Council Vote," *Kansas City Times*, March 12, 1974.

74 It also had to do with the fact that Collins made the best presentation of all the candidates. The candidate who directly preceded her, Inez Kaiser, exceeded her ten-minute allotment by twenty minutes and subjected the Council to a harangue. The personable Collins came next and provided a pleasant change of tone.

75 Interview with author.

76 Mack Alexander, "Collins Returns a Bitter Pill to Freedom, Inc.," *Kansas City Star*, February 26, 1975; George Koppe, "Citizens Screen Four from 3rd District," *Kansas City*

Times, January 9, 1975. In a demonstration of how small the local political world was, Myers's wife worked as Hughes's assistant at the county legislature.

77 In 1970, the voters of Jackson County approved a charter form of government. It did away with the old three-member County Court as well as the host of elected executive officials (e.g., auditor, coroner, etc.) and replaced them with an elected county executive and legislature.

78 William L. McCorkle, "Collins, Hughes Vie in 3rd," *Kansas City Star,* February 19, 1975. Hughes's second husband was Dr. Samuel Rodgers, a nationally respected pioneer of the community health center movement. Rodgers founded Missouri's first community health center at the Wayne Miner housing project in 1968; it was only the fourth such center in the country.

79 This was especially relevant given that the Council's only other female member, Sarah Snow, chose not to pursue reelection in order to run for mayor.

80 The local chapter of the Black Panthers, which had renamed itself the Sons of Malcolm, had by then virtually ceased to exist. The chapter never had more than a few dozen active members, but when its leader, Pete O'Neal, went into exile in Algeria and then Tanzania, the chapter went into hibernation. The other major youth movement, the Social Action Committee of 20 (SAC-20) remained active but inched towards moderation and, in any event, focused its activities on programs like mentoring and neighborhood clean-ups rather than politics per se.

81 Interview with author.

82 He was also one of the council members who supported Myers over Collins.

83 Kate Lahey, "Mayor Alleges Political Trade," *Kansas City Star,* January 5, 1975.

84 Richard D. Ralls, "Wheeler Wins G.O.P. Fight; Gets Freedom Backing," *Kansas City Times,* February 7, 1975.

85 William L. McCorkle, "Close Vote Goes to Shaughnessy," *Kansas City Star,* January 12, 1975; Darrelee Williams, "Collins Almost Loses Citizens Endorsement," *Call,* January 17, 1975.

86 John T. Dauner, "Democrats, Freedom, Inc. Join Forces," *Kansas City Times,* January 21, 1975; Ralls, "Wheeler Wins G.O.P. Fight."

87 *Call,* "For Tuesday's Election, The Call Endorses," March 21, 1975; *Kansas City Star,* "The Six At-Large Council Races," March 17, 1975.

88 Interview with author.

89 Koppe, "Citizens Screen Four from 3rd District;" McCorkle, "Collins, Hughes Vie in 3rd;" *Call,* "Freedom's Team Candidates File for City Council Seats," January 31, 1975; *Call,* "Many Groups Hear Joanne Collins during Campaign," March 21, 1975.

90 Kate Lahey, "Freedom, Inc. Tactics Hit," *Kansas City Star,* February 2, 1975; Robert T. Nelson, "Jail Worker Charge: Holliday Threat on Job," *Kansas City Star,* March 9, 1975; *Kansas City Star,* "Freedom, Inc. Pressure Denied," February 5, 1975; Darrelee Williams, "Freedom Knocked: 'Doc Holliday' Answers Collins Accusations," *Call,* February 7, 1975.

91 Under the City Charter, the top two finishers in the nonpartisan primary advance to the general election. Even when only two candidates file for an office, the primary

election is still held. Collins and Hughes were the only two candidates who filed for the office. Both were thus guaranteed a place in the general election and the primary served to help them identify areas of strength and weakness.

92 Interview with author.

93 Alexander, "Collins Returns a Bitter Pill to Freedom, Inc."

94 Mack Alexander, "Support by Blacks Surprises Collins," *Kansas City Star*, February 26, 1975.

95 Interview with authors.

96 Robert T. Nelson, "Results Bittersweet for Freedom, Inc.," *Kansas City* Star, March 26, 1975; *Call*, "Collins Wins over Difficult Odds," March 28, 1975.

97 Nelson, "Jail Worker Charge: Holliday Threat on Job;" Nelson, "Results Bittersweet for Freedom, Inc."

98 Mamie Hughes, "Mamie Hughes Writes an Open Letter to the Black Community," *Call*, March 14, 1975.

99 John T. Dauner, "Wheeler Wins, Capra Out; Watkins, 3 New Faces in," *Kansas City Times*, March 26, 1975; Nelson, "Results Bittersweet for Freedom, Inc.;" *Call*, "Collins Wins over Difficult Odds."

100 Given the fact that one of the major talking points in Collins's campaign was that it was inappropriate for Hughes to run for council after having just been reelected to the county legislature, it is interesting to note that Collins was the Republican nominee for Congress the very next year. She ran against liberal (and powerful) civil rights stalwart Richard Bolling. On a campaign swing to support Collins, United Negro College Fund president (and former Nixon administration official) Arthur Fletcher engaged in a bit of hyperbole when he said of the nominee that she "is to the Republicans what Barbara Jordan is to the Democrats" (*Call*, "Art Fletcher Says Collins Is Needed to Integrate House of Representatives—Where Money Is," July 22, 1976). In the heavily Democratic district, Collins lost to Bolling in a landslide.

101 Interview with author.

102 Interview with author.

103 It bears noting that Watkins personally and Freedom, Inc. collectively were supporters of the "charter government" movement, in spite of the fact that it was clearly contrary to Watkins's self-interest.

104 *Call*, "Watkins out of Senate Race in Favor of Johnson," June 23, 1972; *Call*, "Bruce Watkins Files for Top Position in County," April 16, 1956.

105 This is by no means to suggest that Watkins's return to the municipal political fray was universally heralded, even within the organization. As will be seen later, some dissatisfaction with his presidency of Freedom began at roughly this same time.

106 William L. McCorkle, "Contest Lively for District Seat in 5th," *Kansas City Star*, February 21, 1975; *Kansas City Times*, "Poll Shows Bruce Watkins in Lead," February 20, 1975. This is consistent with the findings of many political scientists, who have historically argued that districts must have African American populations close to 60 percent in order to command a voting majority.

107 John T. Dauner, "Drops At-Large Bid: Watkins to Seek 5th-District Seat," *Kansas City Times,* January 11, 1975; *Call,* "Citizens Association Will Screen Candidates Next Week," January 3, 1975.

108 Ferns was a naturalized citizen who originally hailed from the United Kingdom. The fact that he still spoke with a heavy British accent was constantly noted by voters and the press.

109 McCorkle, "Contest Lively for District Seat in 5th;" *Call,* "Emanuel Cleaver to Run for City Council Seat," December 20, 1974.

110 *Call,* "'No Tent' City Goes up Sunday," July 21, 1972.

111 Mack Alexander, "Charging Pressure, Cleaver Quits as S.C.L.C. Chief," *Kansas City Star,* February 26, 1975.

112 McCorkle, "Contest Lively for District Seat in 5th."

113 Dauner, "Drops At-Large Bid: Watkins to Seek 5th-District Seat."

114 McCorkle, "Close Vote Goes to Shaughnessy."

115 Dauner, "Democrats, Freedom, Inc. Join Forces."

116 McCorkle, "Contest Lively for District Seat in 5th;" Sally Morris, "Bruce R. Watkins Says He Feels 'Compelled' to Run for City Council again," *Call,* February 21, 1975.

117 Robert T. Nelson, "Freedom, Race 'Nonissue' Hurt Cleaver," *Kansas City Star,* March 9, 1975.

118 John T. Dauner, "Wheeler, Mrs. Snow Win; Bonds Defeated by .5%," *Kansas City Times,* February 26, 1975.

119 Nelson, "Freedom, Race 'Nonissue' Hurt Cleaver."

120 *Kansas City Star,* "Cleaver Favors Watkins," March 4, 1975.

121 Dauner, "Wheeler Wins, Capra out; Watkins, 3 New Faces in;" Nelson, "Results Bittersweet for Freedom, Inc."

122 Immediately after the 1971 inauguration, Hazley was made chair of the powerful Planning and Zoning Committee (P&Z). P&Z regulated land use in the city and was responsible for most economic development matters, including important steps in the tax incentive-granting process.

123 *Call,* "Hazley to Head Committee," April 16, 1971; *Call,* "Mayor Takes Tour of Inner City Ghetto," January 26, 1973.

124 William L. McCorkle, "Burden on Council: Mayor Erratic, Foe Charges," *Kansas City Star,* March 18, 1975; Roger Moore, "Mayoral Candidates Face Weeding out by Voters," *Kansas City Star,* February 23, 1975.

125 *Call,* "Mayor Tussle—but Not Hard—with Real Bear," January 28, 1972.

126 Lahey, "Mayor Alleges Political Trade."

127 Ralls, "Wheeler Wins G.O.P. Fight; Gets Freedom Backing."

128 Dauner, "Democrats, Freedom, Inc. Join Forces;" Ralls, "Wheeler Wins G.O.P. Fight; Gets Freedom Backing."

129 William V. Francis Jr., "Mrs. Snow Overcame Lack of Backing, Funds," *Kansas City Times,* February 26, 1975.

130 *Call,* "Mayor Wheeler Has the Edge," February 21, 1975.

131 Robert L. Carroll, "Wheeler Asserts Issues Lacking," *Kansas City Times*, January 4, 1975; John A. Dvorak, "Mayor's Role the Top Issue in Citizens Interviews," *Kansas City Times*, January 11, 1975.

132 Dauner, "Wheeler, Mrs. Snow Win; Bonds Defeated by .5%;" Roger Moore, "Primary Tally Road Sign on Victory Path," *Kansas City Star*, March 2, 1975.

133 Kate Lahey, "Wait-and-See Donors Expected to Aid Snow," *Kansas City Star*, March 9, 1975; Roger Moore, "Snow Backed by Citizens," *Kansas City Star*, March 2, 1975; *Call*, "Blacks Vote No on Snow Endorsement," March 7, 1975.

134 *Kansas City Star*, "Mayor Charles B. Wheeler, Jr., for Another Four Years," March 18, 1975.

135 Kate Lahey, "Mayoral Hopefuls Value Aid of Factions in Close Vote," *Kansas City Star*, January 13, 1975.

136 *Call*, "Freedom, Inc. Board Tells Why Wheeler Should Be Reelected," March 21, 1975.

137 Wheeler made only one exception to this policy. In a move that can only be described as bizarre, Wheeler did consent to a debate on a cable television station: one based in and viewable only by the residents of suburban Johnson County, Kansas, not one of whom was eligible to vote in the Kansas City, Missouri municipal elections.

138 Dauner, "Wheeler Wins, Capra out; Watkins, 3 New Faces in;" *Kansas City Times*, "Unofficial Ward Totals in Mayoral, Council Races," March 26, 1975.

139 Capra was the senior member of the city council, having first been elected in 1959. The nephew of North End factional leader Alex Presta, Capra was also the last of the old-line factional figures to hold municipal office. In his final two terms in office, Capra had outgrown his image as a factional tool and became a highly respected voice on the budget. Capra's defeat was partly a function of his changing district. The district's large Italian-American population was gradually moving out, while the population of the West Side, the neighborhood where the city's Latino population was historically concentrated, was growing.

140 Dauner, "Wheeler Wins, Capra out; Watkins, 3 New Faces in;" William L. McCorkle, "Capra's Defeat the Surprise in an Unsurprising Election," *Kansas City Star*, March 26, 1975.

141 Nelson, "Results Bittersweet for Freedom, Inc."

142 The most important of the myriad litigation involving the KCSMD during this period began in 1977. In that year, the KCMSD sued the State of Missouri, federal agencies, and surrounding school districts on behalf of its students, alleging that they were responsible for the intense racial segregation found in the district. Federal courts removed the KCMSD as a plaintiff, substituting it with the students themselves, and made the district a defendant in the case. A 1985 federal court order found that the State of Missouri was responsible for racial segregation and as a remedy mandated the creation of a voluntary inter-district busing scheme to racially integrate the district, the creation of a host of themed "magnet" schools, and billions of dollars in state expenditures to address the district's underfunding. The court order remained in effect until the landmark case *Missouri*

v. Jenkins in 1995, when the United States Supreme Court overturned the finding and the remedy.

143 *Call,* "Inner City Property Taxes Too High, Says Freedom Inc.," June 21, 1974.

144 *Time,* "Chief Clarence Kelley: A Dick Tracy for the FBI," June 18, 1973.

145 Harry Jones Jr., "Panther Rise Linked to Ills," *Kansas City Times,* March 7, 1970; Harry Jones Jr., "Doubts Panthers Understand Marxism," *Kansas City Times,* March 5, 1970; Harry Jones Jr., "Kansas Citian Defends Panther Tie," *Kansas City Times,* March 5, 1970; Joe Lastelic, "Two Tell of Panthers Here," *Kansas City Star,* March 6, 1970.

146 James S. Tinney, "Chief Kelley to Direct FBI," *Call,* June 8, 1973.

147 *Time,* "Chief Clarence Kelley: A Dick Tracy for the FBI."

148 *Call,* "Watkins to Oppose Kelley Nomination," June 15, 1973; *Call,* "Watkins to Testify on Monday against Kelley," June 22, 1973; *Call,* "Blacks Speak for and against Kelley as New FBI Director," June 29, 1973.

149 *Time,* "Chief Clarence Kelley: A Dick Tracy for the FBI."

150 *Call,* "Senate Okays Chief 96 to 0," June 29, 1973.

151 Kelley was never again active in local politics, although he returned to Kansas City upon his retirement from the FBI in 1978. At that time, several white civic elites attempted to recruit Kelley as a mayoral candidate. Kelley provided some encouragement to this idea before abandoning it to concentrate is energies on founding a private security firm which is still thriving, years after its namesake's death (Rick E. Abel, "Wheeler's Spark Aimed at Setting Fire to 'Establishment-Backed Candidate,'" *Call,* March 17, 1978; *Call,* "Don't Run for Mayor, Mr. Kelley," February 10, 1978).

152 *Call,* "Public Hearing Likely in James Case," February 11, 1972; *Call,* "Black Leaders Ask for Federal Probe of Police Department," December 23, 1977.

153 *Call,* "Police Dept. Reports Shortage of Blacks," July 18, 1971; *Time,* "Chief Clarence Kelley: A Dick Tracy for the FBI."

154 Louis Blue, "Bloody Week in Kansas City," *Call,* January 19, 1973; John Robinson, "No Money for Crime Prevention in Police Budgets' Watkins," *Call,* August 24, 1973.

155 Raphael J. Sonenshein, *Politics in Black and White: Race and Power in Los Angeles* (Princeton: Princeton University Press, 1993), 191–228; Carl B. Stokes, *Promises of Power: A Political Autobiography* (New York: Simon and Schuster, 1972), 171–205; Clarence N. Stone, *Regime Politics: Governing Atlanta, 1946–1988* (Lawrence: University of Kansas Press, 1989), 156–165.

156 Although it falls outside the scope of this research, it should be noted that the relationship between Freedom and Teasdale was perhaps the *worst* of the three. Freedom endorsed his opponent in the Democratic primary, feeling that Teasdale's record on African American issues as Jackson County prosecutor left something to be desired. After taking office, Teasdale openly feuded with the black LPO, refusing to consult it on gubernatorial appointments, refusing to appoint its members, and going out of his way to scorn the group by appointing known Freedom enemies. Freedom and Teasdale eventually reconciled, but even then the relationship was not a warm one (Jeanne A. Fox, "In Kansas City, Missouri Economic Development Plays Catch-Up to Political Clout," *Black Enterprise,* March, 1978). Teasdale served only one term as governor, badly losing his 1980 reelection bid.

157 There was only one, minor, rather odd exception to this rule. In 1978, the police board voted to dismiss Chief Marvin Van Kirk. The board was previously divided over the chief's performance. His dismissal was made possible by the appointment of Gwendolyn Wells, an African American law professor at the University of Missouri-Kansas City (who, readers will recall, was one of two Freedom precinct captains to endorse Holliday, Sr. over Watkins in the 1963 elections), to the board. One major rationale for the chief's dismissal was his rocky relationship with and insensitivity towards the city's African Americans. Although some African American leaders were pleased that Van Kirk was fired, they quickly restrained their exaltation when it became clear that the charge of racial insensitivity was something of a smokescreen. In fact, the chief was fired to settle an old grudge between the police board chair who hired him (Ilus Davis) and the new board chair (Clinton Kanaga, who was bitter that Davis defeated him for the CA's mayoral endorsement in 1963). Other charges were leveled at Van Kirk to warrant his firing, but at a tempestuous televised hearing of the board where the chief challenged his dismissal and a second vote on the issue was taken, the other board members refused to participate and substantiate those charges. Only Wells questioned the chief and did so in an aggressive manner, causing many white observers to develop a highly negative opinion of the whole proceedings. Black viewers, by contrast, generally felt that it was high time that the police chief be confronted with facts about the racial conduct of his department. Still, in a turnabout that can only be considered bizarre, in the second ballot to confirm the chief's dismissal, Wells changed her position and became the only board member to vote for Van Kirk's retention. She did so, she said, because the black community was being used and scapegoated for political reasons (Louis Blue, "Sudden Firing of Police Chief Shocks Blacks, Too," *Call*, February 10, 1978; Louis Blue, "Why Gwen Wells Voted As She Did, Van Kirk Hearing Didn't Go 'Right,'" *Call*, February 24, 1978; *Call*, "How the Votes Turned Against Chief Van Kirk," February 10, 1978; *Call*, "'Grudges Tend to Last' Mayor Says of 'Political' Ouster," March 3, 1978).

158 Bernard J. Frieden and Marshall Kaplan, *The Politics of Neglect: Urban Aid from Model Cities to Revenue Sharing* (Cambridge: MIT Press, 1977).

159 C.E. Edmondson, "Goals of Model Cities: Part II," *Call*, January 22, 1976; *Call*, "Area Director Says Model Cities Program Has 'Fallen Short,'" August 13, 1971; *Call*, "Model Cities Ready for Third Year, Has Budget of 8 Million," September 10, 1971.

160 *Call*, "Create New City Department to Replace Model Cities," December 14, 1973.

161 Sigman, "Wheeler in Mayor's Race."

162 *Call*, "Councilman Hazley Answers Questions on Bond Election," November 23, 1973; *Call*, "Freedom, Inc. Backs All Fourteen Bond Proposals," November 30, 1973; *Call*, "Freedom, Inc. Opposes Sales Tax for Schools," August 15, 1975.

163 Robert L. Carroll, "9 Vote Margin on City Center; 3 Others Pass," *Kansas City Times*, December 19, 1973; Robert L. Carroll, "Ten Bond Proposals Fail A Second Time," *Kansas City Times*, April 3, 1974; Roger Moore, "Mayor Shoulders Defeat of 10 Bonds," *Kansas City Star*, April 3, 1974; *Kansas City Star*, "Freedom Will Try Again on Bonds," March 11, 1974.

164 Kevin Fox Gotham, "Political Opportunity, Community, Identity, and the Emergence of a Local Anti-Expressway Movement," *Social Problems* 46, no. 3 (1999): 332–354;

Gotham, *Race, Real Estate and Uneven Development,* 83–94; Doris Handy, "'Other Side of Tracks' Now 'Other Side of Freeway,'" *Call,* February 20, 1976; *Call,* "Freedom, Inc., Asks for Active Public Interest in South Midtown Freeway," February 13, 1976.

165 Freedom, Inc., "Freedom, Inc.—10 Years of Progress (Paid political advertisement)."

166 In the eyes of many Freedom members, this one appointment "did not count." The Human Relations Commission was a *commission,* rather than a full-fledged city department (although it later became one), had a small staff, was of recent creation, and there was frequent discussion about removing it from City Hall entirely and making it a nonprofit organization.

167 *Call,* "Create New City Department to Replace Model Cities."

168 *Call,* "Naming of Black Deputy City Manager Causes Stir," June 11, 1971.The number of assistant city managers has increased over time, as has the overall size of the municipal workforce. There is no set number of assistant city managers and city managers have appointed as many as they have seen fit.

169 *Call,* "NAACP Says Figures Show City Discrimination against Women and Minority Groups," December 19, 1975.

170 *Call,* "Freedom, Inc. Board Tells Why Wheeler Should Be Reelected."

171 *Call,* "Hazley to Head Committee."

172 Rick E. Abel, "Blacks Protest Failure to Nominate Black Judge," *Call,* January 7, 1977.

173 M.J. Marlow, "Importance of Committeemen Explained by Freedom, Inc.," *Call,* July 14, 1972.

174 Interview with author; *Call,* "Freedom, Inc. Conducts Christmas Basket Project," December 13, 1974.

175 David Crockett, "Family Fun Festival Registers 490 Voters," *Call,* July 9, 1976; M.J. Marlow, "Food, Drink and 90 Degrees Spark Freedom, Inc., Picnic," *Call,* July 28, 1972; *Call,* "Young Freedom Sponsors Civic Movement Drive," January 14, 1972; *Call,* "Freedom, Inc. to Sponsor Family Fun Festival and Voter Registration Drive," July 2, 1976.

176 *Call,* "Freedom to Hold Coffees for Candidates," February 26, 1971; *Call,* "Coffee Hours for Hazley and Hughes," February 21, 1975.

177 *Call,* "Count Basie and Orchestra to Play at Freedom, Inc. Rally," March 7, 1975.

178 Rick E. Abel, "Speaking on How Black People 'Got Over,' Bishop Brookins Addresses Jordan Award Dinner," *Call,* May 27, 1977; *Call,* "Jordan Awards to 17," May 7, 1971; *Call,* "Bennett and Cosby Thrill 1,000," May 4, 1973; *Call,* "$8,417 Netted from Leon Jordan Dinner," August 24, 1973.

179 Interview with author.

180 Indeed, many interview subjects who asserted that Freedom endorsements in the contemporary era were "for sale" also maintained that the 1970s were halcyon days of ethical activities at Freedom, when endorsements were *not* sold. The archival record proves, though, that even in the 1970s there were opponents making this criticism of Freedom. Given the lack of evidence for this view during any time period and the strong correlation between the emergence of this criticism and the intra-community splits already discussed here (e.g., Blankinship vs. Hazley or Collins vs. Hughes), it seems far

more likely that this critique has its origin in politically inspired disagreement instead of actual fact.

181 Mack Alexander, "Watkins Yields Post," *Kansas City Star,* September 4, 1975; Doris Moore, "Freedom Changes Officers, but Aims and Goals Still the Same," *Call,* September 12, 1975; *Call,* "Watkins Steps Down," September 12, 1975.

182 Interview with author.

183 Committee to Re-Elect Orchid Jordan, "An Open Letter to the Community (Paid Political Advertisement);" Freedom, Inc., "We Support Harold Holliday, Sr. (Paid Political Advertisement);" Leonard S. Hughes III, "Fulfill the Dream of Leon Jordan Youth in Politics (Paid Political Advertisement);" *Call,* "Political Climate Getting 'Hot,'" July 27, 1978. Although Johnson would later come to be regarded as an elder statesman among black Kansas Citians, his campaign against the beloved Mrs. Jordan would make him persona non grata in Freedom circles for many years.

184 Leonard S. Hughes III, "Fulfill the Dream of Leon Jordan (Paid Political Advertisement)."

185 Rick E. Abel, "Hughes III Defeats Holliday Sr.," *Call,* August 11, 1978.

186 Ibid; *Call,* "Clint Adams Heads New Political Club," October 27, 1978.

187 Interview with author.

188 *Call,* "Women of Freedom, Inc. Call for 'Doc' to Resign," August 11, 1978.

189 Rick E. Abel, "Holliday Says He's Still Freedom President," *Call,* August 18, 1978.

190 *Call,* "Watkins Heads Reorganized Freedom, Inc.," August 25, 1978.

191 Louis Blue, "Freedom, Inc., Has 12 to 12 Tie Vote on Endorsing Swinton," *Call,* July 11, 1980.

192 Abel, "Holliday Says He's Still Freedom President;" *Call,* "Watkins Heads Reorganized Freedom, Inc."

193 Interview with author.

194 *Call,* "Watkins Enters Mayor Race," August 25, 1978.

195 *Call,* "Chicago Politicians to Hear Bruce Watkins, Rep. Holliday," August 24, 1973.

196 *Call,* "Detroit's Coleman Young to Kick-Off Watkins Campaign," November 10, 1978.

197 John A. Dvorak, "Packed Field for Mayor Leads Spirited Primary," *Kansas City Times,* February 27, 1979; Miriam Pepper, "How Watkins and Berkley Did It," *Kansas City Star,* February 28, 1979; *Kansas City Star,* "Charles Wheeler Still Cares about People," February 25, 1979; Bill Turque, "'We'll See You, Charlie,'" *Kansas City Star,* February 28, 1979.

198 Abel, "Blacks Protest Failure to Nominate Black Judge;" Rick E. Abel, "City Councilmen Say Public Works Funds Being Misused," *Call,* August 26, 1977.

199 *Call,* "Wheeler Blasts Tax Opponents; Watkins, McDonough Return Fire," November 18, 1977.

200 *Call,* "City Center Ministers for Watkins," February 21, 1979.

201 Melba J. Marlow, "1963—The Year When Watkins Began Long Service to City," *Call,* February 21, 1979; *Call,* "Keeping up with Watkins," February 21, 1979.

202 Rick E. Abel, "Citizens' Directors Endorse Adams," *Call*, January 12, 1979.

203 James C. Fitzpatrick, "No Party Disfavor Likely for Democratic 'Strays,'" *Kansas City Times*, March 23, 1979.

204 Abel, "Citizens' Directors Endorse Adams."

205 Dvorak, "Packed Field for Mayor Leads Spirited Primary;" Melba Marlow, "Watkins Makes Strong Bid for Citizens' Nod," *Call*, December 15, 1978; Pepper, "How Watkins and Berkley Did It."

206 *Kansas City Star*, "Charles Wheeler Still Cares about People."

207 James C. Fitzpatrick, "Candidates Hone Attack as Election Nears," *Kansas City Star*, March 24, 1979; Interview with author; *Kansas City Star*, "The Candidates Debate," March 25, 1979.

208 *Call*, "It's Time for Black Community to Take A Stand behind Watkins," February 2, 1979.

209 Pepper, "How Watkins and Berkley Did It."

210 Bleys W. Rose, "Democratic Clubs May Hold Keys to Mayor's Race," *Kansas City Times*, March 23, 1979.

211 Fitzpatrick, "Candidates Hone Attack As Election Nears;" Rick Lyman, "Labor Issue Heats up Mayoral Campaign," *Kansas City Star*, March 22, 1979; *Kansas City Star*, "The Candidates Debate."

212 Robert L. Carroll, "Mondale's Visit Spurs Barb about Potholes," *Kansas City Times*, March 22, 1979; Kathleen Patterson, "Mondale and Eagleton Are Pleased at Turnout for Watkins' Campaign," *Kansas City Star*, March 21, 1979; Kathleen Patterson, "Mondale Sought Ties with Blacks," *Kansas City Times*, March 24, 1979.

213 Interviews with author.

214 *Kansas City Star*, "The Star's Recommendations in Tuesday's Election," March 26, 1979.

215 Miriam Pepper, "Victory Glows with Green, Defeat Shrouded in Black," *Kansas City Star*, March 28, 1979.

216 Arthur S. Brisbane, "Watkins Sensed Defeat Early on," *Kansas City Times*, March 28, 1979.

217 Interview with author.

218 Interview with author.

219 Rick E. Abel, "Richard Berkley Next Mayor," *Call*, March 30, 1979; John A. Dvorak, "Berkley Wins Decisive Victory," *Kansas City Times*, March 28, 1979; David Firestone, "Why Berkley Won and Watkins Lost," *Kansas City Star*, March 28, 1979; *Kansas City Times*, "Mayoral Vote by Ward," March 28, 1979.

220 Abel, "Richard Berkley Next Mayor."

221 Interview with author.

222 Interview with author.

223 Freedom did support a challenger to Collins in the form of Icelean Clark. However, it gave no real support to her campaign outside of the Freedom wards and endorsed her primarily because members simply could not bear to print a Freedom ballot that

featured Collins's name. Clark became one of many candidates who previously campaigned against Freedom only to later find their way into the Freedom tent. She ran against Charles Hazley in 1975, losing badly.

224 *Call,* "Councilman Hazley Files for Re-election to 3rd District," December 15, 1978.

225 Louis Blue, "City Election Campaign Heats up ahead of Time," *Call,* December 8, 1978; Citizens for A Fair Campaign, "Paid Political Advertisement;" People's Committee to Elect Clint Adams, "Ask Your 3rd District Councilman Why (Paid Political Advertisement)."

226 Bleys W. Rose, "Well-Worn 3rd District Scene Furnishes Battlefield," *Kansas City Star,* March 21, 1979.

227 Abel, "Citizens' Directors Endorse Adams."

228 Rick E. Abel, "Swinton Backs Adams against Hazley," *Call,* November 17, 1978. Swinton, like so many before and after him, would later reconcile with Freedom and become the LPO's successful candidate for a state Senate seat in 1980.

229 Bleys W. Rose, "Council Retains Political Makeup," *Kansas City Star,* March 28, 1979.

230 Freedom, Inc., "Your Freedom, Inc. Community Team (Paid Political Advertisement)."

231 John T. Dauner, "Cleaver Says Foe Used Racist Handbills," *Kansas City Times,* March 28, 1979; *Call,* "Voters Felt Cleaver Was Obvious Choice," March 2, 1979.

232 Rose, "Council Retains Political Makeup."

233 Robert L. Carroll, "8 Keep Seats on Council," *Kansas City Times,* March 28, 1979.

234 Melba Marlow, "Bruce Watkins Made History As Elected Official," *Call,* September 19, 1980; *Kansas City Star,* "Bruce Watkins Dies after Long Battle with Cancer," September 14, 1980.

Chapter 4

1 *Call,* "Lee V. Swinton Named to Parks Board by Berkley," May 4, 1979.

2 Louis Blue, "Mayor Berkley Appoints Watkins to Parks Board," *Call,* June 13, 1980; *Kansas City Star,* "Bruce Watkins Dies After Long Battle with Cancer," September 14, 1980.

3 Hazley was later made chair of another new and more significant committee, Policy and Rules. The new appointment still did not compensate for the slight, as the Policy and Rules Committee lacked the prestige or power of Planning and Zoning.

4 John A. Dvorak, "Mayoral Candidates Vie for Endorsement of Freedom, Inc.," *Kansas City Times,* January 28, 1983; *Call,* "New Mayor Would Be Wise to Keep Chairman Hazley," April 6, 1979; *Call,* "Hazley Loses His Chairmanship; Mrs. Joanne Collins," April 13, 1979.

5 Melissa Berg, "Low-key Berkley Has A Fondness for Details," *Kansas City Times,* March 19, 1983; Louis Blue, "Councilmen Cleaver and Hazley Oppose Sales Tax; Tell Why," *Call,* April 10, 1981; *Call,* "Cleaver Names Blacks' 'Enemies,'" March 20, 1980.

6 Louis Blue, "Freedom's Major Thrust Is Reelection of Wheat," *Call,* May 30, 1980.

7 Louis Blue, "Primary Brings 'Sweet' Victory to Freedom, Inc.," *Call,* August 6, 1980; Lewis W. Diuguid and Mark Schlinkmann, "Swinton Is Charged with Stealing," *Kansas City Times,* March 23, 1983; *Call,* "Lee Swinton Endorsed by Freedom, Inc., for 9th District Senator," July 25, 1980.

8 Blue, "Primary Brings 'Sweet' Victory to Freedom, Inc.;" Louise Blue, "Swinton Defeats Mary Gant," *Call,* August 9, 1980. These three seats were lost during the next decennial redistricting, when the state legislature approved a plan that conjoined the seven black-held districts into four (Rick E. Abel, "Freedom, Inc., and Black Community Lose Three House Seats after Redistricting," *Call,* September 18, 1981).

9 Office of History and Preservation, "Alan Dupree Wheat," *Black Americans in Congress* (Washington: Government Printing Office, 2008).

10 Interview with author.

11 Rick E. Abel, "Wheat Edges Carnes in Final Sprint," *Call,* August 6, 1982.

12 Louis Blue, "It's Congressman Alan Wheat," *Call,* November 5, 1982; Interview with author; Justin Mitchell, "Wheat, Sharp Leave Campaign Rancor Behind," *Kansas City Times,* February 14, 1983. Despite being a Republican, Sharp would later go on to be Freedom's successful candidate for city council on three separate occasions. Married to an African American woman in the early 1990s, he was also subjected to crude white supremacist attacks in several of his campaigns for a school board seat.

13 This reputation was only enhanced two years later, when Wheat was challenged in the Democratic primary by Kansas City councilman Frank Palermo (who was accused of using racist tactics) and a liberal activist attorney. In the three-person race, Wheat crushed his opponents, winning 53,150 votes to Palermo's 9,479 votes and the third candidate's 2,400 votes (Mack Alexander, "Wheat Rolls Over Palermo," *Call,* August 10, 1984).

14 Melissa Berg, "Berkley Poll Buoys Mayor and Supporters," *Kansas City Star,* January 6, 1983.

15 Kevin Murphy, Rick Alm, and Carol Power, *The Last Dance: The Skywalks Disaster and a City Changed* (Kansas City: Kansas City Star Books, 2011).

16 Berg, "Low-key Berkley Has A Fondness for Details," *Kansas City Star,* "The Men Who Want to Lead KC: Their Views and Goals for the Future," February 6, 1983.

17 Melissa Berg, "Democrats Seek Unity to Defeat Berkley," *Kansas City Star,* February 4, 1983.

18 Michael Yablonski, "Freedom Inc. Backs Serviss in KC Mayor's Race," *Kansas City Times,* February 4, 1983.

19 *Call,* "Freedom for Serviss," February 4, 1983; Yablonski, "Freedom Inc. Backs Serviss in KC Mayor's Race."

20 Melissa Berg, "Wheeler Looks for Warm Welcome Back," *Kansas City Star,* January 5, 1983.

21 Melissa Berg, "Berkley, Serviss Accused of Making Scandal Political," *Kansas City Star,* February 17, 1983; John A. Dvorak, "Berkley, Serviss and Wheeler Snap Up Public

Works Football," *Kansas City Times,* February 3, 1983; Lee Judge, "Editorial Cartoon," *Kansas City Star,* February 13, 1983.

22 *Call,* "Baptists Back Berkley," February 4, 1983; *Kansas City Star,* "Baptist Ministers Group Backs Mayor Berkley," February 2, 1983.

23 Lewis W. Diuguid, "Inner-city Black Ministers Meet Over Endorsements," *Kansas City Times,* February 24, 1983; *Call,* "AME Ministers Endorse Richard Berkley for Mayor," February 18, 1983.

24 Rich Hood, "13 Ministers Back Freedom Inc.," *Kansas City Star,* March 16, 1983.

25 *Call,* "Don't Believe Rumors!," March 25, 1983.

26 Celeste Hadrick, "Ministers Insist Berkley Is Their Choice," *Kansas City Star,* March 17, 1983.

27 Interview with author.

28 Rich Hood and Barbara Shelly, "Cash Buys Love in KC Politics," *Kansas City Star,* March 15, 1987; James Kuhnhenn, "Serviss Decision Not to Run Shows Clubs' Clout," *Kansas City Times,* January 31, 1987.

29 Freedom would not forget the slight of the bounced check. When Serviss attempted to reclaim his council seat four years later, Freedom declined to endorse him because of that incident. Serviss quit the race as a result (Kuhnhenn, "Serviss Decision Not to Run Shows Clubs' Clout").

30 Berg, "Berkley Poll Buoys Mayor and Supporters."

31 Hood, "13 Ministers Back Freedom Inc."

32 Ibid.

33 James C. Fitzpatrick, "Report Will Show That Berkley Raised $102,916, Spent $98,480," *Kansas City Times,* January 23, 1987.

34 UPI, "Kansas City Victor Vows Unity Drive," *New York Times,* March 31, 1983.

35 Donna F. Stewart and Valerie Nicholson, "Berkley's Machine Beats Wheeler in Mayor's Race," *Call,* April 1, 1983.

36 Florestine Purnell, "Scenario of Holding Four Council Seats Elates KC's Black Representatives," *Kansas City Star,* February 6, 1983.

37 The CA in 1983 was but a shell of its former self, almost ceasing to exist outside of municipal election years. While its electoral machinery and direct influence with voters had virtually disappeared, it remained a useful indicator of the sentiments of the white political elite.

38 Interview with author.

39 John A. Dvorak and Michael Yablonski, "Veteran Councilman, Young Lawyer Square Off in 5th District," *Kansas City Times,* February 25, 1983; Rich Hood and Melissa Berg, "Trade-Offs Mark City Election Endorsements," *Kansas City Star,* February 9, 1983; Michael Yablonski, "Jolts in Primary Stir Incumbents in Council Races," *Kansas City Times,* March 16, 1983.

40 *Call,* "Mark Bryant Election No. 1 Priority March 29," March 18, 1983.

41 Rich Hood, "Black Ministers' Group Reportedly Shifts Stance," *Kansas City Star,* March 22, 1983.

42 Interview with author.

43 *Kansas City Times,* "For 5th District," March 23, 1983.

44 Rick E. Abel, "City Jubilant Over Bryant Win," *Call,* April 1, 1983.

45 Joanne Collins was endorsed by Freedom in 1983, but was not a member of the LPO.

46 James C. Fitzpatrick, "Berkley Routs Heeter for Third Term," *Kansas City Times,* April 1, 1987.

47 Rich Hood, "Blandness Seen As A Plus for Berkley," *Kansas City Star,* January 18, 1987.

48 Joe Popper, "The Rev: The Passions and Politics of Emanuel Cleaver," *Kansas City Star: Star Magazine,* April 12, 1987. Cleaver almost certainly would have benefitted from widespread black support had he run in 1987, but there was no popular groundswell for his candidacy. Mimicking an experiment in Chicago that resulted in Harold Washington's candidacy, *The Call* printed a "ballot" in its pages for several weeks in the fall of 1986, asking readers to vote on whether Cleaver should run or not. By the end of the experiment, just 26 people had voted and only 16 of those said that Cleaver should run (*Call,* "Early Poll Results Say CALL Readers Want Cleaver to Run for Mayor," October 24, 1986).

49 Waldo—born Kay Cronkite and a cousin of the famed journalist Walter Cronkite—later remarried and, at the time of her election as mayor, was known as Kay Barnes.

50 Melissa Berg, "Brisk Contest Developing for 4th District At-Large Post," *Kansas City Star,* February 7, 1983; Hood and Berg, "Trade-Offs Mark City Election Endorsements." Heeter won Freedom's support over Waldo and Katheryn Shields, a white attorney and future elected official, who served as Alan Wheat's campaign manager in his successful 1982 congressional bid. The decision to back Heeter was taken because he was favored by the CA; Freedom's endorsement of him secured the CA's endorsement of Mark Bryant.

51 *Call,* "Minority Councilmen Filibuster Job Training Program Vote," May 17, 1985; *Call,* "Jobs Program Dispute Settled," June 7, 1985.

52 *Call,* "Contractors Ordered to Repay City $86,704," March 15, 1985.

53 James Kuhnhenn, "Berkley Makes Choices with Harmony in Mind," *Kansas City Times,* April 11, 1987.

54 James Kuhnhenn, "Eight Return, 4 New Faces Join Council," *Kansas City* Times, April 1, 1987; Barbara Shelly, "Hazley Moves Into Fifth Term, Wielding Quiet Power," *Kansas City Star,* April 1, 1987.

55 *Call,* "Minority Councilmen Filibuster Job Training Program Vote."

56 Interview with author.

57 James C. Fitzpatrick, "Seven City Council Members Endorse Berkley," *Kansas City* Times, March 28, 1987; Barbara Shelly, "Heeter Personifies Yuppie Image," *Kansas City Star,* January 18, 1987.

58 Popper, "The Rev."

59 James C. Fitzpatrick, "Berkley Sails Along as Heeter Hits Choppy Seas," *Kansas City Times,* January 31, 1987; James C. Fitzpatrick, "Businessman's Donations Fueling

Heeter Campaign," *Kansas City Times*, March 24, 1987; Shelly, "Heeter Personifies Yuppie Image."

60 James C. Fitzpatrick, "Freedom Inc. May Follow Lead Set by Cleaver," *Kansas City Times*, January 8, 1987.

61 The mayor *pro tem* presides over the city council in the mayor's absence and is considered the official leader of the city council. It has also been considered a good launching post for mayoral candidacies; in the nine elections since 1979, five mayors *pro tem* have run for mayor and four have advanced to the general election, though just two have actually been elected. The method of selection of the mayor *pro tem* has varied over the years. In the 1970s, the twelve council members elected their own mayor *pro tem*. In the 1980s, Berkley initiated a system where the office rotated among council members, with none holding the post for more than a few months. In 1987, Berkley recommended that Cleaver hold the post for the life of the council term (four years), but the choice still had to be formally ratified by the council. Charter amendments in the 1990s gave the mayor the power to fill the office.

62 Popper, "The Rev."

63 Dan Margolies, "Welch Leaving KC Spotlight for the Sunlight of Phoenix," *Kansas City Business Journal*, February 9, 1997.

64 James C. Fitzpatrick, "Citizens Endorse Berkley Despite Move by Heeter," *Kansas City Times*, January 23, 1987; James C. Fitzpatrick, "Freedom Inc. Endorses Berkley Over Heeter in Mayor's Contest," *Kansas City Times*, January 30, 1987.

65 Popper, "The Rev."

66 Interview with author.

67 *Call*, "Mayor Richard Berkley Should Be Reelected," March 27, 1987.

68 Himanee Gupta, "Freedom Offshoot Backs Heeter," *Kansas City Star*, January 18, 1987. The dissent of Bruce Watkins Jr. was not so radical as it at first appears. Watkins was denied Freedom's endorsement in his 1986 campaign for state representative, because other activists felt he was trading on his father's famous name. Watkins lost the race to Freedom's candidate, Vernon Thompson, by 40 votes and was deeply embittered (*Call*, "Vernon Thompson Wins by 40 Votes in Squeaker over Bruce Watkins Jr.," August 8, 1986).

69 Rich Hood, "Party Leaders Endorse Heeter's Mayoral Bid," *Kansas City Star*, January 21, 1987; *Kansas City Star*, "Heeter Gets Backing from Some Lawmakers," March 15, 1987.

70 Louis Blue, "Oust Thompson From Freedom, Inc.," *Call*, March 27, 1987.

71 *Call*, "Freedom, Inc., President Calls Campaign Tactics A Scheme to Divide Community," March 27, 1987.

72 Fitzpatrick, "Freedom Inc. May Follow Lead Set by Cleaver;" James C. Fitzpatrick, "Citizens Board Backs Berkley for Third Term," *Kansas City Times*, January 16, 1987.

73 Ibid.

74 Shelly, "Hazley Moves into Fifth Term, Wielding Quiet Power."

75 Barbara Shelly, "Adviser Hired by Heeter," *Kansas City Star*, January 2, 1987.

76 Fitzpatrick, "Berkley Sails Along as Heeter Hits Choppy Seas;" Rich Hood, "Publicity from Events Part of Candidate's Plan," *Kansas City Star,* January 15, 1987.

77 James C. Fitzpatrick, "Heeters Bid Savings on Campaign," *Kansas City Times,* January 13, 1987.

78 Berkley and Heeter were the only two candidates in the race, guaranteeing them both a place in the general election.

79 James C. Fitzpatrick, "KC Margin Is Biggest Since 1967," *Kansas City Times,* March 4, 1987.

80 *Kansas City Times,* "Polluting an Election," March 26, 1987; *Kansas City Times,* "Election Endorsements," March 31, 1987; *Kansas City Times,* "The Heeter Campaign," March 31, 1987.

81 Rich Hood, "Donations to Heeter Criticized," *Kansas City Star,* January 18, 1987; Jeff Taylor, "Dunmire Not Fazed by Outcome of Vote," *Kansas City Times,* April 1, 1987. The businessman in question, Delbert Dunmire, was colorful, to say the least. In 1958, Dunmire robbed the Commercial State Bank in Abilene, Kansas to pay off a gambling debt. He served two years in prison for the robbery, and then borrowed $3,000 to start Growth Industries, the aircraft parts manufacturer that was the source of his wealth. The advertisements that Dunmire funded for Heeter were, ironically, about the need for the mayor to crack down on crime. Dunmire has made millions of dollars in charitable contributions in the years since, but remains controversial for the manner in which he has managed his considerable real estate holdings and for his eccentric public persona.

82 Hood, "Donations to Heeter Criticized."

83 *Call,* "Mayor Richard Berkley Should Be Reelected."

84 Fitzpatrick, "Berkley Routs Heeter for Third Term."

85 Sam Smith, "Mayor Berkley Wins in All Black Wards," *Call,* April 3, 1987.

86 Kuhnhenn, "Berkley Makes Choices with Harmony in Mind." The CA was enraged that Berkley appointed Hazley, who won reelection with 82 percent of the vote, to chair Plans and Zoning. Robert Lutz went so far as to state that had the CA known that Berkley would name Hazley to chair that crucial committee, it would have endorsed Heeter instead.

87 Adolph L. Reed, *Stirrings in the Jug: Black Politics in the Post-Segregation Era* (Minneapolis: University of Minnesota Press, 1999), 117–159.

88 Louis Blue, "Regional HUD Job Pending for Watkins; Will Resign as President of Freedom," *Call,* June 22, 1979.

89 Margolies, "Welch Leaving KC Spotlight for the Sunlight of Phoenix."

90 *Call,* "Freedom's Future Questioned after Major Losses in Primary," August 10, 1990.

91 Al Ansare, "Archie Welch Says Freedom, Inc., Didn't Lose Election," *Call,* August 17, 1990.

92 *Call,* "Senator Phil Curls New President of Freedom," August 31, 1990.

93 Yael T. Abouhalkah, "Freedom Inc.'s Plight in Upcoming Elections Delights Foes," *Kansas City Star,* January 5, 1991.

94 Ansare, "Archie Welch Says Freedom, Inc., Didn't Lose Election." Individual members paid $5 in annual dues, while institutional members paid $100 (*Call,* "Freedom, Inc. to Launch Membership Drive," June 9, 1989).

95 *Call,* "Freedom, Inc. Volunteers Help to Ready 62,000-Piece Mass Mailing," March 4, 1988.

96 Interview with author.

97 The term "professionalized" is used with some reluctance, as it perhaps suggests a level of internal sophistication (formal structures, hierarchical leadership, strategy, etc.) that had long been present within Freedom. Here, professionalized is intended to communicate primarily the use of paid labor, the presence of intense pragmatism, and the orientation away from mobilizing the masses to relying on a core group of devoted political activists.

98 Louis Blue, "Freedom's Voter Registration Drive Launched with Speech by Andrew Young at Breakfast," *Call,* September 12, 1980; *Call,* "Freedom, Inc., Says 'Get Registered Now,'" February 5, 1988.

99 *Call,* "Gospel Extravaganza for Freedom, Inc., Candidates Sunday," July 9, 1982.

100 *Call,* "Youth Group of Freedom, Inc., Formed; to Learn Government Principles and Procedures," March 27, 1980.

101 *Call,* "Over 500 Attend Freedom, Inc. Gala," September 25, 1987.

102 *Call,* "Freedom Awards Four at Formal Ceremony," July 29, 1989.

103 Interview with author.

104 Interview with author.

105 Interview with author.

106 Interview with author.

107 Diuguid and Schlinkmann, "Swinton Is Charged with Stealing."

108 *Call,* "Swinton Pleads Guilty; Resigns from Missouri Senate; Gets Probation," October 21, 1983.

109 *Call,* "Phil Curls Wins State Senate Seat," December 23, 1983. At the time of Swinton's disgrace, there was ample speculation that Freedom was dissatisfied with his performance in office and would challenge him in the 1984 primary. Phil Curls was the most frequently mentioned potential challenger.

110 *Call,* "Time for Answers," November 25, 1983; *Call,* "Watkins Takes Scholarship Reins," December 2, 1983; *Call,* "Citizens Give Comments on Jordan Scholarship Fund," March 2, 1984; *Call,* "IRS Seizes Apartment Building of Holliday for Tax Non-Payment," March 2, 1984.

111 David Goldstein, "Bruce Watkins Jr. Is Indicted in Theft," *Kansas City Times,* April 25, 1987.

112 *Call,* "Freedom Inc. Criticizes Move to Oust Holliday," May 18, 1984.

113 *Call,* "Watkins Pleads Guilty in Fund Theft; Repays $15,000," October 9, 1987.

114 Goldstein, "Bruce Watkins Jr. Is Indicted in Theft."

115 Al Ansare, "Hazley Remains on Council but Gives up Committee Chair Pending Investigation," *Call,* May 6, 1988.

116 *Call*, "Hazley to Serve 30 Days at Indiana Prison," August 5, 1988; *Call*, "Hazley Home Early for Good Behavior," September 9, 1988.

117 Al Ansare, "Community Leaders Continue to Support Hazley," *Call*, July 15, 1988.

118 Interview with author.

119 *Call*, "Carol Coe Sworn in as County Legislator," February 15, 1985.

120 *Call*, "Remarks Attributed to Carol Coe 'Talk of the Town,'" February 15, 1985; *Kansas City Star* Magazine, "In Search of the Real Carol Coe," May 15, 1988.

121 Dunstan McNichol, "Freedom Inc. to Probe Vote," *Kansas City Star*, January 9, 1987.

122 Tim O'Connor, "In the Wake of Her Vote for Carnes, Coe Leaves Board of Political Club," *Kansas City Times*, January 17, 1987.

123 David Hayes, "Coe to Be Investigated on Bribery Allegation," *Kansas City Times*, February 18, 1987.

124 Karen Blakeman, "Report Clears Coe of Bribery Allegations," *Kansas City Times*, April 17, 1987.

125 *Call*, "Freedom Not among 34 Violators," September 30, 1983.

126 V.P. Howard, "Black Leaders Rally Against Daily Paper," *Call*, May 30, 1986; *Call*, "Black Leaders in Campaign Against K.C. Star-Times," May 16, 1986; *Call*, "Press Conference on K.C. Star Friday Noon at 18th and Grand," May 23, 1986.

127 James C. Fitzpatrick, "Steve Penn: A Horrible Way to Pack up Your Pencils," *JimmyCSays: At the Juncture of Journalism and Daily Life in Kansas City*, July 13, 2011.

128 *Call*, "McGee, Coe to Make Plea for Unity," August 5, 1988.

129 Interview with author.

130 Interview with author.

131 Interview with author.

132 Shelly, "Hazley Moves into Fifth Term, Wielding Quiet Power."

133 Interview with author.

134 Al Ansare, "Freedom Opposes Two-Term Limits," *Call*, October 26, 1990.

135 Yael T. Abouhalkah, "The Berkley Style Gets Results," *Kansas City Star*, February 17, 1991.

136 Nosakhere Makalani, "Five Black Males Are Homicide Victimrs within 5-Day Period," *Call*, August 7, 1987.

137 Al Ansare, "Ad Hoc's Story of Cooperation Attracts Nationwide Attention," *Call*, May 19, 1989; Donna Stewart, "10 Years of Fighting Crime," *Call*, November 20, 1987; *Call*, "City's Black Homicides Decline in 1979; Ad Hoc Group to Continue Efforts," January 25, 1980; *Call*, "Ad Hoc Group, Southeast Community Organizations, Join to Wage War on Sexual Assaults in the Area," December 30, 1983; *Call*, "Ad Hoc Declares War on Drug Houses," September 20, 1985.

138 Rick E. Abel, "Solution to Salty Police/Community Relations Moving in Several Circles," *Call*, November 21, 1980; Al Ansare, "Police Brutality Complaints under Investigation by OCC," *Call*, April 21, 1989; Al Ansare, "Community Outraged by Police Killing," *Call*, June 22, 1990; Al Ansare, "Reports of Police Brutality Complaints Rise,"

Call, June 22, 1990; *Call,* "Black Leaders Shocked at 90-Day Sentence to Man Beaten by Police," October 21, 1980; *Call,* "Are Police Tests Fair?," August 16, 1985.

139 *Call,* "City's Affirmative Action Plan Approved," December 6, 1985.

140 Rick E. Abel, "Edward Wilson Jr. Named Fire Department Chief by City Manager Robert Kipp," *Call,* April 10, 1981.

141 Shelly, "Hazley Moves into Fifth Term, Wielding Quiet Power;" *Call,* "Jim Threatt to Continue Handling Federal Grants," May 11, 1984.

142 Donna Stewart, "Rumors, Motives and More Questions Revolve around Threatt Controversy," *Call,* May 23, 1986.

143 *Call,* "City Manager Makes Changes in Budget in Response to Citizens," April 13, 1984.

144 Donna Stewart, "Troubles of Vista Hotel Still Taking New Twists," *Call,* June 5, 1987.

145 Rick E. Abel, "Black Leaders Want Pact Kept," *Call,* January 13, 1984.

146 Tamar Jacoby, *Someone Else's House: America's Unfinished Struggle for Integration* (New York: Basic Books, 1998), 377–403.

147 William Julius Wilson, *When Work Disappears: The World of the New Urban Poor* (New York: Vintage Books, 1996).

148 *Call,* "City to Kick-off Enterprise Zone Campaign on January 12," January 9, 1987.

149 Sandra Nicholson, "12th Street Heritage Development Corp. Has Area Residents Showing Optimism for the Future," *Call,* December 27, 1985; *Call,* "Plans and Zoning Committee Approves Lakeview II," March 21, 1986; *Call,* "New Program Helps Families Buy Houses," July 31, 1987.

150 Mack Alexander, "Shopping Center to Provide Jobs, Fill Need for Quality Retail Stores," *Call,* October 19, 1984; Donna Stewart, "Blight Turns to Pride as Shopping Center Opens," *Call,* February 14, 1986.

151 *Call,* "HDCIC President Gives Response to Article Regarding Agency," May 2, 1986.

152 Louis Blue, Rick E. Abel, and Donna F. Stewart, "Black Votes Help Push Tax to Victory," *Call,* August 5, 1983.

153 Sam Smith, "Black Community May Decide Future of Zoo," *Call,* August 3, 1990; *Call,* "Freedom, Inc. Endorses Waris; Opposed to K.C. Zoo Proposition," July 20, 1990.

154 Al Ansare, "Council Passes Cleaver Plan," *Call,* November 24, 1989; Steve Farnsworth, "Cleaver's Plan Is Expanded, Wins," *Kansas City Times,* November 23, 1989.

155 Farnsworth, "Cleaver's Plan Is Expanded, Wins."

156 Al Ansare, "19 Groups Push Cleaver's Plan," *Call,* November 17, 1989.

157 *Call,* "Freedom, Inc., Answers Criticism Made by K.C. Star," October 27, 1989; *Kansas City Star,* "Freedom Inc. Makes A Foolish Threat," October 19, 1989.

158 Farnsworth, "Cleaver's Plan Is Expanded, Wins."

159 Bobby Hernandez, typically Freedom's strongest nonblack ally, voted against the Cleaver Plan. He refused to support the proposal because it did not also include $75 million for housing rehabilitation and new housing for low-income residents. That proposal

was supported by the African American members but was strongly opposed by white council members whose votes were needed.

160 Interview with author.

161 Kevin Q. Murphy, "Years Have Modified Cleaver's Stance," *Kansas City Star*, February 18, 1991.

162 Al Ansare, "Black Community Kills Move to Change Charter," *Call*, April 7, 1989; James C. Fitzpatrick, "KC Voters Trounce Proposition 4," *Kansas City Times*, April 5, 1989; James C. Fitzpatrick, "Opinions Changed Quickly," *Kansas City Times*, April 5, 1989; *Call*, "Fight over Charter Picking up Steam," March 17, 1989; Archie W. Welch Jr., "Passage of Charter Amendment Could Polarize Our Community," *Call*, March 31, 1989.

163 Ansare, "Freedom Opposes Two-Terms Limits;" Sam Smith and Al Ansare, "Two-Term Limit Fails in Inner City but Voters Approve It City-wide," *Call*, November 9, 1990.

164 Shelly, "Hazley Moves into Fifth Term, Wielding Quiet Power;" Welch, "Passage of Charter Amendment Could Polarize Our Community."

165 Al Ansare, "Term Limits Challenged," *Call*, November 23, 1990.

166 James C. Fitzpatrick, "Abolish KC's At-Large Districts? Some See Big Problem in Idea," *Kansas City Star*, January 1, 1991; James C. Fitzpatrick, "Charter Plan Not on Ballot," *Kansas City Star*, January 25, 1991.

167 Al Ansare and Renee Sutherland, "KKK May Go on Cablevision," *Call*, May 27, 1988; Al Ansare, "KKK Show Sparks Debate," *Call*, May 13, 1988; Al Ansare, "Council Passes Cable Resolution," *Call*, June 17, 1988; J.M. Balkin, "Some Realism about Pluralism: Legal Realist Approaches to the First Amendment," *Duke Law Journal* 1990 (1990): 375–430; Steve Farnsworth, "KC Abandons Effort to Keep Klan off TV," *Kansas City Times*, July 14, 1989; Steve Farnsworth, "Council Pays All Legal Fees of ACLU in TV Case," *Kansas City Times*, September 29, 1989; Stacy Overman, "City Council Drops out of Suit with Klan," *Call*, July 14, 1989.

Chapter 5

1 Interview with author.

2 Interview with author.

3 Laura Gordon, "Cleaver Makes It Official," *Call*, November 16, 1990.

4 Yael T. Abouhalkah, "Leadership Put to Test in Crowded Mayoral Campaign," *Kansas City Star*, February 9, 1991; Yael T. Abouhalkah, "Four Mayoral Contenders Have Ambitious Ideas for City," *Kansas City Star*, February 14, 1991; Yael T. Abouhalkah, "Surge of Activity in Last Lap of Mayoral Primary," *Kansas City Star*, February 21, 1991; James C. Fitzpatrick, "Cleaver's Low-Key Campaign Puzzles Foes King, Harris," February 2, 1991.

5 James C. Fitzpatrick, "King Became a Contender Years Ago," *Kansas City Star*, February 21, 1991.

6 Yael T. Abouhalkah, "Candidates for Mayor Zero in on Some Issues," *Kansas City Star*, January 16, 1991; James C. Fitzpatrick, "No More Mr. Nice Guy for Mayoral Foes as Race Takes Off," *Kansas City Star*, February 6, 1991.

7 James C. Fitzpatrick, "King Leads Harris and Cleaver in Raising Cash for Mayor's Race," *Kansas City Star*, January 19, 1991; Fitzpatrick, "Cleaver's Low-Key Campaign Puzzles Foes King, Harris."

8 James C. Fitzpatrick, "Brice Harris Eager to Win KC's Top Job," *Kansas City Star,* February 20, 1991.

9 Fitzpatrick, "King Leads Harris and Cleaver in Raising Cash for Mayor's Race;" James C. Fitzpatrick, "Mayoral Race Attracts Money," February 22, 1991.

10 Abouhalkah, "Surge of Last Activity in Last Lap of Mayoral Primary;" Audrey McKinney, "Joanne Collins To Run For Mayor," *Call,* October 12, 1990; Kevin Q. Murphy, "This Campaign Is No Joke," *Kansas City Star,* February 22, 1991; Diane Stafford, "Joanne Collins Feels Her Time Is Now," *Kansas City Star,* February 19, 1991.

11 Interview with author.

12 J.D. Tindall, "Redistricting Request Will Diminish Black Representation," *Call,* April 20, 1990.

13 Fitzpatrick, "No More Mr. Nice Guy for Mayoral Foes as Race Takes Off."

14 Cleaver for Mayor Campaign, "You've Got To Believe! (Paid Political Advertisement);" Glenn E. Rice, "Campaign Song to Hit Air," *Kansas City Star,* February 16, 1991; *Call,* "Cleaver for Mayor," February 22, 1991.

15 Kevin Q. Murphy, "Cleaver a Key Issue in Panel's Questions," *Kansas City Star,* January 13, 1991; *Kansas City Star,* "Freedom Inc. Backs Cleaver for Mayor," January 18, 1991.

16 Interview with author; *Call,* "Kansas City Ministers Endorse Rev. Cleaver," February 1, 1991; *Call,* "A.M.E. Ministers Endorse Rev. Cleaver for Mayor," February 8, 1991.

17 Kevin Q. Murphy, "Collins Wins Support of Pastor at Big Church," *Kansas City Star,* February 16, 1991.

18 Backers of Cleaver and Collins alike chafed when asked whether Collins was "splitting the black vote" and hurting Cleaver, finding the question spurious and racist. Cleaver supporter Charles Hazley, for example, "bristle[d] at comments that [Collins's] candidacy will serve mainly to take votes away from Emanuel Cleaver. 'Why don't people say he'll take votes from her?'" (Stafford, "Joanne Collins Feels Her Time Is Now").

19 Interview with author.

20 Louis Blue, "Desperate to Win, Candidate Resorts to Fraudulent Ballots," *Call,* March 29, 1991.

21 Interview with author.

22 James C. Fitzpatrick, "Cleaver Stands Clear as Other Candidates Slug Away," *Kansas City Star,* January 12, 1991.

23 Yael T. Abouhalkah, "Voters Set the Tone of Mayoral Runoff," *Kansas City Star,* February 28, 1991; Yael T. Abouhalkah, "Funny Thing Happened on the Way to the Mayoral Runoff," *Kansas City Star,* March 9, 1991; James C. Fitzpatrick, "Harris, King Back Their Ads," *Kansas City Star,* February 23, 1991; James C. Fitzpatrick, "For Harris, King, Losing Mayor's Race Was Costly," *Kansas City Star,* March 29, 1991.

24 The district was then hiring a new superintendent. The school board opted to make an offer to a white candidate, rather than to several African American finalists for the position. This enraged, among others, Clinton Adams. Adams and an organization he then led, the Black Agenda Group, stated that hiring a white superintendent in a district with an overwhelmingly black student population would be regarded as an act of "war" on the black community and called for a boycott. These comments were not well-received by voters or the individual offered the superintendent's position, who remarked that he was "appalled

by the fact you would have such bigoted people in the community." Cleaver was drawn into the fray because his campaign paid Adams several thousand dollars for consulting services, a fact of which the mayoral candidate said he was unaware (Art Brisbane, "School Fiasco Fallout," *Kansas City Star,* February 15, 1991; Kevin Q. Murphy, "Concern over Backlash," *Kansas City Star,* February 16, 1991; Kevin Q. Murphy, "Cleaver Erasing Campaign's Links with Outspoken Clinton Adams," *Kansas City Star,* February 19, 1991).

25 Kevin Q. Murphy, "KC's Cleaver, Lewellen Top Mayoral Field," *Kansas City Star,* February 27, 1991.

26 James C. Fitzpatrick, "AFL-CIO Endorses Cleaver," *Kansas City Star,* March 15, 1991.

27 James C. Fitzpatrick, "Candidates Add Endorsements," *Kansas City Star,* March 12, 1991; James C. Fitzpatrick, "Cleaver Wins Allies of Foe to His Side," *Kansas City Star,* March 16, 1991.

28 Kevin Q. Murphy, "Lewellen Gets Endorsement," *Kansas City Star,* March 1, 1991.

29 Louis Blue, "You Need to Vote," *Call,* March 15, 1991; *Call,* "Emanuel Cleaver Best Man for Mayor," March 22, 1991.

30 Interview with author.

31 Yael T. Abouhalkah, "Candidates Hit Out in Final Round," *Kansas City Star,* March 25, 1991; James C. Fitzpatrick, "Candidates Spar Over Gay Rights," *Kansas City Star,* March 24, 1991; Kevin Q. Murphy, "Cleaver's Portable Phone Becomes a Campaign Issue," *Kansas City Star,* February 16, 1991.

32 Rick Montgomery, "Clues to Cleaver Victory and Lewellen Loss," *Kansas City Star,* March 31, 1991.

33 Kevin Q. Murphy, "Cleaver Maintains Big Lead," *Kansas City Star,* March 17, 1991.

34 Kevin Q. Murphy, "Cleaver Wins, Proclaims 'New Era,'" *Kansas City Star,* March 27, 1991; Donna Stewart, "It's Mayor Cleaver," *Kansas City Star,* March 29, 1991.

35 *Kansas City Star,* "Cleaver for Mayor," March 20, 1991.

36 John T. Ferguson, "Guilt Trip," *Kansas City Star,* March 2, 1991.

37 United States Census Bureau.

38 Freedom, Inc., "Freedom, Inc.—Support the Bridge That Brought Us Across (Paid Political Advertisement)."

39 James C. Fitzpatrick, "Chances of Write-In Campaign by Hazley Seem to be Fading," *Kansas City Star,* January 4, 1991; Kevin Q. Murphy, "Hazley, Hernandez Are Abandoning Fight to Stay on KC Ballot," *Kansas City Star,* January 9, 1991.

40 *Call,* "Freedom's Future Questioned After Major Losses in Primary," August 10, 1990. Coe also ran for a school board seat in 1990, a campaign which she lost. One of her opponents in that race was Kit Carson Roque, who also lost (Louis Blue, "Five Elected to School Board," *Call,* April 6, 1990).

41 Blue, "Desperate to Win, Candidate Resorts to Fraudulent Ballots;" James C. Fitzpatrick, "Coe's Presence on Slate Hinders Cleaver," *Kansas City Star,* January 22, 1991.

42 *Kansas City Star,* "Freedom Inc. Backs Cleaver for Mayor."

43 *Call,* "Carol Coe Says Remarks on T.V. Program 'Overblown,'" May 15, 1987.

44 Yael T. Abouhalkah, "Freedom's Message," *Kansas City Star,* January 22, 1991; Fitzpatrick, "Coe's Presence on Slate Hinders Cleaver."

45 Abouhalkah, "Freedom's Message."

46 Committee to Elect Carol Coe, "Strong Black Women Keep on Coming (Paid Political Advertisement)."

47 Melissa Berg, "Bitterness Marks KC Council Races," *Kansas City Star,* March 3, 1991; Blue, "Desperate to Win, Candidate Resorts to Fraudulent Ballots;" April D. McLellan, "Rival Files Challenge to Coe's Address Claim," *Kansas City Star,* February 14, 1991.

48 Blue, "Desperate to Win, Candidate Resorts to Fraudulent Ballots;" Amy Snider, "'Freedom Now' Ballots in KC Being Investigated," *Kansas City Star,* March 26, 1991. Similar tactics had been attempted sporadically in the past, as in 1979. From this point forward, *every* municipal election would feature at least one "fake Freedom" ballot that substituted one or more candidate passed over for the endorsement for genuine members of the slate.

49 Abouhalkah, "Voters Set the Tone of Mayoral Runoff;" Louis Blue, "Defeat of Jim Wilson a Blow to Freedom," *Call,* March 29, 1991; David Goldstein, "Issues Fail to Divide 5th District Candidates," *Kansas City Star,* March 14, 1991; Interview with author.

50 Blue, "Defeat of Jim Wilson a Blow to Freedom."

51 Jim Wilson would never again seek public office, though he would be named by the governor to the KCPD Board of Police Commissioners. His wife, Yvonne, would later have a distinguished career as a member of the state House of Representatives and state Senate. Yvonne Wilson was endorsed by Freedom in all of her campaigns for public office.

52 April McLellan, "Allies Are Opponents in 3rd District-At-Large," *Kansas City Star,* March 20, 1991; *Kansas City Star,* "Freedom Inc. Backs Cleaver for Mayor."

Like Coe and Roque, Ron Finley was also a losing candidate for the school board in 1990 (Blue, "Five Elected to School Board").

53 Yael T. Abouhalkah, "Several Good Races Slated in Final City Council Sweeps," *Kansas City Star,* March 1, 1991; April McLellan, "5th District Visions Clash, Not Candidates," *Kansas City Star,* March 22, 1991.

54 Shields was also campaign manager for Alan Wheat in his 1982 congressional bid.

55 Interview with author.

56 Kevin Q. Murphy, "Labor Denounces Freedom Endorsements," *Kansas City Star,* February 9, 1991.

57 Berg, "Bitterness Marks KC Council Races."

58 Steve Penn, "Shields, Weber Object to Freedom Inc. Flier," *Kansas City Star,* March 27, 1991.

59 Yael T. Abouhalkah, "A Turning Point in City's History," *Kansas City Star,* March 28, 1991.

60 Martin Connolly and Kevin Q. Murphy, "Mayor Vacations with Free Tickets," *Kansas City Star,* February 2, 1991; Michael Phillips, "Ethics Report Is Critical of Mayor Cleaver," *Call,* April 10, 1992.

61 Jeffrey Spivak, "Tax Boost Is a Big Loser in KC Vote;" *Call,* "Voters Say No to Odyssey 2000."

62 James C. Fitzpatrick, "Contests in KC for Mayor, Council Could Be Spirited," *Kansas City Star,* January 1, 1995.

63 Yael T. Abouhalkah, "Cleaver Dumped Cofran After Relations Soured," *Kansas City Star,* September 17, 1993. Cleaver removed Cofran from the chairmanship because the councilman publicly attacked the Odyssey 2000 plan and said he and the mayor were on "divergent paths." In 2004, when Cleaver announced that he was running for Congress, he was again challenged by Cofran. Cofran made no secret of the fact that his campaign was exclusively about needling Cleaver.

64 Fitzpatrick, "Contests in KC for Mayor, Council Could Be Spirited."

65 Mark Morris, "Cofran Is in Line for Citizen's Nod," *Kansas City Star,* January 20, 1995; *Call,* "Citizens Endorses Cofran for Mayor," January 20, 1995.

66 Yael T. Abouhalkah, "Cleaver Cruises as Cofran Seeks Traction," *Kansas City Star,* March 16, 1995.

67 Yael T. Abouhalkah, "The Money Trail Leading to City Hall," *Kansas City Star,* April 27, 1995.

68 The ten predominantly black wards of 1991 had been reduced to eight after the decennial redistricting process.

69 The CA was damaged by its then-chairman Henry Lyons, a strong opponent of Cleaver. Lyons was an African American who spear-headed the successful 1990 term limits initiative, leading some to consider him an "Uncle Tom" or, in the words of Phil Curls, "point man for the Mission Hills Mafia" [Mission Hills is a wealthy suburb in Johnson County, Kansas.] (Donna Stewart, "The Man Behind the Plan to Limit Terms," *Call,* October 26, 1990). In 1995, Lyons attracted several days of negative attention with press accounts that he was anti-Semitic.

70 Gromer Jeffers Jr., "A Divisive History Haunts Carol Coe, Freedom Inc.," *Kansas City Star,* July 30, 1995.

71 *Call,* "The Mayor Should Make Clear What He Says and Means," September 27, 1991.

72 Al Ansare, "Mary Williams Neal in Surprise Win Over Carol Coe," *Call,* March 31, 1995.

73 Morris, "Cofran Is in Line for Citizen's Nod."

74 Ansare, "Mary Williams Neal in Surprise Win Over Carol Coe." McCaskill was supported by Freedom in the 1992 Democratic primary and some saw a debt-repaying conspiracy in the speed with which Coe was charged. McCaskill had her own history with Coe. McCaskill, then a state representative, filed for Jackson County prosecutor in 1988, believing she would have the support of black voters. Coe filed for the same office a few days later. McCaskill subsequently withdrew, believing that Coe's unexpected entry had ruined her chances (and that Coe was enticed into the race for precisely that reason). McCaskill then ran against Coe for the latter's seat on the Jackson County Legislature, defeating her by more than 30,000 votes (*Call,* "Freedom's Future Questioned after Major Losses in Primary," August 10, 1990). The enmity between the two was further cemented when Coe charged that McCaskill ran a racist campaign against her.

75 Ibid.

76 Yael T. Abouhalkah, "Stop the Sleaze, Now!," *Kansas City Star,* March 24, 1995.

77 Audrey L. McKinney, "Third District At-Large Race Close," *Call,* March 31, 1995.

78 Interview with the author.

79 Interview with author.

80 Interview with author.

81 *Call*, "Tindall Now President of Freedom," March 11, 1994.

82 Gromer Jeffers Jr., "Leader Leaves Legislature in Uncertainty," *Kansas City Star,* September 29, 1996; Gromer Jeffers Jr., "Freedom Searches for Chief, Direction," *Kansas City Star,* November 10, 1996.

83 Al Ansare, "Bishop Tindall: 'I Feel Exonerated,'" *Call,* Januray 29, 1999; Mark Morris, "Tindall Cleared of Corruption," *Kansas City Star,* January 25, 1999.

84 Al Ansare, "Kelvin Simmons Wins 5th District City Council Seat With Over 63 Percent of Vote," *Call,* January 10, 1997; Jeffers, "Freedom searches for chief, direction."

85 *Call*, "Mary Groves Bland New President of Freedom," June 20, 1997.

86 Hughes's only foray into seeking elective office ended ignominiously in 1988, when she was resoundingly defeated for a seat in the state House of Representatives by Jackie McGee. At the time of her campaign for the Freedom presidency, Hughes was the affirmative action compliance officer for Jackson County.

87 Gromer Jeffers Jr., "Freedom political club elects state lawmaker," *Kansas City Star,* June 20, 1997.

88 *Call*, "Massive Voter Drive Saturday," July 10, 1992.

89 Jeffers, "Freedom Searches for Chief, Direction."

90 Abouhalkah, "Freedom's Message."

91 Interview with author.

92 Interview with author.

93 Interview with author.

94 Interview with author.

95 Matt Campbell, "Freedom Chastised for Choice," *Kansas City Star,* July 6, 1994; *Call*, "Group Challenges Freedom Endorsement," July 8, 1994.

96 Interview with author.

97 Al Ansare, "Councilwoman Indicted on Six Counts of Fraud," *Call,* July 19, 1996; *Call*, "Robinson Pleads Guilty, Resigns," September 13, 1996.

98 Morris, "Tindall Cleared of Corruption."

99 Mark Morris and Tom Jackman, "Weber Accused of Role in Bribery," *Kansas City Star,* July 26, 1995.

100 Ironically, Freedom was attacked by the forces of good government for not endorsing Hernandez in 1991. The *Star* revealed that Hernandez's opponent, Joseph Spinello, received campaign contributions from individuals that the paper claimed were associated with organized crime or were otherwise embarrassing (e.g., the owner of a "gentleman's club"). Hernandez claimed that electing Spinello would open the door for illegal activity at City Hall.

101 Morris, "Tindall Cleared of Corruption;" *Call*, "Jury Convicts Anderson," September 26, 1997.

102 Interview with author.

103 Freedom, Inc., "Freedom, Inc.—Please Vote! (Paid Political Advertisement)."

104 Interview with author.

105 Interview with author.

106 Interviews with author.

107 Phil B. Curls Sr., "The Empty Bag Cannot Stand Up," *Call*, February 28, 1997; Lloyd Daniel, "Why I Got Kicked Out of Freedom, Inc. Or Breaking the Conspiracy of Silence," *Call*, February 28, 1997; Kevin Murphy and Gromer Jeffers Jr., "Freedom Threatens to Expel Members," *Kansas City Star*, February 20, 1997; *Call*, "Freedom, Inc. Official Says 'No One' Expelled," February 28, 1997.

108 Interview with author.

109 *Call*, "Freedom, Inc., in Process of Reorganization," November 15, 1996.

110 Interview with author.

111 Interview with author.

112 Interview with author.

113 Interview with author.

114 Murphy and Jeffers, "Freedom Threatens to Expel Members."

115 Interview with author.

116 Interview with author.

117 Federal Bureau of Investigation, "Crime Reported by Kansas City Police Department, Missouri," *Uniform Crime Reporting Statistics* (Washington: Federal Bureau of Investigation, 2010).

118 *Call*, "Council for Urban Peace and Justice Summit in Kansas City," April 30, 1993.

119 Sheri Baker, "Cleaver's 'State of the City' Speech Proclaims Progress Against Crime," *Call*, February 10, 1995; *Call*, "Police Say Efforts Lower Crime in '93," February 4, 1994.

120 Al Ansare, "Police Shooting of Fleeing Drug Suspect Sparks Angry Response," *Call*, June 7, 1996; *Call*, "Mayor Cleaver Responds to Events at 27th and Benton," June 7, 1996.

121 Donna Stewart, "Mayor's First Year A Mixture of Accomplishments and Controversy," *Call*, March 27, 1992.

122 To be sure, some of these appointments *did* have substantive results. For example, a more diverse Parks Board demanded that more funds be spent on community centers and activities for youth in the urban core, which contributed to falling rates of youth crime.

123 *Call*, "Council Unanimously Approves Disparity Ordinance That Ensures Fair Participation of Minorities in Bidding," March 15, 1996.

124 James C. Fitzpatrick, "Vaughn Pulls Out of Race," *Kansas City Star*, October 30, 1993; *Call*, "Vaughn Withdraws From Manager's Race," November 5, 1993.

125 The Vaughn incident was provoked when a council majority was assembled to fire city manager Dave Olson. Cleaver was unaware that this coup was brewing. He returned from an out of town trip to be informed by his chief antagonist on the Council, Chuck Weber, that Weber had gathered the votes to fire Olson. This lack of awareness on Cleaver's part was highly irregular and never again repeated (Yael T. Abouhalkah, "Turbulence on Surface at 12th and Oak May Run Deep," *Kansas City Star*, September 23, 1993).

126 *Call*, "Will 18th and Vine Fly?," March 19, 1993.

127 *Call*, "Jazz Hall Dropping Out of 18th and Vine," May 28, 1993; *Call*, "Negro Leagues Baseball Museum to Stadium," October 15, 1993.

128 Donna Stewart, "Everything's Fine at 18th and Vine," *Call,* September 5, 1997.

129 Some were incensed that city funds were used to purchase artifacts for the American Jazz Museum. The purchase of Charlie Parker's saxophone for $150,000 was particularly controversial.

130 Matt Campbell, "Williams-Neal, Coe Face Rematch," *Kansas City Star,* February 18, 1999.

131 *Call,* "Voters Say No to Odyssey 2000," August 6, 1993.

132 Michael P. Kelsay, *Uneven Patchwork: Tax Increment Financing in Kansas City* (Kansas City: ReclaimDemocracy.org, 2007).

133 It deserves to be noted that even the abuse of economic development programs produced significant economic benefits for the city. Some of the developments so sponsored, including those in thriving neighborhoods, genuinely would not have been located in Kansas City, Missouri in the absence of such programs. These programs were also essential in catalyzing large-scale redevelopment, like a downtown entertainment district, that had a significant impact on the economic success of the entire city.

134 Interview with author.

135 *Call,* "Tenants Pleased with Receivership," July 16, 1993.

136 *Call,* "Cleaver Reflects on 'Colorful Hands' He Appointed to Boards," December 4, 1998.

137 J. Philip Thompson III, *Double Trouble: Black Mayors, Black Communities, and the Call for a Deep Democracy* (New York: Oxford University Press, 2006).

138 Interview with author.

139 Interview with author.

140 *Call,* "City Primary Just A Few Days Away," February 26, 1999. The author served as Director of Communications, Policy, and Research for Ellis's second mayoral campaign in 2007.

141 Gromer Jeffers Jr., "Ellis Focuses on Executive Experience," *Kansas City Star,* February 18, 1999.

142 Interview with author.

143 Interview with author; Gromer Jeffers Jr., "Race for Mayor Puts Freedom on the Spot," *Kansas City Star,* January 20, 1999; Gromer Jeffers Jr., "Ellis Wins Freedom Inc. Endorsement," *Kansas City Star,* January 29, 1999; Gromer Jeffers Jr., "With A Chat and Hug, Hard Feelings Vanish," *Kansas City Star,* February 14, 1999.

144 Interview with author.

145 Steve Kraske, "Mayoral Race Rests on Neighborhood Blocs," *Kansas City Star,* March 14, 1999; Steve Kraske, "Northland Displays Its Expanding Political Influence," *Kansas City Star,* April 1, 1999; Steve Kraske, "City Gets Back on Landslide Track," *Kansas City Star,* April 6, 1999.

146 Interview with author.

147 The researcher later served as a member of Nash's City Council staff for eight years.

148 Jeffers, "With A Chat and Hug, Hard Feelings Vanish."

149 *Call,* "Riley Wins 43rd District State Representative Special Election," April 9, 1999.

150 Interview with author.

151 Shawn Edwards, "Former Councilman Promises A New Freedom Inc.," *Pitch,* March 30, 2000.

152 Interview with author.

153 Interview with author.

154 Interview with author.

155 Allie Johnson, "Hughes Blues," *Pitch,* February 13, 2003.

156 Matt Campbell, Mike Rice, and Benita Y. Williams, "Glover Heads Back to Council, Nace Easily Overcomes Challenger Fields," *Kansas City Star,* March 26, 2003.

157 Federal Election Commission, "Freedom Inc. Pays $45,000 Penalty for Failing to Register as Political Committee." Freedom subsequently created a new committee, Freedom Federal, that it did register with the FEC and which would handle its future involvement in federal races.

158 Trish Mehaffy, "Federal Jury Finds Former Kansas City Council Member Guilty of Mortgage Fraud," *Daily Record,* August 17, 2007.

159 Interview with author.

160 Interview with author.

161 Interview with author.

162 Interview with author.

163 Interview with author.

164 Interview with author.

165 Interview with author.

166 Interview with author.

167 Tom Bogdon, "Bland Wants to Reinvigorate Freedom Inc.," *eKC,* July 6, 2007.

168 Interview with author.

169 Interviews with author.

170 Steve Kraske, "Freedom Inc. Administrators Fined for Mishandling Finances," *Kansas City Star,* March 4, 2012.

171 Interview with author.

Chapter 6

1 Quoted in Amy Hart, "The Founding of Freedom: A Kansas City Civil Rights Organization Since 1962" (MA thesis, Central Missouri State University, 2006).

2 Interview with author.

3 Adolph Reed, *Stirrings in the Jug: Black Politics in the Post-Segregation Era* (Minneapolis: University of Minnesota Press, 1999), 1–52, 197–224.

4 Tommie Shelby, *We Who Are Dark: The Philosophical Foundations of Black Solidarity* (Cambridge: The Belknap Press of Harvard University Press, 2005).

5 Raphael J. Sonenshein, *Politics in Black and White: Race and Power in Los Angeles* (Princeton: Princeton University Press, 1993), 67–84, 269–282.

6 Richard P. Coleman, *The Kansas City Establishment: Leadership Through Two Centuries in a Midwestern Metropolis* (Manhattan: KS Publishing, 2006), 1–29.

7 Robert C. Smith, *We Have No Leaders: African Americans in the Post-Civil Rights Era* (Albany: State University of New York Press, 1996), 127–138, 255–282.

8 Ronald W. Walters, *White Nationalism, Black Interests: Conservative Public Policy and the Black Community* (Detroit: Wayne State University Press, 2003), 93–222.

Bibliography

Abel, Rick E. "Black Leaders Want Pact Kept." *Call*, January 13, 1984.

———. "Blacks Protest Failure to Nominate Black Judge." *Call*, January 7, 1977.

———. "Citizens' Directors Endorse Adams." *Call*, January 12, 1979.

———. "City Councilmen Say Public Works Funds Being Misused." *Call*, August 26, 1977.

———. "City Jubilant over Bryant Win." *Call*, April 1, 1983.

———. "Edward Wilson Jr. Named Fire Department Chief by City Manager Robert Kipp." *Call*, April 10, 1981.

———. "Freedom, Inc., and Black Community Lose Three House Seats after Redistricting." *Call*, September 18, 1981.

———. "Holliday Says He's Still Freedom, Inc. President." *Call*, August 18, 1978.

———. "Hughes III Defeats Holliday Sr." *Call*, August 11, 1978.

———. "Justice Department Urged to Probe Police Brutality." *Call*, July 18, 1980.

———. "Richard Berkley Next Mayor." *Call*, March 30, 1979.

———. "Solution to Salty Police/Community Relations Moving In Several Circles." *Call*, November 21, 1980.

———. "Speaking on How Black People 'Got Over,' Bishop Brookins Addresses Jordan Award Dinner." *Call*, May 27, 1977.

———. "Swinton Backs Adams against Hazley." *Call*, November 17, 1978.

———. "Wheat Edges Carnes in Final Sprint." *Call*, August 6, 1982.

———. "Wheeler's Spark Aimed at Setting Fire to 'Establishment-Backed Candidate.'" *Call*, March 17, 1978.

Abouhalkah, Yael T. "A Turning Point in City's History." *Kansas City Star*, March 28, 1991.

——— . "Candidates for Mayor Zero in on Some Issues." *Kansas City Star,* January 16, 1991.

——— . "Candidates Hit out in Final Round." *Kansas City Star,* March 25, 1991.

——— . "Cleaver Cruises as Cofran Seeks Traction." *Kansas City Star,* March 16, 1995.

——— . "Cleaver Dumped Cofran after Relations Soured." *Kansas City Star,* September 17, 1993.

——— . "Four Mayoral Contenders Have Ambitious Ideas for City." *Kansas City Star,* February 14, 1991.

——— . "Freedom Inc.'s Plight in Upcoming Elections delights foes." *Kansas City Star,* January 5, 1991.

——— . "Freedom's Message." *Kansas City Star,* January 22, 1991.

——— . "Funny Thing Happened on the Way to the Mayoral Runoff." *Kansas City Star,* March 9, 1991.

——— . "Leadership Put to Test in Crowded Mayoral Campaign." *Kansas City Star,* February 9, 1991.

——— . "Let's Listen to the Candidates, Not the Mayor." *Kansas City Star,* March 22, 2007.

——— . "Several Good Races Slated in Final City Council Sweeps." *Kansas City Star,* March 1, 1991.

——— . "Stop the Sleaze, Now!" *Kansas City Star,* March 24, 1995.

——— . "Surge of Activity in Last Lap of Mayoral Primary." *Kansas City Star,* February 21, 1991.

——— . "The Berkley Style Gets Results." *Kansas City Star,* February 17, 1991.

——— . "The Money Trail Leading to City Hall." *Kansas City Star,* April 27, 1995.

——— . "Turbulence on Surface at 12th and Oak May Run Deep." *Kansas City Star,* September 23, 1993.

——— . "Voters Set the Tone of Mayoral Runoff." *Kansas City Star,* February 28, 1991.

Adrian, Charles R. "A Typology for Nonpartisan Elections." *Western Political Quarterly* 12 (1959): 449–458.

Affiliated Democratic Club. *Vote the True Negro Democratic Ballot.* Paid political advertisement, 1968.

Alexander, Mack. "Charging Pressure, Cleaver Quits As S.C.L.C. Chief." *Kansas City Star,* February 2, 1975.

———. "Collins Returns a Bitter Pill to Freedom, Inc." *Kansas City Star,* February 26, 1975.

———. "Shopping Center To Provide Jobs, Fill Need For Quality Retail Stores." *Call,* October 19, 1984.

———. "Support by Blacks Surprises Collins." *Kansas City Star,* February 26, 1975.

———. "Watkins Yields Post." *Kansas City Star,* September 4, 1975.

———. "Wheat Rolls Over Palermo." *Call,* August 10, 1984.

Alkalimat, Abdul, and Doug Gills. *Harold Washington and the Crisis of Black Power in Chicago.* Chicago: Twenty-First Century Books and Publications, 1989.

Andrews, Kenneth T., and Bob Edwards. "Advocacy Organizations in the U.S. Political Process." *Annual Review of Sociology* 30 (2004): 479–506.

Ansare, Al, and Renee Sutherland. "KKK May Go On Cablevision." *Call,* May 27, 1988.

Ansare, Al, and Sheri Baker. "Charges Filed Against Coe." *Call,* March 17, 1995.

Ansare, Al. "19 Groups Push Cleaver's Plan." *Call,* November 17, 1989.

———. "Ad Hoc's Story of Cooperation Attracts Nationwide Attention." *Call,* May 19, 1989.

———. "Archie Welch Says Freedom, Inc., Didn't Lose Election." *Call,* August 17, 1990.

———. "Bishop Tindall: 'I Feel Exonerated.'" *Call,* January 29, 1999.

———. "Black Community Kills Move To Change Charter." *Call,* April 7, 1989.

———. "Community Leaders Continue To Support Hazley." *Call,* July 15, 1988.

———. "Community Outraged By Police Killing." *Call,* June 22, 1990.

———. "Council Passes Cable Resolution." *Call,* June 17, 1988.

———. "Council Passes Cleaver Plan." *Call,* November 24, 1989.

———. "Councilwoman Indicted On Six Counts Of Fraud." *Call,* July 19, 1996.

———. "Freedom Opposes Two-Term Limits." *Call,* October 26, 1990.

———. "Hazley Remains On Council But Gives Up Committee Chair Pending Investigation." *Call,* May 6, 1988.

———. "Kelvin Simmons Wins 5th District City Council Seat With Over 63 Percent Of Vote." *Call,* January 10, 1997.

———. "KKK Show Sparks Debate." *Call,* May 13, 1988.

———. "Mary Williams Neal In Surprise Win Over Carol Coe." *Call,* March 31, 1995.

———. "Police Brutality Complaints Under Investigation by OCC." *Call,* April 21, 1989.

———. "Police Shooting Of Fleeing Drug Suspect Sparks Angry Response." *Call,* June 7, 1996.

———. "Reports Of Police Brutality Complaints Rise." *Call,* June 22, 1990.

———. "Term Limits Challenged." *Call,* November 23, 1990.

Arrington, Richard. *There's Hope for the World: The Memoir of Birmingham, Alabama's First African American Mayor.* Tuscaloosa: University of Alabama Press, 2008.

Bacote, C.A. "The Negro in Atlanta Politics." *Phylon* 16, no.4 (1955): 335–350.

Baker, Sheri, and Louis Blue. "Cleaver Wins Another Term." *Call,* March 31, 1995.

Baker, Sheri. "Cleaver's 'State Of The City' Speech Proclaims Progress against Crime." *Call,* February 10, 1995.

Balkin, J.M. "Some Realism About Pluralism: Legal Realist Approaches to the First Amendment." *Duke Law Journal* 1990, no. 3 (1990):375–430.

Banfield, Edward C. and James Q. Wilson. *City Politics.* Cambridge: Harvard University Press, 1967.

Banfield, Edward C. *Big City Politics: A Comparative Guide to the Political Systems of Atlanta, Boston, Detroit, El Paso, Los Angeles, Miami, St. Louis, and Seattle.* New York: Random House, 1965.

Bayor, Ronald H. *Race and the Shaping of Twentieth-Century Atlanta.* Chapel Hill: University of North Carolina Press, 1996.

Bent, Devin. "Partisan Elections and Public Policy: Response to Black Demands in Large American Cities." *Journal of Black Studies* 12, no. 3 (1982): 291–314.

Berg, Melissa. "Berkley Poll Buoys Mayor and Supporters." *Kansas City Star,* January 6, 1983.

———. "Berkley, Serviss Accused of Making Scandal Political." *Kansas City Star,* February 17, 1983.

———. "Bitterness Marks KC Council Races." *Kansas City Star,* March 3, 1991.

———. "Brisk Contest Developing for 4th District At-Large Post." *Kansas City Star,* February 7, 1983.

———. "Democrats Seek Unity to Defeat Berkley." *Kansas City Star,* February 4, 1983.

———. "Low-key Berkley Has a Fondness for Details." *Kansas City Times,* March 19, 1983.

———. "Wheeler Looks for Warm Welcome Back." *Kansas City Star,* January 5, 1983.

Blakeman, Karen. "Report Clears Coe of Bribery Allegations." *Kansas City Times,* April 17, 1987.

Blankinship, G. L. "Open Letter to Third District Voters ." *Call,* February 26, 1971.

Blue, Louis, Rick E. Abel, and Donna F. Stewart. "Black Votes Help Push Tax to Victory." *Call,* August 5, 1983.

Blue, Louis. "Bloody Week in Kansas City." *Call,* January 19, 1973.

———. "City Election Campaign Heats up Ahead of Time." *Call,* December 8, 1978.

———. "Councilmen Cleaver and Hazley Oppose Sales Tax; Tell Why." *Call,* April 10, 1981.

———. "Defeat of Jim Wilson a Blow to Freedom." *Call,* March 29, 1991.

———. "Desperate to Win, Candidate Resorts to Fraudulent Ballots." *Call,* March 29, 1991.

———. "Five Elected to School Board." *Call,* April 6, 1990.

———. "Freedom Wins Despite Smears." *Call,* August 11, 1972.

———. "Freedom, Inc., Has 12 to 12 Tie Vote on Endorsing Swinton." *Call,* July 11, 1980.

———. "Freedom, Inc., Wins Six Top Demo Party Posts." *Call,* August 29, 1980.

———. "Freedom's Major Thrust Is Reelection of Wheat." *Call,* May 30, 1980.

———. "Freedom's Voter Registration Drive Launched with Speech by Andrew Young at Breakfast." *Call,* September 12, 1980.

———. "It's Congressman Alan Wheat." *Call,* November 5, 1982.

———. "Kansas City Passes Rights Bill." *Call,* April 17, 1964.

———. "Kansas City to Send Two Blacks to Demo Convention for 1st Time." *Call,* May 26, 1972.

———. "Leon Jordan Takes over 14th Ward from Moran." *Call,* August 10, 1962.

———. "Mayor Berkley Appoints Watkins to Parks Board." *Call,* June 13, 1980.

———. "Oust Thompson from Freedom, Inc." *Call,* March 27, 1987.

———. "Primary Brings 'Sweet' Victory to Freedom, Inc." *Call,* August 8, 1980.

———. "Regional HUD Job Pending for Watkins; Will Resign as President Of Freedom." *Call,* June 22, 1979.

———. "Sudden Firing of Police Chief Shocks Blacks, Too." *Call,* February 10, 1978.

——. "Swinton Defeats Mary Gant." *Call,* August 9, 1980.

——. "Why Gwen Wells Voted as She Did, Van Kirk Hearing Didn't Go 'Right.'" *Call,* February 24, 1978.

——. "You Need to Vote." *Call,* March 15, 1991.

Bobo, Lawrence, and Franklin D. Gilliam Jr. "Race, Sociopolitical Participation, and Empowerment." *The American Political Science Review* 84, no. 2 (1990): 377–393.

Bogdon, Tom. "Bland Wants to Reinvigorate Freedom Inc." *eKC,* July 6, 2007.

Bond, Julian. "Practical Politician: Julian Bond." *The Black Politician* 1, no. 2 (1969): 28.

Bridges, Amy. *Morning Glories: Municipal Reform in the Southwest.* Princeton: Princeton University Press, 1997.

Brisbane, Art. "School Fiasco Fallout." *Kansas City Star,* February 15, 1991.

Brisbane, Arthur S. "Watkins Sensed Defeat Early on." *Kansas City Times,* March 28, 1979.

Brown, A. Theodore, and Lyle W. Dorsett. *K.C.: A History of Kansas City, Missouri.* Boulder: Pruett, 1978.

Brown, A. Theodore. *The Politics of Reform: Kansas City's Municipal Government.* Kansas City: Community Studies, Inc., 1958.

Brown, Jim. "Slim Chance for 2nd Negro State Lawmaker." *Call,* July 10, 1964.

——. "Wide Support for Rights Bill." *Call,* February 28, 1964.

Brown, Ronald E., and Carolyn Hartfield. "Black Churches and the Formation of Political Action Committees in Detroit." In *Black Churches and Local Politics: Clergy Influence, Organizational Partnerships, and Civic Empowerment,* edited by R. Drew Smith and Fredrick C. Harris, 151–170. Lanham: Rowman and Littlefield, 2005.

Browning, Rufus P., Dale Rogers Marshall, and David H. Tabb. *Protest Is Not Enough: The Struggle of Blacks and Hispanics for Equality in Urban Politics.* Berkley: University of California Press, 1984.

——. *Racial Politics in American Cities.* New York: Longman, 1990.

——. *Racial Politics in American Cities, Third Edition.* New York: Longman, 2003.

Burgess, M. Elaine. *Negro Leadership in a Southern City.* New Haven: College and University Press, 1961.

Call, "$8,417 Netted from Leon Jordan Dinner," August 24, 1973.

Call, "'Freedom, Inc.' Name of New Political Group," May 4, 1962.

Call, "A.M.E. Ministers Endorse Rev. Cleaver for Mayor," February 8, 1991.

Call, "Ad Hoc Declares War on Drug Houses," September 20, 1985.

Call, "Ad Hoc Group, Southeast Community Organizations, Join to Wage War on Sexual Assaults in the Area," December 30, 1983.

Call, "AME Ministers Endorse Richard Berkley for Mayor," February 18, 1983.

Call, "Another Business Man Tells Why He Supports Lawrence Blankinship," February 5, 1971.

Call, "Are Police Tests Fair?," August 16, 1985.

Call, "Area Director Says Model Cities Program Has 'Fallen Short,'" August 13, 1971.

Call, "Art Fletcher Says Collins Is Needed to Integrate House of Representatives—Where Money Is," July 22, 1976.

Call, "Baptist Union Reaffirms Support of Michael Myers," February 8, 1974.

Call, "Baptists Back Berkley," February 4, 1983.

Call, "Bennett and Cosby Thrill 1,000," May 4, 1973.

Call, "Bernard Powell Says Young People Support Blankinship," February 19, 1971.

Call, "Black Leaders Ask for Federal Probe of Police Department," December 23, 1977.

Call, "Black Leaders in Campaign Against K.C. Star-Times," May 16, 1986.

Call, "Black Leaders Shocked at 90-Day Sentence to Man Beaten by Police," October 31, 1980.

Call, "Blacks Speak for and against Kelley as New FBI Director," June 29, 1973.

Call, "Blacks Vote No on Snow Endorsement," March 7, 1975.

Call, "Blankinship Asks Where Opponent Is," February 19, 1971.

Call, "Blankinship Speaks out Where Its (sic) Counts," March 26, 1971.

Call, "Brookfield Our Choice," March 19, 1971.

Call, "Brookfield, Thomas, and Blankinship," March 26, 1971.

Call, "Bruce R. Watkins Files For State Legislature On Republican Ticket," April 16, 1956.

Call, "Bruce Watkins Files for Top Position in County," May 3, 1974.

Call, "Carol Coe Says Remarks on T.V. Program 'Overblown,'" May 15, 1987.

Call, "Carol Coe Sworn in as County Legislator," February 15, 1985.

Call, "Chicago Politicians to Hear Bruce Watkins, Rep. Holliday," August 24, 1973.

Call, "Citizens Association Will Screen Candidates Next Week," January 3, 1975.

Call, "Citizens Endorse Cofran for Mayor," January 20, 1995.

Call, "Citizens Give Comments on Jordan Scholarship Fund," March 2, 1984.

Call, "City Center Ministers for Watkins," February 21, 1979.

Call, "City Manager Makes Changes in Budget in Response to Citizens," April 13, 1984.

Call, "City Primary Just a Few Days Away," February 26, 1999.

Call, "City to Kick-Off Enterprise Zone Campaign on January 12," January 9, 1987.

Call, "City's Affirmative Action Plan Approved," December 6, 1985.

Call, "City's Black Homicides Decline in 1979; Ad Hoc Group to Continue Efforts," January 25, 1980.

Call, "Civic Groups Gird for Fight," January 17, 1964.

Call, "Cleaver for Mayor," February 22, 1991.

Call, "Cleaver Names Blacks' 'Enemies,'" March 20, 1980.

Call, "Cleaver Reflects on 'Colorful Hands' He Appointed to Boards," December 4, 1998.

Call, "Clint Adams Heads New Political Club," October 27, 1978.

Call, "Coffee Hours for Hazley and Hughes," February 21, 1975.

Call, "Collins Wins over Difficult Odds," March 28, 1975.

Call, "Contractors Ordered to Repay City $86,704," March 15, 1985.

Call, "Council for Urban Peace and Justice Summit in Kansas City," April 30, 1993.

Call, "Council Unanimously Approves Disparity Ordinance that Ensures Fair Participation of Minorities in Bidding," March 15, 1996.

Call, "Councilman Hazley Answers Questions On Bond Election," November 23, 1973.

Call, "Councilman Hazley Files for Re-Election to 3rd District," December 15, 1978.

Call, "Councilman Richard Tolbert Forms New Political Party," February 18, 1972.

Call, "Count Basie and Orchestra to Play at Freedom, Inc. Rally," March 7, 1975.

Call, "Create New City Department to Replace Model Cities," December 14, 1973.

Call, "Detroit's Coleman Young to Kick-Off Watkins Campaign," November 10, 1978.

Call, "Don't Believe Rumors!," March 25, 1983.

Call, "Don't Run for Mayor, Mr. Kelley," February 10, 1978.

Call, "Early Poll Results Say CALL Readers Want Cleaver to Run for Mayor," October 24, 1986.

Call, "Emanuel Cleaver Best Man for Mayor," March 22, 1991.

Call, "Emanuel Cleaver to Run for City Council Seat," December 20, 1974.

Call, "Endorsement," March 8, 1963.

Call, " 'Freedom, Inc.' Name of New Political Group," May 4, 1962.

Call, "Fight over Charter Picking up Steam," March 17, 1989.

Call, "First Independent Push by Negroes Defeated," August 10, 1962.

Call, "Five in Race For City Council Spot," February 1, 1974.

Call, "For Tuesday's Election, Call Endorses," March 21, 1975.

Call, "Freedom Awards Four at Formal Ceremony," July 29, 1989.

Call, "Freedom for Serviss," February 4, 1983.

Call, "Freedom Inc. Criticizes Move to Oust Holliday," May 18, 1984.

Call, "Freedom Not among 34 Violators," September 30, 1983.

Call, "Freedom To Hold Coffees For Candidates," February 26, 1971.

Call, "Freedom, Inc. Backs All Fourteen Bond Proposals,"November 30, 1973.

Call, "Freedom, Inc. Board Tells Why Wheeler Should Be Re-elected," March 21, 1975.

Call, "Freedom, Inc. Censures Councilman Tolbert," February 25, 1972.

Call, "Freedom, Inc. Conducts Christmas Basket Project," December 13, 1974.

Call, "Freedom, Inc. Endorses Waris; Opposed to K.C. Zoo Proposition," July 20, 1990.

Call, "Freedom, Inc. Holds Rally," February 26, 1971.

Call, "Freedom, Inc. Official Says 'No One' Expelled," February 28, 1997.

Call, "Freedom, Inc. to Launch Membership Drive," June 9, 1989.

Call, "Freedom, Inc. to Sponsor Family Fun Festival and Voter Registration Drive," July 2, 1976.

Call, "Freedom, Inc. Volunteers Help to Ready 62,000-Piece Mass Mailing," March 4, 1988.

Call, "Freedom, Inc., Answers Criticism Made by K.C. Star," October 27, 1989.

Call, "Freedom, Inc., Asks for Active Public Interest in South Midtown Freeway," February 13, 1976.

Call, "Freedom, Inc., in Process of Reorganization," November 15, 1996.

Call, "Freedom, Inc., Opposes Sales Tax For Schools," August 15, 1975.

Call, "Freedom, Inc., President Calls Campaign Tactics a Scheme to Divide Community," March 27, 1987.

Call, "Freedom, Inc., Says 'Get Registered Now,'" February 5, 1988.

Call, "Freedom-CCP Beat Factions," August 19, 1968

Call, "Freedom's Future Questioned after Major Losses in Primary," August 10, 1990.

Call, "Freedom's Team Candidates File for City Council Seats," January 31, 1975.

Call, "Gospel Extravaganza for Freedom, Inc., Candidates Sunday," July 9, 1982.

Call, "Group Challenges Freedom Endorsement," July 8, 1994.

Call, "'Grudges Tend to Last' Mayor Says of 'Political' Ouster," March 3, 1978.

Call, "Hazley Home Early For Good Behavior," September 9, 1988.

Call, "Hazley Loses His Chairmanship; Mrs. Joanne Collins," April 13, 1979.

Call, "Hazley to Head Committee," April 16, 1971.

Call, "Hazley to Serve 30 Days at Indiana Prison," August 5, 1988.

Call, "HDCIC President Gives Response to Article Regarding Agency," May 2, 1986.

Call, "Herman Johnson Top Choice of Citizens Assn.," February 15, 1974.

Call, "Holliday in Call for Debate with Watkins," March 15, 1963.

Call, "How the Votes Turned against Chief Van Kirk," February 10, 1978.

Call, "Inner City Property Taxes Too High, Says Freedom Inc," June 21, 1974.

Call, "IRS Seizes Apartment Building of Holliday for Tax Non-Payment," March 2, 1984.

Call, "It's Time for Black Community to Take a Stand behind Watkins," February 2, 1979.

Call, "Jazz Hall Dropping out of 18th And Vine," May 28, 1993.

Call, "Jim Threatt to Continue Handling Federal Grants," May 11, 1984.

Call, "Jobs Program Dispute Settled," June 7, 1985.

Call, "Jordan Awards to 17," May 7, 1971.

Call, "Jury Convicts Anderson," September 26, 1997.

Call, "Kansas City Ministers Endorse Rev. Cleaver," February 1, 1991.

Call, "Kansas City Rioting Ends with 6 Dead: Many Questions on Police Action in Riots," April 19, 1968.

Call, "Kansas City Will Send Three to Legislature," August 14, 1964.

Call, "Keeping up with Watkins," February 21, 1979.

Call, "Lee Swinton Endorsed by Freedom, Inc., for 9th District Senator," July 25, 1980.

Call, "Lee V. Swinton Named to Parks Board by Berkley," May 4, 1979.

Call, "Lines Drawn for Political Battle," July 3, 1964.

Call, "Many Groups Hear Joanne Collins during Campaign," March 21, 1975.

Call, "Mark Bryant Election No.1 Priority March 29," March 18, 1983.

Call, "Mary Groves Bland New President of Freedom," June 20, 1997.

Call, "Massive Voter Drive Saturday," July 10, 1992.

Call, "Mayor Cleaver Responds to Events at 27th and Benton," June 7, 1996.

Call, "Mayor Richard Berkley Should Be Reelected," March 27, 1987.

Call, "Mayor Takes Tour of Inner City Ghetto," January 26, 1973.

Call, "Mayor Tussle—But Not Hard—With Real Bear," January 28, 1972.

Call, "Mayor Wheeler Has the Edge," February 21, 1975.

Call, "McGee, Coe to Make Plea for Unity," August 5, 1988.

Call, "Minority Councilmen Filibuster Job Training Program Vote," May 17, 1985.

Call, "Model Cities Ready for Third Year, Has Budget of 8 Million," September 10, 1971.

Call, "Mrs. Fannie Meek Speaks out against Tactics Used against Councilman Larry Blankinship," March 26, 1971.

Call, "NAACP Says Figures Show City Discriminates against Women and Minority Groups," December 19, 1975.

Call, "Naming of Black Deputy City Manager Causes Stir," June 11, 1971.

Call, "Negro Leagues Baseball Museum to Stadium," October 15, 1993.

Call, "Negro Voters Cannot Desert Bolling," April 10, 1964.

Call, "Negroes Unopposed in Third," February 8, 1963.

Call, "Neighborhood Coalition Opposes Continuation of Mid-Town Freeway," March 12, 1976.

Call, "New Mayor Would Be Wise to Keep Chairman Hazley," April 6, 1979.

Call, "New Program Helps Families Buy Houses," July 31, 1987.

Call, "'No Tent' City Goes up Sunday," July 21, 1972.

Call, "Over 500 Attend Freedom, Inc. Gala," September 25, 1987.

Call, "Phil Curls Wins State Senate Seat," December 23, 1983.

Call, "Plans and Zoning Committee Approves Lakeview II," March 21, 1986.

Call, "Police Dept. Reports Shortage of Blacks," July 18, 1971.

Call, "Police Say Efforts Lower Crime in '93," February 4, 1994.

Call, "Political Climate Getting 'Hot,'" July 27, 1978.

Call, "Press Conference on K.C. Star Friday Noon at 18th and Grand," May 23, 1986.

Call, "Public Hearing Likely in James Case," February 11, 1972.

Call, "Remarks Attributed to Carol Coe 'Talk of Town,'" February 15, 1985.

Call, "Rev. Charles Briscoe Predicts G.L. Blankinship Re-election," February 12, 1971.

Call, "Riley Wins 43rd District State Representative Special Election," April 9, 1999.

Call, "Robinson Pleads Guilty, Resigns," September 13, 1996.

Call, "Says Blankinship Will Win Support of Black Community," January 29, 1971.

Call, "Senate Okays Chief 96 to 0," June 29, 1973.

Call, "Senator Phil Curls New President of Freedom," August 31, 1990.

Call, "Set for Fight over Council Seat," January 22, 1971.

Call, "Swinton Pleads Guilty; Resigns from Missouri Senate; Gets Probation," October 21, 1983.

Call, "Tenants Pleased with Receivership," July 16, 1993.

Call, "The Council Seat Vacancy," March 1, 1974.

Call, "The Mayor Should Make Clear What He Says and Means," September 27, 1991.

Call, "Third District Race 'Hottest' One in Town," March 19, 1971.

Call, "Three Groups Endorse Mrs. Joanne Collins," February 8, 1974.

Call, "Time for Answers," November 25, 1983.

Call, "Tindall Now President of Freedom," March 11, 1994.

Call, "Tolbert Defies Council, Ignores Council Session," March 3, 1972.

Call, "Tolbert Gains Community Support through Friends," September 14, 1973.

Call, "Tolbert Gets No Support on Resolution Calling for Own Impeachment," March 31, 1972.

Call, "Tolbert in Squabble over City Car," July 13, 1973.

Call, "Tolbert to Run for Mayor," June 8, 1973.

Call, "Vaughn Withdraws from Manager's Race," November 5, 1993.

Call, "Vernon Thompson Wins by 40 Votes in Squeaker over Bruce Watkins Jr.," August 8, 1986.

Call, "Voters Felt Cleaver Was Obvious Choice," March 2, 1979.

Call, "Voters Say No to Odyssey 2000," August 6, 1993.

Call, "Watkins Charges 'Racism,'" February 26, 1971.

Call, "Watkins Enters Mayor Race," August 25, 1978.

Call, "Watkins Heads Reorganized Freedom, Inc.," August 25, 1978.

Call, "Watkins Named Coordinator of Freedom," 1994.

Call, "Watkins out of Senate Race in Favor of Johnson," June 23, 1972.

Call, "Watkins Pleads Guilty in Fund Theft; Repays $15,000," October 9, 1987.

Call, "Watkins Steps down," September 12, 1975.

Call, "Watkins Takes Scholarship Reins," December 2, 1983.

Call, "Watkins to Oppose Kelley Nomination," June 15, 1973.

Call, "Watkins to Testify on Monday against Kelley," June 22, 1973.

Call, "Wheeler and Freedom Win City Election," April 2, 1971.

Call, "Wheeler Blasts Tax Opponents; Watkins, McDonough Return Fire," November 18, 1977.

Call, "Wheeler for Mayor," March 25, 1983.

Call, "Will 18th And Vine Fly?," March 19, 1993.

Call, "Women of Freedom, Inc. Call for 'Doc' to Resign," August 11, 1978.

Call, "Young Freedom Sponsors Civic Movement Drive," January 14, 1972.

Call, "Youth Group of Freedom, Inc., Formed; To Learn Government Principles & Procedures," March 27, 1980.

Campbell, Matt, Mike Rice, and Benita Y. Williams. "Glover Heads back to Council, Nace Easily Overcomes Challenger Fields." *Kansas City Star,* March 26, 2003.

Campbell, Matt. "Freedom Chastised for Choice." *Kansas City Star,* July 6, 1994.

———. "Williams-Neal, Coe Face Rematch." *Kansas City Star,* February 18, 1999.

Cannato, Vincent J. *The Ungovernable City: John Lindsay and His Struggle to Save New York.* New York: Basic Books, 2001.

Carmichael, Stokely, and Charles V. Hamilton. *Black Power: The Politics of Liberation in America.* New York: Vintage Books, 1967.

Carroll, Robert L. "8 Keep Seats on Council." *Kansas City Times,* March 28, 1979.

———. "9 Vote Margin on City Center; 3 Others Pass." *Kansas City Times,* December 19, 1973.

———. "Mondale's Visit Spurs Barb about Potholes." *Kansas City Times,* March 22, 1979.

———. "Myers Serving Probation." *Kansas City Star,* February 26, 1974.

———. "Ten Bond Proposals Fail a Second Time." *Kansas City Times,* April 3, 1974.

———. "Wheeler Asserts Issues Lacking." *Kansas City Times,* January 4, 1975.

Cigler, Allan J., and Burdett A. Loomis. *Interest Group Politics, Seventh Edition.* Washington: CQ Press, 2007.

Citizens for a Fair Campaign. *Citizens for a Fair Campaign.* Paid political advertisement, 1978.

Clay, William L. *Just Permanent Interests: Black Americans in Congress, 1870–1991*. New York: Amistad Press, 1992.

Clayton, Merle. *Union Station Massacre: The Shootout that Started the FBI's War on Crime*. Indianapolis: Bobbs-Merrill, 1975.

Cleaver for Mayor Campaign. *You've Got To Believe!* Paid political advertisement, 1991.

Coleman, Richard P. *The Kansas City Establishment: Leadership through Two Centuries in a Midwestern Metropolis*. Manhattan: KS Publishing, 2006.

Coleman, Richard P., and Bernice L. Neugarten. *Social Status in the City*. San Francisco: Jossey-Bass, 1971.

Committee to Elect Carol Coe. *Strong Black Women Keep on Coming*. Paid political advertisement, 1991.

Committee to Re-Elect Orchid Jordan. *An Open Letter To The Community*. Paid political advertisement, 1978.

Connolly, Martin, and Kevin Q. Murphy. "Mayor Vacations with Free Tickets." *Kansas City Star,* February 2, 1991.

Conway, M. Margaret. "Voter Information Sources in a Nonpartisan Local Election." *Western Political Quarterly* 21, no. 1 (1968): 69–77.

Coulter, Charles E. *Take Up the Black Man's Burden: Kansas City's African American Communities, 1865–1939*. Columbia: University of Missouri Press, 2006.

Crockett, David. "Family Fun Festival Registers 490 Voters." *Call,* July 9, 1976.

Curls, Sr., Phil B. "The Empty Bag Cannot Stand up." *Call,* February 28, 1997.

Dahl, Robert A. *Who Governs? Democracy and Power in an American City*. New Haven: Yale University Press, 1961.

Daniel, Lloyd. "Why I Got Kicked out of Freedom, Inc. or Breaking the Conspiracy of Silence." *Call,* February 28, 1997.

Dauner, John T. "Cleaver Says Foe Used Racist Handbills." *Kansas City Times,* March 28, 1979.

———. "Council Vacancy Delay." *Kansas City Times,* March 2, 1974.

———. "Democrats, Freedom, Inc. Join Forces." *Kansas City Times,* January 21, 1975.

———. "Drops At-Large Bid: Watkins to Seek 5th-District Seat." *Kansas City Times,* January 11, 1975.

———. "Freedom Backs Wheeler." *Kansas City Times,* February 19, 1971.

———. "New Housing Step Seen." *Kansas City Times,* April 13, 1968.

———. "Wheeler Wins, Capra out; Watkins, 3 New Faces in." *Kansas City Times*, March 26, 1975.

———. "Wheeler, Brookfield Square off again." *Kansas City Times*, March 5, 1971.

———. "Wheeler, Mrs. Snow Win; Bonds Defeated by .5%." *Kansas City Times*, February 26, 1975.

Davidson, Chandler, and Luis Ricardo Fraga. "Slating Groups as Parties in a 'Nonpartisan' Setting." *Western Political Quarterly* 41, no. 2 (1988): 373–390.

Davidson, Chandler. *Biracial Politics: Conflict and Coalition in the Metropolitan South*. Baton Rouge: Louisiana State University Press, 1972.

Dawson, Michael C. *Behind the Mule: Race and Class in African-American Politics*. Princeton: Princeton University Press, 1994.

———. *Black Visions: The Roots of Contemporary African-American Political Ideologies*. Chicago: University of Chicago Press, 2001.

Diuguid, Lewis W. "Inner-city Black Ministers Meet over Endorsements." *Kansas City Times*, February 24, 1983.

Diuguid, Lewis W., and Mark Schlinkmann. "Swinton Is Charged with Stealing." *Kansas City Times*, March 23, 1983.

Dorsett, Lyle. *The Pendergast Machine*. New York: Oxford University Press, 1968.

Dvorak, John A. "Berkley Wins Decisive Victory." *Kansas City Times*, March 28, 1979.

———. "Berkley, Serviss and Wheeler Snap up Public Works Football." *Kansas City Times*, February 3, 1983.

———. "Mayoral Candidates Vie for Endorsement of Freedom, Inc." *Kansas City Times*, January 28, 1983.

———. "Mayor's Role the Top Issue in Citizens Interviews." *Kansas City Times*, January 11, 1975.

———. "Packed Field for Mayor Leads Spirited Primary." *Kansas City Times*, February 27, 1979.

Dvorak, John A., and Michael Yabonski. "Veteran Councilman, Young Lawyer Square off in 5th District." *Kansas City Times*, February 25, 1983.

Dye, Robert M. "Watkins Charges Funds Offered for Black Vote." *Kansas City Times*, March 27, 1971.

———. "Wheeler Dodges Debate, Tags Citizens as G.O.P." *Kansas City Times*, March 19, 1971.

Earle, Susan. *Aaron Douglas: African American Modernist.* New Haven: Yale University Press, 2007.

Edmondson, C. E. "Goals of Model Cities: Part II." *Call,* January 22, 1976.

———. "Model Cities Program: The War On Poverty." *Call,* January 9, 1976.

Edwards, Shawn. "Former Councilman Promises a New Freedom Inc." *The Pitch,* March 30, 2000.

Fancher, Mike. "Fifth District Has Option." *Kansas City Times,* March 23, 1971.

Farney, Dennis. "Good Marks Given the Outgoing Mayor." *Kansas City Star,* March 13, 1971.

Farnsworth, Steve. "Cleaver's Plan Is Expanded, Wins." *Kansas City Times,* November 23, 1989.

———. "Council Pays All Legal Fees of ACLU in TV Case." *Kansas City Times,* September 29, 1989.

———. "KC Abandons Effort to Keep Klan Off TV." *Kansas City Times,* July 14, 1989.

Federal Bureau of Investigation. "Crime reported by Kansas City Police Department, Missouri." *Uniform Crime Reporting Statistics.* Washington: Federal Bureau of Investigation, 2010.

Federal Election Commission. *Freedom Inc. Pays $45,000 Penalty For Failing To Register As Political Committee.* Washington: Federal Election Commission, 2006.

Ferguson, John T. "Guilt Trip." *Kansas City Star,* March 2, 1991.

Firestone, David. "Why Berkley Won and Watkins Lost." *Kansas City Star,* March 28, 1979.

Fitzpatrick, James C. "Abolish KC's At-Large Districts? Some See Big Problem in Idea." *Kansas City Star,* January 1, 1991.

———. "AFL-CIO Endorses Cleaver." *Kansas City Star,* March 15, 1991.

———. "Berkley Routs Heeter for Third Term." *Kansas City Times,* April 1, 1987.

———. "Berkley Sails along as Heeter Hits Choppy Seas." *Kansas City Times,* January 31, 1987.

———. "Brice Harris Eager to Win KC's Top Job." *Kansas City Star,* February 20, 1991.

———. "Brownfield Explains Council Vote." *Kansas City Times,* March 12, 1974.

———. "Businessman's Donations Fueling Heeter Campaign." *Kansas City Times,* March 24, 1987.

———. "Candidates Add Endorsements." *Kansas City Star,* March 12, 1991.

———. "Candidates Hone Attack as Election Nears." *Kansas City Star,* March 24, 1979.

———. "Candidates Spar over Gay Rights." *Kansas City Star,* March 24, 1991.

———. "Chances of Write-in Campaign by Hazley Seem to Be Fading." *Kansas City Star,* January 4, 1991.

———. "Charter Plan Not on Ballot." *Kansas City Star,* January 25, 1991.

———. "Citizens Board Backs Berkley for Third Term." *Kansas City Times,* January 16, 1987.

———. "Citizens Endorse Berkley Despite Move by Heeter." *Kansas City Times,* January 23, 1987.

———. "Cleaver Stands Clear as Other Candidates Slug away." *Kansas City Star,* January 12, 1991.

———. "Cleaver Wins Allies of Foe to His Side." *Kansas City Star,* March 16, 1991.

———. "Cleaver's Low-Key Campaign Puzzles Foes King, Harris." *Kansas City Star,* February 2, 1991.

———. "Coe's Presence on Slate Hinders Cleaver." *Kansas City Star,* January 22, 1991.

———. "Contests in KC for Mayor, Council Could Be Spirited." *Kansas City Star,* January 1, 1995.

———. "For Harris, King, Losing Mayor's Race Was Costly." *Kansas City Star,* March 29, 1991.

———. "Freedom Inc. Endorses Berkley over Heeter in Mayor's Contest." *Kansas City Times,* January 30, 1987.

———. "Freedom Inc. May Follow Lead Set by Cleaver." *Kansas City Times,* January 8, 1987.

———. "Harris, King Back Their Ads." *Kansas City Star,* February 23, 1991.

———. "Heeters Bid Savings on Campaign." *Kansas City Times,* January 13, 1987.

———. "KC Margin Is Biggest since 1967." *Kansas City Times,* March 4, 1987.

———. "KC Voters Trounce Proposition 4." *Kansas City Times,* April 5, 1989.

———. "King Became a Contender Years Ago." *Kansas City Star,* February 21, 1991.

———. "King Leads Harris and Cleaver in Raising Cash for Mayor's Race." *Kansas City Star,* January 19, 1991.

———. "Mayoral Race Attracts Money." *Kansas City Star,* February 22, 1991.

———. "No More Mr. Nice Guy for Mayoral Foes as Race Takes off." *Kansas City Star,* February 6, 1991.

———. "No Party Disfavor Likely for Democratic 'Strays.'" *Kansas City Times,* March 23, 1979.

———. "Opinions Changed Quickly." *Kansas City Times,* April 5, 1989.

———. "Report Will Show that Berkley Raised $102,916, Spent $98,480." *Kansas City Times,* January 23, 1987.

———. "Seven City Council Members Endorse Berkley." *Kansas City Times,* March 28, 1987.

———. "Steve Penn: A Horrible Way to Pack up Your Pencils." *JimmyCsays: At the Juncture of Journalism and Daily Life in Kansas City.* July 13, 2011. http://jimmycsays.com/2011/07/13/steve-penn-a-horrible-way-to-pack-up-your-pencils/.

———. "Vaughn Pulls out of Race." *Kansas City Star,* October 30, 1993.

Fox, Jeanne A. "In Kansas City, Missouri Economic Development Plays Catch-Up to Political Clout." *Black Enterprise,* March, 1978.

Francis Jr., William V. "Mrs. Snow Overcame Lack of Backing, Funds." *Kansas City Times,* February 26, 1975.

Freedom, Inc. *Freedom, Inc.—10 Years of Progress.* Paid political advertisement, 1972.

———. *Freedom, Inc.—Please Vote!* Paid political advertisement, 1996.

———. *Freedom, Inc.—Support the Bridge That Brought Us Across.* Paid political advertisement, 1991.

———. *Men Who Care.* Paid political advertisement, 1971.

———. *Vote the Freedom, Inc. Democratic Ballot.* Paid Political Advertisement, 1971.

———. *We Support Harold Holliday Sr.* Paid political advertisement, 1978.

———. *Your Freedom, Inc. Community Team.* Paid political advertisement, 1979.

Frieden, Bernard J., and Marshall Kaplan. *The Politics of Neglect: Urban Aid from Model Cities to Revenue Sharing.* Cambridge: MIT Press, 1977.

Gillespie, Andra, and Emma Tolbert. "Racial Authenticity and Redistricting: A Comparison of Artur Davis's 2000 and 2002 Congressional Campaigns." In *Whose Black Politics? Cases in Post-Racial Black Leadership,* edited by Andra Gillespie, 45–66. New York: Routledge, 2010.

Gillis, Delia. *Kansas City.* Charleston: Acadia, 2007.

Glorioso, Steven A. "Fight Against the Factions: The 1964 and 1966 Democratic Primaries." Master's thesis, University of Missouri-Kansas City, 1974.

Gold, Henry C. "Bolling Victory Easy: Gets Negro Aid." *Kansas City Times,* August 5., 1964.

Goldstein, David. "Bruce Watkins Jr. Is Indicted in Theft." *Kansas City Times,* April 25, 1987.

———. "Issues Fail to Divide 5th District Candidates." *Kansas City Star,* March 14, 1991.

Gordon, Laura. "Cleaver Makes It Official." *Call,* November 16, 1990.

Gotham, Kevin Fox. "Political Opportunity, Community Identity, and the Emergence of a Local Anti-Expressway Movement." *Social Problems* 46, no. 3 (1999): 332–354.

———. *Race, Real Estate, and Uneven Development.* Albany: State University of New York Press, 2002.

Graves, William R. "Citizens Name 2 for Council." *Kansas City Times,* December 8, 1966.

———. "Citizens Plan All-Out Drive." *Kansas City Times,* February 6, 1967.

———. "Close Race Bill Victory." *Kansas City Times,* April 8, 1964.

———. "Council Reins Won by Citizens." *Kansas City Times,* March 27, 1963.

———. "Davis, Brookfield Win." *Kansas City Times,* February 27, 1963.

———. "O.K. 6–6 by Nearly 4–1." *Kansas City Times,* March 7, 1962.

———. "Ten Citizens Candidates Elected." *Kansas City Times,* March 29, 1967.

Graves, William R., and John T. Dauner. "Back Brookfield." *Kansas City Times,* January 8, 1971.

Gray, Kenneth E. *A Report on Politics in Kansas City, Missouri.* Cambridge: Joint Center for Urban Studies, 1959.

Greene, Lorenzo J., Gary R. Kremer, and Antonio F. Holland. *Missouri's Black Heritage, Revised Edition.* Columbia: University of Missouri Press, 1993.

Gupta, Himanee. "Freedom Offshoot Backs Heeter." *Kansas City Star,* January 18, 1987.

Hadley, Charles D. "The Transformation of the Role of Black Ministers and Black Political Organizations in Louisiana Politics." In *Blacks and Southern Politics,* edited by Laurence W. Moreland, Robert P. Steed, and Tod A. Baker, 133–148. New York: Praeger, 1987.

Hadrick, Celeste. "Ministers Insist Berkley Is Their Choice." *Kansas City Star,* March 17, 1983.

Hajnal, Zoltan L. "White Residents, Black Incumbents, and a Declining Racial Divide." *The American Political Science Review* 95, no. 3 (2001): 603–617.

Hammer, Charles. "Davis Dispels Fair Housing Fear." *Kansas City Star,* April 7, 1967.

———. "Rights Leader Hits Police Tactics." *Kansas City Times,* April 10, 1968.

———. "Varied Ballot after Primary." *Kansas City Star,* March 5, 1967.

Handy, Doris. "'Other Side of Tracks' Now 'Other Side of Freeway.'" *Call,* February 20, 1976.

Hart, Amy. "The Founding of Freedom: A Kansas City Civil Rights Organization Since 1962." Master's thesis, Central Missouri State University, 2006.

Hayes, David. "Coe to Be Investigated on Bribery Allegation." *Kansas City Times,* February 18, 1987.

Heaney, Michael T. "Identity Crisis: How Interest Groups Struggle to Define Themselves in Washington." In *Interest Group Politics, Seventh Edition,* edited by Allan J. Cigler and Burdett C. Loomis, 279–300. Washington: CQ Press, 2007.

Holloway, Harry. "Negro Political Strategy: Coalition or Independent Power Politics." *Social Science Quarterly* 49 (1968): 534–547.

Hood, Rich, and Barbara Shelly. "Cash Buys Love in KC Politics." *Kansas City Star,* March 15, 1987.

Hood, Rich, and Melissa Berg. "Trade-offs Mark City Election Endorsements." *Kansas City Star,* February 9, 1983.

Hood, Rich. "13 Ministers Back Freedom Inc." *Kansas City Star,* March 16, 1983.

———. "Black Ministers' Group Reportedly Shifts Stance." *Kansas City Star,* March 22, 1983.

———. "Blandness Seen as a Plus for Berkley." *Kansas City Star,* January 18, 1987.

———. "Donations to Heeter Criticized." *Kansas City Star,* March 24, 1987.

———. "Party Leaders Endorse Heeter's Mayoral Bid." *Kansas City Star,* January 21, 1987.

———. "Publicity from Events Part of Candidate's Plan." *Kansas City Star,* January 15, 1987.

Howard, V.P. "Black Leaders Rally against Daily Paper." *Call,* May 30, 1986.

Hughes III, Leonard S. *Fulfill The Dream Of Leon Jordan Youth In Politics.* Paid political advertisement, 1978.

———. *Fulfill The Dream Of Leon Jordan.* Paid political advertisement, 1978.

Hughes, Mamie. "Mamie Hughes Writes an Open Letter to the Black Community." *Call,* March 14, 1975.

Hunter, Floyd. *Community Power Structure: A Study of Decision Makers.* Chapel Hill: University of North Carolina Press, 1953.

———. *Community Power Succession: Atlanta's Policy-Makers Revisited.* Chapel Hill: University of North Carolina Press, 1980.

Hyra, Derek S. "City Politics and Black Protest: The Economic Transformation of Harlem and Bronzeville." *Souls* 8, no. 3 (2006): 176–196.

Jacoby, Tamar. *Someone Else's House: America's Unfinished Struggle for Integration.* New York: Basic Books, 1998.

Jeffers Jr., Gromer. "With a Chat and Hug, Hard Feelings Vanish." *Kansas City Star,* February 14, 1999.

———. "A Divisive History Haunts Carol Coe, Freedom Inc." *Kansas City Star,* July 30, 1995.

———. "Ellis Focuses on Executive Experience." *Kansas City Star,* February 18, 1999.

———. "Ellis Wins Freedom Inc. Endorsement." *Kansas City Star,* January 29, 1999.

———. "Freedom Political Club Elects State Lawmaker." *Kansas City Star,* June 20, 1997.

———. "Freedom Searches for Chief, Direction." *Kansas City Star,* November 10, 1996.

———. "Leader Leaves Legislature in Uncertainty." *Kansas City Star,* September 29, 1996.

———. "Race for Mayor Puts Freedom on the Spot." *Kansas City Star,* January 20, 1999.

Jennings, James, and Mel King. *From Access to Power: Black Politics in Boston.* Cambridge: Schenkman Books, 1986.

Jennings, James. *Blacks, Latinos, and Asians in Urban America: Status and Prospects for Politics and Activism.* Westport: Praeger, 1994.

———. *The Politics of Black Empowerment: The Transformation of Black Activism in Urban America.* Detroit: Wayne State University Press, 1992.

Johnson, Allie. "Hughes Blues." *The Pitch,* February 13, 2003.

Jones Jr., Harry. "A Dilemma in Council Plans." *Kansas City Star,* December 24, 1961.

——. "Citizens Back Bruce Watkins." *Kansas City Times,* March 5, 1963.

——. "Doubts Panthers Understand Marxism." *Kansas City Times,* March 5, 1970.

——. "Kansas Citian Defends Panther Tie." *Kansas City Times,* March 5, 1970.

——. "Panther Rise Linked to Ills." *Kansas City Times,* March 7, 1970.

——. "Sad, Stunned by Loss." *Kansas City Star,* August 3, 1966.

——. "Step up Drives in Rights Vote." *Kansas City Star,* March 18, 1964.

——. "Third District Races Pit Youth vs. Experience." *Kansas City Star,* February 25, 1971.

——. "Vote Fight Looms in a Council Shift." *Kansas City Star,* November 12, 1961.

——. "Votes Realign Base of Power." *Kansas City Star,* March 27, 1963.

Jones, Mack H. "Politics and Organizational Options: Comments on Essay VI: 'The Next Five Years: II. Organizational Options." *National Political Science Review* 8 (2001): 50–57.

Judge, Lee. "Editorial Cartoon." *Kansas City Star,* February 13, 1983.

Kansas City Citizens Council. *Don't Be an April Fool!* Paid political advertisement, 1968.

Kansas City Star Magazine, "In Search of the Real Carol Coe," May 15, 1988.

Kansas City Star, "A Heavy Vote on Racial Law," April 7, 1964.

Kansas City Star, "A Racial Fear on Home Plan," December 6, 1966.

Kansas City Star, "An All-Out Effort by Tavern Owners," March 30, 1964.

Kansas City Star, "Ask No by Voters on Bias Ordinance," March 11, 1964.

Kansas City Star, "Baptist Ministers Group Backs Mayor Berkley," February 2, 1983.

Kansas City Star, "Blankinship Blasts 'Bossism' in City," March 29, 1971.

Kansas City Star, "Blankinship Cites Record of Projects," February 5, 1971.

Kansas City Star, "Bohannon View on Slaying," July 15, 1970.

Kansas City Star, "Both Parties for Rights Law," April 2, 1964.

Kansas City Star, "Both Sides Offer Rights Bill Views," April 3, 1964.

Kansas City Star, "Brookfield Replies to Watkins Charge," March 28, 1971.

Kansas City Star, "Bruce Watkins Dies after Long battle with Cancer," September 14, 1980.

Kansas City Star, "Call Support to Brookfield," March 15, 1963.

Kansas City Star, "Charles Hazely (sic) Files for Council Seat," January 19, 1971.

Kansas City Star, "Charles Wheeler Still Cares about People," February 25, 1979.

Kansas City Star, "Citizens Headquarters," February 16, 1971.

Kansas City Star, "Citizens List 3 for Council," February 10, 1974.

Kansas City Star, "Cleaver Favors Watkins," March 4, 1975.

Kansas City Star, "Cleaver for Mayor," March 20, 1991.

Kansas City Star, "Cleaver on the Outside, Looking in," April 9, 1975.

Kansas City Star, "Favor Racial Move in Poll," March 11, 1964.

Kansas City Star, "Fiscal Acumen Makes Mark Funkhouser the Best Choice for KC Mayor," March 22, 2007.

Kansas City Star, "Freedom Inc. Backs Cleaver for Mayor," January 18, 1991.

Kansas City Star, "Freedom Inc. Makes a Foolish Threat," October 19, 1989.

Kansas City Star, "Freedom Will Try again on Bonds," March 11, 1974.

Kansas City Star, "Freedom, Inc. Pressure Denied," February 5, 1975.

Kansas City Star, "Funkhouser Is the Best Choice for KC Mayor," February 11, 2007.

Kansas City Star, "Giant Step for Kansas City," March 29, 1991.

Kansas City Star, "Happy to Receive Wagner's Support," February 22, 1963.

Kansas City Star, "Heeter Gets Backing from Some Lawmakers," March 15, 1987.

Kansas City Star, "Holliday Denies Faction Control," March 7, 1963.

Kansas City Star, "Hunt for 3 Killers," July 15, 1970.

Kansas City Star, "Kansas City's Reputation on Civil Rights," March 26, 1964.

Kansas City Star, "Mayor and Councilmen for the Hard City Job," March 22, 1963.

Kansas City Star, "Mayor Charles B. Wheeler,Jr., for Another Four Years," March 18, 1975.

Kansas City Star, "Politics Bid in City Districts," November 14, 1961.

Kansas City Star, "Registration for April 7 Election Close to 187,000," March 11, 1964.

Kansas City Star, "Shute Resigns as CBAR Head," November 24, 1961.

Kansas City Star, "Suit on Secret Meeting," February 18, 1974.

Kansas City Star, "Take 2 Whites in Sniper Area," April 12, 1968.

Kansas City Star, "The Candidates Debate," March 25, 1979.

Kansas City Star, "The District Candidates for The City Council," February 26, 1971.

Kansas City Star, "The Election Results by Wards," March 27, 1963.

Kansas City Star, "The Factions Are A Major Issue In This City Campaign," March 26, 1971.

Kansas City Star, "The Men Who Want to Lead KC: Their Views and Goals for the Future," February 6, 1983.

Kansas City Star, "The Moral and Economic Issues of Public Accommodations," March 19, 1964.

Kansas City Star, "The Six At-Large Council Races," March 17, 1975.

Kansas City Star, "The Star's Recommendations in Tuesday's Election," March 26, 1979.

Kansas City Star, "Third District to Place Two Negroes on Council," February 6, 1963.

Kansas City Star, "Watkins Charges Ties with Wagner," March 6, 1963.

Kansas City Star, "Youths in March Here," April 9, 1967

Kansas City Times, "A Hard Fight on Mrs. Hagan," February 17, 1967.

Kansas City Times, "Apart on Role of Mrs. Hagan," February 14, 1967.

Kansas City Times, "Blankinship Enters Race," January 29, 1971.

Kansas City Times, "Citizens Endorsed by Freedom Inc.," March 14, 1963.

Kansas City Times, "Civil Rights Stand Recalled by Davis," February 5, 1963.

Kansas City Times, "Davis Asks OK on Rights Bill," March 10, 1964.

Kansas City Times, "Disorder in City Wanes," April 10, 1968.

Kansas City Times, "Election Endorsements," March 31, 1987.

Kansas City Times, "Few Breaks in Calm," April 12, 1968.

Kansas City Times, "For 5th District," March 23, 1983.

Kansas City Times, "Freedom, Inc. President Scolds Council Candidate," March 9, 1963.

Kansas City Times, "Guard in City Numbers 2,200," April 10, 1968.

Kansas City Times, "Jackson County Election Results," August 3, 1966.

Kansas City Times, "Labor Council to Rights Bill," March 11, 1964.

Kansas City Times, "Mayoral Vote by Ward," March 28, 1979.

Kansas City Times, "Moved by Tragedy," April 5, 1968.

Kansas City Times, "Named to Head Race Campaign," March 5, 1964.

Kansas City Times, "Order in City, Curfew Lifted," April 15, 1968.

Kansas City Times, "Poll Shows Bruce Watkins in Lead," February 20, 1975.

Kansas City Times, "Polluting an Election," March 26, 1987.

Kansas City Times, "Rights Bill Given Citizens Support," March 13, 1964.

Kansas City Times, "Rival Council Plans Offered," November 15, 1961.

Kansas City Times, "Tavern Men Wage Their Own Battle," March 2, 1964.

Kansas City Times, "Test Case Blamed in Disorder," April 10, 1968.

Kansas City Times, "The At-Large Candidates for the City Council," February 26, 1971.

Kansas City Times, "The City Vote," February 27, 1963.

Kansas City Times, "The Heeter Campaign," March 31, 1987.

Kansas City Times, "The Six District Races for the Kansas City Council," March 15, 1975.

Kansas City Times, "Unofficial Ward Totals in Mayoral, Council Races," March 26, 1975.

Kansas City Times, "Urban Renewal Funds Sought," March 24, 1967.

Kansas City Times, "Urge Approval of Racial Bill," April 6, 1964.

Kansas City Times, "Watkins Charges Ties with Wagner," March 6, 1963.

Kansas City Times. "Voting Reform Plan Advances," November 14, 1961.

Kansas City Times, "Watkins Cites Black Needs," December 8, 1970.

Kansas City, Missouri Mayor's Commission on Civil Disorder. "Final Report." Kansas City, 1968.

Kaufmann, Karen M. "Black and Latino Voters in Denver: Responses to Each Other's Political Leadership." *Political Science Quarterly* 118, no. 1 (2003): 107–125.

———. *The Urban Voter: Group Conflict & Mayoral Voting Behavior in American Cities.* Ann Arbor: University of Michigan Press, 2004.

Keiser, Richard A. *Subordination or Empowerment? African-American Leadership and the Struggle for Urban Political Power.* New York: Oxford University Press, 1997.

Keiser, Richard A., and Katherine Underwood. *Minority Politics at the Millennium.* New York: Garland Publishing, 2000.

Kelley, Michael J. "C.C.P. Unhurt by Ticket Splitting." *Kansas City Times,* November 6, 1968.

———. "Curry Slate Sweeps 8 Offices." *Kansas City Times,* August 3, 1966.

———. "Factions Shun City Elections." *Kansas City Times,* February 2, 1967.

———. "Heat Builds in Council Race." *Kansas City Star,* March 15, 1967.

———. "Wide Contrast in 3rd District." *Kansas City Times,* March 24, 1967.

Kelsay, Michael P. "Uneven Patchwork: Tax Increment Financing in Kansas City." Kansas City: ReclaimDemocracy.org, 2007.

Kerbo, Harold R., and L. Richard Della Fave. "The Empirical Side of the Power Elite Debate: An Assessment and Critique of Recent Research." *The Sociological Quarterly* 20, no. 1(1979): 5–22.

Kiewit, Fred. "Riot Tempo Mounted Quickly." *Kansas City Star,* April 14, 1968.

Klinkner, Philip A., and Rogers M. Smith. *The Unsteady March: The Rise and Decline of Racial Equality in America.* Chicago: University of Chicago Press, 1999.

Koppe, George. "Citizens Screen Four from 3rd District." *Kansas City Times,* January 9, 1975.

Kraske, Steve. "Kansas City Needs a Strong-Mayor System of Government." *Kansas City Star,* March 12, 2011.

———. "City Gets Back on Landslide Track." *Kansas City Star,* April 6, 1999.

———. "Freedom Inc. Administrators Fined for Mishandling Finances." *Kansas City Star,* March 4, 2012.

———. "Mayoral Race Rests on Neighborhood Blocs." *Kansas City Star,* March 14, 1999.

———. "Northland Displays Its Expanding Political Influence." *Kansas City Star,* April 1, 1999.

Kuhnhenn, James. "Berkley Makes Choices with Harmony in Mind." *Kansas City Times,* April 11, 1987.

———. "Eight Return, 4 New Faces Join Council." *Kansas City Times,* April 1, 1987.

———. "Serviss Decision Not to Run Shows Clubs' Clout." *Kansas City Times,* January 31, 1987.

Lahey, Kate. "Freedom, Inc. Tactics Hit." *Kansas City Star,* February 2, 1975.

———. "Mayor Alleges Political Trade." *Kansas City Star,* January 5, 1975.

———. "Mayoral Hopefuls Value Aid of Factions in Close Vote." *Kansas City Star,* January 13, 1975.

———. "Third Ballot Ends Tension, Fills Vacant Council Seat." *Kansas City Star,* March 10, 1974.

———. "Wait-and-See Donors Expected to Aid Snow." *Kansas City Star,* March 9, 1975.

Larsen, Lawrence H. and Nancy J. Hulston. *Pendergast!* Columbia: University of Missouri Press, 1997.

Lastelic, Joe. "Two Tell of Panthers Here." *Kansas City Star,* March 6, 1970.

Leuellyn, Lois. "Council Candidate Backed." *Kansas City Star,* January 28, 1974.

Lewis, Melvin D. "Neighbors Silent on Jordan Murder." *Kansas City Star,* July 15, 1970.

Liu, Baodong, and James M. Vanderleeuw. *Race Rules: Electoral Politics in New Orleans, 1965–2006.* Lanham: Lexington Books, 2007.

Lyman, Rick. "Labor Issue Heats up Mayoral Campaign." *Kansas City Star,* March 22, 1979.

Makalani, Nosakhere. "Five Black Males Are Homicide Victims Within 5-Day Period." *Call,* August 7, 1987.

Marable, Manning. *Race, Reform, and Rebellion: The Second Reconstruction in Black America, 1945–1990 (Revised Second Edition).* Jackson: University Press of Mississippi, 1991.

Margolies, Dan. "Welch Leaving KC Spotlight for the Sunlight of Phoenix." *Kansas City Business Journal,* February 9, 1997.

Marlow, M.J. "Food, Drink and 90 Degrees Spark Freedom, Inc., Picnic." *Call,* July 28, 1972.

———. "Importance of Committeemen Explained by Freedom, Inc." *Call,* July 14, 1972.

Marlow, Melba J. "1963—The Year When Watkins Began Long Service to City." *Call,* February 21, 1979.

———. "Bruce Watkins Made History as Elected Official." *Call,* September 19, 1980.

———. "Tolbert Accuses Council and Press of 'Personal Vendetta' Against Him." *Call,* July 20, 1973.

———. "Watkins Makes Strong Bid for Citizens' Nod." *Call,* December 15, 1978.

Massey, Douglas S., and Nancy M. Denton. *American Apartheid: Segregation and the Making of the Underclass.* Cambridge: Harvard University Press, 1993.

Mattox, Joe L. "What Barbershop Talk Says Is Needed to Reduce Crime." *Call,* August 30, 1974.

McAdam, Doug. *Political Process and the Development of Black Insurgency 1930–1970.* Chicago: University of Chicago Press, 1982.

McCorkle, William L. "Burden on Council: Mayor Erratic, Foe Charges." *Kansas City Star,* March 18, 1975.

———. "Capra's Defeat the Surprise in an Unsurprising Election." *Kansas City Star,* March 26, 1975.

———. "Close Vote Goes to Shaughnessy." *Kansas City Star*, January 12, 1975.

———. "Collins, Hughes Vie in 3rd." *Kansas City Star*, February 19, 1975.

———. "Contest Lively for District Seat in 5th." *Kansas City Star*, February 21, 1975.

———. "Races Tight in 2nd-at-Large and 5th as Election Nears." *Kansas City Star*, March 16, 1975.

McCullough, David G. *Truman*. New York: Simon and Schuster, 1992.

McGraw, Mike, and Glenn E. Rice. "Case Closed." *Kansas City Star*, June 21, 2011.

———. "Unsolved Killing of Leon Jordan Echoes Civil Rights Era." *Kansas City Star*, September 9, 2010.

McKinney, Audrey L. "Third District At-Large Race Close." *Call*, March 31, 1995.

McKinney, Audrey, and Al Ansare. "Four New Black Members on Council." *Call*, March 29, 1991.

McKinney, Audrey. "Joanne Collins to Run for Mayor." *Call*, October 12, 1990.

McLellan, April D. "5th District Visions Clash, Not Candidates." *Kansas City Star*, March 22, 1991.

———. "Allies Are Opponents in 3rd District-At-Large." *Kansas City Star*, March 20, 1991.

———. "Rival Files Challenge to Coe's Address Claim." *Kansas City Star*, February 14, 1991.

McNichol, Dunstan. "Freedom Inc. to Probe Vote." *Kansas City Star*, January 9, 1987.

Mearsheimer, John J., and Stephen M. Walt. *The Israel Lobby and U.S. Foreign Policy*. New York: Farrar, Straus, and Giroux, 2007.

Mehaffy, Trish. "Federal Jury Finds Former Kansas City Council Member Guilty of Mortgage Fraud." *The Daily Record*, August 17, 2007.

Mintz, Beth, Peter Freitag, Carol Hendricks, and Michael Schwartz. "Problems of Proof in Elite Research." *Social Problems* 23, no. 3(1976): 314–324.

Mitchell, Justin. "Wheat, Sharp Leave Campaign Rancor behind." *Kansas City Times*, February 14, 1983.

Mladenka, Kenneth R. "Blacks and Hispanics in Urban Politics." *The American Political Science Review* 83, no. 1 (1989): 165–191.

Mollenkopf, John H. "New York: The Great Anomaly." In *Racial Politics in American Cities*, edited by Rufus P. Browning, Dale Rogers Marshall, and David H. Tabb, 75–87. New York: Longman, 1990.

Molotch, Harvey. "The City as Growth Machine." *American Journal of Sociology* 82 (1976): 309–332.

Montgomery, Rick. "Clues to Cleaver Victory and Lewellen Loss." *Kansas City Star,* March 31, 1991.

Moore, Bill. "Mission to Liberia, Acrimony at Home." *Kansas City Star,* July 15, 1970.

Moore, Doris. "Freedom Changes Officers, but Aims and Goals Still the Same." *Call,* September 12, 1975.

Moore, Leonard N. *Carl B. Stokes and the Rise of Black Political Power.* Urbana: University of Illinois Press, 2002.

Moore, Roger. "Candidates for Vacancy on City Council Outline Goals." *Kansas City Star,* February 4, 1974.

———. "Mayor Shoulders Defeat of 10 Bonds." *Kansas City Star,* April 3, 1974.

———. "Mayoral Candidates Face Weeding out by Voters." *Kansas City Star,* February 23, 1975.

———. "Primary Tally Road Sign on Victory Path." *Kansas City Star,* March 2, 1975.

———. "Snow Backed by Citizens." *Kansas City Star,* March 2, 1975.

———. "Tolbert Decides to Leave Council." *Kansas City Star,* January 25, 1974.

———. "Tolbert Gone. Puzzlement Lingers on." *Kansas City Star,* January 27, 1974.

Morris, Aldon D. *The Origins of the Civil Rights Movement.* New York: The Free Press, 1984.

Morris, Mark, and Tom Jackman. "Weber Accused of Role in Bribery." *Kansas City Star,* July 26, 1995.

Morris, Mark. "Cofran Is in Line for Citizen's Nod." *Kansas City Star,* January 20, 1995.

———. "Tindall Cleared of Corruption." *Kansas City Star,* January 25, 1999.

Morris, Sally. "Bruce R. Watkins Says He Feels 'Compelled' to Run for City Council Again." *Call,* February 21, 1975.

Murphy, Kevin Q. "Cleaver a Key Issue in Panel's Questions." *Kansas City Star,* January 13, 1991.

———. "Cleaver Erasing Campaign's Links with Outspoken Clinton Adams." *Kansas City Star,* February 19, 1991.

———. "Cleaver Maintains Big Lead." *Kansas City Star,* March 17, 1991.

———. "Cleaver Wins, Proclaims 'New Era.'" *Kansas City Star,* March 27, 1991.

———. "Cleaver's Portable Phone Becomes a Campaign Issue." *Kansas City Star,* March 18, 1991.

———. "Collins Wins Support of Pastor at Big Church." *Kansas City Star,* February 16, 1991.

———. "Concern over Backlash." *Kansas City Star,* February 16, 1991.

———. "Hazley, Hernandez Are Abandoning Fight to Stay on KC Ballot." *Kansas City Star,* January 9, 1991.

———. "KC's Cleaver, Lewellen Top Mayoral Field." *Kansas City Star,* 1991.

———. "Labor Denounces Freedom Endorsements." *Kansas City Star,* February 9, 1991.

———. "Lewellen Gets Endorsement." *Kansas City Star,* March 1, 1991.

———. "This Campaign Is No Joke." *Kansas City Star,* February 22, 1991.

———. "Years Have Modified Cleaver's Stance." *Kansas City Star,* February 18, 1991.

Murphy, Kevin, and Gromer Jeffers Jr. "Freedom Threatens to Expel Members." *Kansas City Star,* February 20, 1997.

Murphy, Kevin, Rick Alm, and Carol Powers. *The Last Dance: The Skywalks Disaster and a City Changed.* Kansas City: Kansas City Star Books, 2011.

Nelson Jr., William E. "Cleveland: The Rise and Fall of the New Black Politics." In *The New Black Politics: The Search for Political Power,* edited by Michael B. Preston and Lenneal J. Henderson, 187–208. New York: Longman, 1982.

Nelson Jr., William E., and Philip J. Meranto. *Electing Black Mayors: Political Action in the Black Community.* Columbus: Ohio State University Press, 1977.

Nelson, Robert T. "Freedom, Race 'Nonissue' Hurt Cleaver." *Kansas City Star,* February 26, 1975.

———. "Jail Worker Charge: Holliday Threat on Job." *Kansas City Star,* March 9, 1975.

———. "Results Bittersweet for Freedom, Inc." *Kansas City Star,* March 26, 1975.

Nicely, Stephen. "Voting Charges Fly." *Kansas City Star,* March 5, 1971.

Nicholson, Sandra. "12th Street Heritage Development Corp. Has Area Residents Showing Optimism for the Future." *Call,* December 27, 1985.

O'Brien, David J. *Neighborhood Organization and Interest-Group Processes.* Princeton: Princeton University Press, 1975.

O'Connor, Tim. "In the Wake of Her Vote for Carnes, Coe Leaves Board of Political Club." *Kansas City Times,* January 17, 1987.

Office of History and Preservation, Office of the Clerk of the United States House of Representatives. "Alan Dupree Wheat." In *Black Americans in Congress, 1870–2007.* Washington: Government Printing Office, 2008.

Olson, Mancur. *The Logic of Collective Action: Public Goods and the Theory of Groups.* Cambridge: Harvard University Press, 1965.

Overman, Stacy. "City Council Drops out of Suit with Klan." *Call,* July 14, 1989.

Patterson, Kathleen. "Mondale and Eagleton Are Pleased at Turnout for Watkins' Campaign." *Kansas City Star,* March 21, 1979

———. "Mondale Sought Ties with Blacks." *Kansas City Times,* March 24, 1979.

Patterson, Kelly D., and Matthew M. Singer. "Targeting Success: The Enduring Power of the NRA." In *Interest Group Politics, Seventh Edition,* edited Allan J. Cigler and Burdett A. Loomis, 37–64. Washington: CQ Press, 2007.

Penn, Steve. "Shields, Weber Object to Freedom Inc. Flier." *Kansas City Star,* March 27, 1991.

People's Committee To Elect Clint Adams. *Ask Your 3rd District Councilman Why.* Paid political advertisement, 1978.

Pepper, Miriam. "How Watkins and Berkley Did It." *Kansas City Star,* February 28, 1979.

———. "Victory Glows with Green; Defeat Shrouded in Black." *Kansas City Star,* March 28, 1979.

Perry, Huey L. "The Evolution and Impact of Biracial Coalitions and Black Mayors in Birmingham and New Orleans." In *Racial Politics in American Cities,* edited by Rufus P. Browning, Dale Rogers Marshall, and David H. Tabb, 140–152. New York: Longman, 1990.

———. "The Evolution and Impact of Biracial Coalitions and Black Mayors in Birmingham and New Orleans." In *Racial Politics in American Cities, Third Edition,* edited by Rufus P. Browning, Dale Rogers Marshall, and David H. Tabb, 227–254. New York: Longman, 2003.

Phillips Committee for Congress. *Vote for Judge Hunter Phillips.* Paid political advertisement, 1964.

Phillips, Michael. "Ethics Report Is Critical of Mayor Cleaver." *Call,* April 10, 1992.

Piliawsky, Monte. "Black Political Empowerment in Kansas City." In *The State of Black Kansas City 1991,* edited by Sandra V. Walker, 163–190. Kansas City: The Urban League of Greater Kansas City, 1991.

Pohlmann, Marcus D., and Michael P. Kirby. *Racial Politics at the Crossroads: Memphis Elects Dr. W.W. Herenton.* Knoxville: University of Tennessee Press, 1996.

Poinsett, Alex. *Black Power, Gary Style: The Making of Mayor Richard Gordon Hatcher.* Chicago: Johnson Publishing Company, 1970.

Popper, Joe. "The Rev: The Passions and Politics of Emanuel Cleaver." *Kansas City Star: Star Magazine,* April 12, 1987.

Purnell, Florestine. "Scenario of Holding Four Council Seats Elates KC's Black Representatives." *Kansas City Star,* February 6, 1983.

Ralls, Richard D. "Wheeler Wins G.O.P. Fight; Gets Freedom Backing." *Kansas City Times,* February 7, 1975.

Reddig, William M. *Tom's Town: Kansas City and the Pendergast Legend.* Philadelphia: J.B. Lippincott Company, 1947.

Reed, Adolph L. *Stirrings in the Jug: Black Politics in the Post-Segregation Era.* Minneapolis: University of Minnesota Press, 1999.

Rice, Glenn E. "Campaign Song to Hit Air." *Kansas City Star,* February 16, 1991.

Rich, Wilbur C. *Coleman Young and Detroit Politics: From Social Activist to Power Broker.* Detroit: Wayne State University Press, 1989.

Robinson, Armstead L., and Patricia Sullivan. *New Directions in Civil Rights Studies.* Charlottesville: University Press of Virginia, 1991.

Robinson, John. "'No Money for Crime Prevention in Police Budgets' Watkins." *Call,* August 24, 1973.

Rose, Bleys W. "Council Retains Political Makeup." *Kansas City Star,* March 28, 1979.

———. "Democratic Clubs May Hold Keys to Mayor's Race." *Kansas City Times,* March 23, 1979.

———. "Well-Worn 3rd District Scene Furnishes Battlefield." *Kansas City Star,* March 21, 1979.

Satchell, Michael J. "Faction Support Debated by Mayor Candidates." *Kansas City Star,* March 14, 1971.

Schattschneider, E.E. *The Semisovereign People: A Realist's View of Democracy in America.* New York: Holt, Rinehart and Winston, 1960.

Schexnider, Alvin J. "Political Mobilization in the South: The Election of a Black Mayor in New Orleans." In *The New Black Politics: The Search for Political Power,* edited by Michael B. Preston, Lenneal J. Henderson Jr., and Paul Puryear, 221–240. New York: Longman, 1982.

Schirmer, Sherry Lamb. *A City Divided: The Racial Landscape of Kansas City, 1900–1960.* Columbia: University of Missouri Press, 2002.

Schneider, Anne, and Helen M. Ingram. *Deserving and Entitled: Social Constructions and Public Policy.* Albany: State University of New York Press, 2005.

Shaw, Todd C. *Now Is The Time! Detroit Black Politics and Grassroots Activism.* Durham: Duke University Press, 2009.

Shelby, Tommie. *We Who Are Dark: The Philosophical Foundations of Black Solidarity.* Cambridge: The Belknap Press of Harvard University Press, 2005.

Shelly, Barbara. "Adviser Hired by Heeter." *Kansas City Star,* January 2, 1987.

———. "Hazley Moves into Fifth Term, Wielding Quiet Power." *Kansas City Star,* April 1, 1987.

———. "Heeter Personifies Yuppie Image." *Kansas City Star,* January 18, 1987.

Sides, Josh. "A Simple Quest for Dignity: African American Los Angeles Since World War II." In *City of Promise: Race and Historical Change in Los Angeles,* edited by Martin Schiesl and Mark M. Dodge, 109–126. Claremont: Regina Books, 2006.

Sigman, Robert P. "Blacks Bid for Backing." *Kansas City Star,* January 6, 1971.

———. "Citizens Association Ready to Chalk Up Slate." *Kansas City Star,* January 3, 1971.

———. "Council Races Warm up." *Kansas City Star,* March 21, 1971.

———. "Faction Edge to Wheeler." *Kansas City Star,* March 3, 1971.

———. "Factions Hold to Courthouse." *Kansas City Times,* August 5, 1964.

———. "Thomas Unsure on Race." *Kansas City Star,* January 8, 1971.

———. "Wheeler in Mayor's Race." *Kansas City Star,* January 12, 1971.

———. "Wheeler, 8 Citizens Victors." *Kansas City Times,* March 31, 1971.

Smith, Lena R. "Add 5,000 New Voters." *Call,* March 20, 1964.

Smith, R. Drew, and Fredrick C. Harris. *Black Churches and Local Politics: Clergy Influence, Organizational Partnerships, and Civic Empowerment.* Lanham: Rowman and Littlefield, 2005.

Smith, Richard A. 1995. "Interest Group Influence in the U.S. Congress." *Legislative Studies Quarterly* 20, no. 1 (1995): 89–139.

Smith, Robert C. *We Have No Leaders: African Americans in the Post-Civil Rights Era.* Albany: State University of New York Press, 1996.

Smith, Sam, and Al Ansare. "Two-Term Limit Fails in Inner City but Voters Approve It City-wide." *Call,* November 9, 1990.

Smith, Sam. "Black Community May Decide Future of Zoo." *Call,* August 3, 1990.

———. "Mayor Berkley Wins In All Black Wards." *Call,* April 3, 1987.

Snider, Amy. "'Freedom Now' Ballots in KC Being Investigated." *Kansas City Star,* March 26, 1991.

Sonenshein, Raphael J. "The Dynamics of Biracial Coalitions: Crossover Politics in Los Angeles." *The Western Political Quarterly* 42, no. 2 (1989): 333–353.

———. *Politics in Black and White: Race and Power in Los Angeles.* Princeton: Princeton University Press, 1993.

Spivak, Jeffrey. "Tax Boost a Big Loser in KC Vote." *Kansas City Star,* August 4, 1993.

Stafford, Diane. "Joanne Collins Feels Her Time Is Now." *Kansas City Star,* February 19, 1991.

Stewart, Donna F., and Valerie Nicholson. "Berkley's Machine Beats Wheeler in Mayor's Race." *Call,* April 1, 1983.

Stewart, Donna. "10 Years of Fighting Crime." *Call,* November 20, 1987.

———. "Blight Turns to Pride as Shopping Center Opens." *Call,* February 14, 1986.

———. "Everything's Fine at 18th and Vine." *Call,* September 5, 1997.

———. "It's Mayor Cleaver." *Kansas City Star,* March 29, 1991.

———. "Mayor's First Year a Mixture of Accomplishments and Controversy." *Call,* March 27, 1992.

———. "Rumors, Motives and More Questions Revolve around Threatt Controversy." *Call,* May 23, 1986.

———. "The Man behind the Plan to Limit Terms." *Call,* October 26, 1990.

———. "Troubles of Vista Hotel Still Taking New Twists." *Call,* June 5, 1987.

Stokes, Carl B. *Promises of Power: A Political Autobiography.* New York: Simon & Schuster, 1973.

Stone, Clarence N. *Regime Politics: Governing Atlanta, 1946–1988.* Lawrence: University of Kansas Press, 1989.

Taylor, Jeff. "Dunmire Not Fazed by Outcome of Vote." *Kansas City Times,* April 1, 1987.

Teaford, Jon C. "New Life for an Old Subject: Investigating the Structure of Urban Rule." *American Quarterly* 37, no. 3 (1985): 346–356.

The Committeemen and Women of the Inner City. *An Open Letter to the Public.* Paid political advertisement, 1971.

Theoharis, Jeanne, and Komozi Woodard. *Freedom North: Black Freedom Struggles Outside the South, 1940–1980.* New York: Palgrave Macmillan, 2003.

———. *Groundwork: Local Black Freedom Movements in America.* New York: New York University Press, 2005.

Thomas, Tracy, and Walt Bodine. *Right Here in River City: A Portrait of Kansas City.* Garden City, New York: Doubleday, 1976.

Thompson III, J. Phillip. *Double Trouble: Black Mayors, Black Communities, and Call for a Deep Democracy.* New York: Oxford University Press, 2006.

Thornton III, J. Mills. *Dividing Lines: Municipal Politics and the Struggle for Civil Rights in Montgomery, Birmingham, and Selma.* Tuscaloosa: University of Alabama Press, 2002.

Time, "Chief Clarence Kelley: A Dick Tracy for the FBI," June 18, 1973.

Tindall, Rev. J. D. "Redistricting Request Will Diminish Black Representation." *Call,* April 20, 1990.

Tinney, James S. "Chief Kelley to Direct FBI." *Call,* June 8, 1973.

Turque, Bill. "'We'll See Ya, Charlie.'" *Kansas City Star,* February 28, 1979.

United States Census Bureau. "Table 26. Missouri—Race and Hispanic Origin for Selected Large Cities and Other Places: Earliest Census to 1990." *Historical Census Statistics on Population Totals by Race, 1790 to 1990, and By Hispanic Origin, 1970 to 1990, for Large Cities and Other Urban Places in the United States.* Washington: United States Census Bureau, 1991.

UPI. "Kansas City Victor Vows Unity Drive." *New York Times,* March 31, 1983.

Walker, Jack L. "Protest and Negotiation: A Case Study of Negro Leadership in Atlanta, Georgia." *Midwest Journal of Political Science* 7, no. 2 (1963): 99–124.

Walters, Ronald W. *Black Presidential Politics in America: A Strategic Approach.* Albany: State University of New York Press, 1988.

———. *Freedom Is Not Enough: Black Voters, Black Candidates, and American Presidential Politics.* Lanham: Rowman and Littlefield, 2005.

———. *White Nationalism, Black Interests: Conservative Public Policy and the Black Community.* Detroit: Wayne State University Press, 2003.

Watkins, Bruce R. "Watkins Tells Why He Doesn't Want Blankinship Re-Elected." *Call,* February 19, 1971.

Welch Jr., Archie W. "Passage of Charter Amendment Could Polarize Our Community." *Call,* March 31, 1989.

Wheeler, Charles B. *Doctor in Politics.* Kansas City: Inform, Inc., 1974.

Williams, Darrelee. "Collins Almost Loses Citizens Endorsement." *Call,* January 17, 1975.

———. "Freedom Knocked: 'Doc Holliday' Answers Collins Accusations." *Call,* February 7, 1975.

Wilson, James Q. *Negro Politics: The Search for Leadership.* New York: Free Press, 1960.

Wilson, William J. *When Work Disappears: The World of the New Urban Poor.* New York: Vintage Books, 1996.

Woodard, Komozi. *A Nation Within A Nation: Amiri Baraka (LeRoi Jones) and Black Power Politics.* Chapel Hill: University of North Carolina Press, 1999.

Woody, Bette. *Managing Crisis Cities: The New Black Leadership and the Politics of Resource Allocation.* Westport: Greenwood Press, 1982.

Yablonski, Michael. "Freedom Inc. Backs Serviss in KC Mayor's Race." *Kansas City Times,* February 4, 1983.

———. "Jolts in Primary Stir Incumbents in Council Races." *Kansas City Times,* March 16, 1983.

Yates, Douglas. *The Ungovernable City: The Politics of Urban Problems and Policy Making.* Cambridge: MIT Press, 1977.

Zisk, Betty H. *Local Interest Politics: A One-Way Street.* Indianapolis: The Bobbs-Merrill Company, 1973.

Zisk, Betty H., Heinz Eulau, and Kenneth Prewitt. "City Councilmen and the Group Struggle: A Typology of Role Orientation." *The Journal of Politics* 27, no. 3 (1965): 618–646.

Index

*An italic *f* indicates a figure; an italic *t*, a table.